THE MESSAGE
THE PROPHETS

The Message is *a contemporary rendering*
of the Bible from the original languages,
crafted to present its tone, rhythm, events,
and ideas in everyday language.

Other editions of *The Message*:

The New Testament, Psalms and Proverbs
The New Testament
The Old Testament Wisdom Books
Psalms
Proverbs
Job
The Message Promise Book
Sayings of Jesus
Stories of Jesus
His Unfolding Grace
Messages of the Heart (60-minute audio cassette)

THE PROPHETS

EUGENE H. PETERSON

NAVPRESS

BRINGING TRUTH TO LIFE

P.O. Box 35001, Colorado Springs, Colorado 80935

Old Testament Exegetical Consultants:

Dr. Lamar E. Cooper, Sr.
The Criswell College
Dallas, Texas

Prof. Donald R. Glenn
Dallas Theological Seminary
Dallas, Texas

Dr. Tremper Longman III
Westmont College
Santa Barbara, California

Dr. John N. Oswalt
Wesley Biblical Seminary
Jackson, Mississippi

Dr. Marvin R. Wilson
Gordon College
Wenham, Massachusetts

THE MESSAGE: The Prophets

Library of Congress Catalog Card Number: 00-033253
ISBN 1 57683 1957

Bible. O.T. Prophets. English. Peterson. 2000
  The message : Old Testament prophets in contemporary language / [compiled by]
Eugene Peterson.
    p. cm.
  ISBN 1-57683-195-7
    I. Peterson, Eugene H., 1932- II.Title

  BS1502.P48 2000
  224'.05209—dc21

                                                                    00-033253

Published in association with the literary agency of Alive Communications, Inc., 7680 Goddard St., Suite 200, Colorado Springs, CO 80920.

Printed in the United States of America

2 3 4 5 6 7 8 9 10 11 12 13 14 15 16 / 09 08 07 06 05 04 03 02 01 00

CONTENTS

INTRODUCTION TO
THE PROPHETS

Over a period of several hundred years, the Hebrew people gave birth to an extraordinary number of prophets—men and women distinguished by the power and skill with which they presented the reality of God. They delivered God's commands and promises and living presence to communities and nations who had been living on god-fantasies and god-lies.

Everyone more or less believes in God. But most of us do our best to keep God on the margins of our lives or, failing that, refashion God to suit our convenience. Prophets insist that God is the sovereign center, not off in the wings awaiting our beck and call. And prophets insist that we deal with God as God reveals himself, not as we imagine him to be.

These men and women woke people up to the sovereign presence of God in their lives. They yelled, they wept, they rebuked, they soothed, they challenged, they comforted. They used words with power and imagination, whether blunt or subtle.

⌒

Sixteen of these prophets wrote what they spoke. We call them "the writing prophets." They comprise the section from Isaiah to Malachi in our Bibles. These sixteen Hebrew prophets provide the help we so badly need if we are to stay alert and knowledgeable regarding the conditions in which we cultivate faithful and obedient lives before God. For the ways of the world—its assumptions, its values, its methods of going about its work—are never on the side of God. Never.

The prophets purge our imaginations of this world's assumptions on how life is lived and what counts in life. Over and over again, God the Holy Spirit uses these prophets to separate his people from the cultures in which they live, putting them back on the path of simple faith and obedience and worship in defiance of all that the world admires and rewards. Prophets train us in discerning the difference between the ways of the world and the ways of the gospel, keeping us present to the Presence of God.

⌒

We don't read very many pages into the Prophets before realizing that there was nothing easygoing about them. Prophets were not popular figures. They never achieved celebrity status. They were decidedly uncongenial to the temperaments and dispositions of the people with whom they lived. And the centuries have not mellowed them. It's understandable that we should have a difficult time coming to terms with them. They aren't particularly sensitive to our feelings. They have very modest, as we would say, "relationship skills." We like leaders, especially religious leaders, who understand our problems ("come alongside us" is our idiom for it), leaders with a touch of glamour, leaders who look good on posters and on television.

The hard-rock reality is that prophets don't fit into our way of life.

For a people who are accustomed to "fitting God" into their lives, or, as we like to say, "making room for God," the prophets are hard to take and easy to dismiss. The God of which the prophets speak is far too large to fit into our lives. If we want anything to do with God, we have to fit into him.

The prophets are not "reasonable," accommodating themselves to what makes sense to us. They are not diplomatic, tactfully negotiating an agreement that allows us a "say" in the outcome. What they do is haul us unceremoniously into a reality far too large to be accounted for by our explanations and expectations. They plunge us into mystery, immense and staggering.

Their words and visions penetrate the illusions with which we cocoon ourselves from reality. We humans have an enormous capacity for denial and for self-deceit. We incapacitate ourselves from dealing with the consequences of sin, for facing judgment, for embracing truth. Then the prophets step in and help us to first recognize and then enter the new life God has for us, the life that hope in God opens up.

They don't explain God. They shake us out of old conventional habits of small-mindedness, of trivializing god-gossip, and set us on our feet in wonder and obedience and worship. If we insist on understanding them before we live into them, we will never get it.

⌒

Basically, the prophets did two things: They worked to get people to accept the worst as *God's* judgment — not a religious catastrophe or a political disaster, but *judgment.* If what seems like the worst turns out to be *God's* judgment, it can be embraced, not denied or avoided, for God is good and intends our salvation. So judgment, while certainly not what we human beings anticipate in our planned future, can never be the worst that can happen. It is the best, for it is the work of God to set the world, and us, right.

And the prophets worked to get people who were beaten down to open themselves up to hope in God's future. In the wreckage of exile and death and humiliation and sin, the prophet ignited hope, opening lives to the new work of salvation that God is about at all times and everywhere.

One of the bad habits that we pick up early in our lives is separating things and people into secular and sacred. We assume that the secular is what we are more or less in charge of: our jobs, our time, our entertainment, our government, our social relations. The sacred is what God has charge of: worship and the Bible, heaven and hell, church and prayers. We then contrive to set aside a sacred place for God, designed, we say, to honor God but really intended to keep God in his place, leaving us free to have the final say about everything else that goes on.

Prophets will have none of this. They contend that everything, absolutely everything, takes place on sacred ground. God has something to say about every aspect of our lives: the way we feel and act in the so-called privacy of our hearts and homes, the way we make our money and the way we spend it, the politics we embrace, the wars we fight, the catastrophes we endure, the people we hurt and the people we help. Nothing is hidden from the scrutiny of God, nothing is exempt from the rule of God, nothing escapes the purposes of God. Holy, holy, holy.

Prophets make it impossible to evade God or make detours around God. Prophets insist on receiving God in every nook and cranny of life. For a prophet, God is more real than the next-door neighbor.

ISAIAH

F or Isaiah, words are watercolors and melodies and chisels
to make truth and beauty and goodness. Or, as the case
may be, hammers and swords and scalpels to *unmake* sin
and guilt and rebellion. Isaiah does not merely convey informa-
tion. He creates visions, delivers revelation, arouses belief. He is
a poet in the most fundamental sense — a *maker*, making God
present and that presence urgent. Isaiah is the supreme poet-
prophet to come out of the Hebrew people.

Isaiah is a large presence in the lives of people who live by
faith in God, who submit themselves to being shaped by the
Word of God and are on the lookout for the holy. *The Holy*. The
characteristic name for God in Isaiah is "The Holy." As we read
this large and comprehensive gathering of messages that were
preached to the ancient people of Israel, we find ourselves
immersed in both the presence and the action of The Holy.

The more hours we spend pondering the words of Isaiah,
the more the word "holy" changes in our understanding. If
"holy" was ever a pious, pastel-tinted word in our vocabularies,
the Isaiah-preaching quickly turns it into something blazing.
Holiness is the most attractive quality, the most intense experience we ever get of sheer *life* — authentic, firsthand living, not
life looked at and enjoyed from a distance. We find ourselves in
on the operations of God himself, not talking about them or
reading about them. Holiness is a furnace that transforms the
men and women who enter it. "Holy, Holy, Holy" is not needle-
point. It is the banner of a revolution, *the* revolution.

The book of Isaiah is expansive, dealing with virtually
everything that is involved in being a people of God on this
planet Earth. The impressive art of Isaiah involves taking the
stuff of our ordinary and often disappointing human experience
and showing us how it is the very stuff that God uses to create
and save and give hope. As this vast panorama opens up before
us, it turns out that nothing is unusable by God. He uses everything and everybody as material for his work, which is the
remaking of the mess we have made of our lives.

"Symphony" is the term many find useful to capture the
fusion of simplicity and complexity presented in the book of
Isaiah. The major thrust is clearly God's work of salvation: "The

Salvation Symphony" (the name Isaiah means "God Saves"). The prominent themes repeated and developed throughout this vast symphonic work are judgment, comfort, and hope. All three elements are present on nearly every page, but each also gives distinction to the three "movements" of the book that so powerfully enact salvation: Messages of Judgment (chapters 1–39), Messages of Comfort (chapters 40–55), and Messages of Hope (chapters 56–66).

ISAIAH

1

QUIT YOUR WORSHIP CHARADES

The vision that Isaiah son of Amoz saw regarding Judah and Jerusalem during the times of the kings of Judah: Uzziah, Jotham, Ahaz, and Hezekiah.

Heaven and earth, you're the jury.
    Listen to GOD's case:
"I had children and raised them well,
    and they turned on me.
The ox knows who's boss,
    the mule knows the hand that feeds him,
But not Israel.
    My people don't know up from down.
Shame! Misguided GOD-dropouts,
    staggering under their guilt-baggage,
Gang of miscreants,
    band of vandals—
My people have walked out on me, their GOD,
    turned their backs on The Holy of Israel,
    walked off and never looked back.

"Why bother even trying to do anything with you
    when you just keep to your bullheaded ways?
You keep beating your heads against brick walls.
    Everything within you protests against you.
From the bottom of your feet to the top of your head,
    nothing's working right.
Wounds and bruises and running sores—
    untended, unwashed, unbandaged.
Your country is laid waste,
    your cities burned down.
Your land is destroyed by outsiders while you watch,
    reduced to rubble by barbarians.
Daughter Zion is deserted—

like a tumbledown shack on a dead-end street,
Like a tarpaper shanty on the wrong side of the tracks,
   like a sinking ship abandoned by the rats.
If GOD-of-the-Angel-Armies hadn't left us a few survivors,
   we'd be as desolate as Sodom, doomed just like Gomorrah.

"Listen to my Message,
   you Sodom-schooled leaders.
Receive God's revelation,
   you Gomorrah-schooled people.

"Why this frenzy of sacrifices?"
   GOD's asking.
"Don't you think I've had my fill of burnt sacrifices,
   rams and plump grain-fed calves?
Don't you think I've had my fill
   of blood from bulls, lambs, and goats?
When you come before me,
   who ever gave you the idea of acting like this,
Running here and there, doing this and that—
   all this sheer *commotion* in the place provided for worship?

"Quit your worship charades.
   I can't stand your trivial religious games:
Monthly conferences, weekly sabbaths, special meetings—
   meetings, meetings, meetings—I can't stand one more!
Meetings for this, meetings for that. I hate them!
   You've worn me out!
I'm sick of your religion, religion, religion,
   while you go right on sinning.
When you put on your next prayer-performance,
   I'll be looking the other way.
No matter how long or loud or often you pray,
   I'll not be listening.
And do you know why? Because you've been tearing
   people to pieces, and your hands are bloody.
Go home and wash up.
   Clean up your act.
Sweep your lives clean of your evildoings
   so I don't have to look at them any longer.

Say no to wrong.
 Learn to do good.
Work for justice.
 Help the down-and-out.
Stand up for the homeless.
 Go to bat for the defenseless.

LET'S ARGUE THIS OUT

"Come. Sit down. Let's argue this out."
 This is GOD's Message:
"If your sins are blood-red,
 they'll be snow-white.
If they're red like crimson,
 they'll be like wool.
If you'll willingly obey,
 you'll feast like kings.
But if you're willful and stubborn,
 you'll die like dogs."
That's right. GOD says so.

THOSE WHO WALK OUT ON GOD

Oh! Can you believe it? The chaste city
 has become a whore!
She was once all justice,
 everyone living as good neighbors,
And now they're all
 at one another's throats.
Your coins are all counterfeits.
 Your wine is watered down.
Your leaders are turncoats
 who keep company with crooks.
They sell themselves to the highest bidder
 and grab anything not nailed down.
They never stand up for the homeless,
 never stick up for the defenseless.

This Decree, therefore, of the Master, GOD-of-the-Angel-Armies,
 the Strong One of Israel:
"This is it! I'll get my oppressors off my back.

I'll get back at my enemies.
I'll give you the back of my hand,
    purge the junk from your life, clean you up.
I'll set honest judges and wise counselors among you
    just like it was back in the beginning.
Then you'll be renamed
    City-That-Treats-People-Right, the True-Blue City."
GOD's right ways will put Zion right again.
    GOD's right actions will restore her penitents.
But it's curtains for rebels and GOD-traitors,
    a dead end for those who walk out on GOD.
"Your dalliances in those oak grove shrines
    will leave you looking mighty foolish,
All that fooling around in god and goddess gardens
    that you thought was the latest thing.
You'll end up like an oak tree
    with all its leaves falling off,
Like an unwatered garden,
    withered and brown.
'The Big Man' will turn out to be dead bark and twigs,
    and his 'work,' the spark that starts the fire
That exposes man and work both
    as nothing but cinders and smoke."

2

CLIMB GOD'S MOUNTAIN

The Message Isaiah got regarding Judah and Jerusalem:

There's a day coming
    when the mountain of GOD's House
Will be The Mountain—
    solid, towering over all mountains.
All nations will river toward it,
    people from all over set out for it.
They'll say, "Come,
    let's climb GOD's Mountain,
    go to the House of the God of Jacob.
He'll show us the way he works

17

so we can live the way we're made."
Zion's the source of the revelation.
>   GOD's Message comes from Jerusalem.
He'll settle things fairly between nations.
>   He'll make things right between many peoples.
They'll turn their swords into shovels,
>   their spears into hoes.
No more will nation fight nation;
>   they won't play war anymore.
Come, family of Jacob,
>   let's live in the light of GOD.

GOD, you've walked out on your family Jacob
>   because their world is full of hokey religion,
Philistine witchcraft, and pagan hocus-pocus,
>   a world rolling in wealth,
Stuffed with things,
>   no end to its machines and gadgets,
And gods—gods of all sorts and sizes.
>   These people make their own gods and worship what they
>   make.
A degenerate race, facedown in the gutter.
>   Don't bother with them! They're not worth forgiving!

PRETENTIOUS EGOS BROUGHT DOWN TO EARTH

Head for the hills,
>   hide in the caves
From the terror of GOD,
>   from his dazzling presence.

People with a big head are headed for a fall,
>   pretentious egos brought down a peg.
It's GOD alone at front-and-center
>   on the Day we're talking about,
The Day that GOD-of-the-Angel-Armies
>   is matched against all big-talking rivals,
>   against all swaggering big names;
Against all giant sequoias
>   hugely towering,

18

and against the expansive chestnut;
Against Kilimanjaro and Annapurna,
    against the ranges of Alps and Andes;
Against every soaring skyscraper,
    against all proud obelisks and statues;
Against ocean-going luxury liners,
    against elegant three-masted schooners.
The swelled big heads will be punctured bladders,
    the pretentious egos brought down to earth,
Leaving GOD alone at front-and-center
    on the Day we're talking about.

And all those sticks and stones
    dressed up to look like gods
    will be gone for good.

Clamber into caves in the cliffs,
    duck into any hole you can find.
Hide from the terror of GOD,
    from his dazzling presence,
When he assumes his full stature on earth,
    towering and terrifying.

On that Day men and women will take
    the sticks and stones
They've decked out in gold and silver
    to look like gods and then worshiped,
And they will dump them
    in any ditch or gully,
Then run for rock caves
    and cliff hideouts
To hide from the terror of GOD,
    from his dazzling presence,
When he assumes his full stature on earth,
    towering and terrifying.

Quit scraping and fawning over mere humans,
    so full of themselves, so full of hot air!
    Can't you see there's nothing to them?

3

JERUSALEM ON ITS LAST LEGS

The Master, GOD-of-the-Angel-Armies,
   is emptying Jerusalem and Judah
Of all the basic necessities,
   plain bread and water to begin with.
He's withdrawing police and protection,
      judges and courts,
      pastors and teachers,
      captains and generals,
      doctors and nurses,
      and, yes, even the repairmen and jacks-of-all-trades.
He says, "I'll put little kids in charge of the city.
   Schoolboys and schoolgirls will order everyone around.
People will be at each other's throats,
   stabbing one another in the back:
Neighbor against neighbor, young against old,
   the no-account against the well-respected.
One brother will grab another and say,
   'You look like you've got a head on your shoulders.
Do something!
   Get us out of this mess.'
And he'll say, 'Me? Not me! I don't have a clue.
   Don't put me in charge of anything.'

"Jerusalem's on its last legs.
   Judah is soon down for the count.
Everything people say and do
   is at cross-purposes with GOD,
   a slap in my face.
Brazen in their depravity,
   they flaunt their sins like degenerate Sodom.
Doom to their eternal souls! They've made their bed;
   now they'll sleep in it.

"Reassure the righteous
   that their good living will pay off.
But doom to the wicked! Disaster!
   Everything they did will be done to them.

"Skinny kids terrorize my people.
     Silly girls bully them around.
My dear people! Your leaders are taking you down a blind alley.
     They're sending you off on a wild goose chase."

A City Brought to Her Knees by Her Sorrows

God enters the courtroom.
     He takes his place at the bench to judge his people.
God calls for order in the court,
     hauls the leaders of his people into the dock:
"You've played havoc with this country.
     Your houses are stuffed with what you've stolen from the poor.
What is this anyway? Stomping on my people,
     grinding the faces of the poor into the dirt?"
That's what the Master,
     God-of-the-Angel-Armies, says.

God says, "Zion women are stuck-up,
     prancing around in their high heels,
Making eyes at all the men in the street,
     swinging their hips,
Tossing their hair,
     gaudy and garish in cheap jewelry."
The Master will fix it so those Zion women
     will all turn bald—
Scabby, bald-headed women.
     The Master will do it.

The time is coming when the Master will strip them of their fancy baubles—the dangling earrings, anklets and bracelets, combs and mirrors and silk scarves, diamond brooches and pearl necklaces, the rings on their fingers and the rings on their toes, the latest fashions in hats, exotic perfumes and aphrodisiacs, gowns and capes, all the world's finest in fabrics and design.

Instead of wearing seductive scents,
     these women are going to smell like rotting cabbages;
Instead of modeling flowing gowns,
     they'll be sporting rags;

21

Instead of their stylish hairdos,
    scruffy heads;
Instead of beauty marks,
    scabs and scars.

Your finest fighting men will be killed,
    your soldiers left dead on the battlefield.
The entrance gate to Zion will be clotted
    with people mourning their dead—
A city stooped under the weight of her loss,
    brought to her knees by her sorrows.

✝

4

That will be the day when seven women
    will gang up on one man, saying,
"We'll take care of ourselves,
    get our own food and clothes.
Just give us a child. Make us pregnant
    so we'll have something to live for!"

GOD'S BRANCH

And that's when GOD's Branch will sprout green and lush. The produce of the country will give Israel's survivors something to be proud of again. Oh, they'll hold their heads high! Everyone left behind in Zion, all the discards and rejects in Jerusalem, will be reclassified as "holy"—alive and therefore precious. GOD will give Zion's women a good bath. He'll scrub the bloodstained city of its violence and brutality, purge the place with a firestorm of judgment.

Then GOD will bring back the ancient pillar of cloud by day and the pillar of fire by night and mark Mount Zion and everyone in it with his glorious presence, his immense, protective presence, shade from the burning sun and shelter from the driving rain.

5

LOOKING FOR A CROP OF JUSTICE

I'll sing a ballad to the one I love,
    a love ballad about his vineyard:
The one I love had a vineyard,
    a fine, well-placed vineyard.
He hoed the soil and pulled the weeds,
    and planted the very best vines.
He built a lookout, built a winepress,
    a vineyard to be proud of.
He looked for a vintage yield of grapes,
    but for all his pains he got junk grapes.

"Now listen to what I'm telling you,
    you who live in Jerusalem and Judah.
What do you think is going on
    between me and my vineyard?
Can you think of anything I could have done
    to my vineyard that I didn't do?
When I expected good grapes,
    why did I get bitter grapes?

"Well now, let me tell you
    what I'll do to my vineyard:
I'll tear down its fence
    and let it go to ruin.
I'll knock down the gate
    and let it be trampled.
I'll turn it into a patch of weeds, untended, uncared for—
    thistles and thorns will take over.
I'll give orders to the clouds:
    'Don't rain on that vineyard, ever!'"

Do you get it? The vineyard of GOD-of-the-Angel-Armies
    is the country of Israel.
All the men and women of Judah
    are the garden he was so proud of.
He looked for a crop of justice

and saw them murdering each other.
He looked for a harvest of righteousness
    and heard only the moans of victims.

YOU WHO CALL EVIL GOOD AND GOOD EVIL

Doom to you who buy up all the houses
    and grab all the land for yourselves—
Evicting the old owners,
        posting NO TRESPASSING signs,
Taking over the country,
        leaving everyone homeless and landless.
I overheard GOD-of-the-Angel-Armies say:
"Those mighty houses will end up empty.
        Those extravagant estates will be deserted.
A ten-acre vineyard will produce a pint of wine,
        a fifty-pound sack of seed, a quart of grain."

Doom to those who get up early
        and start drinking booze before breakfast,
Who stay up all hours of the night
        drinking themselves into a stupor.
They make sure their banquets are well-furnished
        with harps and flutes and plenty of wine,
But they'll have nothing to do with the work of GOD,
        pay no mind to what he is doing.
Therefore my people will end up in exile
        because they don't know the score.
Their "big men" will starve to death
        and the common people die of thirst.
Sheol developed a huge appetite,
        swallowing people nonstop!
Big people and little people alike
        down that gullet, to say nothing of all the drunks.
The down-and-out on a par
        with the high-and-mighty,
Windbag boasters crumpled,
        flaccid as a punctured bladder.
But by working justice,
        GOD-of-the-Angel-Armies will be a mountain.

By working righteousness,
    Holy God will show what "holy" is.
And lambs will graze
    as if they owned the place,
Kids and calves
    right at home in the ruins.

Doom to you who use lies to sell evil,
    who haul sin to market by the truckload,
Who say, "What's God waiting for?
    Let him get a move on so we can see it.
Whatever The Holy of Israel has cooked up,
    we'd like to check it out."

Doom to you who call evil good
    and good evil,
Who put darkness in place of light
    and light in place of darkness,
Who substitute bitter for sweet
    and sweet for bitter!

Doom to you who think you're so smart,
    who hold such a high opinion of yourselves!
All you're good at is drinking—champion boozers
    who collect trophies from drinking bouts
And then line your pockets with bribes from the guilty
    while you violate the rights of the innocent.

But they won't get by with it. As fire eats stubble
    and dry grass goes up in smoke,
Their souls will atrophy,
    their achievements crumble into dust,
Because they said no to the revelation
    of GOD-of-the-Angel-Armies,
Would have nothing to do
    with The Holy of Israel.

That's why GOD flamed out in anger against his people,
    reached out and knocked them down.
The mountains trembled

as their dead bodies piled up in the streets.
But even after that, he was still angry,
   his fist still raised, ready to hit them again.
He raises a flag, signaling a distant nation,
   whistles for people at the ends of the earth.
And here they come—
   on the run!
None drag their feet, no one stumbles,
   no one sleeps or dawdles.
Shirts are on and pants buckled,
   every boot is spit-polished and tied.
Their arrows are sharp,
   bows strung,
The hooves of their horses shod,
   chariot wheels greased.
Roaring like a pride of lions,
   the full-throated roars of young lions,
They growl and seize their prey,
   dragging it off—no rescue for that one!
They'll roar and roar and roar on that Day,
   like the roar of ocean billows.
Look as long and hard as you like at that land,
   you'll see nothing but darkness and trouble.
Every light in the sky
   will be blacked out by the clouds.

6

HOLY, HOLY, HOLY!

In the year that King Uzziah died, I saw the Master sitting on a throne—high, exalted!—and the train of his robes filled the Temple. Angel-seraphs hovered above him, each with six wings. With two wings they covered their faces, with two their feet, and with two they flew. And they called back and forth one to the other,

> "Holy, Holy, Holy is GOD-of-the-Angel-Armies.
> His bright glory fills the whole earth."

The foundations trembled at the sound of the angel voices, and then the whole house filled with smoke. I said,

"Doom! It's Doomsday!
    I'm as good as dead!
Every word I've ever spoken is tainted—
    blasphemous even!
And the people I live with talk the same way,
    using words that corrupt and desecrate.
And here I've looked God in the face!
    The King! GOD-of-the-Angel-Armies!"

Then one of the angel-seraphs flew to me. He held a live coal that he
had taken with tongs from the altar. He touched my mouth with the coal
and said,

"Look. This coal has touched your lips.
    Gone your guilt,
    your sins wiped out."
And then I heard the voice of the Master:
    "Whom shall I send?
    Who will go for us?"
I spoke up,
    "I'll go.
    Send me!"

☩

He said, "Go and tell this people:

"'Listen hard, but you aren't going to get it;
    look hard, but you won't catch on.'
Make these people blockheads,
    with fingers in their ears and blindfolds on their eyes,
So they won't see a thing,
    won't hear a word,
So they won't have a clue about what's going on
    and, yes, so they won't turn around and be made whole."

Astonished, I said,
    "And Master, how long is this to go on?"
He said, "Until the cities are emptied out,
    not a soul left in the cities—

Houses empty of people,
    countryside empty of people.
Until I, GOD, get rid of everyone, sending them off,
    the land totally empty.
And even if some should survive, say a tenth,
    the devastation will start up again.
The country will look like pine and oak forest
    with every tree cut down—
Every tree a stump, a huge field of stumps.
    But there's a holy seed in those stumps."

7

A VIRGIN WILL BEAR A SON

During the time that Ahaz son of Jothan, son of Uzziah, was king of Judah, King Rezin of Aram and King Pekah son of Remaliah of Israel attacked Jerusalem, but the attack sputtered out. When the Davidic government learned that Aram had joined forces with Ephraim (that is, Israel), Ahaz and his people were badly shaken. They shook like trees in the wind.

Then GOD told Isaiah, "Go and meet Ahaz. Take your son Shear-jashub ["A-Remnant-Will-Return"] with you. Meet him south of the city at the end of the aqueduct where it empties into the upper pool on the road to the public laundry. Tell him, 'Listen, calm down. Don't be afraid. And don't panic over these two burnt-out cases, Rezin of Aram and the son of Remaliah. They talk big but there's nothing to them. Aram, along with Ephraim's son of Remaliah, have plotted to do you harm. They've conspired against you, saying, "Let's go to war against Judah, dismember it, take it for ourselves, and set the son of Tabeel up as a puppet king over it."

"'But GOD, the Master, says,

"'"It won't happen.
    Nothing will come of it
Because the capital of Aram is Damascus
    and the king of Damascus is a mere man, Rezin.
As for Ephraim, in sixty-five years
    it will be rubble, nothing left of it.

The capital of Ephraim is Samaria,
    and the king of Samaria is the mere son of Remaliah.
If you don't take your stand in faith,
    you won't have a leg to stand on.""

+

GOD spoke again to Ahaz. This time he said, "Ask for a sign from your GOD. Ask anything. Be extravagant. Ask for the moon!"

But Ahaz said, "I'd never do that. I'd never make demands like that on GOD!"

So Isaiah told him, "Then listen to this, government of David! It's bad enough that you make people tired with your pious, timid hypocrisies, but now you're making God tired. So the Master is going to give you a sign anyway. Watch for this: A girl who is presently a virgin will get pregnant. She'll bear a son and name him Immanuel ["God-With-Us"]. By the time the child is twelve years old, able to make moral decisions, the threat of war will be over. Relax, those two kings that have you so worried will be out of the picture. But also be warned: GOD will bring on you and your people and your government a judgment worse than anything since the time the kingdom split, when Ephraim left Judah. The king of Assyria is coming!"

That's when GOD will whistle for the flies at the headwaters of Egypt's Nile, and whistle for the bees in the land of Assyria. They'll come and infest every nook and cranny of this country. There'll be no getting away from them.

And that's when the Master will take the razor rented from across the Euphrates—the king of Assyria no less!—and shave the hair off your heads and genitals, leaving you shamed, exposed, and denuded. He'll shave off your beards while he's at it.

It will be a time when survivors will count themselves lucky to have a cow and a couple of sheep. At least they'll have plenty of milk! Whoever's left in the land will learn to make do with the simplest foods — curds, say, and honey.

But that's not the end of it. This country that used to be covered with fine vineyards — thousands of them, worth millions!—will revert to a weed patch. Weeds and thorn bushes everywhere! Good for nothing except, perhaps, hunting rabbits. Cattle and sheep will forage as best they can in the fields of weeds—but there won't be a trace of all those fertile and well-tended gardens and fields.

✛

8

Then GOD told me, "Get a big sheet of paper and write in indelible ink, 'This belongs to Maher-shalal-hash-baz ["Spoil-Speeds-Plunder-Hurries"].'"

I got two honest men, Uriah the priest and Zechariah son of Jeberekiah, to witness the document. Then I went home to my wife, the prophetess. She conceived and gave birth to a son.

GOD told me, "Name him Maher-shalal-hash-baz. Before that baby says 'Daddy' or 'Mamma' the king of Assyria will have plundered the wealth of Damascus and the riches of Samaria."

✛

GOD spoke to me again, saying:

"Because this people has turned its back
    on the gently flowing stream of Shiloah
And gotten all excited over Rezin
    and the son of Remaliah,
I'm stepping in and facing them with
    the wild floodwaters of the Euphrates,
The king of Assyria and all his fanfare,
    a river in flood, bursting its banks,
Pouring into Judah, sweeping everything before it,
    water up to your necks,
A huge wingspan of a raging river,
    oh Immanuel, spreading across your land."

✛

But face the facts, all you oppressors, and then wring your hands.
    Listen, all of you, far and near.
Prepare for the worst, and wring your hands.
    Yes, prepare for the worst and wring your hands!

Plan and plot all you want—nothing will come of it.
    All your talk is mere talk, empty words,
Because when all is said and done,
    the last word is Immanuel—God-With-Us.

A Boulder Blocking Your Way

God spoke strongly to me, grabbed me with both hands and warned
me not to go along with this people. He said:

"Don't be like this people,
    always afraid somebody is plotting against them.
Don't fear what they fear.
    Don't take on their worries.
If you're going to worry,
    worry about The Holy. Fear God-of-the-Angel-Armies.
The Holy can be either a Hiding Place
    or a Boulder blocking your way,
The Rock standing in the willful way
    of both houses of Israel,
A barbed-wire Fence preventing trespass
    to the citizens of Jerusalem.
Many of them are going to run into that Rock
    and get their bones broken,
Get tangled up in that barbed wire
    and not get free of it."

✝

Gather up the testimony,
    preserve the teaching for my followers,
While I wait for God as long as he remains in hiding,
    while I wait and hope for him.
I stand my ground and hope,
    I and the children God gave me as signs to Israel,
Warning signs and hope signs from God-of-the-Angel-Armies,
    who makes his home in Mount Zion.

When people tell you, "Try out the fortunetellers.
    Consult the spiritualists.
Why not tap into the spirit-world,

get in touch with the dead?"
Tell them, "No, we're going to study the Scriptures."
    People who try the other ways get nowhere—a dead end!
Frustrated and famished,
    they try one thing after another.
When nothing works out they get angry,
    cursing first this god and then that one,
Looking this way and that,
    up, down, and sideways—and seeing nothing,
A blank wall, an empty hole.
    They end up in the dark with nothing.

9

A Child Has Been Born—For Us!

But there'll be no darkness for those who were in trouble. Earlier he did bring the lands of Zebulun and Naphtali into disrepute, but the time is coming when he'll make that whole area glorious—the road along the Sea, the country past the Jordan, international Galilee.

The people who walked in darkness
    have seen a great light.
For those who lived in a land of deep shadows—
    light! sunbursts of light!
You repopulated the nation,
    you expanded its joy.
Oh, they're so glad in your presence!
    Festival joy!
The joy of a great celebration,
    sharing rich gifts and warm greetings.
The abuse of oppressors and cruelty of tyrants—
    all their whips and cudgels and curses—
Is gone, done away with, a deliverance
    as surprising and sudden as Gideon's old victory over Midian.
The boots of all those invading troops,
    along with their shirts soaked with innocent blood,
Will be piled in a heap and burned,
    a fire that will burn for days!

For a child has been born—for us!
    the gift of a son—for us!
He'll take over
    the running of the world.
His names will be: Amazing Counselor,
    Strong God,
Eternal Father,
    Prince of Wholeness.
His ruling authority will grow,
    and there'll be no limits to the wholeness he brings.
He'll rule from the historic David throne
    over that promised kingdom.
He'll put that kingdom on a firm footing
    and keep it going
With fair dealing and right living,
    beginning now and lasting always.
The zeal of GOD-of-the-Angel-Armies
    will do all this.

GOD ANSWERED FIRE WITH FIRE

The Master sent a message against Jacob.
    It landed right on Israel's doorstep.
All the people soon heard the message,
    Ephraim and the citizens of Samaria.
But they were a proud and arrogant bunch.
    They dismissed the message, saying,
"Things aren't that bad.
    We can handle anything that comes.
If our buildings are knocked down,
    we'll rebuild them bigger and finer.
If our forests are cut down,
    we'll replant them with finer trees."

So GOD incited their adversaries against them,
    stirred up their enemies to attack:
From the east, Arameans; from the west, Philistines.
    They made hash of Israel.
But even after that, he was still angry,
    his fist still raised, ready to hit them again.

But the people paid no mind to him who hit them,
    didn't seek GOD-of-the-Angel-Armies.
So GOD hacked off Israel's head and tail,
    palm branch and reed, both on the same day.
The big-head elders were the head,
    the lying prophets were the tail.
Those who were supposed to lead this people
    led them down blind alleys,
And those who followed the leaders
    ended up lost and confused.
That's why the Master lost interest in the young men,
    had no feeling for their orphans and widows.
All of them were godless and evil,
    talking filth and folly.
And even after that, he was still angry,
    his fist still raised, ready to hit them again.

Their wicked lives raged like an out-of-control fire,
    the kind that burns everything in its path—
Trees and bushes, weeds and grasses—
    filling the skies with smoke.
GOD-of-the-Angel-Armies answered fire with fire,
    set the whole country on fire,
Turned the people into consuming fires,
    consuming one another in their lusts—
Appetites insatiable, stuffing and gorging
    themselves left and right with people and things.
But still they starved. Not even their children
    were safe from their rapacious hunger.
Manasseh ate Ephraim, and Ephraim Manasseh,
    and then the two ganged up against Judah.
And after that, he was still angry,
    his fist still raised, ready to hit them again.

✠

10

YOU WHO LEGISLATE EVIL

Doom to you who legislate evil,
    who make laws that make victims—
Laws that make misery for the poor,
    that rob my destitute people of dignity,
Exploiting defenseless widows,
    taking advantage of homeless children.
What will you have to say on Judgment Day,
    when Doomsday arrives out of the blue?
Who will you get to help you?
    What good will your money do you?
A sorry sight you'll be then, huddled with the prisoners,
    or just some corpses stacked in the street.
Even after all this, God is still angry,
    his fist still raised, ready to hit them again.

DOOM TO ASSYRIA!

"Doom to Assyria, weapon of my anger.
    My wrath is a cudgel in his hands!
I send him against a godless nation,
    against the people I'm angry with.
I command him to strip them clean, rob them blind,
    and then push their faces in the mud and leave them.
But Assyria has another agenda;
    he has something else in mind.
He's out to destroy utterly,
    to stamp out as many nations as he can.
Assyria says, 'Aren't my commanders all kings?
    Can't they do whatever they like?
Didn't I destroy Calno as well as Carchemish?
    Hamath as well as Arpad? Level Samaria as I did Damascus?
I've eliminated kingdoms full of gods
    far more impressive than anything in Jerusalem and Samaria.
So what's to keep me from destroying Jerusalem
    in the same way I destroyed Samaria and all her god-idols?'"

When the Master has finished dealing with Mount Zion and
Jerusalem, he'll say, "Now it's Assyria's turn. I'll punish the bragging arro-

gance of the king of Assyria, his high and mighty posturing, the way
he goes around saying,

"'I've done all this by myself.
  I know more than anyone.
I've wiped out the boundaries of whole countries.
  I've walked in and taken anything I wanted.
I charged in like a bull
  and toppled their kings from their thrones.
I reached out my hand and took all that they treasured
  as easily as a boy taking a bird's eggs from a nest.
Like a farmer gathering eggs from the hen house,
  I gathered the world in my basket,
And no one so much as fluttered a wing
  or squawked or even chirped.'"

Does an ax take over from the one who swings it?
  Does a saw act more important than the sawyer?
As if a shovel did its shoveling by using a ditch digger!
  As if a hammer used the carpenter to pound nails!
Therefore the Master, GOD-of-the-Angel-Armies,
  will send a debilitating disease on his robust Assyrian fighters.
Under the canopy of God's bright glory
  a fierce fire will break out.
Israel's Light will burst into a conflagration.
  The Holy will explode into a firestorm,
And in one day burn to cinders
  every last Assyrian thornbush.
GOD will destroy the splendid trees and lush gardens.
  The Assyrian body and soul will waste away to nothing
  like a disease-ridden invalid.
A child could count what's left of the trees
  on the fingers of his two hands.

✝

And on that Day also, what's left of Israel, the ragtag survivors of Jacob,
will no longer be fascinated by abusive, battering Assyria. They'll lean
on GOD, The Holy—yes, truly. The ragtag remnant—what's left of
Jacob—will come back to the Strong God. Your people Israel were once

like the sand on the seashore, but only a scattered few will return. Destruction is ordered, brimming over with righteousness. For the Master, GOD-of-the-Angel-Armies, will finish here what he started all over the globe.

Therefore the Master, GOD-of-the-Angel-Armies, says: "My dear, dear people who live in Zion, don't be terrorized by the Assyrians when they beat you with clubs and threaten you with rods like the Egyptians once did. In just a short time my anger against you will be spent and I'll turn my destroying anger on them. I, GOD-of-the-Angel-Armies, will go after them with a cat-o'-nine-tails and finish them off decisively— as Gideon downed Midian at the rock Oreb, as Moses turned the tables on Egypt. On that day, Assyria will be pulled off your back, and the yoke of slavery lifted from your neck."

✝

Assyria's on the move: up from Rimmon,
    on to Aiath,
through Migron,
    with a bivouac at Michmash.
They've crossed the pass,
    set camp at Geba for the night.
Ramah trembles with fright.
    Gibeah of Saul has run off.
Cry for help, daughter of Gallim!
    Listen to her, Laishah!
    Do something, Anathoth!
Madmenah takes to the hills.
    The people of Gebim flee in panic.
The enemy's soon at Nob—nearly there!
    In sight of the city he shakes his fist
At the mount of dear daughter Zion,
    the hill of Jerusalem.

But now watch this: The Master, GOD-of-the-Angel-Armies,
    swings his ax and lops the branches,
Chops down the giant trees,
    lays flat the towering forest-on-the-march.
His ax will make toothpicks of that forest,
    that Lebanon-like army reduced to kindling.

37

11

A GREEN SHOOT FROM JESSE'S STUMP

A green Shoot will sprout from Jesse's stump,
     from his roots a budding Branch.
The life-giving Spirit of GOD will hover over him,
     the Spirit that brings wisdom and understanding,
The Spirit that gives direction and builds strength,
     the Spirit that instills knowledge and Fear-of-GOD.
Fear-of-GOD
     will be all his joy and delight.
He won't judge by appearances,
     won't decide on the basis of hearsay.
He'll judge the needy by what is right,
     render decisions on earth's poor with justice.
His words will bring everyone to awed attention.
     A mere breath from his lips will topple the wicked.
Each morning he'll pull on sturdy work clothes and boots,
     and build righteousness and faithfulness in the land.

A LIVING KNOWLEDGE OF GOD

The wolf will romp with the lamb,
     the leopard sleep with the kid.
Calf and lion will eat from the same trough,
     and a little child will tend them.
Cow and bear will graze the same pasture,
     their calves and cubs grow up together,
     and the lion eat straw like the ox.
The nursing child will crawl over rattlesnake dens,
     the toddler stick his hand down the hole of a serpent.
Neither animal nor human will hurt or kill
     on my holy mountain.
The whole earth will be brimming with knowing God-Alive,
     a living knowledge of God ocean-deep, ocean-wide.

✠

On that day, Jesse's Root will be raised high, posted as a rallying banner for the peoples. The nations will all come to him. His headquarters will be glorious.

Also on that day, the Master for the second time will reach out to bring back what's left of his scattered people. He'll bring them back from Assyria, Egypt, Pathros, Ethiopia, Elam, Sinar, Hamath, and the ocean islands.

And he'll raise that rallying banner high, visible to all nations,
    gather in all the scattered exiles of Israel,
Pull in all the dispersed refugees of Judah
    from the four winds and the seven seas.
The jealousy of Ephraim will dissolve,
    the hostility of Judah will vanish—
Ephraim no longer the jealous rival of Judah,
    Judah no longer the hostile rival of Ephraim!
Blood brothers united, they'll pounce on the Philistines in the west,
    join forces to plunder the people in the east.
They'll attack Edom and Moab.
    The Ammonites will fall into line.
GOD will once again dry up Egypt's Red Sea,
    making for an easy crossing.
He'll send a blistering wind
    down on the great River Euphrates,
Reduce it to seven mere trickles.
    None even need get their feet wet!
In the end there'll be a highway all the way from Assyria,
    easy traveling for what's left of God's people—
A highway just like the one Israel had
    when he marched up out of Egypt.

12

MY STRENGTH AND SONG

And you will say in that day,
    "I thank you, GOD.
You were angry
    but your anger wasn't forever.
You withdrew your anger
    and moved in and comforted me.

"Yes, indeed—God is my salvation.
    I trust, I won't be afraid.

GOD—yes GOD!—is my strength and song,
     best of all, my salvation!"

Joyfully you'll pull up buckets of water
     from the wells of salvation.
And as you do it, you'll say,
     "Give thanks to GOD.
Call out his name.
     Ask him anything!
Shout to the nations, tell them what he's done,
     spread the news of his great reputation!

Sing praise-songs to GOD. He's done it all!
     Let the whole earth know what he's done!
Raise the roof! Sing your hearts out, oh Zion!
     The Greatest lives among you: The Holy of Israel.

13

BABYLON IS DOOMED!

The Message on Babylon. Isaiah son of Amoz saw it:

"Run up a flag on an open hill.
     Yell loud. Get their attention.
Wave them into formation.
     Direct them to the nerve center of power.
I've taken charge of my special forces,
     called up my crack troops.
They're bursting with pride and passion
     to carry out my angry judgment."

Thunder rolls off the mountains
     like a mob huge and noisy—
Thunder of kingdoms in an uproar,
     nations assembling for war.
GOD-of-the-Angel-Armies is calling
     his army into battle formation.
They come from far-off countries,
     they pour in across the horizon.

It's GOD on the move with the weapons of his wrath,
    ready to destroy the whole country.

Wail! GOD's Day of Judgment is near—
    an avalanche crashing down from the Strong God!
Everyone paralyzed in the panic,
    hysterical and unstrung,
Doubled up in pain
    like a woman giving birth to a baby.
Horrified—everyone they see
    is like a face out of a nightmare.

✝

"Watch now. GOD's Judgment Day comes.
    Cruel it is, a day of wrath and anger,
A day to waste the earth
    and clean out all the sinners.
The stars in the sky, the great parade of constellations,
    will be nothing but black holes.
The sun will come up as a black disk,
    and the moon a blank nothing.
I'll put a full stop to the evil on earth,
    terminate the dark acts of the wicked.
I'll gag all braggarts and boasters—not a peep anymore from them—
    and trip strutting tyrants, leave them flat on their faces.
Proud humanity will disappear from the earth.
    I'll make mortals rarer than hens' teeth.
And yes, I'll even make the sky shake,
    and the earth quake to its roots
Under the wrath of GOD-of-the-Angel-Armies,
    the Judgment Day of his raging anger.
Like a hunted white-tailed deer,
    like lost sheep with no shepherd,
People will huddle with a few of their own kind,
    run off to some makeshift shelter.
But tough luck to stragglers—they'll be killed on the spot,
    throats cut, bellies ripped open,
Babies smashed on the rocks
    while mothers and fathers watch,

Houses looted,
    wives raped.

"And now watch this:
    Against Babylon, I'm inciting the Medes,
A ruthless bunch indifferent to bribes,
    the kind of brutality that no one can blunt.
They massacre the young,
    wantonly kick and kill even babies.
And Babylon, most glorious of all kingdoms,
    the pride and joy of Chaldeans,
Will end up smoking and stinking like Sodom,
    and, yes, like Gomorrah, when God had finished with them.
No one will live there anymore,
    generation after generation a ghost town.
Not even Bedouins will pitch tents there.
    Shepherds will give it a wide berth.
But strange and wild animals will like it just fine,
    filling the vacant houses with eerie night sounds.
Skunks will make it their home,
    and unspeakable night hags will haunt it.
Hyenas will curdle your blood with their laughing,
    and the howling of coyotes will give you the shivers.

"Babylon is doomed.
    It won't be long now."

14

Now You Are Nothing

But not so with Jacob. GOD will have compassion on Jacob. Once again he'll choose Israel. He'll establish them in their own country. Outsiders will be attracted and throw their lot in with Jacob. The nations among whom they lived will actually escort them back home, and then Israel will pay them back by making slaves of them, men and women alike, possessing them as slaves in GOD's country, capturing those who had captured them, ruling over those who had abused them.

When GOD has given you time to recover from the abuse and trouble and harsh servitude that you had to endure, you can amuse yourselves by taking up this satire, a taunt against the king of Babylon:

Can you believe it? The tyrant is gone!
    The tyranny is over!
GOD has broken the rule of the wicked,
    the power of the bully-rulers
That crushed many people.
    A relentless rain of cruel outrage
Established a violent rule of anger
    rife with torture and persecution.

And now it's over, the whole earth quietly at rest.
    Burst into song! Make the rafters ring!
Ponderosa pine trees are happy,
    giant Lebanon cedars are relieved, saying,
"Since you've been cut down,
    there's no one around to cut us down."
And the underworld dead are all excited,
    preparing to welcome you when you come.
Getting ready to greet you are the ghostly dead,
    all the famous names of earth.
All the buried kings of the nations
    will stand up on their thrones
With well-prepared speeches,
    royal invitations to death:
"Now you are as nothing as we are!
    Make yourselves at home with us dead folks!"

This is where your pomp and fine music led you, Babylon,
    to your underworld private chambers,
A king-size mattress of maggots for repose
    and a quilt of crawling worms for warmth.

What a come-down this, oh Babylon!
    Daystar! Son of Dawn!
Flat on your face in the underworld mud,
    you, famous for flattening nations!

You said to yourself,
    "I'll climb to heaven.
I'll set my throne
    over the stars of God.

I'll run the assembly of angels
    that meets on sacred Mount Zaphon.
I'll climb to the top of the clouds.
    I'll take over as King of the Universe!"

But you didn't make it, did you?
    Instead of climbing up, you came down—
Down with the underground dead,
    down to the abyss of the Pit.
People will stare and muse:
    "Can this be the one
Who terrorized earth and its kingdoms,
    turned earth to a moonscape,
Wasted its cities,
    shut up his prisoners to a living death?"

Other kings get a decent burial,
    honored with eulogies and placed in a tomb.
But you're dumped in a ditch unburied,
    like a stray dog or cat,
Covered with rotting bodies,
    murdered and indigent corpses.
Your dead body desecrated, mutilated—
    no state funeral for you!
You've left your land in ruins,
    left a legacy of massacre.
The progeny of your evil life
    will never be named. Oblivion!

Get a place ready to slaughter the sons of the wicked
    and wipe out their father's line.
Unthinkable that they should own a square foot of land
    or desecrate the face of the world with their cities!

"I will confront them"—Decree of GOD-of-the-Angel-Armies—
"and strip Babylon of name and survivors, children and grandchildren."
GOD's Decree. "I'll make it a worthless swamp and give it as a prize to
the hedgehog. And then I'll bulldoze it out of existence." Decree of GOD-
of-the-Angel-Armies.

WHO COULD EVER CANCEL SUCH PLANS?

GOD-of-the-Angel-Armies speaks:

"Exactly as I planned,
    it will happen.
Following my blueprints,
    it will take shape.
I will shatter the Assyrian who trespasses my land
    and stomp him into the dirt on my mountains.
I will ban his taking and making of slaves
    and lift the weight of oppression from all shoulders."
This is the plan,
    planned for the whole earth,
And this is the hand that will do it,
    reaching into every nation.
GOD-of-the-Angel-Armies has planned it.
    Who could ever cancel such plans?
His is the hand that's reached out.
    Who could brush it aside?

In the year King Ahaz died, this Message came:

Hold it, Philistines! It's too soon to celebrate
    the defeat of your cruel oppressor.
From the death throes of that snake a worse snake will come,
    and from that, one even worse.
The poor won't have to worry.
    The needy will escape the terror.
But you Philistines will be plunged into famine,
    and those who don't starve, God will kill.
Wail and howl, proud city!
    Fall prostrate in fear, Philistia!
On the northern horizon, smoke from burned cities,
    the wake of a brutal, disciplined destroyer.

What does one say to
    outsiders who ask questions?
Tell them, "GOD has established Zion.
    Those in need and in trouble find refuge in her."

15

POIGNANT CRIES REVERBERATE THROUGH MOAB

A Message concerning Moab:

Village Ar of Moab is in ruins,
    destroyed in a night raid.
Village Kir of Moab is in ruins,
    destroyed in a night raid.
Village Dibon climbs to its chapel in the hills,
    goes up to lament.
Moab weeps and wails
    over Nebo and Medba.
Every head is shaved bald,
    every beard shaved clean.
They pour into the streets wearing black,
    go up on the roofs, take to the town square,
Everyone in tears,
    everyone in grief.
Towns Heshbon and Elealeh cry long and loud.
    The sound carries as far as Jahaz.
Moab sobs, shaking in grief.
    The soul of Moab trembles.

Oh, how I grieve for Moab!
    Refugees stream to Zoar
    and then on to Eglath-shelishiyah.
Up the slopes of Luhith they weep;
    on the road to Horonaim they cry their loss.
The springs of Nimrim are dried up—
    grass brown, buds stunted, nothing grows.
They leave, carrying all their possessions
    on their backs, everything they own,
Making their way as best they can
    across Willow Creek to safety.
Poignant cries reverberate
    all through Moab,
Gut-wrenching sobs as far as Eglaim,
    heart-racking sobs all the way to Beer-elim.

The banks of the Dibon crest with blood,
>	but God has worse in store for Dibon:
A lion—a lion to finish off the fugitives,
>	to clean up whoever's left in the land.

16

A New Government in the David Tradition

"Dispatch a gift of lambs," says Moab,
>	"to the leaders in Jerusalem—
Lambs from Sela sent across the desert
>	to buy the goodwill of Jerusalem.
The towns and people of Moab
>	are at a loss,
New-hatched birds knocked from the nest,
>	fluttering helplessly
At the banks of the Arnon River,
>	unable to cross:
'Tell us what to do,
>	help us out!
Protect us,
>	hide us!
Give the refugees from Moab
>	sanctuary with you.
Be a safe place for those on the run
>	from the killing fields.'"

"When this is all over," Judah answers,
>	"the tyrant toppled,
The killing at an end,
>	all signs of these cruelties long gone,
A new government of love will be established
>	in the venerable David tradition.
A Ruler you can depend upon
>	will head this government,
A Ruler passionate for justice,
>	a Ruler quick to set things right."

✝

We've heard—everyone's heard!—of Moab's pride,
    world-famous for pride—
Arrogant, self-important, insufferable,
    full of hot air.
So now let Moab lament for a change,
    with antiphonal mock-laments from the neighbors!
What a shame! How terrible!
    No more fine fruitcakes and Kir-haresheth candies!
All those lush Heshbon fields dried up,
    the rich Sibmah vineyards withered!
Foreign thugs have crushed and torn out
    the famous grapevines
That once reached all the way to Jazer,
    right to the edge of the desert,
Ripped out the crops in every direction
    as far as the eye can see.
I'll join the weeping. I'll weep right along with Jazer,
    weep for the Sibmah vineyards.
And yes, Heshbon and Elealeh,
    I'll mingle my tears with your tears!
The joyful shouting at harvest is gone.
    Instead of song and celebration, dead silence.
No more boisterous laughter in the orchards,
    no more hearty work songs in the vineyards.
Instead of the bustle and sound of good work in the fields,
    silence—deathly and deadening silence.
My heartstrings throb like harp strings for Moab,
    my soul in sympathy for sad Kir-heres.
When Moab trudges to the shrine to pray,
    he wastes both time and energy.
Going to the sanctuary and praying for relief
    is useless. Nothing ever happens.

This is GOD's earlier Message on Moab. GOD's updated Message is, "In three years, no longer than the term of an enlisted soldier, Moab's impressive presence will be gone, that splendid hot-air balloon will be punctured, and instead of a vigorous population, just a few shuffling bums cadging handouts."

17
DAMASCUS: A PILE OF DUST AND RUBBLE

A Message concerning Damascus:

"Watch this: Damascus undone as a city,
    a pile of dust and rubble!
Her towns emptied of people.
    The sheep and goats will move in
And take over the towns
    as if they owned them—which they will!
Not a sign of a fort is left in Ephraim,
    not a trace of government left in Damascus.
What's left of Aram?
        The same as what's left of Israel—not much."
            Decree of GOD-of-the-Angel-Armies.

THE DAY IS COMING

"The Day is coming when Jacob's robust splendor goes pale
    and his well-fed body turns skinny.
The country will be left empty, picked clean
    as a field harvested by field hands.
She'll be like a few stalks of barley left standing
    in the lush Valley of Rephaim after harvest,
Or like the couple of ripe olives overlooked
    in the top of the olive tree,
Or the four or five apples
    that the pickers couldn't reach in the orchard."
        Decree of the GOD of Israel.

Yes, the Day is coming when people will notice The One Who Made Them, take a long hard look at The Holy of Israel. They'll lose interest in all the stuff they've made—altars and monuments and rituals, their homemade, handmade religion—however impressive it is.

And yes, the Day is coming when their fortress cities will be abandoned—the very same cities that the Hivites and Amorites abandoned when Israel invaded! And the country will be empty, desolate.

You Have Forgotten God

And why? Because you have forgotten God-Your-Salvation,
    not remembered your Rock-of-Refuge.
And so, even though you are very religious,
    planting all sorts of bushes and herbs and trees
    to honor and influence your fertility gods,
And even though you make them grow so well,
    bursting with buds and sprouts and blossoms,
Nothing will come of them. Instead of a harvest
    you'll get nothing but grief and pain, pain, pain.

Oh my! Thunder! A thundering herd of people!
    Thunder like the crashing of ocean waves!
Nations roaring, roaring,
    like the roar of a massive waterfall,
Roaring like a deafening niagara!
    But God will silence them with a word,
And then he'll blow them away like dead leaves off a tree,
    like down from a thistle.

At bedtime, terror fills the air.
    By morning it's gone—not a sign of it anywhere!
This is what happens to those who would ruin us,
    this is the fate of those out to get us.

18

People Mighty and Merciless

Doom to the land of flies and mosquitoes
    beyond the Ethiopian rivers,
Shipping emissaries all over the world,
    down rivers and across seas.

Go, swift messengers,
    go to this people tall and handsome,
This people held in respect everywhere,
    this people mighty and merciless,
    from the land crisscrossed with rivers.

Everybody everywhere,
    all earth-dwellers:
When you see a flag flying on the mountain, look!
    When you hear the trumpet blown, listen!

For here's what GOD told me:

"I'm not going to say anything,
    but simply look on from where I live,
Quiet as warmth that comes from the sun,
    silent as dew during harvest."
And then, just before harvest, after the blossom
    has turned into a maturing grape,
He'll step in and prune back the new shoots,
    ruthlessly hack off all the growing branches.
He'll leave them piled on the ground
    for birds and animals to feed on—
Fodder for the summering birds,
    fodder for the wintering animals.

Then tribute will be brought to GOD-of-the-Angel-Armies,
    brought from this people tall and handsome,
This people once held in respect everywhere,
    this people once mighty and merciless,
From the land crisscrossed with rivers,
    to Mount Zion, GOD's place.

19

ANARCHY AND CHAOS AND KILLING!

A Message concerning Egypt:

Watch this! GOD riding on a fast-moving cloud,
    moving in on Egypt!
The god-idols of Egypt shudder and shake,
    Egyptians paralyzed by panic.

God says, "I'll make Egyptian fight Egyptian,
    brother fight brother, neighbor fight neighbor,

City fight city, kingdom fight kingdom—
    anarchy and chaos and killing!
I'll knock the wind out of the Egyptians.
    They won't know coming from going.
They'll go to their god-idols for answers;
    they'll conjure ghosts and hold seances, desperate for answers.
But I'll turn the Egyptians
    over to a tyrant most cruel.
I'll put them under the rule of a mean, merciless king."
    Decree of the Master, GOD-of-the-Angel-Armies.

The River Nile will dry up,
    the riverbed baked dry in the sun.
The canals will become stagnant and stink,
    every stream touching the Nile dry up.
River vegetation will rot away
    the banks of the Nile-baked clay,
The riverbed hard and smooth,
    river grasses dried up and gone with the wind.
Fishermen will complain
    that the fishing's been ruined.
Textile workers will be out of work, all weavers
    and workers in linen and cotton and wool
Dispirited, depressed in their forced idleness—
    everyone who works for a living, jobless.

The princes of Zoan are fools,
    the advisors of Pharaoh stupid.
How could any of you dare tell Pharaoh,
    "Trust me: I'm wise. I know what's going on.
    Why, I'm descended from the old wisdom of Egypt"?
There's not a wise man or woman left in the country.
    If there were, one of them would tell you
    what GOD-of-the-Angel-Armies has in mind for Egypt.
As it is, the princes of Zoan are all fools
    and the princes of Memphis, dunces.
The honored pillars of your society
    have led Egypt into detours and dead ends.
GOD has scrambled their brains,
    Egypt's become a falling-down-in-his-own-vomit drunk.

Egypt's hopeless, past helping,
  a senile, doddering old fool.

✜

On that Day, Egyptians will be like hysterical schoolgirls, screaming at
the first hint of action from GOD-of-the-Angel-Armies. Little Judah will
strike terror in Egyptians! Say "Judah" to an Egyptian and see panic. The
word triggers fear of the GOD-of-the-Angel-Armies' plan against Egypt.

  On that Day, more than one city in Egypt will learn to speak the
language of faith and promise to follow GOD-of-the-Angel-Armies. One
of these cities will be honored with the title "City of the Sun."

  On that Day, there will be a place of worship to GOD in the center
of Egypt and a monument to GOD at its border. It will show how the
GOD-of-the-Angel-Armies has helped the Egyptians. When they cry out
in prayer to GOD because of oppressors, he'll send them help, a savior
who will keep them safe and take care of them. GOD will openly show
himself to the Egyptians and they'll get to know him on that Day. They'll
worship him seriously with sacrifices and burnt offerings. They'll make
vows and keep them. GOD will wound Egypt, first hit and then heal.
Egypt will come back to GOD, and GOD will listen to their prayers and
heal them, heal them from head to toe.

  On that Day, there will be a highway all the way from Egypt to
Assyria: Assyrians will have free range in Egypt and Egyptians in Assyria.
No longer rivals, they'll worship together, Egyptians and Assyrians!

  On that Day, Israel will take its place alongside Egypt and Assyria,
sharing the blessing from the center. GOD-of-the-Angel-Armies, who
blessed Israel, will generously bless them all: "Blessed be Egypt, my
people! . . . Blessed be Assyria, work of my hands! . . . Blessed be Israel,
my heritage!"

20

EXPOSED TO MOCKERY AND JEERS

In the year the field commander, sent by King Sargon of Assyria, came
to Ashdod and fought and took it, GOD told Isaiah son of Amoz, "Go,
take off your clothes and sandals," and Isaiah did it, going about naked
and barefooted.

  Then GOD said, "Just as my servant Isaiah has walked around town
naked and barefooted for three years as a warning sign to Egypt and

Ethiopia, so the king of Assyria is going to come and take the Egyptians as captives and the Ethiopians as exiles. He'll take young and old alike and march them out of there naked and barefooted, exposed to mockery and jeers—the bared buttocks of Egypt on parade! Everyone who has put hope in Ethiopia and expected help from Egypt will be thrown into confusion. Everyone who lives along this coast will say, 'Look at them! Naked and barefooted, shuffling off to exile! And we thought they were our best hope, that they'd rescue us from the king of Assyria. *Now* what's going to happen to us? How are we going to get out of this?'"

21

THE BETRAYER BETRAYED

A Message concerning the desert at the sea:

As tempests drive through the Negev Desert,
    coming out of the desert, that terror-filled place,
A hard vision is given me:
    The betrayer betrayed, the plunderer plundered.
Attack, Elam!
    Lay siege, Media!
Persians, attack!
    Attack, Babylon!
I'll put an end to
    all the moaning and groaning.
Because of this news I'm doubled up in pain,
    writhing in pain like a woman having a baby,
Baffled by what I hear,
    undone by what I see.
Absolutely stunned,
    horror-stricken,
I had hoped for a relaxed evening,
    but it has turned into a nightmare.

The banquet is spread,
    the guests reclining in luxurious ease,
Eating and drinking, having a good time,
    and then, "To arms, princes! The fight is on!"

The Master told me, "Go, post a lookout.
    Have him report whatever he spots.
When he sees horses and wagons in battle formation,
    lines of donkeys and columns of camels,
Tell him to keep his ear to the ground,
    note every whisper, every rumor."
Just then, the lookout shouted,
    "I'm at my post, Master,
Sticking to my post day after day
    and all through the night!
I watched them come,
    the horses and wagons in battle formation.
I heard them call out the war news in headlines:
    'Babylon fallen! Fallen!
And all its precious god-idols
    smashed to pieces on the ground.'"

Dear Israel, you've been through a lot,
    you've been put through the mill.
The good news I get from GOD-of-the-Angel-Armies,
    the God of Israel, I now pass on to you.

✠

A Message concerning Edom:

A voice calls to me
    from the Seir mountains in Edom,
"Night watchman! How long till daybreak?
    How long will this night last?"
The night watchman calls back,
    "Morning's coming,
But for now it's still night.
    If you ask me again, I'll give the same answer."

✠

A Message concerning Arabia:

You'll have to camp out in the desert badlands,
    you caravans of Dedanites.

Haul water to the thirsty,
    greet fugitives with bread.
Show your desert hospitality,
    you who live in Tema.
The desert's swarming with refugees
    escaping the horrors of war.

The Master told me, "Hang on. Within one year—I'll sign a contract on it!—the arrogant brutality of Kedar, those hooligans of the
desert, will be over, nothing much left of the Kedar toughs." The GOD
of Israel says so.

22

A COUNTRY OF COWARDS

A Message concerning the Valley of Vision:

What's going on here anyway?
    All this partying and noisemaking,
Shouting and cheering in the streets,
    the city noisy with celebrations!
You have no brave soldiers to honor,
    no combat heroes to be proud of.
Your leaders were all cowards,
    captured without even lifting a sword,
A country of cowards
    captured escaping the battle.

YOU LOOKED, BUT YOU NEVER LOOKED TO HIM

In the midst of the shouting, I said, "Let me alone.
    Let me grieve by myself.
Don't tell me it's going to be all right.
    These people are doomed. It's *not* all right."
For the Master, GOD-of-the-Angel-Armies,
    is bringing a day noisy with mobs of people,
Jostling and stampeding in the Valley of Vision,
    knocking down walls
    and hollering to the mountains, "Attack! Attack!"

Old enemies Elam and Kir arrive armed to the teeth—
  weapons and chariots and cavalry.
Your fine valleys are noisy with war,
  chariots and cavalry charging this way and that.
  God has left Judah exposed and defenseless.

You assessed your defenses that Day, inspected your arsenal of
weapons in the Forest Armory. You found the weak places in the city
walls that needed repair. You secured the water supply at the Lower
Pool. You took an inventory of the houses in Jerusalem and tore down
some to get bricks to fortify the city wall. You built a large cistern to
ensure plenty of water.
  You looked and looked and looked, but you never looked to him
who gave you this city, never once consulted the One who has long had
plans for this city.

The Master, GOD-of-the-Angel-Armies,
  called out on that Day,
Called for a day of repentant tears,
  called you to dress in somber clothes of mourning.
But what do *you* do? You throw a party!
  Eating and drinking and dancing in the streets!
You barbecue bulls and sheep, and throw a huge feast—
  slabs of meat, kegs of beer.
"Seize the day! Eat and drink!
  Tomorrow we die!"

GOD-of-the-Angel-Armies whispered to me his verdict on this fri-
volity: "You'll pay for this outrage until the day you die." The Master,
GOD-of-the-Angel-Armies, says so.

THE KEY OF THE DAVIDIC HERITAGE

The Master, GOD-of-the-Angel-Armies, spoke: "Come. Go to this steward, Shebna, who is in charge of all the king's affairs, and tell him: What's
going on here? You're an outsider here and yet you act like you own the
place, make a big, fancy tomb for yourself where everyone can see it,
making sure everyone will think you're important. GOD is about to sack
you, to throw you to the dogs. He'll grab you by the hair, swing you
round and round dizzyingly, and then let you go, sailing through the

air like a ball, until you're out of sight. Where you'll land, nobody knows. And there you'll die, and all the stuff you've collected heaped on your grave. You've disgraced your master's house! You're fired—and good riddance!

"On that Day I'll replace Shebna. I will call my servant Eliakim son of Hilkiah. I'll dress him in your robe. I'll put your belt on him. I'll give him your authority. He'll be a father-leader to Jerusalem and the government of Judah. I'll give him the key of the Davidic heritage. He'll have the run of the place—open any door and keep it open, lock any door and keep it locked. I'll pound him like a nail into a solid wall. He'll secure the Davidic tradition. Everything will hang on him—not only the fate of Davidic descendants but also the detailed daily operations of the house, including cups and cutlery.

"And then the Day will come," says GOD-of-the-Angel-Armies, "when that nail will come loose and fall out, break loose from that solid wall—and everything hanging on it will go with it." That's what will happen. GOD says so.

23

IT WAS ALL NUMBERS, DEAD NUMBERS, PROFIT AND LOSS

Wail, ships of Tarshish,
    your strong seaports all in ruins!
When the ships returned from Cyprus,
    they saw the destruction.
Hold your tongue, you who live on the seacoast,
    merchants of Sidon.
Your people sailed the deep seas,
    buying and selling,
Making money on wheat from Shihor,
    grown along the Nile—
    multinational broker in grains!
Hang your head in shame, Sidon. The Sea speaks up,
    the powerhouse of the ocean says,
"I've never had labor pains, never had a baby,
    never reared children to adulthood,
Never gave life, never worked with life.
    It was all numbers, dead numbers, profit and loss."

When Egypt gets the report on Tyre,
    what wailing! what wringing of hands!

NOTHING LEFT HERE TO BE PROUD OF

Visit Tarshish, you who live on the seacoast.
    Take a good, long look and wail—yes, cry buckets of tears!
Is this the city you remember as energetic and alive,
    bustling with activity, this historic old city,
Expanding throughout the globe,
    buying and selling all over the world?
And who is behind the collapse of Tyre,
    the Tyre that controlled the world markets?
Tyre's merchants were the business tycoons.
    Tyre's traders called all the shots.
GOD-of-the-Angel-Armies ordered the crash
    to show the sordid backside of pride
    and puncture the inflated reputations.
Sail for home, oh ships of Tarshish.
    There are no docks left in this harbor.
GOD reached out to the sea and sea traders,
    threw the sea kingdoms into turmoil.
GOD ordered the destruction
    of the seacoast cities, the centers of commerce.
GOD said, "There's nothing left here to be proud of,
    bankrupt and bereft Sidon.
Do you want to make a new start in Cyprus?
    Don't count on it. Nothing there will work out for you either."

Look at what happened to Babylon: There's nothing left of it.
Assyria turned it into a desert, into a refuge for wild dogs and stray cats.
They brought in their big siege engines, tore down the buildings, and
left nothing behind but rubble.

Wail, ships of Tarshish,
    your strong seaports all in ruins!

✠

For the next seventy years, a king's lifetime, Tyre will be forgotten. At
the end of the seventy years, Tyre will stage a comeback, but it will be
the comeback of a worn-out whore, as in the song:

"Take a harp, circle the city,
   unremembered whore.
Sing your old songs, your many old songs.
   Maybe someone will remember."

At the end of the seventy years, GOD will look in on Tyre. She'll go back to her old whoring trade, selling herself to the highest bidder, doing anything with anyone—promiscuous with all the kingdoms of earth— for a fee. But everything she gets, all the money she takes in, will be turned over to GOD. It will not be put in banks. Her profits will be put to the use of GOD-Aware, GOD-Serving-People, providing plenty of food and the best of clothing.

24

THE LANDSCAPE WILL BE A MOONSCAPE

Danger ahead! GOD's about to ravish the earth
   and leave it in ruins,
Rip everything out by the roots
   and send everyone scurrying:
         priests and laypeople alike,
         owners and workers alike,
         celebrities and nobodies alike,
         buyers and sellers alike,
         bankers and beggars alike,
         the haves and have-nots alike.
The landscape will be a moonscape,
   totally wasted.
And why? Because GOD says so.
   He's issued the orders.

The earth turns gaunt and gray,
   the world silent and sad,
   sky and land lifeless, colorless.

EARTH POLLUTED BY ITS VERY OWN PEOPLE

Earth is polluted by its very own people,
   who have broken its laws,
Disrupted its order,

violated the sacred and eternal covenant.
Therefore a curse, like a cancer,
    ravages the earth.
Its people pay the price of their sacrilege.
    They dwindle away, dying out one by one.
No more wine, no more vineyards,
    no more songs or singers.
The laughter of castanets is gone,
    the shouts of celebrants, gone,
    the laughter of fiddles, gone.
No more parties with toasts of champagne.
    Serious drinkers gag on their drinks.
The chaotic cities are unlivable. Anarchy reigns.
    Every house is boarded up, condemned.
People riot in the streets for wine,
    but the good times are gone forever—
    no more joy for this old world.
The city is dead and deserted,
    bulldozed into piles of rubble.
That's the way it will be on this earth.
    This is the fate of all nations:
An olive tree shaken clean of its olives,
    a grapevine picked clean of its grapes.

But there are some who will break into glad song.
    Out of the west they'll shout of GOD's majesty.
Yes, from the east GOD's glory will ascend.
    Every island of the sea
Will broadcast GOD's fame,
    the fame of the God of Israel.
From the four winds and the seven seas we hear the singing:
    "All praise to the Righteous One!"

But I said, "That's all well and good for somebody,
    but all I can see is doom, doom, and more doom."
All of them at one another's throats,
    yes, all of them at one another's throats.
Terror and pits and booby-traps
    are everywhere, whoever you are.
If you run from the terror,

you'll fall into the pit.
If you climb out of the pit,
　　you'll get caught in the trap.
Chaos pours out of the skies.
　　The foundations of earth are crumbling.
Earth is smashed to pieces,
　　earth is ripped to shreds,
　　earth is wobbling out of control,
Earth staggers like a drunk,
　　sways like a shack in a high wind.
Its piled-up sins are too much for it.
　　It collapses and won't get up again.

That's when GOD will call on the carpet
　　rebel powers in the skies and
Rebel kings on earth.
　　They'll be rounded up like prisoners in a jail,
Corralled and locked up in a jail,
　　and then sentenced and put to hard labor.
Shamefaced moon will cower, humiliated,
　　red-faced sun will skulk, disgraced,
Because GOD-of-the-Angel-Armies will take over,
　　ruling from Mount Zion and Jerusalem,
Splendid and glorious
　　before all his leaders.

25

GOD'S HAND RESTS ON THIS MOUNTAIN

GOD, you are *my* God.
　　I celebrate you. I praise you.
You've done your share of miracle-wonders,
　　well-thought-out plans, solid and sure.
Here you've reduced the city to rubble,
　　the strong city to a pile of stones.
The enemy Big City is a non-city,
　　never to be a city again.
Superpowers will see it and honor you,
　　brutal oppressors bow in worshipful reverence.

They'll see that you take care of the poor,
  that you take care of poor people in trouble,
Provide a warm, dry place in bad weather,
  provide a cool place when it's hot.
Brutal oppressors are like a winter blizzard
  and vicious foreigners like high noon in the desert.
But you, shelter from the storm and shade from the sun,
  shut the mouths of the big-mouthed bullies.

But here on this mountain, GOD-of-the-Angel-Armies
  will throw a feast for all the people of the world,
A feast of the finest foods, a feast with vintage wines,
  a feast of seven courses, a feast lavish with gourmet desserts.
And here on this mountain, GOD will banish
  the pall of doom hanging over all peoples,
The shadow of doom darkening all nations.
  Yes, he'll banish death forever.
And GOD will wipe the tears from every face.
  He'll remove every sign of disgrace
From his people, wherever they are.
  Yes! GOD says so!

Also at that time, people will say,
  "Look at what's happened! This is our God!
We waited for him and he showed up and saved us!
  This GOD, the one we waited for!
Let's celebrate, sing the joys of his salvation.
  GOD's hand rests on this mountain!"

As for the Moabites, they'll be treated like refuse,
  waste shoveled into a cesspool.
Thrash away as they will,
  like swimmers trying to stay afloat,
They'll sink in the sewage.
  Their pride will pull them under.
Their famous fortifications will crumble to nothing,
  those mighty walls reduced to dust.

26

STRETCH THE BORDERS OF LIFE

At that time, this song
 will be sung in the country of Judah:
We have a strong city, Salvation City,
 built and fortified with salvation.
Throw wide the gates
 so good and true people can enter.
People with their minds set on you,
 you keep completely whole,
Steady on their feet,
 because they keep at it and don't quit.
Depend on GOD and keep at it
 because in the LORD GOD you have a sure thing.
Those who lived high and mighty
 he knocked off their high horse.
He used the city built on the hill
 as fill for the marshes.
All the exploited and outcast peoples
 build their lives on the reclaimed land.

The path of right-living people is level.
 The Leveler evens the road for the right-living.
We're in no hurry, GOD. We're content to linger
 in the path sign-posted with your decisions.
Who you are and what you've done
 are all we'll ever want.
Through the night my soul longs for you.
 Deep from within me my spirit reaches out to you.
When your decisions are on public display,
 everyone learns how to live right.
If the wicked are shown grace,
 they don't seem to get it.
In the land of right living, they persist in wrong living,
 blind to the splendor of GOD.

You hold your hand up high, GOD,
 but they don't see it.

Open their eyes to what you do,
    to see your zealous love for your people.
Shame them. Light a fire under them.
    Get the attention of these enemies of yours.
GOD, order a peaceful and whole life for us
    because everything we've done, you've done for us.
Oh GOD, our God, we've had other masters rule us,
    but you're the only Master we've ever known.
The dead don't talk,
    ghosts don't walk,
Because you've said, "Enough—that's all for you,"
    and wiped them off the books.
But the living you make larger than life.
    The more life you give, the more glory you display,
    and stretch the borders to accommodate more living!

Oh GOD, they begged you for help when they were in trouble,
    when your discipline was so heavy
    they could barely whisper a prayer.
Like a woman having a baby,
    writhing in distress, screaming her pain
    as the baby is being born,
That's how we were because of you, oh GOD.
    We were pregnant full-term.
We writhed in labor but bore no baby.
    We gave birth to wind.
Nothing came of our labor.
    We produced nothing living.
    We couldn't save the world.

But friends, your dead will live,
    your corpses will get to their feet.
All you dead and buried,
    wake up! Sing!
Your dew is morning dew
    catching the first rays of sun,
The earth bursting with life,
    giving birth to the dead.

Come, my people, go home
    and shut yourselves in.

Go into seclusion for a while
    until the punishing wrath is past,
Because GOD is sure to come from his place
    to punish the wrong of the people on earth.
Earth itself will point out the blood stains;
    it will show where the murdered have been hidden away.

27

SELECTED GRAIN BY GRAIN

At that time GOD will unsheathe his sword,
    his merciless, massive, mighty sword.
He'll punish the serpent Leviathan as it flees,
    the serpent Leviathan thrashing in flight.
He'll kill that old dragon
    that lives in the sea.

"At that same time, a fine vineyard will appear.
    There's something to sing about!
I, GOD, tend it.
    I keep it well-watered.
I keep careful watch over it
    so that no one can damage it.
I'm not angry. I care.
    Even if it gives me thistles and thornbushes,
I'll just pull them out
    and burn them up.
Let that vine cling to me for safety,
    let it find a good and whole life with me,
    let it hold on for a good and whole life."

The days are coming when Jacob
    shall put down roots,
Israel blossom and grow fresh branches,
    and fill the world with its fruit.

Has GOD knocked them to the ground
    as he knocked down those who hit them? Oh, no.
Were they killed
    as their killers were killed? Again, no.

He was hard on them all right. The exile was a harsh sentence.
    He blew them away on a fierce blast of wind.
But the good news is that through this experience
    Jacob's guilt was taken away.
    The evidence that his sin is removed will be this:
He will tear down the alien altars,
    take them apart stone by stone,
And then crush the stones into gravel
    and clean out all the sex-and-religion shrines.
For there's nothing left of that pretentious grandeur.
    Nobody lives there anymore. It's unlivable.
But animals do just fine,
    browsing and bedding down.
And it's not a bad place to get firewood.
    Dry twigs and dead branches are plentiful.
It's the leavings of a people with no sense of God.
    So, the God who made them
Will have nothing to do with them.
    He who formed them will turn his back on them.

At that time GOD will thresh
    from the River Euphrates to the Brook of Egypt,
And you, people of Israel,
    will be selected grain by grain.
At that same time a great trumpet will be blown,
    calling home the exiles from Assyria,
Welcoming home the refugees from Egypt
    to come and worship GOD on the holy mountain, Jerusalem.

28

GOD WILL SPEAK IN BABY TALK

Doom to the pretentious drunks of Ephraim,
    shabby and washed out and seedy—
Tipsy, sloppy-fat, beer-bellied parodies
    of a proud and handsome past.
Watch closely: GOD has someone picked out,
    someone tough and strong to flatten them.
Like a hailstorm, like a hurricane, like a flash flood,

one-handed he'll throw them to the ground.
Samaria, the party hat on Israel's head,
    will be knocked off with one blow.
It will disappear quicker than
    a piece of meat tossed to a dog.

At that time, GOD-of-the-Angel-Armies will be
    the beautiful crown on the head of what's left of his people:
Energy and insights of justice to those who guide and decide,
    strength and prowess to those who guard and protect.

These also, the priest and prophet, stagger from drink,
    weaving, falling-down drunks,
Besotted with wine and whiskey,
    can't see straight, can't talk sense.
Every table is covered with vomit.
    They *live* in vomit.

"Is that so? And who do you think you are to teach us?
    Who are you to lord it over us?
We're not babies in diapers
    to be talked down to by such as you—
'Da, da, da, da,
    blah, blah, blah, blah.
That's a good little girl,
    that's a good little boy.'"

But that's exactly how you will be addressed.
    God will speak to this people
In baby talk, one syllable at a time—
    and he'll do it through foreign oppressors.
He said before, "This is the time and place to rest,
    to give rest to the weary.
This is the place to lay down your burden."
    But they won't listen.

So GOD will start over with the simple basics
    and address them in baby talk, one syllable at a time—
"Da, da, da, da,
    blah, blah, blah, blah.

That's a good little girl,
    that's a good little boy."
And like toddlers, they will get up and fall down,
    get bruised and confused and lost.

Now listen to GOD's Message, you scoffers,
    you who rule this people in Jerusalem.
You say, "We've taken out good life insurance.
    We've hedged all our bets, covered all our bases.
No disaster can touch us. We've thought of everything.
    We're advised by the experts. We're set."

THE MEANING OF THE STONE

But the Master, GOD, has something to say to this:

"Watch closely. I'm laying a foundation in Zion,
    a solid granite foundation, squared and true.
And this is the meaning of the stone:
    A TRUSTING LIFE WON'T TOPPLE.
I'll make justice the measuring stick
    and righteousness the plumb line for the building.
A hailstorm will knock down the shantytown of lies,
    and a flash flood will wash out the rubble.

"Then you'll see that your precious life insurance policy
    wasn't worth the paper it was written on.
Your careful precautions against death
    were a pack of illusions and lies.
When the disaster happens,
    you'll be crushed by it.
Every time disaster comes, you'll be in on it—
    disaster in the morning, disaster at night."
Every report of disaster
    will send you cowering in terror.
There will be no place where you can rest,
    nothing to hide under.
GOD will rise to full stature,
    raging as he did long ago on Mount Perazim
And in the valley of Gibeon against the Philistines.

But this time it's against *you*.
Hard to believe, but true.
    Not what you'd expect, but it's coming.
Sober up, friends, and don't scoff.
    Scoffing will just make it worse.
I've heard the orders issued for destruction, orders from
    God-of-the-Angel-Armies—ending up in an international
        disaster.

☩

Listen to me now.
    Give me your closest attention.
Do farmers plow and plow and do nothing but plow?
    Or harrow and harrow and do nothing but harrow?
After they've prepared the ground, don't they plant?
    Don't they scatter dill and spread cumin,
Plant wheat and barley in the fields
    and raspberries along the borders?
They know exactly what to do and when to do it.
    Their God is their teacher.

And at the harvest, the delicate herbs and spices,
    the dill and cumin, are treated delicately.
On the other hand, wheat is threshed and milled, but still
        not endlessly.
    The farmer knows how to treat each kind of grain.
He's learned it all from God-of-the-Angel-Armies,
    who knows everything about when and how and where.

29

BLIND YOURSELVES SO THAT YOU SEE NOTHING

Doom, Ariel, Ariel,
    the city where David set camp!
Let the years add up,
    let the festivals run their cycles,
But I'm not letting up on Jerusalem.
    The moaning and groaning will continue.

Jerusalem to me is an Ariel.
Like David, I'll set up camp against you.
   I'll set siege, build towers,
      bring in siege engines, build siege ramps.
Driven into the ground, you'll speak,
      you'll mumble words from the dirt—
Your voice from the ground, like the muttering of a ghost.
      Your speech will whisper from the dust.

But it will be your enemies who are beaten to dust,
      the mob of tyrants who will be blown away like chaff.
Because, surprise, as if out of nowhere,
      a visit from GOD-of-the-Angel-Armies,
With thunderclaps, earthquakes, and earsplitting noise,
      backed up by hurricanes, tornadoes, and lightning strikes,
And the mob of enemies at war with Ariel,
   all who trouble and hassle and torment her,
   will turn out to be a bad dream, a nightmare.
Like a hungry man dreaming he's eating steak
   and wakes up hungry as ever,
Like a thirsty woman dreaming she's drinking iced tea
   and wakes up thirsty as ever,
So that mob of nations at war against Mount Zion
   will wake up and find they haven't shot an arrow,
   haven't killed a single soul.

Drug yourselves so you feel nothing.
   Blind yourselves so you see nothing.
Get drunk, but not on wine.
   Black out, but not from whiskey.
For GOD has rocked you into a deep, deep sleep,
   put the discerning prophets to sleep,
   put the farsighted seers to sleep.

YOU HAVE EVERYTHING BACKWARDS

What you've been shown here is somewhat like a letter in a sealed envelope. If you give it to someone who can read and tell her, "Read this," she'll say, "I can't. The envelope is sealed." And if you give it to someone who can't read and tell him, "Read this," he'll say, "I can't read."

71

✠

The Master said:

"These people make a big show of saying the right thing,
      but their hearts aren't in it.
Because they act like they're worshiping me
      but don't mean it,
I'm going to step in and shock them awake,
      astonish them, stand them on their ears.
The wise ones who had it all figured out
      will be exposed as fools.
The smart people who thought they knew everything
      will turn out to know nothing."

Doom to you! You pretend to have the inside track.
      You shut GOD out and work behind the scenes,
Plotting the future as if you knew everything,
      acting mysterious, never showing your hand.
You have everything backwards!
      You treat the potter as a lump of clay.
Does a book say to its author,
      "He didn't write a word of me"?
Does a meal say to the woman who cooked it,
      "She had nothing to do with this"?

And then before you know it,
      and without you having anything to do with it,
Wasted Lebanon will be transformed into lush gardens,
      and Mount Carmel reforested.
At that time the deaf will hear
      word-for-word what's been written.
After a lifetime in the dark,
      the blind will see.
The cast-offs of society will be laughing and dancing in GOD,
      the down-and-outs shouting praise to The Holy of Israel.
For there'll be no more gangs on the street.
      Cynical scoffers will be an extinct species.
Those who never missed a chance to hurt or demean
      will never be heard of again:

Gone the people who corrupted the courts,
 gone the people who cheated the poor,
 gone the people who victimized the innocent.

And finally this, GOD's Message for the family of Jacob,
 the same GOD who redeemed Abraham:
"No longer will Jacob hang his head in shame,
 no longer grow gaunt and pale with waiting.
For he's going to see his children,
 my personal gift to him—lots of children.
And these children will honor me
 by living holy lives.
In holy worship they'll honor the Holy One of Jacob
 and stand in holy awe of the God of Israel.
Those who got off-track will get back on-track,
 and complainers and whiners learn gratitude."

30

ALL SHOW, NO SUBSTANCE

"Doom, rebel children!"
 GOD's Decree.
"You make plans, but not mine.
 You make deals, but not in my Spirit.
You pile sin on sin,
 one sin on top of another,
Going off to Egypt
 without so much as asking me,
Running off to Pharaoh for protection,
 expecting to hide out in Egypt.
Well, some protection Pharaoh will be!
 Some hideout, Egypt!
They look big and important, true,
 with officials strategically established in
Zoan in the north and Hanes in the south,
 but there's nothing to them.
Anyone stupid enough to trust them
 will end up looking stupid—

All show, no substance,
>   an embarrassing farce."

And this note on the animals of the Negev
>   encountered on the road to Egypt:
A most dangerous, treacherous route,
>   menaced by lions and deadly snakes.
And you're going to lug all your stuff down *there*,
>   your donkeys and camels loaded down with bribes,
Thinking you can buy protection
>   from that hollow farce of a nation?
Egypt is all show, no substance.
>   My name for her is Toothless Dragon.

THIS IS A REBEL GENERATION

So, go now and write all this down.
>   Put it in a book
So that the record will be there
>   to instruct the coming generations,
Because this is a rebel generation,
>   a people who lie,
A people unwilling to listen
>   to anything GOD tells them.
They tell their spiritual leaders,
>   "Don't bother us with irrelevancies."
They tell their preachers,
>   "Don't waste our time on impracticalities.
Tell us what makes us feel better.
>   Don't bore us with obsolete religion.
That stuff means nothing to us.
>   Quit hounding us with The Holy of Israel."

Therefore, The Holy of Israel says this:
>   "Because you scorn this Message,
Preferring to live by injustice
>   and shape your lives on lies,
This perverse way of life
>   will be like a towering, badly built wall
That slowly, slowly tilts and shifts,

and then one day, without warning, collapses—
Smashed to bits like a piece of pottery,
      smashed beyond recognition or repair,
Useless, a pile of debris
      to be swept up and thrown in the trash."

GOD TAKES THE TIME TO DO EVERYTHING RIGHT

GOD, the Master, the Holy of Israel,
      has this solemn counsel:
"Your salvation requires you to turn back to me
      and stop your silly efforts to save yourselves.
Your strength will come from settling down
      in complete dependence on me—
The very thing
      you've been unwilling to do.
You've said, 'Nothing doing! We'll rush off on horseback!'
      You'll rush off, all right! Just not far enough!
You've said, 'We'll ride off on fast horses!'
      Do you think your pursuers ride old nags?
Think again: A thousand of you will scatter before one attacker.
      Before a mere five you'll all run off.
There'll be nothing left of you—
      a flagpole on a hill with no flag,
      a signpost on a roadside with the sign torn off."

But GOD's not finished. He's waiting around to be gracious to you.
      He's gathering strength to show mercy to you.
GOD takes the time to do everything right—everything.
      Those who wait around for him are the lucky ones.

Oh yes, people of Zion, citizens of Jerusalem, your time of tears is
over. Cry for help and you'll find it's grace and more grace. The moment
he hears, he'll answer. Just as the Master kept you alive during the hard
times, he'll keep your teacher alive and present among you. Your teacher
will be right there, local and on the job, urging you on whenever you
wander left or right: "This is the right road. Walk down this road." You'll
scrap your expensive and fashionable god-images. You'll throw them in
the trash as so much garbage, saying, "Good riddance!"
      God will provide rain for the seeds you sow. The grain that grows

will be abundant. Your cattle will range far and wide. Oblivious to war and earthquake, the oxen and donkeys you use for hauling and plowing will be fed well near running brooks that flow freely from mountains and hills. Better yet, on the Day GOD heals his people of the wounds and bruises from the time of punishment, moonlight will flare into sunlight, and sunlight, like a whole week of sunshine at once, will flood the land.

✛

Look, GOD's on his way,
    and from a long way off!
Smoking with anger,
    immense as he comes into view,
Words steaming from his mouth,
    searing, indicting words!
A torrent of words, a flash flood of words
    sweeping everyone into the vortex of his words.
He'll shake down the nations in a sieve of destruction,
    herd them into a dead end.

But *you* will sing,
    sing through an all-night holy feast!
Your hearts will burst with song,
    make music like the sound of flutes on parade,
En route to the mountain of GOD,
    on the way to the Rock of Israel.
GOD will sound out in grandiose thunder,
    display his hammering arm,
Furiously angry, showering sparks—
    cloudburst, storm, hail!
Oh yes, at GOD's thunder
    Assyria will cower under the clubbing.
Every blow GOD lands on them with his club
    is in time to the music of drums and pipes,
GOD in all-out, two-fisted battle,
    fighting against them.
Topheth's fierce fires are well prepared,
    ready for the Assyrian king.
The Topheth furnace is deep and wide,

well stoked with hot-burning wood.
GOD's breath, like a river of burning pitch,
    starts the fire.

31

IMPRESSED BY MILITARY MATHEMATICS

Doom to those who go off to Egypt
    thinking that horses can help them,
Impressed by military mathematics,
    awed by sheer numbers of chariots and riders—
And to The Holy of Israel, not even a glance,
    not so much as a prayer to GOD.
Still, he must be reckoned with,
    a most wise God who knows what he's doing.
He can call down catastrophe.
    He's a God who does what he says.
He intervenes in the work of those who do wrong,
    stands up against interfering evildoers.
Egyptians are mortal, not God,
    and their horses are flesh, not Spirit.
When GOD gives the signal, helpers and helped alike
    will fall in a heap and share the same dirt grave.

✛

This is what GOD told me:

"Like a lion, king of the beasts,
    that gnaws and chews and worries its prey,
Not fazed in the least by a bunch of shepherds
    who arrive to chase it off,
So GOD-of-the-Angel-Armies comes down
    to fight on Mount Zion, to make war from its heights.
And like a huge eagle hovering in the sky,
    GOD-of-the-Angel-Armies protects Jerusalem.
I'll protect and rescue it.
    Yes, I'll hover and deliver."

Repent, return, dear Israel, to the One you so cruelly abandoned.
On the day you return, you'll throw away—every last one of you—the
no-gods your sinful hands made from metal and wood.

"Assyrians will fall dead,
    killed by a sword-thrust but not by a soldier,
    laid low by a sword not swung by a mortal.
Assyrians will run from that sword, run for their lives,
    and their prize young men made slaves.
Terrorized, that rock-solid people will fall to pieces,
    their leaders scatter hysterically."
GOD's Decree on Assyria.
    His fire blazes in Zion,
    his furnace burns hot in Jerusalem.

32

SAFE HOUSES, QUIET GARDENS

But look! A king will rule in the right way,
    and his leaders will carry out justice.
Each one will stand as a shelter from high winds,
    provide safe cover in stormy weather.
Each will be cool running water in parched land,
    a huge granite outcrop giving shade in the desert.
Anyone who looks will see,
    anyone who listens will hear.
The impulsive will make sound decisions,
    the tongue-tied will speak with eloquence.
No more will fools become celebrities,
    nor crooks be rewarded with fame.
For fools are fools and that's that,
    thinking up new ways to do mischief.
They leave a wake of wrecked lives
    and lies about GOD,
Turning their backs on the homeless hungry,
    ignoring those dying of thirst in the streets.
And the crooks? Underhanded sneaks they are,
    inventive in sin and scandal,
Exploiting the poor with scams and lies,

unmoved by the victimized poor.
But those who are noble make noble plans,
and stand for what is noble.

✠

Take your stand, indolent women!
Listen to me!
Indulgent, indolent women,
listen closely to what I have to say.
In just a little over a year from now,
you'll be shaken out of your lazy lives.
The grape harvest will fail,
and there'll be no fruit on the trees.
Oh tremble, you indolent women.
Get serious, you pampered dolls!
Strip down and discard your silk fineries.
Put on funeral clothes.
Shed honest tears for the lost harvest,
the failed vintage.
Weep for my people's gardens and farms
that grow nothing but thistles and thornbushes.
Cry tears, real tears, for the happy homes no longer happy,
the merry city no longer merry.
The royal palace is deserted,
the bustling city quiet as a morgue,
The emptied parks and playgrounds
taken over by wild animals,
delighted with their new home.

Yes, weep and grieve until the Spirit is poured
down on us from above
And the badlands desert grows crops
and the fertile fields become forests.
Justice will move into the badlands desert.
Right will build a home in the fertile field.
And where there's Right, there'll be Peace
and the progeny of Right: quiet lives and endless trust.
My people will live in a peaceful neighborhood—
in safe houses, in quiet gardens.

The forest of your pride will be clear-cut,
 the city showing off your power leveled.
But you will enjoy a blessed life,
  planting well-watered fields and gardens,
  with your farm animals grazing freely.

33

The Ground Under Our Feet Mourns

Doom to you, Destroyer,
 not yet destroyed;
And doom to you, Betrayer,
 not yet betrayed.
When you finish destroying,
 your turn will come—destroyed!
When you quit betraying,
 your turn will come—betrayed!

God, treat us kindly. You're our only hope.
 First thing in the morning, be there for us!
 When things go bad, help us out!
You spoke in thunder and everyone ran.
 You showed up and nations scattered.
Your people, for a change, got in on the loot,
 picking the field clean of the enemy spoils.

God is supremely esteemed. His center holds.
 Zion brims over with all that is just and right.
God keeps your days stable and secure—
 salvation, wisdom, and knowledge in surplus,
 and best of all, Zion's treasure, Fear-of-God.

But look! Listen!
 Tough men weep openly.
 Peacemaking diplomats are in bitter tears.
The roads are empty—
 not a soul out on the streets.
The peace treaty is broken,
 its conditions violated,

its signers reviled.
The very ground under our feet mourns,
    the Lebanon mountains hang their heads,
Flowering Sharon is a weed-choked gully,
    and the forests of Bashan and Carmel? Bare branches.

"Now I'm stepping in," GOD says.
    "From now on, I'm taking over.
    The gloves come off. Now see how mighty I am.
There's nothing to you.
    Pregnant with chaff, you produce straw babies;
    full of hot air, you self-destruct.
You're good for nothing but fertilizer and fuel.
    Earth to earth—and the sooner the better.

"If you're far away,
    get the reports on what I've done,
And if you're in the neighborhood,
    pay attention to my record.
The sinners in Zion are rightly terrified;
    the godless are at their wit's end:
'Who among us can survive this firestorm?
    Who of us can get out of this purge with our lives?'"

The answer's simple:
    Live right,
    speak the truth,
    despise exploitation,
    refuse bribes,
    reject violence,
    avoid evil amusements.
This is how you raise your standard of living!
    A safe and stable way to live.
    A nourishing, satisfying way to live.

GOD MAKES ALL THE DECISIONS HERE

Oh, you'll see the king—a beautiful sight!
    And you'll take in the wide vistas of land.
In your mind you'll go over the old terrors:

"What happened to that Assyrian inspector who condemned and
    confiscated?
And the one who gouged us of taxes?
    And that cheating moneychanger?"
Gone! Out of sight forever! Their insolence
    nothing now but a fading stain on the carpet!
No more putting up with a language you can't understand,
    no more sounds of gibberish in your ears.

Just take a look at Zion, will you?
    Centering our worship in festival feasts!
Feast your eyes on Jerusalem,
    a quiet and permanent place to live.
No more pulling up stakes and moving on,
    no more patched-together lean-tos.
Instead, GOD! GOD majestic, God himself the place
    in a country of broad rivers and streams,
But rivers blocked to invading ships,
    off-limits to predatory pirates.
For GOD makes all the decisions here. GOD is our king.
    GOD runs this place and he'll keep us safe.

Ha! Your sails are in shreds,
    your mast wobbling,
    your hold leaking.
The plunder is free for the taking, free for all—
    for weak and strong, insiders and outsiders.

No one in Zion will say, "I'm sick."
    Best of all, they'll all live guilt-free.

34

THE FIRES BURNING DAY AND NIGHT

Draw in close now, nations. Listen carefully,
    you people. Pay attention!
Earth, you too, and everything in you.
    World, and all that comes from you.

And here's why: GOD is angry,
    good and angry with all the nations,
So blazingly angry at their arms and armies
    that he's going to rid earth of them, wipe them out.
The corpses, thrown in a heap,
    will stink like the town dump in midsummer,
Their blood flowing off the mountains
    like creeks in spring runoff.
Stars will fall out of the sky
    like overripe, rotting fruit in the orchard,
And the sky itself will be folded up like a blanket
    and put away in a closet.
All that army of stars, shriveled to nothing,
    like leaves and fruit in autumn, dropping and rotting!

"Once I've finished with earth and sky,
    I'll start in on Edom.
I'll come down hard on Edom,
    a people I've slated for total termination."
GOD has a sword, thirsty for blood and more blood,
    a sword hungry for well-fed flesh,
Lamb and goat blood,
    the suet-rich kidneys of rams.
Yes, GOD has scheduled a sacrifice in Bozrah, the capital,
    the whole country of Edom a slaughterhouse.
A wholesale slaughter, wild animals
    and farm animals alike slaughtered.
The whole country soaked with blood,
    all the ground greasy with fat.

It's GOD's scheduled time for vengeance,
    the year all Zion's accounts are settled.
Edom's streams will flow sluggish, thick with pollution,
    the soil sterile, poisoned with waste,
The whole country
    a smoking, stinking garbage dump—
The fires burning day and night,
    the skies black with endless smoke.
Generation after generation of wasteland—
    no more travelers through this country!

Vultures and skunks will police the streets;
>owls and crows will feel at home there.
God will reverse creation. Chaos!
>He will cancel fertility. Emptiness!
Leaders will have no one to lead.
>They'll name it No Kingdom There,
A country where all kings
>and princes are unemployed.
Thistles will take over, covering the castles,
>fortresses conquered by weeds and thornbushes.
Wild dogs will prowl the ruins,
>ostriches have the run of the place.
Wildcats and hyenas will hunt together,
>demons and devils dance through the night.
The night-demon Lilith, evil and rapacious,
>will establish permanent quarters.
Scavenging carrion birds will breed and brood,
>infestations of ominous evil.

Get and read GOD's book:
>None of this is going away,
>this breeding, brooding evil.
GOD has personally commanded it all.
>His Spirit set it in motion.
GOD has assigned them their place,
>decreed their fate in detail.
This is permanent—
>generation after generation, the same old thing.

35

THE VOICELESS BREAK INTO SONG

Wilderness and desert will sing joyously,
>the badlands will celebrate and flower—
Like the crocus in spring, bursting into blossom,
>a symphony of song and color.
Mountain glories of Lebanon—a gift.
>Awesome Carmel, stunning Sharon—gifts.

GOD's resplendent glory, fully on display.
    GOD awesome, GOD majestic.

Energize the limp hands,
    strengthen the rubbery knees.
Tell fearful souls,
    "Courage! Take heart!
GOD is here, right here,
    on his way to put things right
And redress all wrongs.
    He's on his way! He'll save you!"

Blind eyes will be opened,
    deaf ears unstopped,
Lame men and women will leap like deer,
    the voiceless break into song.
Springs of water will burst out in the wilderness,
    streams flow in the desert.
Hot sands will become a cool oasis,
    thirsty ground a splashing fountain.
Even lowly jackals will have water to drink,
    and barren grasslands flourish richly.

There will be a highway
    called the Holy Road.
No one rude or rebellious
    is permitted on this road.
It's for GOD's people exclusively—
    impossible to get lost on this road.
    Not even fools can get lost on it.
No lions on this road,
    no dangerous wild animals—
Nothing and no one dangerous or threatening.
    Only the redeemed will walk on it.
The people GOD has ransomed
    will come back on this road.
They'll sing as they make their way home to Zion,
    unfading halos of joy encircling their heads,
Welcomed home with gifts of joy and gladness
    as all sorrows and sighs scurry into the night.

36

IT'S THEIR FATE THAT'S AT STAKE

In the fourteenth year of King Hezekiah, Sennacherib king of Assyria made war on all the fortress cities of Judah and took them. Then the king of Assyria sent his general, the "Rabshekah," accompanied by a huge army, from Lachish to Jerusalem to King Hezekiah. The general stopped at the aqueduct where it empties into the upper pool on the road to the public laundry. Three men went out to meet him: Eliakim son of Hilkiah, in charge of the palace; Shebna the secretary; and Joah son of Asaph, the official historian.

The Rabshekah said to them, "Tell Hezekiah, the Great King, the king of Assyria, this: 'What kind of backing do you think you have against me? You're bluffing and I'm calling your bluff. Your words are no match for my weapons. What kind of backup do you have now that you've rebelled against me? Egypt? Don't make me laugh. Egypt is a rubber crutch. Lean on Egypt and you'll end up flat on your face. That's all Pharaoh king of Egypt is to anyone who leans on him. And if you try to tell me, "We're leaning on our GOD," isn't it a bit late? Hasn't Hezekiah just gotten rid of all the places of worship, telling you, "You've got to worship at *this* altar"?

"'Be reasonable. Face the facts: My master the king of Assyria will give you two thousand horses if you can put riders on them. You can't do it, can you? So how do you think, depending on flimsy Egypt's chariots and riders, you can stand up against even the lowest-ranking captain in my master's army?

"'And besides, do you think I came all this way to destroy this land without first getting GOD's blessing? It was your GOD who told me, "Make war on this land. Destroy it."'"

Eliakim, Shebna, and Joah answered the Rabshekah, "Please talk to us in Aramaic. We understand Aramaic. Don't talk to us in Hebrew within earshot of all the people gathered around."

But the Rabshekah replied, "Do you think my master has sent me to give this message to your master and you but not also to the people clustered here? It's their fate that's at stake. They're the ones who are going to end up eating their own excrement and drinking their own urine."

Then the Rabshekah stood up and called out loudly in Hebrew, the common language, "Listen to the message of the great king, the king of Assyria! Don't listen to Hezekiah's lies. He can't save you. And don't pay any attention to Hezekiah's pious sermons telling you to lean on GOD, telling you 'GOD will save us, depend on it. GOD won't let this city fall to the king of Assyria.'

"Don't listen to Hezekiah. Listen to the king of Assyria's offer: 'Make peace with me. Come and join me. Everyone will end up with a good life, with plenty of land and water, and eventually something far better. I'll turn you loose in wide open spaces, with more than enough fertile and productive land for everyone.' Don't let Hezekiah mislead you with his lies, 'GOD will save us.' Has that ever happened? Has any god in history ever gotten the best of the king of Assyria? Look around you. Where are the gods of Hamath and Arpad? The gods of Sepharvaim? Did the gods do anything for Samaria? Name one god that has ever saved its countries from me. So what makes you think that GOD could save Jerusalem from me?'"

The three men were silent. They said nothing, for the king had already commanded, "Don't answer him."

Then Eliakim son of Hilkiah, the palace administrator, Shebna the secretary, and Joah son of Asaph, the court historian, tearing their clothes in defeat and despair, went back and reported what the Rabshekah had said to Hezekiah.

37

THE ONLY GOD THERE IS

When King Hezekiah heard the report, he also tore his clothes and dressed in rough, penitential burlap gunnysacks, and went into the sanctuary of GOD. He sent Eliakim the palace administrator, Shebna the secretary, and the senior priests, all of them also dressed in penitential burlap, to the prophet Isaiah son of Amoz.

They said to him, "Hezekiah says, 'This is a black day. We're in crisis. We're like pregnant women without even the strength to have a baby! Do you think your GOD heard what the Rabshekah said, sent by his master the king of Assyria to mock the living God? And do you think your GOD will do anything about it? Pray for us, Isaiah. Pray for those of us left here holding the fort!'"

Then King Hezekiah's servants came to Isaiah. Isaiah said, "Tell your master this: 'GOD's Message: Don't be upset by what you've heard, all those words the servants of the Assyrian king have used to mock me. I personally will take care of him. I'll arrange it so that he'll get a rumor of bad news back home and rush home to take care of it. And he'll die there. Killed—a violent death.'"

✠

The Rabshekah left and found the king of Assyria fighting against Libnah. (He had gotten word that the king had left Lachish.)

Just then the Assyrian king received an intelligence report on King Tirhakah of Ethiopia: "He is on his way to make war on you."

On hearing that, he sent messengers to Hezekiah with instructions to deliver this message: "Don't let your GOD, on whom you so naively lean, deceive you, promising that Jerusalem won't fall to the king of Assyria. Use your head! Look around at what the kings of Assyria have done all over the world—one country after another devastated! And do you think you're going to get off? Have any of the gods of any of these countries ever stepped in and saved them, even one of these nations my predecessors destroyed—Gozan, Haran, Rezeph, and the people of Eden who lived in Telassar? Look around. Do you see anything left of the king of Hamath, the king of Arpad, the king of the city of Sepharvaim, the king of Hena, the king of Ivvah?"

Hezekiah took the letter from the hands of the messengers and read it. Then he went into the sanctuary of GOD and spread the letter out before GOD.

Then Hezekiah prayed to GOD: "GOD-of-the-Angel-Armies, enthroned over the cherubim-angels, you are God, the only God there is, God of all kingdoms on earth. You *made* heaven and earth. Listen, oh GOD, and hear. Look, oh GOD, and see. Mark all these words of Sennacherib that he sent to mock the living God. It's quite true, oh GOD, that the kings of Assyria have devastated all the nations and their lands. They've thrown their gods into the trash and burned them—no great achievement since they were no-gods anyway, gods made in workshops, carved from wood and chiseled from rock. An end to the no-gods! But now step in, oh GOD, our God. Save us from him. Let all the kingdoms of earth know that you and you alone are GOD."

✠

Then Isaiah son of Amoz sent this word to Hezekiah: "GOD's Message, the God of Israel: Because you brought King Sennacherib of Assyria to me in prayer, here is my answer, GOD's answer:

"'She has no use for you, Sennacherib, nothing but contempt,
    this virgin daughter Zion.
She spits at you and turns on her heel,
    this daughter Jerusalem.

"'Who do you think you've been mocking and reviling
    all these years?
Who do you think you've been jeering
    and treating with such utter contempt
All these years?
    The Holy of Israel!
You've used your servants to mock the Master.
    You've bragged, "With my fleet of chariots
I've gone to the highest mountain ranges,
    penetrated the far reaches of Lebanon,
Chopped down its giant cedars,
    its finest cypresses.
I conquered its highest peak,
    explored its deepest forest.
I dug wells
    and drank my fill.
I emptied the famous rivers of Egypt
    with one kick of my foot."

"'Haven't you gotten the news
    that I've been behind this all along?
This is a longstanding plan of mine
    and I'm just now making it happen,
using you to devastate strong cities,
    turning them into piles of rubble
and leaving their citizens helpless,
    bewildered, and confused,
drooping like unwatered plants,
    stunted like withered seedlings.

"'I know all about your pretentious poses,
    your officious comings and goings,
        and, yes, the tantrums you throw against me.
Because of all your wild raging against me,
    your unbridled arrogance that I keep hearing of,

I'll put my hook in your nose
     and my bit in your mouth.
I'll show you who's boss. I'll turn you around
     and take you back to where you came from.

"'And this, Hezekiah, will be your confirming sign: This year's crops
will be slim pickings, and next year it won't be much better. But in three
years, farming will be back to normal, with regular sowing and reap-
ing, planting and harvesting. What's left of the people of Judah will put
down roots and make a new start. The people left in Jerusalem will get
moving again. Mount Zion survivors will take hold again. The zeal of
GOD-of-the-Angel-Armies will do all this.'

✚

"Finally, this is GOD's verdict on the king of Assyria:

"'Don't worry, he won't enter this city,
     won't let loose a single arrow,
Won't brandish so much as one shield,
     let alone build a siege ramp against it.
He'll go back the same way he came.
     He won't set a foot in this city.
          GOD's Decree.
I've got my hand on this city
     to save it,
Save it for my very own sake,
     but also for the sake of my David dynasty.'"

Then the Angel of GOD arrived and struck the Assyrian camp—
185,000 Assyrians died. By the time the sun came up, they were all
dead—an army of corpses! Sennacherib, king of Assyria, got out of
there fast, back home to Nineveh. As he was worshiping in the sanctuary of his god Nisroch, he was murdered by his sons Adrammelech
and Sharezer. They escaped to the land of Ararat. His son Esar-haddon
became the next king.

38

Time Spent in Death's Waiting Room

At that time, Hezekiah got sick. He was about to die. The prophet Isaiah son of Amoz visited him and said, "God says, 'Prepare your affairs and your family. This is it: You're going to die. You're not going to get well.'"

Hezekiah turned away from Isaiah and, facing the wall, prayed to God: "God, please, I beg you: Remember how I've lived my life. I've lived faithfully in your presence, lived out of a heart that was totally yours. You've seen how I've lived, the good that I have done." And Hezekiah wept as he prayed—painful tears.

Then God told Isaiah, "Go and speak with Hezekiah. Give him this Message from me, God, the God of your ancestor David: 'I've heard your prayer. I have seen your tears. Here's what I'll do: I'll add fifteen years to your life. And I'll save both you and this city from the king of Assyria. I have my hand on this city.

"'And this is your confirming sign, confirming that I, God, will do exactly what I have promised. Watch for this: As the sun goes down and the shadow lengthens on the sundial of Ahaz, I'm going to reverse the shadow ten notches on the dial.'" And that's what happened: The declining sun's shadow reversed ten notches on the dial.

☩

This is what Hezekiah king of Judah wrote after he'd been sick and then recovered from his sickness:

"In the very prime of life
    I have to leave.
Whatever time I have left
    is spent in death's waiting room.
No more glimpses of God
    in the land of the living,
No more meetings with my neighbors,
    no more rubbing shoulders with friends.
This body I inhabit is taken down
    and packed away like a camper's tent.
Like a weaver, I've rolled up the carpet of my life
    as God cuts me free of the loom

And at day's end sweeps up the scraps and pieces.
    I cry for help until morning.
Like a lion, God pummels and pounds me,
    relentlessly finishing me off.
I squawk like a doomed hen,
    moan like a dove.
My eyes ache from looking up for help:
    Master, I'm in trouble! Get me out of this!"
But what's the use? God himself gave me the word.
    He's done it to me.
I can't sleep—
    I'm that upset, that troubled.

Oh Master, these are the conditions in which people live,
    and yes, in these very conditions my spirit is still alive—
    fully recovered with a fresh infusion of life!
It seems it was good for me
    to go through all those troubles.
Throughout them all you held tight to my lifeline.
    You never let me tumble over the edge into nothing.
But my sins you let go of,
    threw them over your shoulder—good riddance!
The dead don't thank you,
    and choirs don't sing praises from the morgue.
Those buried six feet under
    don't witness to your faithful ways.
It's the living—live men, live women—who thank you,
    just as I'm doing right now.
Parents give their children
    full reports on your faithful ways.

✢

GOD saves and will save me.
    As fiddles and mandolins strike up the tunes,
We'll sing, oh we'll sing, sing,
    for the rest of our lives in the Sanctuary of GOD.

    Isaiah had said, "Prepare a poultice of figs and put it on the boil so he may recover."

Hezekiah had said, "What is my cue that it's all right to enter again the Sanctuary of GOD?"

39

THERE WILL BE NOTHING LEFT

Sometime later, King Merodach-baladan son of Baladan of Babylon sent messengers with greetings and a gift to Hezekiah. He had heard that Hezekiah had been sick and was now well.

Hezekiah received the messengers warmly. He took them on a tour of his royal precincts, proudly showing them all his treasures: silver, gold, spices, expensive oils, all his weapons—everything out on display. There was nothing in his house or kingdom that Hezekiah didn't show them.

Later the prophet Isaiah showed up. He asked Hezekiah, "What were these men up to? What did they say? And where did they come from?"

Hezekiah said, "They came from a long way off, from Babylon."

"And what did they see in your palace?"

"Everything," said Hezekiah. "I showed them the works, opened all the doors and impressed them with it all."

Then Isaiah said to Hezekiah, "Now listen to this Message from GOD-of-the-Angel-Armies: I have to warn you, the time is coming when everything in this palace, along with everything your ancestors accumulated before you, will be hauled off to Babylon. GOD says that there will be nothing left. Nothing. And not only your things but your *sons*. Some of your sons will be taken into exile, ending up as eunuchs in the palace of the king of Babylon."

Hezekiah replied to Isaiah, "Good. If GOD says so, it's good." Within himself he was thinking, "But surely nothing bad will happen in my lifetime. I'll enjoy peace and stability as long as I live."

40   MESSAGES OF COMFORT

PREPARE FOR GOD'S ARRIVAL

"Comfort, oh comfort my people,"
    says your God.
"Speak softly and tenderly to Jerusalem,

but also make it very clear
That she has served her sentence,
    that her sin is taken care of—forgiven!
She's been punished enough and more than enough,
    and now it's over and done with."

Thunder in the desert!
    "Prepare for GOD's arrival!
Make the road straight and smooth,
    a highway fit for our God.
Fill in the valleys,
    level off the hills,
Smooth out the ruts,
    clear out the rocks.
Then GOD's bright glory will shine
    and everyone will see it.
    Yes. Just as GOD has said."

A voice says, "Shout!"
    I said, "What shall I shout?"

"These people are nothing but grass,
    their love fragile as wildflowers.
The grass withers, the wildflowers fade,
    if GOD so much as puffs on them.
    Aren't these people just so much grass?
True, the grass withers and the wildflowers fade,
    but our God's Word stands firm and forever."

Climb a high mountain, Zion.
    You're the preacher of good news.
Raise your voice. Make it good and loud, Jerusalem.
    You're the preacher of good news.
    Speak loud and clear. Don't be timid!
Tell the cities of Judah,
    "Look! Your God!"
Look at him! GOD, the Master, comes in power,
    ready to go into action.
He is going to pay back his enemies
    and reward those who have loved him.

Like a shepherd, he will care for his flock,
    gathering the lambs in his arms,
Hugging them as he carries them,
    leading the nursing ewes to good pasture.

THE CREATOR OF ALL YOU CAN SEE OR IMAGINE

Who has scooped up the ocean
    in his two hands,
    or measured the sky between his thumb and little finger,
Who has put all the earth's dirt in one of his baskets,
    weighed each mountain and hill?
Who could ever have told GOD what to do
    or taught him his business?
What expert would he have gone to for advice,
    what school would he attend to learn justice?
What god do you suppose might have taught him what he knows,
    showed him how things work?
Why, the nations are but a drop in a bucket,
    a mere smudge on a window.
Watch him sweep up the islands
    like so much dust off the floor!
There aren't enough trees in Lebanon
    nor enough animals in those vast forests
    to furnish adequate fuel and offerings for his worship.
All the nations add up to simply nothing before him—
    less than nothing is more like it. A minus.

So who even comes close to being like God?
    To whom or what can you compare him?
Some no-god idol? Ridiculous!
    It's made in a workshop, cast in bronze,
Given a thin veneer of gold,
    and draped with silver filigree.
Or, perhaps someone will select a fine wood—
    olive wood, say—that won't rot,
Then hire a woodcarver to make a no-god,
    giving special care to its base so it won't tip over!

Have you not been paying attention?
    Have you not been listening?

Haven't you heard these stories all your life?
>Don't you understand the foundation of all things?
God sits high above the round ball of earth.
>The people look like mere ants.
He stretches out the skies like a canvas—
>yes, like a tent canvas to live under.
He ignores what all the princes say and do.
>The rulers of the earth count for nothing.
Princes and rulers don't amount to much.
>Like seeds barely rooted, just sprouted,
They shrivel when God blows on them.
>Like flecks of chaff, they're gone with the wind.

"So—who is like me?
>Who holds a candle to me?" says The Holy.
Look at the night skies:
>Who do you think made all this?
Who marches this army of stars out each night,
>counts them off, calls each by name
—so magnificent! so powerful!—
>and never overlooks a single one?

Why would you ever complain, oh Jacob,
>or, whine, Israel, saying,
"GOD has lost track of me.
>He doesn't care what happens to me"?
Don't you know anything? Haven't you been listening?
GOD doesn't come and go. God *lasts*.
>He's Creator of all you can see or imagine.
He doesn't get tired out, doesn't pause to catch his breath.
>And he knows *everything*, inside and out.
He energizes those who get tired,
>gives fresh strength to dropouts.
For even young people tire and drop out,
>young folk in their prime stumble and fall.
But those who wait upon GOD get fresh strength.
>They spread their wings and soar like eagles,
They run and don't get tired,
>they walk and don't lag behind.

41

DO YOU FEEL LIKE A LOWLY WORM?

"Quiet down, far-flung ocean islands. Listen!
      Sit down and rest, everyone. Recover your strength.
Gather around me. Say what's on your heart.
      Together let's decide what's right.

"Who got things rolling here,
      got this champion from the east on the move?
Who recruited him for this job,
      then rounded up and corralled the nations
      so he could run roughshod over kings?
He's off and running,
      pulverizing nations into dust,
      leaving only stubble and chaff in his wake.
He chases them and comes through unscathed,
      his feet scarcely touching the path.

"Who did this? Who made it happen?
      Who always gets things started?
I did. GOD. I'm first on the scene.
      I'm also the last to leave.

"Far-flung ocean islands see it and panic.
      The ends of the earth are shaken.
      Fearfully they huddle together.
They try to help each other out,
      making up stories in the dark.
The godmakers in the workshops
      go into overtime production, crafting new models of no-gods,
Urging one another on—'Good job!' 'Great design!'—
      pounding in nails at the base
      so that the things won't tip over.

"But you, Israel, are my servant.
      You're Jacob, my first choice,
      descendants of my good friend Abraham.
I pulled you in from all over the world,
      called you in from every dark corner of the earth,

Telling you, 'You're my servant, serving on my side.
  I've picked you. I haven't dropped you.'
Don't panic. I'm with you.
  There's no need to fear for I'm your God.
I'll give you strength. I'll help you.
  I'll hold you steady, keep a firm grip on you.

"Count on it: Everyone who had it in for you
  will end up out in the cold—
  real losers.
Those who worked against you
  will end up empty-handed—
  nothing to show for their lives.
When you go out looking for your old adversaries
  you won't find them—
Not a trace of your old enemies,
  not even a memory.
That's right. Because I, your GOD,
  have a firm grip on you and I'm not letting go.
I'm telling you, 'Don't panic.
  I'm right here to help you.'

"Do you feel like a lowly worm, Jacob?
  Don't be afraid.
Feel like a fragile insect, Israel?
  I'll help you.
I, GOD, want to reassure you.
  The God who buys you back, The Holy of Israel.
I'm transforming you from worm to harrow,
  from insect to iron.
As a sharp-toothed harrow you'll smooth out the mountains,
  turn those tough old hills into loamy soil.
You'll open the rough ground to the weather,
  to the blasts of sun and wind and rain.
But you'll be confident and exuberant,
  expansive in The Holy of Israel!

"The poor and homeless are desperate for water,
  their tongues parched and no water to be found.
But *I'm* there to be found, I'm there for them,

and I, God of Israel, will not leave them thirsty.
I'll open up rivers for them on the barren hills,
    spout fountains in the valleys.
I'll turn the baked-clay badlands into a cool pond,
    the waterless waste into splashing creeks.
I'll plant the red cedar in that treeless wasteland,
    also acacia, myrtle, and olive.
I'll place the cypress in the desert,
    with plenty of oaks and pines.
Everyone will see this. No one can miss it—
    unavoidable, indisputable evidence
That I, GOD, personally did this.
    It's created and signed by The Holy of Israel.

"Set out your case for your gods," says GOD.
    "Bring your evidence," says the King of Jacob.
"Take the stand on behalf of your idols, offer arguments,
    assemble reasons.
Spread out the facts before us
    so that we can assess them ourselves.
Ask them, 'If you are gods, explain what the past means—
    or, failing that, tell us what will happen in the future.
Can't do that?
    How about doing something—anything!
Good or bad—whatever.
    Can you hurt us or help us? Do we need to be afraid?'
They say nothing, because they *are* nothing—
    sham gods, no-gods, fool-making gods.

"I, God, started someone out from the north and he's come.
    He was called out of the east by name.
He'll stomp the rulers into the mud
    the way a potter works the clay.
Let me ask you, Did anyone guess that this might happen?
    Did anyone tell us earlier so we might confirm it
    with 'Yes, he's right!'?
No one mentioned it, no one announced it,
    no one heard a peep out of you.
But I told Zion all about this beforehand.
    I gave Jerusalem a preacher of good news.

But around here there's no one—
    no one who knows what's going on.
    I ask, but no one can tell me the score.
Nothing here. It's all smoke and hot air—
    sham gods, hollow gods, no-gods.

42

GOD'S SERVANT WILL SET EVERYTHING RIGHT

"Take a good look at my servant.
    I'm backing him to the hilt.
He's the one I chose,
    and I couldn't be more pleased with him.
I've bathed him with my Spirit, my *life*.
    He'll set everything right among the nations.
He won't call attention to what he does
    with loud speeches or gaudy parades.
He won't brush aside the bruised and the hurt
    and he won't disregard the small and insignificant,
    but he'll steadily and firmly set things right.
He won't tire out and quit. He won't be stopped
    until he's finished his work—to set things right on earth.
Far-flung ocean islands
    wait expectantly for his teaching."

THE GOD WHO MAKES US ALIVE WITH HIS OWN LIFE

GOD'S Message,
    the God who created the cosmos, stretched out the skies,
    laid out the earth and all that grows from it,
Who breathes life into earth's people,
    makes them alive with his own life:
"I am GOD. I have called you to live right and well.
    I have taken responsibility for you, kept you safe.
I have set you among my people to bind them to me,
    and provided you as a lighthouse to the nations,
To make a start at bringing people into the open, into light:
    opening blind eyes,
    releasing prisoners from dungeons,
    emptying the dark prisons.

I am GOD. That's my name.
    I don't franchise my glory,
    don't endorse the no-god idols.
Take note: The earlier predictions of judgment have been fulfilled.
    I'm announcing the new salvation work.
Before it bursts on the scene,
    I'm telling you all about it."

Sing to GOD a brand-new song,
    sing his praises all over the world!
Let the sea and its fish give a round of applause,
    with all the far-flung islands joining in.
Let the desert and its camps raise a tune,
    calling the Kedar nomads to join in.
Let the villagers in Sela round up a choir
    and perform from the tops of the mountains.
Make GOD's glory resound;
    echo his praises from coast to coast.
GOD steps out like he means business.
    You can see he's primed for action.
He shouts, announcing his arrival;
    he takes charge and his enemies fall into line:
"I've been quiet long enough.
    I've held back, biting my tongue.
But now I'm letting loose, letting go,
    like a woman who's having a baby—
Stripping the hills bare,
    withering the wildflowers,
Drying up the rivers,
    turning lakes into mudflats.
But I'll take the hand of those who don't know the way,
    who can't see where they're going.
I'll be a personal guide to them,
    directing them through unknown country.
I'll be right there to show them what roads to take,
    make sure they don't fall into the ditch.
These are the things I'll be doing for them—
    sticking with them, not leaving them for a minute."

But those who invested in the no-gods
    are bankrupt—dead broke.

You've Seen a Lot, But Looked at Nothing

Pay attention! Are you deaf?
    Open your eyes! Are you blind?
You're my servant, and you're not looking!
    You're my messenger, and you're not listening!
The very people I depended upon, servants of God,
    blind as a bat—willfully blind!
You've seen a lot, but looked at nothing.
    You've heard everything, but listened to nothing.
God intended, out of the goodness of his heart,
    to be lavish in his revelation.
But this is a people battered and cowed,
    shut up in attics and closets,
Victims licking their wounds,
    feeling ignored, abandoned.
But is anyone out there listening?
    Is anyone paying attention to what's coming?
Who do you think turned Jacob over to the thugs,
    let loose the robbers on Israel?
Wasn't it God himself, this God against whom we've sinned—
    not doing what he commanded,
    not listening to what he said?
Isn't it God's anger that's behind all this,
    God's punishing power?
Their whole world collapsed but they still didn't get it;
    their life is in ruins but they don't take it to heart.

43

When You're Between a Rock and a Hard Place

But now, God's Message,
    the God who made you in the first place, Jacob,
    the One who got you started, Israel:
"Don't be afraid, I've redeemed you.
    I've called your name. You're mine.
When you're in over your head, I'll be there with you.
    When you're in rough waters, you will not go down.
When you're between a rock and a hard place,
    it won't be a dead end—

Because I am GOD, your personal God,
    The Holy of Israel, your Savior.
I paid a huge price for you:
    all of Egypt, with rich Cush and Seba thrown in!
That's how much you mean to me!
    That's how much I love you!
I'd sell off the whole world to get you back,
    trade the creation just for you.

"So don't be afraid: I'm with you.
    I'll round up all your scattered children,
    pull them in from east and west;
I'll send orders north and south:
    'Send them back.
Return my sons from distant lands,
    my daughters from faraway places.
I want them back, every last one who bears my name,
    every man, woman, and child
Whom I created for my glory,
    yes, personally formed and made each one.'"

✛

Get the blind and deaf out here and ready—
    the blind (though there's nothing wrong with their eyes)
    and the deaf (though there's nothing wrong with their ears).
Then get the other nations out here and ready.
    Let's see what they have to say about this,
    how they account for what's happened.
Let them present their expert witnesses
    and make their case;
    let them try to convince us what they say is true.
"But *you* are my witnesses." GOD's Decree.
    "You're my handpicked servant
So that you'll come to know and trust me,
    understand both *that* I am and *who* I am.
Previous to me there was no such thing as a god,
    nor will there be after me.
I, yes I, am GOD.
    I'm the only Savior there is.

I spoke, I saved, I told you what existed
    long before these upstart gods appeared on the scene.
And you know it, you're my witnesses,
    you're the evidence." GOD's Decree.
"Yes, I am God.
    I've always been God
    and I always will be God.
No one can take anything from me.
    I make; who can unmake it?"

YOU DIDN'T EVEN DO THE MINIMUM

GOD, your Redeemer,
    The Holy of Israel, says:
"Just for you, I will march on Babylon.
    I'll turn the tables on the Babylonians.
Instead of whooping it up,
    they'll be wailing.
I am GOD, your Holy One,
    Creator of Israel, your King."

This is what GOD says,
    the God who builds a road right through the ocean,
    who carves a path through pounding waves,
The God who summons horses and chariots and armies—
    they lie down and then can't get up;
    they're snuffed out like so many candles:
"Forget about what's happened;
    don't keep going over old history.
Be alert, be present. I'm about to do something brand-new.
    It's bursting out! Don't you see it?
There it is! I'm making a road through the desert,
    rivers in the badlands.
Wild animals will say 'Thank you!'
    —the coyotes and the buzzards—
Because I provided water in the desert,
    rivers through the sun-baked earth,
Drinking water for the people I chose,
    the people I made especially for myself,
    a people custom-made to praise me.

"But you didn't pay a bit of attention to me, Jacob.
    You so quickly tired of me, Israel.
You wouldn't even bring sheep for offerings in worship.
    You couldn't be bothered with sacrifices.
It wasn't that I asked that much from you.
    I didn't expect expensive presents.
But you didn't even do the minimum—
    so stingy with me, so closefisted.
Yet you haven't been stingy with your sins.
    You've been plenty generous with them—and I'm fed up.

"But I, yes I, am the one
    who takes care of your sins—that's what I do.
    I don't keep a list of your sins.

"So, make your case against me. Let's have this out.
    Make your arguments. Prove you're in the right.
Your original ancestor started the sinning,
    and everyone since has joined in.
That's why I had to disqualify the Temple leaders,
    repudiate Jacob and discredit Israel.

44

Proud to Be Called Israel

"But for now, dear servant Jacob, listen—
    yes, you, Israel, my personal choice.
God who made you has something to say to you;
    the God who formed you in the womb wants to help you.
Don't be afraid, dear servant Jacob,
    Jeshurun, the one I chose.
For I will pour water on the thirsty ground
    and send streams coursing through the parched earth.
I will pour my Spirit into your descendants
    and my blessing on your children.
They shall sprout like grass on the prairie,
    like willows alongside creeks.
This one will say, 'I am God's,'
    and another will go by the name Jacob;

That one will write on his hand 'GOD's property'—
>   and be proud to be called Israel."

GOD, King of Israel,
>   your Redeemer, GOD-of-the-Angel-Armies, says:
"I'm first, I'm last, and everything in between.
>   I'm the only God there is.
Who compares with me?
>   Speak up. See if you measure up.
From the beginning, who else has always announced what's coming?
>   So what is coming next? Anybody want to venture a try?
Don't be afraid, and don't worry:
>   Haven't I always kept you informed, told you what was going on?
You're my eyewitnesses:
>   Have you ever come across a God, a real God, other than me?
>   There's no Rock like me that I know of."

LOVER OF EMPTINESS

All those who make no-god idols don't amount to a thing, and what they work so hard at making is nothing. Their little puppet-gods see nothing and know nothing—they're total embarrassments! Who would bother making gods that can't do anything, that can't "*god*"? Watch all the no-god worshipers hide their faces in shame. Watch the no-god makers slink off humiliated when their idols fail them. Get them out here in the open. Make them face God-reality.

The blacksmith makes his no-god, works it over in his forge, hammering it on his anvil—such hard work! He works away, fatigued with hunger and thirst.

The woodworker draws up plans for his no-god, traces it on a block of wood. He shapes it with chisels and planes into human shape—a beautiful woman, a handsome man, ready to be placed in a chapel. He first cuts down a cedar, or maybe picks out a pine or oak, and lets it grow strong in the forest, nourished by the rain. Then it can serve a double purpose: Part he uses as firewood for keeping warm and baking bread; from the other part he makes a god that he worships—carves it into a god shape and prays before it. With half he makes a fire to warm himself and barbecue his supper. He eats his fill and sits back satisfied with his stomach full and his feet warmed by the fire: "Ah, this is the life." And he still has half left for a god, made to his personal

design—a handy, convenient no-god to worship whenever so inclined.
Whenever the need strikes him he prays to it, "Save me. You're my god."

Pretty stupid, wouldn't you say? Don't they have eyes in their heads?
Are their brains working at all? Doesn't it occur to them to say, "Half
of this tree I used for firewood: I baked bread, roasted meat, and enjoyed
a good meal. And now I've used the rest to make an abominable no-
god. Here I am praying to a stick of wood!"

This lover of emptiness, of nothing, is so out of touch with reality,
so far gone, that he can't even look at what he's doing, can't even look
at the no-god stick of wood in his hand and say, "This is crazy."

⊹

"Remember these things, oh Jacob.
    Take it seriously, Israel, that you're my servant.
I made you, *shaped* you: You're my servant.
    Oh Israel, I'll never forget you.
I've wiped the slate of all your wrongdoings.
    There's nothing left of your sins.
Come back to me, come back.
    I've redeemed you."

High heavens, sing!
    GOD has done it.
Deep earth, shout!
    And you mountains, sing!
    A forest choir of oaks and pines and cedars!
GOD has redeemed Jacob.
    GOD's glory is on display in Israel.

GOD, your Redeemer,
    who shaped your life in your mother's womb, says:
"I am GOD. I made all that is.
    With no help from you I spread out the skies
    and laid out the earth."

He makes the magicians look ridiculous
    and turns fortunetellers into jokes.
He makes the experts look trivial
    and their latest knowledge look silly.

But he backs the word of his servant
    and confirms the counsel of his messengers.
He says to Jerusalem, "Be inhabited,"
    and to the cities of Judah, "Be rebuilt,"
    and to the ruins, "I raise you up."
He says to Ocean, "Dry up.
    I'm drying up your rivers."
He says to Cyrus, "My shepherd—
    everything I want, you'll do it."
He says to Jerusalem, "Be built,"
    and to the Temple, "Be established."

45

THE GOD WHO FORMS LIGHT AND DARKNESS

GOD's Message to his anointed,
    to Cyrus, whom he took by the hand
To give the task of taming the nations,
    of terrifying their kings—
He gave him free rein,
    no restrictions:
"I'll go ahead of you,
    clearing and paving the road.
I'll break down bronze city gates,
    smash padlocks, kick down barred entrances.
I'll lead you to buried treasures,
    secret caches of valuables—
Confirmations that it is, in fact, I, GOD,
    the God of Israel, who call you by your name.
It's because of my dear servant Jacob,
    Israel my chosen,
That I've singled you out, called you by name,
    and given you this privileged work.
    And you don't even know me!
I am GOD, the only God there is.
    Besides me there are no real gods.
I'm the one who armed you for this work,
    though you don't even know me,
So that everyone, from east to west, will know

that I have no god-rivals.
    I am GOD, the only God there is.
I form light and create darkness,
    I make harmonies and create discords.
    I, GOD, do all these things.

"Open up, heavens, and rain.
    Clouds, pour out buckets of my goodness!
Loosen up, earth, and bloom salvation;
    sprout right living.
    I, GOD, generate all this.
But doom to you who fight your Maker—
    you're a pot at odds with the potter!
Does clay talk back to the potter:
    'What are you doing? What clumsy fingers!'
Would a sperm say to a father,
    'Who gave you permission to use me to make a baby?'
Or a fetus to a mother,
    'Why have you cooped me up in this belly?'"

Thus GOD, The Holy of Israel, Israel's Maker, says:
    "Do you question who or what I'm making?
    Are you telling me what I can or cannot do?
I made earth,
    and I created man and woman to live on it.
I handcrafted the skies
    and direct all the constellations in their turnings.
And now I've got Cyrus on the move.
    I've rolled out the red carpet before him.
He will build my city.
    He will bring home my exiles.
I didn't hire him to do this. I *told* him.
    I, GOD-of-the-Angel-Armies."

☩

GOD says:

"The workers of Egypt, the merchants of Ethiopia,
    and those statuesque Sabeans

Will all come over to you—all yours.
 Docile in chains, they'll follow you,
Hands folded in reverence, praying before you:
 'Amazing! God is with you!
 There is no other God—none.'"

LOOK AT THE EVIDENCE

Clearly, you are a God who works behind the scenes,
 God of Israel, Savior God.
Humiliated, all those others
 will be ashamed to show their faces in public.
Out of work and at loose ends, the makers of no-god idols
 won't know what to do with themselves.
The people of Israel, though, are saved by you, GOD,
 saved with an eternal salvation.
They won't be ashamed,
 they won't be at loose ends, ever.

GOD, Creator of the heavens—
 he is, remember, *God*.
Maker of earth—
 he put it on its foundations, built it from scratch.
He didn't go to all that trouble
 to just leave it empty, nothing in it.
 He made it to be lived in.

 This GOD says:

"I am GOD,
 the one and only.
I don't just talk to myself
 or mumble under my breath.
I never told Jacob,
 'Seek me in emptiness, in dark nothingness.'
I am GOD. I work out in the open,
 saying what's right, setting things right.
So gather around, come on in,
 all you refugees and cast-offs.
They don't seem to know much, do they—

110

those who carry around their no-god blocks of wood,
    praying for help to a dead stick?
So tell me what you think. Look at the evidence.
    Put your heads together. Make your case.
Who told you, and a long time ago, what's going on here?
    Who made sense of things for you?
Wasn't I the one? GOD?
    It had to be me. I'm the only God there is—
The only God who does things right
    and knows how to help.
So turn to me and be helped—saved!—
    everyone, whoever and wherever you are.
I am GOD,
    the only God there is, the one and only.
I promise in my own name:
    Every word out of my mouth does what it says.
    I never take back what I say.
Everyone is going to end up kneeling before me.
    Everyone is going to end up saying of me,
    'Yes! Salvation and strength are in GOD!'"

All who have raged against him
    will be brought before him,
    disgraced by their unbelief.
And all who are connected with Israel
    will have a robust, praising, good life in GOD!

46

THIS IS SERIOUS BUSINESS, REBELS

The god Bel falls down, god Nebo slumps.
    The no-god hunks of wood are loaded on mules
And have to be hauled off,
    wearing out the poor mules—
Dead weight, burdens who can't bear burdens,
    hauled off to captivity.

"Listen to me, family of Jacob,
    everyone that's left of the family of Israel.

I've been carrying you on my back
    from the day you were born,
And I'll keep on carrying you when you're old.
    I'll be there, bearing you when you're old and gray.
I've done it and will keep on doing it,
    carrying you on my back, saving you.

"So to whom will you compare me, the Incomparable?
    Can you picture me without reducing me?
People with a lot of money
    hire craftsmen to make them gods.
The artisan delivers the god,
    and they kneel and worship it!
They carry it around in holy parades,
    then take it home and put it on a shelf.
And there it sits, day in and day out,
    a dependable god, always right where you put it.
Say anything you want to it, it never talks back.
    Of course, it never *does* anything either!

"Think about this. Wrap your minds around it.
    This is serious business, rebels. Take it to heart.
Remember your history,
    your long and rich history.
I am GOD, the only God you've had or ever will have—
    incomparable, irreplaceable—
From the very beginning
    telling you what the ending will be,
All along letting you in
    on what is going to happen,
Assuring you, 'I'm in this for the long haul,
    I'll do exactly what I set out to do,'
Calling that eagle, Cyrus, out of the east,
    from a far country the man I chose to help me.
I've said it, and I'll most certainly do it.
    I've planned it, so it's as good as done.

"Now listen to me:
    You're a hardheaded bunch and hard to help.
I'm ready to help you right now.

Deliverance is not a long-range plan.
    Salvation isn't on hold.
I'm putting salvation to work in Zion now,
      and glory in Israel.

47

THE PARTY'S OVER

"Get off your high horse and sit in the dirt,
      virgin daughter of Babylon.
No more throne for you—sit on the ground,
      daughter of the Chaldeans.
Nobody will be calling you 'charming'
      and 'alluring' anymore. Get used to it.
Get a job, any old job:
      Clean gutters, scrub toilets.
Hock your gowns and scarves,
      put on overalls—the party's over.
Your nude body will be on public display,
      exposed to vulgar taunts.
It's vengeance time, and I'm taking vengeance.
      No one gets let off the hook."

YOU'RE ACTING LIKE THE CENTER OF THE UNIVERSE

Our Redeemer speaks,
      named GOD-of-the-Angel-Armies, The Holy of Israel:
"Shut up and get out of the way,
      daughter of Chaldeans.
You'll no longer be called
      'First Lady of the Kingdoms.'
I was fed up with my people,
      thoroughly disgusted with my progeny.
I turned them over to you,
      but you had no compassion.
You put old men and women
      to cruel, hard labor.
You said, 'I'm the First Lady.
      I'll always be the pampered darling.'
You took nothing seriously, took nothing to heart,

never gave tomorrow a thought.
Well, start thinking, playgirl.
　　You're acting like the center of the universe,
Smugly saying to yourself, 'I'm Number One. There's nobody but me.
　　I'll never be a widow, I'll never lose my children.'
Those two things are going to hit you both at once,
　　suddenly, on the same day:
Spouse and children gone, a total loss,
　　despite your many enchantments and charms.
You were so confident and comfortable in your evil life,
　　saying, 'No one sees me.'
You thought you knew so much, had everything figured out.
　　What delusion!
　　Smugly telling yourself, 'I'm Number One. There's nobody
　　　　but me.'
Ruin descends—
　　you can't charm it away.
Disaster strikes—
　　you can't cast it off with spells.
Catastrophe, sudden and total—
　　and you're totally at sea, totally bewildered!
But don't give up. From your great repertoire
　　of enchantments there must be one you haven't yet tried.
You've been at this a long time.
　　Surely *something* will work.
I know you're exhausted trying out remedies,
　　but don't give up.
Call in the astrologers and stargazers.
　　They're good at this. Surely they can work up something!

"Fat chance. You'd be grasping at straws
　　that are already in the fire,
A fire that is even now raging.
　　Your 'experts' are in it and won't get out.
It's not a fire for cooking venison stew,
　　not a fire to warm you on a winter night!
That's the fate of your friends in sorcery, your magician buddies
　　you've been in cahoots with all your life.
They reel, confused, bumping into one another.
　　None of them bother to help you.

48

TESTED IN THE FURNACE OF AFFLICTION

"And now listen to this, family of Jacob,
    you who are called by the name Israel:
Who got you started in the loins of Judah,
    you who use GOD's name to back up your promises
    and pray to the God of Israel?
But do you mean it?
    Do you live like it?
You claim to be citizens of the Holy City;
    you act as though you lean on the God of Israel,
    named GOD-of-the-Angel-Armies.
For a long time now, I've let you in on the way I work:
    I told you what I was going to do beforehand,
    then I did it and it was done, and that's that.
I know you're a bunch of hardheads,
    obstinate and flint-faced,
So I got a running start and began telling you
    what was going on before it even happened.
That is why you can't say,
    'My god-idol did this.'
    'My favorite god-carving commanded this.'
You have all this evidence
    confirmed by your own eyes and ears.
    Shouldn't you be talking about it?
And that was just the beginning.
    I have a lot more to tell you,
    things you never knew existed.
This isn't a variation on the same old thing.
    This is new, brand-new,
    something you'd never guess or dream up.
When you hear this you won't be able to say,
    'I knew that all along.'
You've never been good listeners to me.
    You have a history of ignoring me,
A sorry track record of fickle attachments—
    rebels from the womb.
But out of the sheer goodness of my heart,

115

because of who I am,
I keep a tight rein on my anger and hold my temper.
    I don't wash my hands of you.
Do you see what I've done?
    I've refined you, but not without fire.
    I've tested you like silver in the furnace of affliction.
Out of myself, simply because of who I am, I do what I do.
    I have my reputation to keep up.
    I'm not playing second fiddle to either gods or people.

"Listen, Jacob. Listen, Israel—
    I'm the One who named you!
I'm the One.
    I got things started and, yes, I'll wrap them up.
Earth is my work, handmade.
    And the skies—I made them too, horizon to horizon.
When I speak, they're on their feet, at attention.

"Come everybody, gather around, listen:
    Who among the gods has delivered the news?
I, GOD, love this man Cyrus, and I'm using him
    to do what I want with Babylon.
I, yes I, have spoken. I've called him.
    I've brought him here. He'll be successful.
Come close, listen carefully:
    I've never kept secrets from you.
    I've always been present with you."

YOUR PROGENY, LIKE GRAINS OF SAND

And now, the Master, GOD, sends me and his Spirit
    with this Message from GOD,
    your Redeemer, The Holy of Israel:
"I am GOD, your God,
    who teaches you how to live right and well.
    I show you what to do, where to go.
If you had listened all along to what I told you,
    your life would have flowed full like a river,
    blessings rolling in like waves from the sea.
Children and grandchildren are like sand,

116

your progeny like grains of sand.
There would be no end of them,
    no danger of losing touch with me."

Get out of Babylon! Run from the Babylonians!
    Shout the news. Broadcast it.
Let the world know, the whole world.
    Tell them, "GOD redeemed his dear servant Jacob!"

They weren't thirsty when he led them through the deserts.
    He made water pour out of the rock;
    he split the rock and the water gushed.

"There is no peace," says GOD, "for the wicked."

49

A LIGHT FOR THE NATIONS

Listen, far-flung islands,
    pay attention, faraway people:
GOD put me to work from the day I was born.
    The moment I entered the world he named me.
He gave me speech that would cut and penetrate.
    He kept his hand on me to protect me.
He made me his straight arrow
    and hid me in his quiver.
He said to me, "You're my dear servant,
    Israel, through whom I'll shine."

But I said, "I've worked for nothing.
    I've nothing to show for a life of hard work.
Nevertheless, I'll let GOD have the last word.
    I'll let him pronounce his verdict."

"And now," GOD says,
    this God who took me in hand
    from the moment of birth to be his servant,
To bring Jacob back home to him,
    to set a reunion for Israel—

What an honor for me in GOD's eyes!
    That God should be my strength!
He says, "But that's not a big enough job for my servant—
    just to recover the tribes of Jacob,
        merely to round up the strays of Israel.
I'm setting you up as a light for the *nations*
    so that my salvation becomes *global*!"

GOD, Redeemer of Israel, The Holy of Israel,
    says to the despised one, kicked around by the nations,
        slave labor to the ruling class:
"Kings will see, get to their feet—the princes, too—
    and then fall on their faces in homage
Because of GOD, who has faithfully kept his word,
    The Holy of Israel, who has chosen you."

    GOD also says:

"When the time's ripe, I answer you.
    When victory's due, I help you.
I form you and use you
    to reconnect the people with me,
To put the land in order,
    to resettle families on the ruined properties.
I tell prisoners, 'Come on out. You're free!'
    and those huddled in fear, 'It's all right. It's safe now.'
There'll be foodstands along all the roads,
    picnics on all the hills—
Nobody hungry, nobody thirsty,
    shade from the sun, shelter from the wind,
For the Compassionate One guides them,
    takes them to the best springs.
I'll make all my mountains into roads,
    turn them into a superhighway.
Look: These coming from far countries,
    and those, out of the north,
These streaming in from the west,
    and those from all the way down the Nile!"

Heavens, raise the roof! Earth, wake the dead!
    Mountains, send up cheers!

GOD has comforted his people.
>   He has tenderly nursed his beaten-up, beaten-down people.

But Zion said, "I don't get it. GOD has left me.
>   My Master has forgotten I even exist."

"Can a mother forget the infant at her breast,
>   walk away from the baby she bore?
But even if mothers forget,
>   I'd never forget you—never.
Look, I've written your names on the backs of my hands.
>   The walls you're rebuilding are never out of my sight.
Your builders are faster than your wreckers.
>   The demolition crews are gone for good.
Look up, look around, look well!
>   See them all gathering, coming to you?
As sure as I am the living God"—GOD's Decree—
>   "you're going to put them on like so much jewelry,
>   you're going to use them to dress up like a bride.

"And your ruined land?
>   Your devastated, decimated land?
Filled with more people than you know what to do with!
>   And your barbarian enemies, a fading memory.
The children born in your exile will be saying,
>   'It's getting too crowded here. I need more room.'
And you'll say to yourself,
>   'Where on earth did these children come from?
I lost everything, had nothing, was exiled and penniless.
>   So who reared these children?
>   How did these children get here?'"

The Master, GOD, says:

"Look! I signal to the nations,
>   I raise my flag to summon the people.
Here they'll come: women carrying your little boys in their arms,
>   men carrying your little girls on their shoulders.
Kings will be your babysitters,
>   princesses will be your nursemaids.
They'll offer to do all your drudge work—

scrub your floors, do your laundry.
You'll know then that I am GOD.
No one who hopes in me ever regrets it."

Can plunder be retrieved from a giant,
prisoners of war gotten back from a tyrant?
But GOD says, "Even if a giant grips the plunder
and a tyrant holds my people prisoner,
I'm the one who's on your side,
defending your cause, rescuing your children.
And your enemies, crazed and desperate, will turn on themselves,
killing each other in a frenzy of self-destruction.
Then everyone will know that I, GOD,
have saved you—I, the Mighty One of Jacob."

50

WHO OUT THERE FEARS GOD?

GOD says:

"Can you produce your mother's divorce papers
proving I got rid of her?
Can you produce a receipt
proving I sold you?
Of course you can't.
It's your sins that put you here,
your wrongs that got you shipped out.
So why didn't anyone come when I knocked?
Why didn't anyone answer when I called?
Do you think I've forgotten how to help?
Am I so decrepit that I can't deliver?
I'm as powerful as ever,
and can reverse what I once did:
I can dry up the sea with a word,
turn river water into desert sand,
And leave the fish stinking in the sun,
stranded on dry land . . .
Turn all the lights out in the sky
and pull down the curtain."

✝

The Master, GOD, has given me
    a well-taught tongue,
So I know how to encourage tired people.
    He wakes me up in the morning,
Wakes me up, opens my ears
    to listen as one ready to take orders.
The Master, GOD, opened my ears,
    and I didn't go back to sleep,
    didn't pull the covers back over my head.
I followed orders,
    stood there and took it while they beat me,
    held steady while they pulled out my beard,
Didn't dodge their insults,
    faced them as they spit in my face.
And the Master, GOD, stays right there and helps me,
    so I'm not disgraced.
Therefore I set my face like flint,
    confident that I'll never regret this.
My champion is right here.
    Let's take our stand together!
Who dares bring suit against me?
    Let him try!
Look! the Master, GOD, is right here.
    Who would dare call me guilty?
Look! My accusers are a clothes bin of threadbare
    socks and shirts, fodder for moths!

✝

Who out there fears GOD,
    actually listens to the voice of his servant?
For anyone out there who doesn't know where you're going,
    anyone groping in the dark,
Here's what: Trust in GOD.
    Lean on your God!
But if all you're after is making trouble,
    playing with fire,

Go ahead and see where it gets you.
   Set your fires, stir people up, blow on the flames,
But don't expect me to just stand there and watch.
   I'll hold your feet to those flames.

51

COMMITTED TO SEEKING GOD

"Listen to me, all you who are serious about right living
      and committed to seeking GOD.
Ponder the rock from which you were cut,
      the quarry from which you were dug.
Yes, ponder Abraham, your father,
      and Sarah, who bore you.
Think of it! One solitary man when I called him,
      but once I blessed him, he multiplied.
Likewise I, GOD, will comfort Zion,
      comfort all her mounds of ruins.
I'll transform her dead ground into Eden,
      her moonscape into the garden of GOD,
A place filled with exuberance and laughter,
      thankful voices and melodic songs.

"Pay attention, my people.
      Listen to me, nations.
Revelation flows from me.
      My decisions light up the world.
My deliverance arrives on the run,
      my salvation right on time.
      I'll bring justice to the peoples.
Even faraway islands will look to me
      and take hope in my saving power.
Look up at the skies,
      ponder the earth under your feet.
The skies will fade out like smoke,
      the earth will wear out like work pants,
      and the people will die off like flies.
But my salvation will last forever,
      my setting-things-right will never be obsolete.

"Listen now, you who know right from wrong,
    you who hold my teaching inside you:
Pay no attention to insults, and when mocked
    don't let it get you down.
Those insults and mockeries are moth-eaten,
    from brains that are termite-ridden,
But my setting-things-right lasts,
    my salvation goes on and on and on."

Wake up, wake up, flex your muscles, GOD!
    Wake up as in the old days, in the long ago.
Didn't you once make mincemeat of Rahab,
    dispatch the old chaos-dragon?
And didn't you once dry up the sea,
    the powerful waters of the deep,
And then made the bottom of the ocean a road
    for the redeemed to walk across?
In the same way GOD's ransomed will come back,
    come back to Zion cheering, shouting,
Joy eternal wreathing their heads,
    exuberant ecstasies transporting them—
    and not a sign of moans or groans.

WHAT ARE YOU AFRAID OF—OR WHO?
"I, I'm the One comforting you.
    What are you afraid of—or who?
Some man or woman who'll soon be dead?
    Some poor wretch destined for dust?
You've forgotten me, GOD, who made you,
    who unfurled the skies, who founded the earth.
And here you are, quaking like an aspen
    before the tantrums of a tyrant
    who thinks he can kick down the world.
But what will come of the tantrums?
    The victims will be released before you know it.
They're not going to die.
    They're not even going to go hungry.
For I am GOD, your very own God,
    who stirs up the sea and whips up the waves,

named GOD-of-the-Angel-Armies.
I teach you how to talk, word by word,
    and personally watch over you,
Even while I'm unfurling the skies,
    setting earth on solid foundations,
    and greeting Zion: 'Welcome, my people!'"

So wake up! Rub the sleep from your eyes!
    Up on your feet, Jerusalem!
You've drunk the cup GOD handed you,
    the strong drink of his anger.
You drank it down to the last drop,
    staggered and collapsed, dead-drunk.
And nobody to help you home,
    no one among your friends or children
    to take you by the hand and put you in bed.
You've been hit with a double dose of trouble
    —does anyone care?
Assault and battery, hunger and death
    —will anyone comfort?
Your sons and daughters have passed out,
    strewn in the streets like stunned rabbits,
Sleeping off the strong drink of GOD's anger,
    the rage of your God.

Therefore listen, please,
    you with your splitting headaches,
You who are nursing the hangovers
    that didn't come from drinking wine.
Your Master, your GOD, has something to say,
    your God has taken up his people's case:
"Look, I've taken back the drink that sent you reeling.
    No more drinking from that jug of my anger!
I've passed it over to your abusers to drink, those who ordered you,
    'Down on the ground so we can walk all over you!'
And you had to do it. Flat on the ground,
    you were the dirt under their feet."

52

GOD IS LEADING YOU OUT OF HERE

Wake up, wake up! Pull on your boots, Zion!
    Dress up in your Sunday best, Jerusalem, holy city!
Those who want no part of God have been culled out.
    They won't be coming along.
Brush off the dust and get to your feet, captive Jerusalem!
    Throw off your chains, captive daughter of Zion!

    GOD says, "You were sold for nothing. You're being bought back for
nothing."
    Again, the Master, GOD, says, "Early on, my people went to Egypt
and lived, strangers in the land. At the other end, Assyria oppressed
them. And now, what have I here?" GOD's Decree. "My people are
hauled off again for no reason at all. Tyrants on the warpath, whooping it up, and day after day, incessantly, my reputation blackened. Now
it's time that my people know who I am, what I'm made of— yes, that
I have something to say. Here I am!"

How beautiful on the mountains
    are the feet of the messenger bringing good news,
Breaking the news that all's well,
    proclaiming good times, announcing salvation,
    telling Zion, "Your God reigns!"
Voices! Listen! Your scouts are shouting, thunderclap shouts,
    shouting in joyful unison.
They see with their own eyes
    GOD coming back to Zion.
Break into song! Boom it out, ruins of Jerusalem:
    "GOD has comforted his people!
    He's redeemed Jerusalem!"
GOD has rolled up his sleeves.
    All the nations can see his holy, muscled arm.
Everyone, from one end of the earth to the other,
    sees him at work, doing his salvation work.

Out of here! Out of here! Leave this place!
    Don't look back. Don't contaminate yourselves with plunder.

Just leave, but leave clean. Purify yourselves
    in the process of worship, carrying the holy vessels of GOD.
But you don't have to be in a hurry.
    You're not running from anybody!
GOD is leading you out of here,
    and the God of Israel is also your rear guard.

IT WAS OUR PAINS HE CARRIED

"Just watch my servant blossom!
    Exalted, tall, head and shoulders above the crowd!
But he didn't begin that way.
    At first everyone was appalled.
He didn't even look human—
    a ruined face, disfigured past recognition.
Nations all over the world will be in awe, taken aback,
    kings shocked into silence when they see him.
For what was unheard of they'll see with their own eyes,
    what was unthinkable they'll have right before them."

53

Who believes what we've heard and seen?
    Who would have thought GOD's saving power would look like
        this?

The servant grew up before God—a scrawny seedling,
    a scrubby plant in a parched field.
There was nothing attractive about him,
    nothing to cause us to take a second look.
He was looked down on and passed over,
    a man who suffered, who knew pain firsthand.
One look at him and people turned away.
    We looked down on him, thought he was scum.
But the fact is, it was *our* pains he carried—
    our disfigurements, all the things wrong with *us*.
We thought he brought it on himself,
    that God was punishing him for his own failures.
But it was our sins that did that to him,
    that ripped and tore and crushed him—*our sins!*

He took the punishment, and that made us whole.
    Through his bruises we get healed.
We're all like sheep who've wandered off and gotten lost.
    We've all done our own thing, gone our own way.
And GOD has piled all our sins, everything we've done wrong,
    on him, on him.

He was beaten, he was tortured,
    but he didn't say a word.
Like a lamb taken to be slaughtered
    and like a sheep being sheared,
    he took it all in silence.
Justice miscarried, and he was led off—
    and did anyone really know what was happening?
He died without a thought for his own welfare,
    beaten bloody for the sins of my people.
They buried him with the wicked,
    threw him in a grave with criminals,
Even though he'd never hurt a soul
    or said one word that wasn't true.

Still, it's what GOD had in mind all along,
    to crush him with pain.
The plan was that he give himself as an offering for sin
    so that he'd see life come from it—life, life, and more life.
    And GOD's plan will deeply prosper through him.

Out of that terrible travail of soul,
    he'll see that it's worth it and be glad he did it.
Through what he experienced, my righteous one, my servant,
    will make many "righteous ones,"
    as he himself carries the burden of their sins.
Therefore I'll reward him extravagantly—
    the best of everything, the highest honors—
Because he looked death in the face and didn't flinch,
    because he embraced the company of the lowest.
He took on his own shoulders the sin of the many,
    he took up the cause of all the black sheep.

54

SPREAD OUT! THINK BIG!

"Sing, barren woman, who has never had a baby.
    Fill the air with song, you who've never experienced childbirth!
You're ending up with far more children
    than all those childbearing women." GOD says so!
"Clear lots of ground for your tents!
    Make your tents large. Spread out! Think big!
Use plenty of rope,
    drive the tent pegs deep.
You're going to need lots of elbow room
    for your growing family.
You're going to take over whole nations;
    you're going to resettle abandoned cities.
Don't be afraid—you're not going to be embarrassed.
    Don't hold back—you're not going to come up short.
You'll forget all about the humiliations of your youth,
    and the indignities of being a widow will fade from memory.
For your Maker is your bridegroom,
    his name, GOD-of-the-Angel-Armies!
Your Redeemer is The Holy of Israel,
    known as God of the whole earth.
You were like an abandoned wife, devastated with grief,
    and GOD welcomed you back,
Like a woman married young
    and then left," says your God.

    Your Redeemer GOD says:

"I left you, but only for a moment.
    Now, with enormous compassion, I'm bringing you back.
In an outburst of anger I turned my back on you—
    but only for a moment.
It's with lasting love
    that I'm tenderly caring for you.

"This exile is just like the days of Noah for me:
    I promised then that the waters of Noah
    would never again flood the earth.

I'm promising now no more anger,
no more dressing you down.
For even if the mountains walk away
and the hills fall to pieces,
My love won't walk away from you,
my covenant commitment of peace won't fall apart."
The GOD who has compassion on you says so.

"Afflicted city, storm-battered, unpitied:
I'm about to rebuild you with stones of turquoise,
Lay your foundations with sapphires,
construct your towers with rubies,
Your gates with jewels,
and all your walls with precious stones.
All your children will have GOD for their teacher—
what a mentor for your children!
You'll be built solid, grounded in righteousness,
far from any trouble—nothing to fear!
far from terror—it won't even come close!
If anyone attacks you,
don't for a moment suppose that I sent them,
And if any should attack,
nothing will come of it.
I create the blacksmith
who fires up his forge
and makes a weapon designed to kill.
I also create the destroyer—
but no weapon that can hurt you has ever been forged.
Any accuser who takes you to court
will be dismissed as a liar.
This is what GOD's servants can expect.
I'll see to it that everything works out for the best."
GOD's Decree.

55

BUY WITHOUT MONEY

"Hey there! All who are thirsty,
come to the water!
Are you penniless?

Come anyway—buy and eat!
Come, buy your drinks, buy wine and milk.
    Buy without money—everything's free!
Why do you spend your money on junk food,
    your hard-earned cash on cotton candy?
Listen to me, listen well: Eat only the best,
    fill yourself with only the finest.
Pay attention, come close now,
    listen carefully to my life-giving, life-nourishing words.
I'm making a lasting covenant commitment with you,
    the same that I made with David: sure, solid, enduring love.
I set him up as a witness to the nations,
    made him a prince and leader of the nations,
And now I'm doing it to you:
    You'll summon nations you've never heard of,
and nations who've never heard of you
    will come running to you
Because of me, your GOD,
    because The Holy of Israel has honored you."

Seek GOD while he's here to be found,
    pray to him while he's close at hand.
Let the wicked abandon their way of life
    and the evil their way of thinking.
Let them come back to GOD, who is merciful,
    come back to our God, who is lavish with forgiveness.

"I don't think the way you think.
    The way you work isn't the way I work."
        GOD's Decree.
"For as the sky soars high above earth,
    so the way I work surpasses the way you work,
    and the way I think is beyond the way you think.
Just as rain and snow descend from the skies
    and don't go back until they've watered the earth,
Doing their work of making things grow and blossom,
    producing seed for farmers and food for the hungry,
So will the words that come out of my mouth
    not come back empty-handed.

They'll do the work I sent them to do,
    they'll complete the assignment I gave them.

"So you'll go out in joy,
    you'll be led into a whole and complete life.
The mountains and hills will lead the parade,
    bursting with song.
All the trees of the forest will join the procession,
    exuberant with applause.
No more thistles, but giant sequoias,
    no more thornbushes, but stately pines—
Monuments to me, to GOD,
    living and lasting evidence of GOD."

56   MESSAGES OF HOPE

SALVATION IS JUST AROUND THE CORNER

GOD's Message:

"Guard my common good:
    Do what's right and do it in the right way,
For salvation is just around the corner,
    my setting-things-right is about to go into action.
How blessed are you who enter into these things,
    you men and women who embrace them,
Who keep Sabbath and don't defile it,
    who watch your step and don't do anything evil!
Make sure no outsider who now follows GOD
    ever has occasion to say, 'GOD put me in second-class.
    I don't really belong.'
And make sure no physically mutilated person
    is ever made to think, 'I'm damaged goods.
    I don't really belong.'"

For GOD says:

"To the mutilated who keep my Sabbaths
    and choose what delights me
    and keep a firm grip on my covenant,

I'll provide them an honored place
    in my family and within my city,
    even more honored than that of sons and daughters.
I'll confer permanent honors on them
    that will never be revoked.

"And as for the outsiders who now follow me,
    working for me, loving my name,
    and wanting to be my servants—
All who keep Sabbath and don't defile it,
    holding fast to my covenant—
I'll bring them to my holy mountain
    and give them joy in my house of prayer.
They'll be welcome to worship the same as the 'insiders,'
    to bring burnt offerings and sacrifices to my altar.
Oh yes, my house of worship
    will be known as a house of prayer for all people."
The Decree of the Master, GOD himself,
    who gathers in the exiles of Israel:
"I will gather others also,
    gather them in with those already gathered."

☩

A call to the savage beasts: Come on the run.
    Come, devour, beast barbarians!
For Israel's watchmen are blind, the whole lot of them.
    They have no idea what's going on.
They're dogs without sense enough to bark,
    lazy dogs, dreaming in the sun—
But hungry dogs, they do know how to eat,
    voracious dogs, with never enough.
And these are Israel's shepherds!
    They know nothing, understand nothing.
They all look after themselves,
    grabbing whatever's not nailed down.
"Come," they say, "let's have a party.
    Let's go out and get drunk!"
And tomorrow, more of the same:
    "Let's live it up!"

57

NEVER TIRED OF TRYING NEW RELIGIONS

Meanwhile, right-living people die
and no one gives them a thought.
God-fearing people are carted off
and no one even notices.
The right-living people are out of their misery,
they're finally at rest.
They lived well and with dignity
and now they're finally at peace.

✛

"But you, children of a witch, come here!
Sons of a slut, daughters of a whore.
What business do you have taunting,
sneering, and sticking out your tongue?
Do you have any idea what wretches you've turned out to be?
A race of rebels, a generation of liars.
You satisfy your lust any place you find some shade
and fornicate at whim.
You kill your children at any convenient spot—
any cave or crevasse will do.
You take stones from the creek
and set up your sex-and-religion shrines.
You've chosen your fate.
Your worship will be your doom.
You've climbed a high mountain
to practice your foul sex-and-death religion.
Behind closed doors
you assemble your precious gods and goddesses.
Deserting me, you've gone all out, stripped down
and made your bed your place of worship.
You've climbed into bed with the 'sacred' whores
and loved every minute of it,
adoring every curve of their naked bodies.
You anoint your king-god with ointments
and lavish perfumes on yourselves.

You send scouts to search out the latest in religion,
    send them all the way to hell and back.
You wear yourselves out trying the new and the different,
    and never see what a waste it all is.
You've always found strength for the latest fad,
    never got tired of trying new religions.

"Who talked you into the pursuit of this nonsense,
    leaving me high and dry,
    forgetting you ever knew me?
Because I don't yell and make a scene
    do you think I don't exist?
I'll go over, detail by detail, all your 'righteous' attempts at religion,
    and expose the absurdity of it all.
Go ahead, cry for help to your collection of no-gods:
    A good wind will blow them away.
    They're smoke, nothing but smoke.

"But anyone who runs to me for help
    will inherit the land,
    will end up owning my holy mountain!"

☩

Someone says: "Build, build! Make a road!
    Clear the way, remove the rocks
    from the road my people will travel."

A Message from the high and towering God,
    who lives in Eternity,
    whose name is Holy:
"I live in the high and holy places,
    but also with the low-spirited, the spirit-crushed,
And what I do is put new spirit in them,
    get them up and on their feet again.
For I'm not going to haul people into court endlessly,
    I'm not going to be angry forever.
Otherwise, people would lose heart.
    These souls I created would tire out and give up.
I *was* angry, good and angry, because of Israel's sins.

I struck him hard and turned away in anger,
while he kept at his stubborn, willful ways.
When I looked again and saw what he was doing,
I decided to heal him, lead him, and comfort him,
creating a new language of praise for the mourners.
Peace to the faroff, peace to the near-at-hand," says GOD—
"and yes, I will heal them.
But the wicked are storm-battered seas
that can't quiet down.
The waves stir up garbage and mud.
There's no peace," God says, "for the wicked.

58

YOUR PRAYERS WON'T GET OFF THE GROUND

"Shout! A full-throated shout!
Hold nothing back—a trumpet-blast shout!
Tell my people what's wrong with their lives,
face my family Jacob with their sins!
They're busy, busy, busy at worship,
and love studying all about me.
To all appearances they're a nation of right-living people—
law-abiding, God-honoring.
They ask me, 'What's the right thing to do?'
and love having me on their side.
But they also complain,
'Why do we fast and you don't look our way?
Why do we humble ourselves and you don't even notice?'

"Well, here's why:

"The bottom line on your 'fast days' is profit.
You drive your employees much too hard.
You fast, but at the same time you bicker and fight.
You fast, but you swing a mean fist.
The kind of fasting you do
won't get your prayers off the ground.
Do you think this is the kind of fast day I'm after:
a day to show off humility?

To put on a pious long face
    and parade around solemnly in black?
Do you call *that* fasting,
    a fast day that I, GOD, would like?

"This is the kind of fast day I'm after:
    to break the chains of injustice,
    get rid of exploitation in the workplace,
    free the oppressed,
    cancel debts.
What I'm interested in seeing you do is:
    sharing your food with the hungry,
    inviting the homeless poor into your homes,
    putting clothes on the shivering ill-clad,
    being available to your own families.
Do this and the lights will turn on,
    and your lives will turn around at once.
Your righteousness will pave your way.
    The GOD of glory will secure your passage.
Then when you pray, GOD will answer.
    You'll call out for help and I'll say, 'Here I am.'

A FULL LIFE IN THE EMPTIEST OF PLACES

"If you get rid of unfair practices,
    quit blaming victims,
    quit gossiping about other people's sins,
If you are generous with the hungry
    and start giving yourselves to the down-and-out,
Your lives will begin to glow in the darkness,
    your shadowed lives will be bathed in sunlight.
I will always show you where to go.
    I'll give you a full life in the emptiest of places—
    firm muscles, strong bones.
You'll be like a well-watered garden,
    a gurgling spring that never runs dry.
You'll use the old rubble of past lives to build anew,
    rebuild the foundations from out of your past.
You'll be known as those who can fix anything,

restore old ruins, rebuild and renovate,
    make the community livable again.

"If you watch your step on the Sabbath
    and don't use my holy day for personal advantage,
If you treat the Sabbath as a day of joy,
    GOD's holy day as a celebration,
If you honor it by refusing 'business as usual,'
    making money, running here and there—
Then you'll be free to enjoy GOD!
    Oh, I'll make you ride high and soar above it all.
I'll make you feast on the inheritance of your ancestor Jacob."
    Yes! GOD says so!

59

WE LONG FOR LIGHT BUT SINK INTO DARKNESS

Look! Listen!
    GOD's arm is not amputated—he can still save.
    GOD's ears are not stopped up—he can still hear.
There's nothing wrong with God; the wrong is in *you*.
    Your wrongheaded lives caused the split between you and God.
    Your sins got between you so that he doesn't hear.
Your hands are drenched in blood,
    your fingers dripping with guilt,
Your lips smeared with lies,
    your tongue swollen from muttering obscenities.
No one speaks up for the right,
    no one deals fairly.
They trust in illusion, they tell lies,
    they get pregnant with mischief and have sin-babies.
They hatch snake eggs and weave spider webs.
    Eat an egg and die; break an egg and get a snake!
The spider webs are no good for shirts or shawls.
    No one can wear these weavings!
They weave wickedness,
    they hatch violence.
They compete in the race to do evil
    and run to be the first to murder.

They plan and plot evil, think and breathe evil,
    and leave a trail of wrecked lives behind them.
They know nothing about peace
    and less than nothing about justice.
They make tortuously twisted roads.
    No peace for the wretch who walks down those roads!

Which means that we're a far cry from fair dealing,
    and we're not even close to right living.
We long for light but sink into darkness,
    long for brightness but stumble through the night.
Like the blind, we inch along a wall,
    groping eyeless in the dark.
We shuffle our way in broad daylight,
    like the dead, but somehow walking.
We're no better off than bears, groaning,
    and no worse off than doves, moaning.
We look for justice—not a sign of it;
    for salvation—not so much as a hint.

Our wrongdoings pile up before you, God,
    our sins stand up and accuse us.
Our wrongdoings stare us down;
    we know in detail what we've done:
Mocking and denying GOD,
    not following our God,
Spreading false rumors, inciting sedition,
    pregnant with lies, muttering malice.
Justice is beaten back,
    Righteousness is banished to the sidelines,
Truth staggers down the street,
    Honesty is nowhere to be found,
Good is missing in action.
    Anyone renouncing evil is beaten and robbed.

GOD looked and saw evil looming on the horizon—
    so much evil and no sign of Justice.
He couldn't believe what he saw:
    not a soul around to correct this awful situation.
So he did it himself, took on the work of Salvation,

fueled by his own Righteousness.
He dressed in Righteousness, put it on like a suit of armor,
    with Salvation on his head like a helmet,
Put on Judgment like an overcoat,
    and threw a cloak of Passion across his shoulders.
He'll make everyone pay for what they've done:
    fury for his foes, just deserts for his enemies.
    Even the faroff islands will get paid off in full.
In the west they'll fear the name of GOD,
    in the east they'll fear the glory of GOD,
For he'll arrive like a river in flood stage,
    whipped to a torrent by the wind of GOD.

"I'll arrive in Zion as Redeemer,
    to those in Jacob who leave their sins."
        GOD's Decree.

"As for me," GOD says, "this is my covenant with them: My Spirit that I've placed upon you and the words that I've given you to speak, they're not going to leave your mouths nor the mouths of your children nor the mouths of your grandchildren. You will keep repeating these words and won't ever stop." GOD's orders.

60

PEOPLE RETURNING FOR THE REUNION

"Get out of bed, Jerusalem!
    Wake up. Put your face in the sunlight.
    GOD's bright glory has risen for you.
The whole earth is wrapped in darkness,
    all people sunk in deep darkness,
But GOD rises on you,
    his sunrise glory breaks over you.
Nations will come to your light,
    kings to your sunburst brightness.
Look up! Look around!
    Watch as they gather, watch as they approach you:
Your sons coming from great distances,
    your daughters carried by their nannies.

When you see them coming you'll smile—big smiles!
    Your heart will swell and, yes, burst!
All those people returning by sea for the reunion,
    a rich harvest of exiles gathered in from the nations!
And then streams of camel caravans as far as the eye can see,
    young camels of nomads in Midian and Ephah,
Pouring in from the south from Sheba,
    loaded with gold and frankincense,
    preaching the praises of GOD.
And yes, a great roundup
    of flocks from the nomads in Kedar and Nebaioth,
Welcome gifts for worship at my altar
    as I bathe my glorious Temple in splendor.

WHAT'S THAT WE SEE IN THE DISTANCE?

"What's that we see in the distance,
    a cloud on the horizon, like doves darkening the sky?
It's ships from the distant islands,
    the famous Tarshish ships
Returning your children from faraway places,
    loaded with riches, with silver and gold,
And backed by the name of your GOD, The Holy of Israel,
    showering you with splendor.
Foreigners will rebuild your walls,
    and their kings assist you in the conduct of worship.
When I was angry I hit you hard.
    It's my desire now to be tender.
Your Jerusalem gates will always be open
    —open house day and night!—
Receiving deliveries of wealth from all nations,
    and their kings, the delivery boys!
Any nation or kingdom that doesn't deliver will perish;
    those nations will be totally wasted.
The rich woods of Lebanon will be delivered
    —all that cypress and oak and pine—
To give a splendid elegance to my Sanctuary,
    as I make my footstool glorious.
The descendants of your oppressor
    will come bowing and scraping to you.

All who looked down at you in contempt
    will lick your boots.
They'll confer a title on you: City of GOD,
    Zion of The Holy of Israel.
Not long ago you were despised refuse—
    out-of-the-way, unvisited, ignored.
But now I've put you on your feet,
    towering and grand forever, a joy to look at!
When you suck the milk of nations
    and the breasts of royalty,
You'll know that I, GOD, am your Savior,
    your Redeemer, Champion of Jacob.
I'll give you only the best—no more hand-me-downs!
    Gold instead of bronze, silver instead of iron,
    bronze instead of wood, iron instead of stones.
I'll install Peace to run your country,
    make Righteousness your boss.
There'll be no more stories of crime in your land,
    no more robberies, no more vandalism.
You'll name your main street Salvation Way,
    and install Praise Park at the center of town.
You'll have no more need of the sun by day
    nor the brightness of the moon at night.
GOD will be your eternal light,
    your God will bathe you in splendor.
Your sun will never go down,
    your moon will never fade.
I will be your eternal light.
    Your days of grieving are over.
All your people will live right and well,
    in permanent possession of the land.
They're the green shoot that I planted,
    planted with my own hands to display my glory.
The runt will become a great tribe,
    the weakling become a strong nation.
I am GOD.
    At the right time I'll make it happen."

61

ANNOUNCE FREEDOM TO ALL CAPTIVES

The Spirit of GOD, the Master, is on me
    because GOD anointed me.
He sent me to preach good news to the poor,
    heal the heartbroken,
Announce freedom to all captives,
    pardon all prisoners.
GOD sent me to announce the year of his grace—
    a celebration of God's destruction of our enemies—
    and to comfort all who mourn,
To care for the needs of all who mourn in Zion,
    give them bouquets of roses instead of ashes,
Messages of joy instead of news of doom,
    a praising heart instead of a languid spirit.
Rename them "Oaks of Righteousness"
    planted by GOD to display his glory.
They'll rebuild the old ruins,
    raise a new city out of the wreckage.
They'll start over on the ruined cities,
    take the rubble left behind and make it new.
You'll hire outsiders to herd your flocks
    and foreigners to work your fields,
But you'll have the title "Priests of GOD,"
    honored as ministers of our God.
You'll feast on the bounty of nations,
    you'll bask in their glory.
Because you got a double dose of trouble
    and more than your share of contempt,
Your inheritance in the land will be doubled
    and your joy go on forever.

"Because I, GOD, love fair dealing
    and hate thievery and crime,
I'll pay your wages on time and in full,
    and establish my eternal covenant with you.
Your descendants will become well-known all over.
    Your children in foreign countries

Will be recognized at once
    as the people I have blessed."

I will sing for joy in GOD,
    explode in praise from deep in my soul!
He dressed me up in a suit of salvation,
    he outfitted me in a robe of righteousness,
As a bridegroom who puts on a tuxedo
    and a bride a jeweled tiara.
For as the earth bursts with spring wildflowers,
    and as a garden cascades with blossoms,
So the Master, GOD, brings righteousness into full bloom
    and puts praise on display before the nations.

62

LOOK, YOUR SAVIOR COMES!

Regarding Zion, I can't keep my mouth shut,
    regarding Jerusalem, I can't hold my tongue,
Until her righteousness blazes down like the sun
    and her salvation flames up like a torch.
Foreign countries will see your righteousness,
    and world leaders your glory.
You'll get a brand-new name
    straight from the mouth of GOD.
You'll be a stunning crown in the palm of GOD's hand,
    a jeweled gold cup held high in the hand of your God.
No more will anyone call you Rejected,
    and your country will no more be called Ruined.
You'll be called Hephzibah ("My Delight"),
    and your land Beulah ("Married"),
Because GOD delights in you
    and your land will be like a wedding celebration.
For as a young man marries his virgin bride,
    so your builder marries you,
And as a bridegroom is happy in his bride,
    so your God is happy with you.

I've posted watchmen on your walls, Jerusalem.
>Day and night they keep at it, praying, calling out,
>reminding GOD to remember.
They are to give him no peace until he does what he said,
>until he makes Jerusalem famous as the City of Praise.

GOD has taken a solemn oath,
>an oath he means to keep:
"Never again will I open your grain-filled barns
>to your enemies to loot and eat.
Never again will foreigners drink the wine
>that you worked so hard to produce.
No. The farmers who grow the food will eat the food
>and praise GOD for it.
And those who make the wine will drink the wine
>in my holy courtyards."

Walk out of the gates. Get going!
>Get the road ready for the people.
Build the highway. Get at it!
>Clear the debris,
>hoist high a flag, a signal to all peoples!
Yes! GOD has broadcast to all the world:
>"Tell daughter Zion, 'Look! Your Savior comes,
Ready to do what he said he'd do,
>prepared to complete what he promised.'"
Zion will be called new names: Holy People, GOD-Redeemed,
>Sought-Out, City-Not-Forsaken.

63

WHO GOES THERE?

The watchmen call out,
"Who goes there, marching out of Edom,
>out of Bozrah in clothes dyed red?
Name yourself, so splendidly dressed,
>advancing, bristling with power!"

"It is I: I speak what is right,
>I, mighty to save!"

"And why are your robes so red,
    your clothes dyed red like those who tread grapes?"

"I've been treading the winepress alone.
    No one was there to help me.
Angrily, I stomped the grapes;
    raging, I trampled the people.
Their blood spurted all over me—
    all my clothes were soaked with blood.
I was set on vengeance.
    The time for redemption had arrived.
I looked around for someone to help
    —no one.
I couldn't believe it
    —not one volunteer.
So I went ahead and did it myself,
    fed and fueled by my rage.
I trampled the people in my anger,
    crushed them under foot in my wrath,
    soaked the earth with their lifeblood."

ALL THE THINGS GOD HAS DONE THAT NEED PRAISING

I'll make a list of GOD's gracious dealings,
    all the things GOD has done that need praising,
All the generous bounties of GOD,
    his great goodness to the family of Israel—
Compassion lavished,
    love extravagant.
He said, "Without question these are my people,
    children who would never betray me."
So he became their Savior.
    In all their troubles,
    he was troubled, too.
He didn't send someone else to help them.
    He did it himself, in person.
Out of his own love and pity
    he redeemed them.
He rescued them and carried them along
    for a long, long time.

But they turned on him;
    they grieved his Holy Spirit.
So he turned on them,
    became their enemy and fought them.

Then they remembered the old days,
    the days of Moses, God's servant:
"Where is he who brought the shepherds of his flock
    up and out of the sea?
And what happened to the One who set
    his Holy Spirit within them?
Who linked his arm with Moses' right arm,
    divided the waters before them,
Making him famous ever after,
    and led them through the muddy abyss
    as surefooted as horses on hard, level ground?
Like a herd of cattle led to pasture,
    the Spirit of GOD gave them rest."

That's how you led your people!
    That's how you became so famous!
Look down from heaven, look at us!
    Look out the window of your holy and magnificent house!
Whatever happened to your passion,
    your famous mighty acts,
Your heartfelt pity, your compassion?
    Why are you holding back?
You are our Father.
    Abraham and Israel are long dead.
    They wouldn't know us from Adam.
But you're our *living* Father,
    our Redeemer, famous from eternity!
Why, GOD, did you make us wander from your ways?
    Why did you make us cold and stubborn
    so that we no longer worshiped you in awe?
Turn back for the sake of your servants.
    You own us! We belong to you!
For a while your holy people had it good,
    but now our enemies have wrecked your holy place.
For a long time now, you've paid no attention to us.
    It's like you never knew us.

64

CAN WE BE SAVED?

Oh, that you would rip open the heavens and descend,
 make the mountains shudder at your presence—
As when a forest catches fire,
 as when fire makes a pot to boil—
To shock your enemies into facing you,
 make the nations shake in their boots!
You did terrible things we never expected,
 descended and made the mountains shudder at your presence.
Since before time began
 no one has ever imagined,
No ear heard, no eye seen, a God like you
 who works for those who wait for him.
You meet those who happily do what is right,
 who keep a good memory of the way you work.
But how angry you've been with us!
 We've sinned and kept at it so long!
 Is there any hope for us? Can we be saved?
We're all sin-infected, sin-contaminated.
 Our best efforts are grease-stained rags.
We dry up like autumn leaves—
 sin-dried, we're blown off by the wind.
No one prays to you
 or makes the effort to reach out to you
Because you've turned away from us,
 left us to stew in our sins.

Still, GOD, you are our Father.
 We're the clay and you're our potter:
 All of us are what you made us.
Don't be too angry with us, oh GOD.
 Don't keep a permanent account of wrongdoing.
 Keep in mind, please, we *are* your people—all of us.
Your holy cities are all ghost towns:
 Zion's a ghost town,
 Jerusalem's a field of weeds.
Our holy and beautiful Temple,

which our ancestors filled with your praises,
Was burned down by fire,
    all our lovely parks and gardens in ruins.
In the face of all this,
    are you going to sit there unmoved, GOD?
Aren't you going to say something?
    Haven't you made us miserable long enough?

65

THE PEOPLE WHO BOTHERED TO REACH OUT TO GOD

"I've made myself available
    to those who haven't bothered to ask.
I'm here, ready to be found
    by those who haven't bothered to look.
I kept saying 'I'm here, I'm right here'
    to a nation that ignored me.
I reached out day after day
    to a people who turned their backs on me,
People who make wrong turns,
    who insist on doing things their own way.
They get on my nerves,
    are rude to my face day after day,
Make up their own kitchen religion,
    a potluck religious stew.
They spend the night in tombs
    to get messages from the dead,
Eat forbidden foods
    and drink a witch's brew of potions and charms.
They say, 'Keep your distance.
    Don't touch me. I'm holier than thou.'
These people gag me.
    I can't stand their stench.
Look at this! Their sins are all written out—
    I have the list before me.
I'm not putting up with this any longer.
    I'll pay them the wages
They have coming for their sins.
    And for the sins of their parents lumped in,

a bonus." GOD says so.
"Because they've practiced their blasphemous worship,
     mocking me at their hillside shrines,
I'll let loose the consequences
     and pay them in full for their actions."

✚

GOD's Message:

"But just as one bad apple doesn't ruin the whole bushel,
     there are still plenty of good apples left.
So I'll preserve those in Israel who obey me.
     I won't destroy the whole nation.
I'll bring out my true children from Jacob
     and the heirs of my mountains from Judah.
My chosen will inherit the land,
     my servants will move in.
The lush valley of Sharon in the west
     will be a pasture for flocks,
And in the east, the valley of Achor,
     a place for herds to graze.
These will be for the people
     who bothered to reach out to me, who wanted me in their lives,
     who actually bothered to look for me.

✚

"But you who abandon me, your GOD,
     who forget the holy mountains,
Who hold dinners for Lady Luck
     and throw cocktail parties for Sir Fate,
Well, you asked for it. Fate it will be:
     your destiny, Death.
For when I invited you, you ignored me;
     when I spoke to you, you brushed me off.
You did the very things I exposed as evil;
     you chose what I hate."

Therefore, this is the Message from the Master, GOD:

"My servants will eat,
    and you'll go hungry;
My servants will drink,
    and you'll go thirsty;
My servants will rejoice,
    and you'll hang your heads.
My servants will laugh from full hearts,
    and you'll cry out heartbroken,
    yes, wail from crushed spirits.
Your legacy to my chosen
    will be your name reduced to a cuss word.
I, GOD, will put you to death
    and give a new name to my servants.
Then whoever prays a blessing in the land
    will use my faithful name for the blessing,
And whoever takes an oath in the land
    will use my faithful name for the oath,
Because the earlier troubles are gone and forgotten,
    banished far from my sight.

NEW HEAVENS AND A NEW EARTH

"Pay close attention now:
    I'm creating new heavens and a new earth.
All the earlier troubles, chaos, and pain
    are things of the past, to be forgotten.
Look ahead with joy.
    Anticipate what I'm creating:
I'll create Jerusalem as sheer joy,
    create my people as pure delight.
I'll take joy in Jerusalem,
    take delight in my people:
No more sounds of weeping in the city,
    no cries of anguish;
No more babies dying in the cradle,
    or old people who don't enjoy a full lifetime;
One-hundredth birthdays will be considered normal—
    anything less will seem like a cheat.

They'll build houses
 and move in.
They'll plant fields
 and eat what they grow.
No more building a house
 that some outsider takes over,
No more planting fields
 that some enemy confiscates,
For my people will be as long-lived as trees,
 my chosen ones will have satisfaction in their work.
They won't work and have nothing come of it,
 they won't have children snatched out from under them.
For they themselves are plantings blessed by GOD,
 with their children and grandchildren likewise GOD-blessed.
Before they call out, I'll answer.
 Before they've finished speaking, I'll have heard.
Wolf and lamb will graze the same meadow,
 lion and ox eat straw from the same trough,
 but snakes—they'll get a diet of dirt!
Neither animal nor human will hurt or kill
 anywhere on my Holy Mountain," says GOD.

66

LIVING WORSHIP TO GOD

GOD's Message:

"Heaven's my throne,
 earth is my footstool.
What sort of house could you build for me?
 What holiday spot reserve for me?
I made all this! I own all this!"
 GOD's Decree.
"But there *is* something I'm looking for:
 a person simple and plain,
 reverently responsive to what I say.

"Your acts of worship
 are acts of sin:

151

Your sacrificial slaughter of the ox
    is no different from murdering the neighbor;
Your offerings for worship,
    no different from dumping pig's blood on the altar;
Your presentation of memorial gifts,
    no different from honoring a no-god idol.
You choose self-serving worship,
    you delight in self-centered worship—disgusting!
Well, I choose to expose your nonsense
    and let you realize your worst fears,
Because when I invited you, you ignored me;
    when I spoke to you, you brushed me off.
You did the very things I exposed as evil,
    you chose what I hate."

But listen to what GOD has to say
    to you who reverently respond to his Word:
"Your own families hate you
    and turn you out because of me.
They taunt you, 'Let us see GOD's glory!
    If God's so great, why aren't you happy?'
But they're the ones
    who are going to end up shamed."

☩

Rumbles of thunder from the city!
    A voice out of the Temple!
GOD's voice,
    handing out judgment to his enemies:

"Before she went into labor,
    she had the baby.
Before the birth pangs hit,
    she delivered a son.
Has anyone ever heard of such a thing?
    Has anyone seen anything like this?
A country born in a day?
    A nation born in a flash?
But Zion was barely in labor
    when she had her babies!

Do I open the womb
    and not deliver the baby?
Do I, the One who delivers babies,
    shut the womb?

"Rejoice, Jerusalem,
    and all who love her, celebrate!
And all you who have shed tears over her,
    join in the happy singing.
You newborns can satisfy yourselves
    at her nurturing breasts.
Yes, delight yourselves and drink your fill
    at her ample bosom."

    GOD's Message:

"I'll pour robust well-being into her like a river,
    the glory of nations like a river in flood.
You'll nurse at her breasts,
    nestle in her bosom,
    and be bounced on her knees.
As a mother comforts her child,
    so I'll comfort you.
    You will be comforted in Jerusalem."

You'll see all this and burst with joy
    —you'll feel ten feet tall—
As it becomes apparent that GOD is on your side
    and against his enemies.
For GOD arrives like wildfire
    and his chariots like a tornado,
A furious outburst of anger,
    a rebuke fierce and fiery.
For it's by fire that GOD brings judgment,
    a death sentence on the human race.
Many, oh so many,
    are under GOD's sentence of death:

"All who enter the sacred groves for initiation in those unholy rituals that climaxed in that foul and obscene meal of pigs and mice will eat together and then die together." GOD's Decree.

"I know everything they've ever done or thought. I'm going to come and then gather everyone—all nations, all languages. They'll come and see my glory. I'll set up a station at the center. I'll send the survivors of judgment all over the world: Spain and Africa, Turkey and Greece, and the faroff islands that have never heard of me, who know nothing of what I've done nor who I am. I'll send them out as missionaries to preach my glory among the nations. They'll return with all your long-lost brothers and sisters from all over the world. They'll bring them back and offer them in living worship to GOD. They'll bring them on horses and wagons and carts, on mules and camels, straight to my holy mountain Jerusalem," says GOD. "They'll present them just as Israelites present their offerings in a ceremonial vessel in the Temple of GOD. I'll even take some of them and make them priests and Levites," says GOD.

"For just as the new heavens and new earth
    that I am making will stand firm before me"
        —GOD's Decree—
"So will your children
    and your reputation stand firm.
Month after month and week by week,
    everyone will come to worship me," GOD says.

"And then they'll go out and look at what happened
    to those who rebelled against me. Corpses!
Maggots endlessly eating away on them,
    an endless supply of fuel for fires.
Everyone who sees what's happened
    and smells the stench retches."

JEREMIAH

Jeremiah's life and Jeremiah's book are a single piece. He wrote what he lived, he lived what he wrote. There is no dissonance between his life and his book. Some people write better than they live; others live better than they write. Jeremiah, writing or living, was the same Jeremiah.

This is important to know because Jeremiah is the prophet of choice for many when we find ourselves having to live through difficult times and want some trustworthy help in knowing what to think, how to pray, how to carry on. We'd like some verification of credentials. This book provides the verification.

We live in disruptive times. The decades preceding and following the pivotal third millennium are not exactly unprecedented. There have certainly been comparable times of disruption in the past that left everyone reeling, wondering what on earth and in heaven was going on. But whatever their occasion or size, troubles require attention.

Jeremiah's troubled life spanned one of the most troublesome periods in Hebrew history, the decades leading up to the fall of Jerusalem in 587 B.C., followed by the Babylonian exile. Everything that could go wrong *did* go wrong. And Jeremiah was in the middle of all of it, sticking it out, praying and preaching, suffering and striving, writing and believing. He lived through crushing storms of hostility and furies of bitter doubt. Every muscle in his body was stretched to the limit by fatigue; every thought in his mind was subjected to questioning; every feeling in his heart was put through fires of ridicule. He experienced it all agonizingly and wrote it all magnificently.

What happens when everything you believe in and live by is smashed to bits by circumstances? Sometimes the reversals of what we expect from God come to us as individuals, other times as entire communities. When it happens, does catastrophe work to re-form our lives to conform to who God actually is and not the way we imagined or wished him to be? Does it lead to an abandonment of God? Or, worse, does it trigger a stubborn grasping to the old collapsed system of belief, holding on for dear life to an illusion?

Anyone who lives in disruptive times looks for companions who have been through them earlier, wanting to know how they went through it, how they made it, what it was like. In looking for a companion who has lived through catastrophic disruption and survived with grace, biblical people more often than not come upon Jeremiah and receive him as a true, honest, and God-revealing companion for the worst of times.

JEREMIAH

1

DEMOLISH, AND THEN START OVER

The Message of Jeremiah son of Hilkiah of the family of priests who lived in Anathoth in the country of Benjamin. GOD's Message began to come to him during the thirteenth year that Josiah son of Amos reigned over Judah. It continued to come to him during the time Jehoiakim son of Josiah reigned over Judah. And it continued to come to him clear down to the fifth month of the eleventh year of the reign of Zedekiah son of Josiah over Judah, the year that Jerusalem was taken into exile. This is what GOD said:

"Before I shaped you in the womb,
    I knew all about you.
Before you saw the light of day,
    I had holy plans for you:
A prophet to the nations—
    that's what I had in mind for you."

But I said, "Hold it, Master GOD! Look at me.
    I don't know anything. I'm only a boy!"

GOD told me, "Don't say, 'I'm only a boy.'
    I'll tell you where to go and you'll go there.
I'll tell you what to say and you'll say it.
    Don't be afraid of a soul.
I'll be right there, looking after you."
    GOD's Decree.

GOD reached out, touched my mouth, and said,
    "Look! I've just put my words in your mouth—hand-delivered!
See what I've done? I've given you a job to do
    among nations and governments—a red-letter day!
Your job is to pull up and tear down,
    take apart and demolish,
And then start over,
    building and planting."

STAND UP AND SAY YOUR PIECE

GOD's Message came to me: "What do you see, Jeremiah?"
    I said, "A walking stick—that's all."
And GOD said, "Good eyes! I'm sticking with you.
    I'll make every word I give you come true."

GOD's Message came again: "So what do you see now?"
    I said, "I see a boiling pot, tipped down toward us."
Then GOD told me, "Disaster will pour out of the north
    on everyone living in this land.
Watch for this: I'm calling all the kings out of the north."
    GOD's Decree.

"They'll come and set up headquarters
    facing Jerusalem's gates,
Facing all the city walls,
    facing all the villages of Judah.
I'll pronounce my judgment on the people of Judah
    for walking out on me—what a terrible thing to do!—
And courting other gods with their offerings,
    worshiping as gods sticks they'd carved, stones they'd painted.

"But you—up on your feet and get dressed for work!
    Stand up and say your piece. Say exactly what I tell you to say.
Don't pull your punches
    or I'll pull you out of the lineup.

"Stand at attention while I prepare you for your work.
    I'm making you as impregnable as a castle,
Immovable as a steel post,
    solid as a concrete block wall.
You're a one-man defense system
    against this culture,
Against Judah's kings and princes,
    against the priests and local leaders.
They'll fight you, but they won't
    even scratch you.
I'll back you up every inch of the way."
    GOD's Decree.

2

ISRAEL WAS GOD'S HOLY CHOICE

GOD's Message came to me. It went like this:

"Get out in the streets and call to Jerusalem,
  'GOD's Message!
I remember your youthful loyalty,
  our love as newlyweds.
You stayed with me through the wilderness years,
  stuck with me through all the hard places.
Israel was GOD's holy choice,
  the pick of the crop.
Anyone who laid a hand on her
  would soon wish he hadn't!'"
      GOD's Decree.

✠

Hear GOD's Message, House of Jacob!
  Yes, you—House of Israel!
GOD's Message: "What did your ancestors find fault with in me
  that they drifted so far from me,
Took up with Sir Windbag
  and turned into windbags themselves?
It never occurred to them to say, 'Where's GOD,
  the God who got us out of Egypt,
Who took care of us through thick and thin, those rough-and-
      tumble
  wilderness years of parched deserts and death valleys,
A land that no one who enters comes out of,
  a cruel, inhospitable land?'

"I brought you to a garden land
  where you could eat lush fruit.
But you barged in and polluted my land,
  trashed and defiled my dear land.
The priests never thought to ask, 'Where's GOD?'
  The religion experts knew nothing of me.
The rulers defied me.

The prophets preached god Baal
And chased empty god-dreams and silly god-schemes.

"Because of all this, I'm bringing charges against you"
    —GOD's Decree—
    "charging you and your children and your grandchildren.
Look around. Have you ever seen anything quite like this?
    Sail to the western islands and look.
Travel to the Kedar wilderness and look.
    Look closely. Has this ever happened before,
That a nation has traded in its gods
    for gods that aren't even close to gods?
But my people have traded my Glory
    for empty god-dreams and silly god-schemes.

"Stand in shock, heavens, at what you see!
    Throw up your hands in disbelief—this can't be!"
        GOD's Decree.
"My people have committed a compound sin:
    they've walked out on me, the fountain
Of fresh flowing waters, and then dug cisterns—
    cisterns that leak, cisterns that are no better than sieves.

"Isn't Israel a valued servant,
    born into a family with place and position?
So how did she end up a piece of meat
    fought over by snarling and roaring lions?
There's nothing left of her but a few old bones,
    her towns trashed and deserted.
Egyptians from the cities of Memphis and Tahpanhes
    have broken your skulls.
And why do you think all this has happened?
    Isn't it because you walked out on your God
    just as he was beginning to lead you in the right way?

"And now, what do you think you'll get by going off to Egypt?
    Maybe a cool drink of Nile River water?
Or what do you think you'll get by going off to Assyria?
    Maybe a long drink of Euphrates River water?
Your evil ways will get you a sound thrashing, that's what you'll get.

You'll pay dearly for your disloyal ways.
Take a long, hard look at what you've done and its bitter results.
    Was it worth it to have walked out on your God?"
        GOD's Decree, Master GOD-of-the-Angel-Armies.

ADDICTED TO ALIEN GODS

"A long time ago you broke out of the harness.
    You shook off all restraints.
You said, 'I will not serve!'
    and off you went,
Visiting every sex-and-religion shrine on the way,
    like a common whore.
You were a select vine when I planted you
    from completely reliable stock.
And look how you've turned out—
    a tangle of rancid growth, a poor excuse for a vine.
Scrub, using the strongest soaps.
    Scour your skin raw.
The sin-grease won't come out. I can't stand to even look at you!"
        GOD's Decree, the Master's Decree.

"How dare you tell me, 'I'm not stained by sin.
    I've never chased after the Baal sex gods'!
Well, look at the tracks you've left behind in the valley.
    How do you account for what is written in the desert dust—
Tracks of a camel in heat, running this way and that,
    tracks of a wild donkey in rut,
Sniffing the wind for the slightest scent of sex.
    Who could possibly corral her!
On the hunt for sex, sex, and more sex—
    insatiable, indiscriminate, promiscuous.

"Slow down. Take a deep breath. What's the hurry?
    Why wear yourself out? Just what are you after anyway?
But you say, 'I can't help it.
    I'm addicted to alien gods. I can't quit.'

✠

"Just as a thief is chagrined, but only when caught,
    so the people of Israel are chagrined,
Caught along with their kings and princes,
    their priests and prophets.
They walk up to a tree and say, 'My father!'
    They pick up a stone and say, 'My mother! You bore me!'
All I ever see of them is their backsides.
    They never look me in the face.
But when things go badly, they don't hesitate to come running,
    calling out, 'Get a move on! Save us!'
Why not go to your handcrafted gods you're so fond of?
    Rouse them. Let them save you from your bad times.
You've got more gods, Judah,
    than you know what to do with.

TRYING OUT ANOTHER SIN-PROJECT

"What do you have against me,
    running off to assert your 'independence'?"
        GOD's Decree.
"I've wasted my time trying to train your children.
    They've paid no attention to me, ignored my discipline.
And you've gotten rid of your God-messengers,
    treating them like dirt and sweeping them away.

"What a generation you turned out to be!
    Didn't I tell you? Didn't I warn you?
Have I let you down, Israel?
    Am I nothing but a dead-end street?
Why do my people say, 'Good riddance!
    From now on we're on our own'?
Young women don't forget their jewelry, do they?
    Brides don't show up without their veils, do they?
But my people forget me.
    Day after day after day they never give me a thought.

⁜

"What an impressive start you made
    to get the most out of life.

You founded schools of sin,
    taught graduate courses in evil!
And now you're sending out graduates, resplendent in cap and
        gown—
    except the gowns are stained with the blood of your victims!
All that blood convicts you.
    You cut and hurt a lot of people to get where you are.
And yet you have the gall to say, 'I've done nothing wrong.
    God doesn't mind. He hasn't punished me, has he?'
Don't look now, but judgment's on the way,
    aimed at you who say, 'I've done nothing wrong.'

"You think it's just a small thing, don't you,
    to try out another sin-project when the first one fails?
But Egypt will leave you in the lurch
    the same way that Assyria did.
You're going to walk away from there
    wringing your hands.
I, GOD, have blacklisted those you trusted.
    You'll get not a lick of help from them."

3

YOUR SEX-AND-RELIGION OBSESSIONS

GOD's Message came to me as follows:

"If a man's wife
    walks out on him
And marries another man,
    can he take her back as if nothing had happened?
Wouldn't that raise a huge stink
    in the land?
And isn't that what you've done—
    'whored' your way with god after god?
And now you want to come back as if nothing had happened."
    GOD's Decree.

"Look around at the hills.
    Where have you *not* had sex?

You've camped out like hunters stalking deer.
    You've solicited many lover-gods,
Like a streetwalking whore
    chasing after other gods.
And so the rain has stopped.
    No more rain from the skies!
But it doesn't even faze you. Brazen as whores,
    you carry on as if you've done nothing wrong.
Then you have the nerve to call out, 'My father!
    You took care of me when I was a child. Why not now?
Are you going to keep up your anger non-stop?'
    That's your line. Meanwhile you keep sinning nonstop."

Admit Your God-Defiance

God spoke to me during the reign of King Josiah: "You have noticed, haven't you, how fickle Israel has visited every hill and grove of trees as a whore at large? I assumed that after she had gotten it out of her system, she'd come back, but she didn't. Her flighty sister, Judah, saw what she did. She also saw that because of fickle Israel's loose morals I threw her out, gave her her walking papers. But that didn't faze flighty sister Israel. She went out, big as you please, and took up a whore's life also. She took up cheap sex-and-religion as a sideline diversion, an indulgent recreation, and used anything and anyone, flaunting sanity and sanctity alike, stinking up the country. And not once in all this did fickle sister Judah even give me a nod, although she made a show of it from time to time." God's Decree.

Then God told me, "Fickle Israel was a good sight better than flighty Judah. Go and preach this message. Face north toward Israel and say:

"'Turn back, fickle Israel.
    I'm not just hanging back to punish you.
I'm committed in love to you.
    My anger doesn't seethe nonstop.
Just admit your guilt.
    Admit your God-defiance.
Admit to your promiscuous life with casual partners,
    pulling strangers into the sex-and-religion groves
While turning a deaf ear to me.'"
    God's Decree.

"Come back, wandering children!"
　　GOD's Decree.
"I, yes I, am your true husband.
　　I'll pick you out one by one—
This one from the city, these two from the country—
　　and bring you to Zion.
I'll give you good shepherd-rulers who rule my way,
　　who rule you with intelligence and wisdom.

"And this is what will happen: You will increase and prosper in the land. The time will come"—GOD's Decree!—"when no one will say any longer, 'Oh, for the good old days! Remember the Ark of the Covenant?' It won't even occur to anyone to say it—'the good old days.' The so-called good old days of the Ark are gone for good.

"Jerusalem will be the new Ark—'GOD's Throne.' All the godless nations, no longer stuck in the ruts of their evil ways, will gather there to honor GOD.

"At that time, the House of Judah will join up with the House of Israel. Holding hands, they'll leave the north country and come to the land I willed to your ancestors.

✝

"I planned what I'd say if you returned to me:
　　'Good! I'll bring you back into the family.
I'll give you choice land,
　　land that the godless nations would die for.'
And I imagined that you would say, 'Dear father!'
　　and would never again go off and leave me.
But no luck. Like a false-hearted woman walking out
　　　　on her husband,
　　you, the whole family of Israel, have proven false to me."
　　　　GOD's Decree.

The sound of voices comes drifting out of the hills,
　　the unhappy sound of Israel's crying,
Israel lamenting the wasted years,
　　never once giving her God a thought.
"Come back, wandering children!
　　I can heal your wanderlust!"

166

✠

"We're here! We've come back to you.
      You're our own true GOD!
All that popular religion was a cheap lie,
      duped crowds buying up the latest in gods.
We're back! Back to our true GOD,
      the salvation of Israel.
The Fraud picked us clean, swindled us
      of what our ancestors bequeathed us,
Gypped us out of our inheritance—
      God-blessed flocks and God-given children.
We made our bed and now lie in it,
      all tangled up in the dirty sheets of dishonor.
All because we sinned against our GOD,
      we and our fathers and mothers.
From the time we took our first steps, said our first words,
      we've been rebels, disobeying the voice of our GOD."

✠

4

"If you want to come back, oh Israel,
      you must really come back to me.
You must get rid of your stinking sin paraphernalia
      and not wander away from me anymore.
Then you can say words like, 'As GOD lives . . .'
      and have them mean something true and just and right.
And the godless nations will get caught up in the blessing
      and find something in Israel to write home about."

✠

Here's another Message from GOD
      to the people of Judah and Jerusalem:
"Plow your unplowed fields,
      but then don't plant weeds in the soil!
Yes, circumcise your *lives* for God's sake.

Plow your unplowed hearts,
    all you people of Judah and Jerusalem.
Prevent fire—the fire of my anger—
    for once it starts it can't be put out.
Your wicked ways
    are fuel for the fire.

GOD'S SLEDGEHAMMER ANGER

"Sound the alarm in Judah,
    broadcast the news in Jerusalem.
Say, 'Blow the ram's-horn trumpet through the land!'
    Shout out—a bullhorn bellow!—
'Close ranks!
    Run for your lives to the shelters!'
Send up a flare warning Zion:
    'Not a minute to lose! Don't sit on your hands!'
Disaster's descending from the north. I set it off!
    When it lands, it will shake the foundations.
Invaders have pounced like a lion from its cover,
    ready to rip nations to shreds,
Leaving your land in wrack and ruin,
    your cities in rubble, abandoned.
Dress in funereal black.
    Weep and wail,
For GOD's sledgehammer anger
    has slammed into us head-on.

"When this happens"
    —GOD's Decree—
"King and princes will lose heart;
    priests will be baffled and prophets stand dumbfounded."

Then I said, "Alas, Master GOD!
    You've fed lies to this people, this Jerusalem.
You assured them, 'All is well, don't worry,'
    at the very moment when the sword was at their throats."

✢

At that time, this people, yes, this very Jerusalem,
    will be told in plain words:
"The northern hordes are sweeping in
    from the desert steppes—
A wind that's up to no good, a gale-force wind.
    I ordered this wind.
I'm pronouncing
    my hurricane judgment on my people."

YOUR EVIL LIFE IS PIERCING YOUR HEART

Look at them! Like banks of storm clouds,
    racing, tumbling, their chariots a tornado,
Their horses faster than eagles!
    Woe to us! We're done for!
Jerusalem! Scrub the evil from your lives
    so you'll be fit for salvation.
How much longer will you harbor
    devious and malignant designs within you?

What's this? A messenger from Dan?
    Bad news from Ephraim's hills!
Make the report public.
    Broadcast the news to Jerusalem:
"Invaders from far off are
    raising war cries against Judah's towns.
They're all over her, like a dog on a bone.
    And why? Because she rebelled against me."
        GOD's Decree.

"It's the way you've lived
    that's brought all this on you.
The bitter taste is from your evil life.
    That's what's piercing your heart."

✠

I'm doubled up with cramps in my belly—
    a poker burns in my gut.
My insides are tearing me up,
    never a moment's peace.

169

The ram's-horn trumpet blast rings in my ears,
    the signal for all-out war.
Disaster hard on the heels of disaster,
    the whole country in ruins!
In one stroke my home is destroyed,
    the walls flattened in the blink of an eye.
How long do I have to look at the warning flares,
    listen to the siren of danger?

EXPERTS AT EVIL

"What fools my people are!
    They have no idea who I am.
A company of half-wits,
    dopes and donkeys all!
Experts at evil
    but klutzes at good."

I looked at the earth—
    it was back to pre-Genesis chaos and emptiness.
I looked at the skies,
    and not a star to be seen.
I looked at the mountains—
    they were trembling like aspen leaves,
And all the hills
    rocking back and forth in the wind.
I looked—what's this! Not a man or woman in sight,
    and not a bird to be seen in the skies.
I looked—this can't be! Every garden and orchard shriveled up.
    All the towns were ghost towns.
And all this because of GOD,
    because of the blazing anger of GOD.

Yes, this is GOD's Word on the matter:

"The whole country will be laid waste—
    still it won't be the end of the world.
The earth will mourn
    and the skies lament
Because I've given my word and won't take it back.
    I've decided and won't change my mind."

You're Not Going to Seduce Anyone

Someone shouts, "Horsemen and archers!"
    and everybody runs for cover.
They hide in ditches,
    they climb into caves.
The cities are emptied,
    not a person left anywhere.

And you, what do you think you're up to?
    Dressing up in party clothes,
Decking yourselves out in jewelry,
    putting on lipstick and rouge and mascara!
Your primping goes for nothing.
    You're not going to seduce anyone. They're out to *kill* you!
And what's that I hear? The cry of a woman in labor,
    the screams of a mother giving birth to her firstborn.
It's the cry of Daughter Zion, gasping for breath,
    reaching out for help:
"Help, oh help me! I'm dying!
    The killers are on me!"

5

Sins Are Piled Sky-High

"Patrol Jerusalem's streets.
    Look around. Take note.
Search the market squares.
    See if you can find one man, one woman,
A single soul who does what is right
    and tries to live a true life.
    I want to forgive that person."
        God's Decree.
"But if all they do is say, 'As sure as God lives . . .'
    they're nothing but a bunch of liars."

But you, God,
    you have an eye for truth, don't you?
You hit them hard, but it didn't faze them.
    You disciplined them, but they refused correction.

Hardheaded, harder than rock,
    they wouldn't change.
Then I said to myself, "Well, these are just poor people.
    They don't know any better.
They were never taught anything about GOD.
    They never went to prayer meetings.
I'll find some people from the best families.
    I'll talk to them.
They'll know what's going on, the way GOD works.
    They'll know the score."
But they were no better! Rebels all!
    Off doing their own thing.
The invaders are ready to pounce and kill,
    like a mountain lion, a wilderness wolf,
Panthers on the prowl.
    The streets aren't safe anymore.
And why? Because the people's sins are piled sky-high;
    their betrayals are past counting.

"Why should I even bother with you any longer?
    Your children wander off, leaving me,
Taking up with gods
    that aren't even gods.
I satisfied their deepest needs, and then they went off with the
        'sacred' whores,
    left me for orgies in sex shrines!
A bunch of well-groomed, lusty stallions,
    each one pawing and snorting for his neighbor's wife.
Do you think I'm going to stand around and do nothing!"
    GOD's Decree.
"Don't you think I'll take serious measures
    against a people like this?

EYES THAT DON'T REALLY LOOK, EARS THAT DON'T REALLY LISTEN

"Go down the rows of vineyards and rip out the vines,
    but not all of them. Leave a few.
Prune back those vines!
    That growth didn't come from GOD!
They've betrayed me over and over again,

Judah and Israel both."
    GOD's Decree.

"They've spread lies about GOD.
    They've said, 'There's nothing to him.
Nothing bad will happen to us,
    neither famine nor war will come our way.
The prophets are all windbags.
    They speak nothing but nonsense.'"

Therefore, this is what GOD said to me, God-of-the-Angel-Armies:

"Because they have talked this way,
    they are going to eat those words.
Watch now! I'm putting my words
    as fire in your mouth.
And the people are a pile of kindling
    ready to go up in flames.

"Attention! I'm bringing a faroff nation
    against you, oh house of Israel."
    GOD's Decree.
"A solid nation,
    an ancient nation,
A nation that speaks another language.
    You won't understand a word they say.
When they aim their arrows, you're as good as dead.
    They're a nation of real fighters!
They'll clean you out of house and home,
    rob you of crops and children alike.
They'll feast on your sheep and cattle,
    strip your vines and fig trees.
And the fortresses that made you feel so safe—
    leveled with a stroke of the sword!

"Even then, as bad as it will be"—GOD's Decree!—"it will not be the end of the world for you. And when people ask, 'Why did our GOD do all this to us?' you must say to them, 'It's tit for tat. Just as you left me and served foreign gods in your own country, so now you must serve foreigners in their own country.'

"Tell the house of Jacob this,
    put out this bulletin in Judah:
Listen to this,
    you scatterbrains, airheads,
With eyes that see but don't really look,
    and ears that hear but don't really listen.
Why don't you honor me?
    Why aren't you in awe before me?
Yes, *me*, who made the shorelines
    to contain the ocean waters.
I drew a line in the sand
    that cannot be crossed.
Waves roll in but cannot get through;
    breakers crash but that's the end of them.
But this people—what a people!
    Uncontrollable, untameable runaways.
It never occurs to them to say,
    'How can we honor our GOD with our lives,
The God who gives rain in both spring and autumn
    and maintains the rhythm of the seasons,
Who sets aside time each year for harvest
    and keeps everything running smoothly for us?'
Of course you don't! Your bad behavior blinds you to all this.
    Your sins keep my blessings at a distance.

TO STAND FOR NOTHING AND STAND UP FOR NO ONE

"My people are infiltrated by wicked men,
    unscrupulous men on the hunt.
They set traps for the unsuspecting.
    Their victims are innocent men and women.
Their houses are stuffed with ill-gotten gain,
    like a hunter's bag full of birds.
Pretentious and powerful and rich,
    hugely obese, oily with rolls of fat.
Worse, they have no conscience.
    Right and wrong mean nothing to them.
They stand for nothing, stand up for no one,
    throw orphans to the wolves, exploit the poor.
Do you think I'll stand by and do nothing about this?"
    GOD's Decree.

"Don't you think I'll take serious measures
    against a people like this?

✝

"Unspeakable! Sickening!
    What's happened in this country?
Prophets preach lies
    and priests hire on as their assistants.
And my people love it. They eat it up!
    But what will you do when it's time to pick up the pieces?

6

A CITY FULL OF LIES

"Run for your lives, children of Benjamin!
    Get out of Jerusalem, and now!
Give a blast on the ram's horn in Blastville.
    Send up smoke signals from Smoketown.
Doom pours out of the north—
    massive terror!
I have likened my dear daughter Zion
    to a lovely meadow.
Well, now 'shepherds' from the north have discovered her
    and brought in their flocks of soldiers.
They've pitched camp all around her,
    and plan where they'll 'graze.'
And then, 'Prepare to attack! The fight is on!
    To arms! We'll strike at noon!
Oh, it's too late? Day is dying?
    Evening shadows are upon us?
Well, up anyway! We'll attack by night
    and tear apart her defenses stone by stone.'"

GOD-of-the-Angel-Armies gave the orders:

"Chop down her trees.
    Build a siege ramp against Jerusalem,
A city full of brutality,
    bursting with violence.

Just as a well holds a good supply of water,
    she supplies wickedness nonstop.
The streets echo the cries: 'Violence! Rape!'
    Victims, bleeding and moaning, lie all over the place.
You're in deep trouble, Jerusalem.
    You've pushed me to the limit.
You're on the brink of being wiped out,
    being turned into a ghost town."

More orders from GOD-of-the-Angel-Armies:

"Time's up! Harvest the grapes for judgment.
    Salvage what's left of Israel.
Go back over the vines.
    Pick them clean, every last grape.

IS ANYBODY LISTENING?

"I've got something to say. Is anybody listening?
    I've a warning to post. Will anyone notice?
It's hopeless! Their ears are stuffed with wax—
    deaf as a post, blind as a bat.
It's hopeless! They've tuned out GOD.
    They don't want to hear from me.
But I'm bursting with the wrath of GOD.
    I can't hold it in much longer.

"So dump it on the children in the streets.
    Let it loose on the gangs of youth.
For no one's exempt: Husbands and wives will be taken,
    the old and those ready to die;
Their homes will be given away—
    all they own, even their loved ones—
When I give the signal
    against all who live in this country."
        GOD's Decree.

"Everyone's after the dishonest dollar,
    little people and big people alike.
Prophets and priests and everyone in between
    twist words and doctor truth.

My people are broken—shattered!—
    and they put on band-aids,
Saying, 'It's not so bad. You'll be just fine.'
    But things are not 'just fine'!
Do you suppose they are embarrassed
    over this outrage?
No, they have no shame.
    They don't even know how to blush.
There's no hope for them. They've hit bottom
    and there's no getting up.
As far as I'm concerned,
    they're finished."
        GOD has spoken.

DEATH IS ON THE PROWL

GOD's Message yet again:

"Go stand at the crossroads and look around.
    Ask for directions to the old road,
The tried and true road. Then take it.
    Discover the right route for your souls.
But they said, 'Nothing doing.
    We aren't going that way.'
I even provided watchmen for them
    to warn them, to set off the alarm.
But the people said, 'It's a false alarm.
    It doesn't concern us.'
And so I'm calling in the nations as witnesses:
    'Watch, witnesses, what happens to them!'
And, 'Pay attention, earth!
    Don't miss these bulletins.'
I'm visiting catastrophe on this people, the end result
    of the games they've been playing with me.
They've ignored everything I've said,
    had nothing but contempt for my teaching.
What would I want with incense brought in from Sheba,
    rare spices from exotic places?
Your burnt sacrifices in worship give me no pleasure.
    Your religious rituals mean nothing to me."

177

So listen to this. Here's GOD's verdict on your way of life:

"Watch out! I'm putting roadblocks and barriers
    on the road you're taking.
They'll send you sprawling,
    parents and children, neighbors and friends—
    and that will be the end of the lot of you."

And listen to this verdict from GOD:

"Look out! An invasion from the north,
    a mighty power on the move from a faraway place:
Armed to the teeth,
    vicious and pitiless,
Booming like sea storm and thunder—tramp, tramp, tramp—
    riding hard on war horses,
In battle formation
    against you, dear Daughter Zion!"

We've heard the news,
    and we're as limp as wet dishrags.
We're paralyzed with fear.
    Terror has a death grip on our throats.
Don't dare go outdoors!
    Don't leave the house!
Death is on the prowl.
    Danger everywhere!

"Dear Daughter Zion: Dress in black.
    Blacken your face with ashes.
Weep most bitterly,
    as for an only child.
The countdown has begun . . .
    six, five, four, three . . .
    The Terror is on us!"

✢

GOD gave me this task:

"I have made you the examiner of my people,
    to examine and weigh their lives.

They're a thickheaded, hard-nosed bunch,
    rotten to the core, the lot of them.
Refining fires are cranked up to white heat,
    but the ore stays a lump, unchanged.
It's useless to keep trying any longer.
    Nothing can refine evil out of them.
Men will give up and call them 'slag,'
    thrown on the slag heap by me, their GOD."

7

THE NATION THAT WOULDN'T OBEY GOD

The Message from GOD to Jeremiah: "Stand in the gate of GOD's Temple and preach this Message.

"Say, 'Listen, all you people of Judah who come through these gates to worship GOD. GOD-of-the-Angel-Armies, Israel's God, has this to say to you:

"'Clean up your act—the way you live, the things you do—so I can make my home with you in this place. Don't for a minute believe the lies being spoken here—"This is GOD's Temple, GOD's Temple, GOD's Temple!" Total nonsense! Only if you clean up your act (the way you live, the things you do), only if you do a total spring cleaning on the way you live and treat your neighbors, only if you quit exploiting the street people and orphans and widows, no longer taking advantage of innocent people on this very site and no longer destroying your souls by using this Temple as a front for other gods—only *then* will I move into your neighborhood. Only then will this country I gave your ancestors be my permanent home, my Temple.

"'Get smart! Your leaders are handing you a pack of lies, and you're swallowing them! Use your heads! Do you think you can rob and murder, have sex with the neighborhood wives, tell lies nonstop, worship the local gods, and buy every novel religious commodity on the market—and then march into this Temple, set apart for my worship, and say, "We're safe!" thinking that the place itself gives you a license to go on with all this outrageous sacrilege? A cave full of criminals! Do you think you can turn this Temple, set apart for my worship, into something like that? Well, think again. I've got eyes in my head. I can see what's going on.'" GOD's Decree!

"'Take a trip down to the place that was once in Shiloh, where I met

179

my people in the early days. Take a look at those ruins, what I did to it because of the evil ways of my people Israel.

"'So now, because of the way you have lived and failed to listen, even though time and again I took you aside and talked seriously with you, and because you refused to change when I called you to repent, I'm going to do to this Temple, set aside for my worship, this place you think is going to keep you safe no matter what, this place I gave as a gift to your ancestors and you, the same as I did to Shiloh. And as for you, I'm going to get rid of you, the same as I got rid of those old relatives of yours around Shiloh, your fellow Israelites in that former kingdom to the north.'

"And you, Jeremiah, don't waste your time praying for this people. Don't offer to make petitions or intercessions. Don't bother me with them. I'm not listening. Can't you see what they're doing in all the villages of Judah and in the Jerusalem streets? Why, they've got the children gathering wood while the fathers build fires and the mothers make bread to be offered to 'the Queen of Heaven'! And as if that weren't bad enough, they go around pouring out libations to any other gods they come across, just to hurt me.

"But is it me they're hurting?" GOD's Decree! "Aren't they just hurting themselves? Exposing themselves shamefully? Making themselves ridiculous?

"Here's what the Master GOD has to say: 'My white-hot anger is about to descend on this country and everything in it—people and animals, trees in the field and vegetables in the garden—a raging wildfire that no one can put out.'

"The Message from GOD-of-the-Angel-Armies, Israel's God: 'Go ahead! Put your burnt offerings with all your other sacrificial offerings and make a good meal for yourselves. *I* sure don't want them! When I delivered your ancestors out of Egypt, I never said anything to them about wanting burnt offerings and sacrifices as such. But I did say this, *commanded* this: "Obey me. Do what I say and I will be your God and you will be my people. Live the way I tell you. Do what I command so that your lives will go well."

"'But do you think they listened? Not a word of it. They did just what they wanted to do, indulged any and every evil whim and got worse day by day. From the time your ancestors left the land of Egypt until now, I've supplied a steady stream of my servants the prophets, but do you think the people listened? Not once. Stubborn as mules and worse than their ancestors!'

"Tell them all this, but don't expect them to listen. Call out to them, but don't expect an answer. Tell them, 'You are the nation that wouldn't obey GOD, that refused all discipline. Truth has disappeared. There's not a trace of it left in your mouths.

"'So shave your heads.
  Go bald to the hills and lament,
For GOD has rejected and left
  this generation that has made him so angry.'

"The people of Judah have lived evil lives while I've stood by and watched." GOD's Decree. "In deliberate insult to me, they've set up their obscene god-images in the very Temple that was built to honor me. They've constructed Topheth altars for burning babies in prominent places all through the valley of Ben-hinnom, altars for burning their sons and daughters alive in the fire—a shocking perversion of all that I am and all I command.

"But soon, very soon"—GOD's Decree!—"the names Topheth and Ben-hinnom will no longer be used. They'll call the place what it is: Murder Meadow. Corpses will be stacked up in Topheth because there's no room left to bury them! Corpses abandoned in the open air, fed on by crows and coyotes, who have the run of the place. And I'll empty both smiles and laughter from the villages of Judah and the streets of Jerusalem. No wedding songs, no holiday sounds. *Dead* silence.

✠

8

"And when the time comes"—GOD's Decree!—"I'll see to it that they dig up the bones of the kings of Judah, the bones of the princes and priests and prophets, and yes, even the bones of the common people. They'll dig them up and spread them out like a congregation at worship before sun, moon, and stars, all those sky gods they've been so infatuated with all these years, following their 'lucky stars' in doglike devotion. The bones will be left scattered and exposed, to reenter the soil as fertilizer, like manure.

"Everyone left—all from this evil generation unlucky enough to still be alive in whatever godforsaken place I will have driven them to—will wish they were dead." Decree of GOD-of-the-Angel-Armies.

To Know Everything But God's Word

"Tell them this, GOD's Message:

"'Do people fall down and not get up?
  Or take the wrong road and then just keep going?
So why does this people go backwards,
  and just keep on going—*backwards*!
They stubbornly hold on to their illusions,
  refuse to change direction.
I listened carefully
  but heard not so much as a whisper.
No one expressed one word of regret.
  Not a single "I'm sorry" did I hear.
They just kept at it, blindly and stupidly
  banging their heads against a brick wall.
Cranes know when it's time
  to move south for winter.
And robins, warblers, and bluebirds
  know when it's time to come back again.
But my people? My people know nothing,
  not the first thing of GOD and his rule.

"'How can you say, "We know the score.
  We're the proud owners of GOD's revelation"?
Look where it's gotten you—stuck in illusion.
  Your religion experts have taken you for a ride!
Your know-it-alls will be unmasked,
  caught and shown up for what they are.
Look at them! They know everything but GOD's Word.
  Do you call that "knowing"?

"'So here's what will happen to the know-it-alls:
  I'll make them wifeless and homeless.
Everyone's after the dishonest dollar,
  little people and big people alike.
Prophets and priests and everyone in-between
  twist words and doctor truth.
My dear Daughter—my people—broken, shattered,
  and yet they put on band-aids,

182

Saying, "It's not so bad. You'll be just fine."
    But things are not "just fine"!
Do you suppose they are embarrassed
    over this outrage?
Not really. They have no shame.
    They don't even know how to blush.
There's no hope for them. They've hit bottom
    and there's no getting up.
As far as I'm concerned,
    they're finished.'" GOD has spoken.

✠

"'I went out to see if I could salvage anything'"
    —GOD's Decree—
    "'but found nothing:
Not a grape, not a fig,
    just a few withered leaves.
I'm taking back
    everything I gave them.'"

So why are we sitting here, doing nothing?
    Let's get organized.
Let's go to the big city
    and at least die fighting.
We've gotten GOD's ultimatum:
    We're damned if we do and damned if we don't—
    damned because of our sin against him.
We hoped things would turn out for the best,
    but it didn't happen that way.
We were waiting around for healing—
    and terror showed up!
From Dan at the northern borders
    we hear the hooves of horses,
Horses galloping, horses neighing.
    The ground shudders and quakes.
They're going to swallow up the whole country.
    Towns and people alike—fodder for war.

"'What's more, I'm dispatching
    poisonous snakes among you,

183

Snakes that can't be charmed,
   snakes that will bite you and kill you.'"
     GOD's Decree!

ADVANCING FROM ONE EVIL TO THE NEXT

I drown in grief.
   I'm heartsick.
Oh, listen! Please listen! It's the cry of my dear people
   reverberating through the country.
Is GOD no longer in Zion?
   Has the King gone away?
Can you tell me why they flaunt their plaything-gods,
   their silly, imported no-gods before me?
The crops are in, the summer is over,
   but for us nothing's changed.
   We're still waiting to be rescued.
For my dear broken people, I'm heartbroken.
   I weep, seized by grief.
Are there no healing ointments in Gilead?
   Isn't there a doctor in the house?
So why can't something be done
   to heal and save my dear, dear people?

✝

9

I wish my head were a well of water
   and my eyes fountains of tears
So I could weep day and night
   for casualties among my dear, dear people.
At times I wish I had a wilderness hut,
   a backwoods cabin,
Where I could get away from my people
   and never see them again.
They're a faithless, feckless bunch,
   a congregation of degenerates.

✝

"Their tongues shoot out lies
    like a bow shoots arrows—
A mighty army of liars,
    the sworn enemies of truth.
They advance from one evil to the next,
    ignorant of me."
        GOD's Decree.
"Be wary of even longtime neighbors.
    Don't even trust your grandmother!
Brother schemes against brother,
    like old cheating Jacob.
Friend against friend
    spreads malicious gossip.
Neighbors gyp neighbors,
    never telling the truth.
They've trained their tongues to tell lies,
    and now they can't tell the truth.
They pile wrong upon wrong, stack lie upon lie,
    and refuse to know me."
        GOD's Decree.

Therefore, GOD-of-the-Angel-Armies says:

"Watch this! I'll melt them down
    and see what they're made of.
What else can I do
    with a people this wicked?
Their tongues are poison arrows!
    Deadly lies stream from their mouths.
Neighbor greets neighbor with a smile,
    'Good morning! How're things?'
    while scheming to do away with him.
Do you think I'm going to stand around and do nothing!"
        GOD's Decree.
"Don't you think I'll take serious measures
    against a people like this?

"I'm lamenting the loss of the mountain pastures.
    I'm chanting dirges for the old grazing grounds.
They've become deserted wastelands too dangerous for travelers.

185

No sounds of sheep bleating or cattle mooing.
Birds and wild animals, all gone.
  Nothing stirring, no sounds of life.
I'm going to make Jerusalem a pile of rubble,
  fit for nothing but stray cats and dogs.
I'm going to reduce Judah's towns to piles of ruins
  where no one lives!"

✠

I asked, "Is there anyone around bright enough to tell us what's going on here? Anyone who has the inside story from GOD and can let us in on it?
  "Why is the country wasted?
  "Why no travelers in this desert?"
  GOD's answer: "Because they abandoned my plain teaching. They wouldn't listen to anything I said, refused to live the way I told them to. Instead they lived any way they wanted and took up with the Baal gods, who they thought would give them what they wanted—following the example of their parents." And this is the consequence. GOD-of-the-Angel-Armies says so:

  "I'll feed them with pig slop.
  "I'll give them poison to drink.
  "Then I'll scatter them far and wide among godless peoples that neither they nor their parents have ever heard of, and I'll send Death in pursuit until there's nothing left of them."

A LIFE THAT IS ALL OUTSIDE BUT NO INSIDE

A Message from GOD-of-the-Angel-Armies:

"Look over the trouble we're in and call for help.
  Send for some singers who can help us mourn our loss.
Tell them to hurry—
  to help us express our loss and lament,
Help us get our tears flowing,
  make tearful music of our crying.
Listen to it!
  Listen to that torrent of tears out of Zion:
'We're a ruined people,
  we're a shamed people!

We've been driven from our homes
    and must leave our land!'"

⟊

Mourning women! Oh, listen to GOD's Message!
    Open your ears. Take in what he says.
Teach your daughters songs for the dead
    and your friends the songs of heartbreak.
Death has climbed in through the window,
    broken into our bedrooms.
Children on the playgrounds drop dead,
    and young men and women collapse at their games.

    Speak up! "GOD's Message:

"'Dead bodies everywhere, scattered at random
    like sheep and goat dung in the fields,
Like wheat cut down by reapers
    and left to rot where it falls.'"

    GOD's Message:

"Don't let the wise brag of their wisdom.
    Don't let heroes brag of their exploits.
Don't let the rich brag of their riches.
    If you brag, brag of this and this only:
That you understand and know me.
    I'm GOD, and I act in loyal love.
I do what's right and set things right and fair,
    and delight in those who do the same things.
These are my trademarks."
    GOD's Decree.

⟊

"Stay alert! It won't be long now"—GOD's Decree!—"when I will personally deal with everyone whose life is all outside but no inside: Egypt, Judah, Edom, Ammon, Moab. All these nations are big on performance religion—including Israel, who is no better."

10

THE STICK GODS

Listen to the Message that GOD is sending your way, House of Israel. Listen most carefully:

"Don't take the godless nations as your models.
    Don't be impressed by their glamour and glitz,
        no matter how much they're impressed.
The religion of these peoples
    is nothing but smoke.
An idol is nothing but a tree chopped down,
    then shaped by a woodsman's ax.
They trim it with tinsel and balls,
    use hammer and nails to keep it upright.
It's like a scarecrow in a cabbage patch—can't talk!
    Dead wood that has to be carried—can't walk!
Don't be impressed by such stuff.
    It's useless for either good or evil."

All this is nothing compared to you, oh GOD.
    You're wondrously great, famously great.
Who can fail to be impressed by you, King of the nations?
    It's your very nature to be worshiped!
Look far and wide among the elite of the nations.
    The best they can come up with is nothing compared to you.
Stupidly, they line them up—a lineup of sticks,
    good for nothing but making smoke.
Gilded with silver foil from Tarshish,
    covered with gold from Uphaz,
Hung with violet and purple fabrics—
    no matter how fancy the sticks, they're still sticks.

But GOD is the real thing—
    the living God, the eternal King.
When he's angry, Earth shakes.
    Yes, and the godless nations quake.

"Tell them this: 'The stick gods
    who made nothing, neither sky nor earth,

Will come to nothing
    on the earth and under the sky.'"
But it is God whose power made the earth,
    whose wisdom gave shape to the world,
    who crafted the cosmos.
He thunders, and rain pours down.
    He sends the clouds soaring.
He embellishes the storm with lightnings,
    launches wind from his warehouse.
Stick-god worshipers looking mighty foolish,
    god-makers embarrassed by their handmade gods!
Their gods are frauds—dead sticks,
    deadwood gods, tasteless jokes.
    When the fires of judgment come, they'll be ashes.

But the Portion-of-Jacob is the real thing.
    He put the whole universe together
And pays special attention to Israel.
    His name? GOD-of-the-Angel-Armies!

✠

Grab your bags,
    all you who are under attack.
GOD has given notice:
    "Attention! I'm evicting
Everyone who lives here,
    And right now—yes, right now!
I'm going to press them to the limit,
    squeeze the life right out of them."

✠

But it's a black day for me!
    Hopelessly wounded,
I said, "Why, oh why
    did I think I could bear it?"
My house is ruined—
    the roof caved in.

Our children are gone—
    we'll never see them again.
No one left to help in rebuilding,
    no one to make a new start!

It's because our leaders are stupid.
    They never asked GOD for counsel,
And so nothing worked right.
    The people are scattered all over.

But listen! Something's coming!
    A big commotion from the northern borders!
Judah's towns about to be smashed,
    left to all the stray dogs and cats!

I know, GOD, that mere mortals
    can't run their own lives,
That men and women
    don't have what it takes to take charge of life.
So correct us, GOD, as you see best.
    Don't lose your temper. That would be the end of us.
Vent your anger on the godless nations,
    who refuse to acknowledge you,
And on the people
    who won't pray to you—
The very ones who've made hash out of Jacob,
    yes, made hash
And devoured him whole,
    people and pastures alike.

·

11

THE TERMS OF THIS COVENANT

The Message that came to Jeremiah from GOD:

"Preach to the people of Judah and citizens of Jerusalem. Tell them this: 'This is GOD's Message, the Message of Israel's God to you. Anyone who does not keep the terms of this covenant is cursed. The terms are clear. I made them plain to your ancestors when I delivered them from Egypt, out of the iron furnace of suffering.

"'Obey what I tell you. Do exactly what I command you. Your obedience will close the deal. You'll be mine and I'll be yours. This will provide the conditions in which I will be able to do what I promised your ancestors: to give them a fertile and lush land. And, as you know, that's what I did.'"

"Yes, GOD," I replied. "That's true."

GOD continued: "Preach all this in the towns of Judah and the streets of Jerusalem. Say, 'Listen to the terms of this covenant and carry them out! I warned your ancestors when I delivered them from Egypt and I've kept up the warnings. I haven't quit warning them for a moment. I warned them from morning to night: "Obey me or else!" But they didn't obey. They paid no attention to me. They did whatever they wanted to do, whenever they wanted to do it, until finally I stepped in and ordered the punishments set out in the covenant, which, despite all my warnings, they had ignored.'"

Then GOD said, "There's a conspiracy among the people of Judah and the citizens of Jerusalem. They've plotted to reenact the sins of their ancestors—the ones who disobeyed me and decided to go after other gods and worship them. Israel and Judah are in this together, mindlessly breaking the covenant I made with their ancestors."

"Well, your God has something to say about this: Watch out! I'm about to visit doom on you, and no one will get out of it. You're going to cry for help but I won't listen. Then all the people in Judah and Jerusalem will start praying to the gods you've been sacrificing to all these years, but it won't do a bit of good. You've got as many gods as you have villages, Judah! And you've got enough altars for sacrifices to that impotent sex god Baal to put one on every street corner in Jerusalem!"

"And as for you, Jeremiah, I don't want you praying for this people. Nothing! Not a word of petition. Indeed, I'm not going to listen to a single syllable of their crisis-prayers."

PROMISES AND PIOUS PROGRAMS

"What business do the ones I love have figuring out
    how to get off the hook? And right in the house of worship!
Do you think making promises and devising pious programs
    will save you from doom?
Do you think you can get out of this
    by becoming more religious?

A mighty oak tree, majestic and glorious—
  that's how I once described you.
But it will only take a clap of thunder and a bolt of lightning
  to leave you a shattered wreck.

"I, GOD-of-the-Angel-Armies, who planted you—yes, I have pronounced doom on you. Why? Because of the disastrous life you've lived, Israel and Judah alike, goading me to anger with your continuous worship and offerings to that sorry god Baal."

✝

GOD told me what was going on. That's how I knew.
  You, GOD, opened my eyes to their evil scheming.
I had no idea what was going on—naive as a lamb
  being led to slaughter!
I didn't know they had it in for me,
  didn't know of their behind-the-scenes plots:
"Let's get rid of the preacher.
  That will stop the sermons!
Let's get rid of him for good.
  He won't be remembered for long."

Then I said, "GOD-of-the-Angel-Armies,
  you're a fair judge.
You examine and cross-examine
  human actions and motives.
I want to see these people shown up and put down!
  I'm an open book before you. Clear my name."

That sent a signal to GOD, who spoke up: "Here's what I'll do to the men of Anathoth who are trying to murder you, the men who say, 'Don't preach to us in GOD's name or we'll kill you.' Yes, it's GOD-of-the-Angel-Armies speaking. Indeed! I'll call them to account: Their young people will die in battle, their children will die of starvation, and there will be no one left at all, none. I'm visiting the men of Anathoth with doom. Doomsday!"

12

WHAT MAKES YOU THINK YOU CAN RACE AGAINST HORSES?

You are right, oh GOD, and you set things right.
        I can't argue with that. But I do have some questions:
Why do bad people have it so good?
        Why do con artists make it big?
You planted them and they put down roots.
        They flourished and produced fruit.
They talk as if they're old friends with you,
        but they couldn't care less about you.
Meanwhile, you know *me* inside and out.
        You don't let me get by with a thing!
Make them pay for the way they live,
        pay with their lives, like sheep marked for slaughter.
How long do we have to put up with this—
        the country depressed, the farms in ruin—
And all because of wickedness, these wicked lives?
        Even animals and birds are dying off
Because they'll have nothing to do with God
        and think God has nothing to do with them.

✝

"So, Jeremiah, if you're worn out in this footrace with men,
        what makes you think you can race against horses?
And if you can't keep your wits during times of calm,
        what's going to happen when troubles break loose
                like the Jordan in flood?
Those closest to you, your own brothers and cousins,
        are working against you.
They're out to get you. They'll stop at nothing.
        Don't trust them, especially when they're smiling.

✝

"I will abandon the House of Israel,
        walk away from my beloved people.
I will turn over those I most love
        to those who are her enemies.

She's been, this one I held dear,
    like a snarling lion in the jungle,
Growling and baring her teeth at me—
    and I can't take it anymore.
Has this one I hold dear become a preening peacock?
    But isn't she under attack by vultures?
Then invite all the hungry animals at large,
    invite them in for a free meal!
Foreign, scavenging shepherds
    will loot and trample my fields,
Turn my beautiful, well-cared-for fields
    into vacant lots of tin cans and thistles.
They leave them littered with junk—
    a ruined land, a land in lament.
The whole countryside is a wasteland,
    and no one will really care.

✠

"The barbarians will invade,
    swarm over hills and plains.
The judgment sword of GOD will take its toll
    from one end of the land to the other.
    Nothing living will be safe.
They will plant wheat and reap weeds.
    Nothing they do will work out.
They will look at their meager crops and wring their hands.
    All this the result of GOD's fierce anger!"

✠

GOD's Message: "Regarding all the bad neighbors who abused the land I gave to Israel as their inheritance: I'm going to pluck them out of their lands, and then pluck Judah out from among them. Once I've pulled the bad neighbors out, I will relent and take them tenderly to my heart and put them back where they belong, put each of them back in their home country, on their family farms. Then if they will get serious about living my way and pray to me as well as they taught my people to pray to that god Baal, everything will go well for them. But if they won't listen, then I'll pull them out of their land by the roots and cart them off to the dump. Total destruction!" GOD's Decree.

13

People Who Do Only What They Want to Do

God told me, "Go and buy yourself some linen shorts. Put them on and keep them on. Don't even take them off to wash them." So I bought the shorts as God directed and put them on.

Then God told me, "Take the shorts that you bought and go straight to Perath and hide them there in a crack in the rock." So I did what God told me and hid them at Perath.

Next, after quite a long time, God told me, "Go back to Perath and get the linen shorts I told you to hide there." So I went back to Perath and dug them out of the place where I had hidden them. The shorts by then had rotted and were worthless.

God explained, "This is the way I am going to ruin the pride of Judah and the great pride of Jerusalem—a wicked bunch of people who won't obey me, who do only what they want to do, who chase after all kinds of no-gods and worship them. They're going to turn out as rotten as these old shorts. Just as shorts clothe and protect, so I kept the whole family of Israel under my care"—God's Decree—"so that everyone could see they were my people, a people I could show off to the world and be proud of. But they refused to do a thing I said.

"And then tell them this: 'God's Message, personal from the God of Israel: Every wine jug should be full of wine.'

"And they'll say, 'Of course. We know that. Every wine jug should be full of wine!'

"Then you'll say, 'This is what God says: Watch closely. I'm going to fill every person who lives in this country—the kings who rule from David's throne, the priests, the prophets, the citizens of Jerusalem—with wine that will make them drunk. And then I'll smash them, smash the wine-filled jugs—old and young alike. Nothing will stop me. Not an ounce of pity or mercy or compassion will slow me down. Every last drunken jug of them will be smashed!'"

The Light You Always Took for Granted

Then I said, Listen. Listen carefully: Don't stay stuck in your ways!
    It's God's Message we're dealing with here.
Let your lives glow bright before God
    before he turns out the lights,

Before you trip and fall
    on the dark mountain paths.
The light you always took for granted will go out
    and the world will turn black.
If you people won't listen,
    I'll go off by myself and weep over you,
Weep because of your stubborn arrogance,
    bitter, bitter tears,
Rivers of tears from my eyes,
    because GOD's sheep will end up in exile.

☩

Tell the king and the queen-mother,
    "Come down off your high horses.
Your dazzling crowns
    will tumble off your heads."
The villages in the Negev will be surrounded,
    everyone trapped,
And Judah dragged off to exile,
    the whole country dragged to oblivion.

☩

Look, look, Jerusalem!
    Look at the enemies coming out of the north!
What will become of your flocks of people,
    the beautiful flocks in your care?
How are you going to feel when the people
    you've played up to, looked up to all these years
Now look down on you? You didn't expect this?
    Surprise! The pain of a woman having a baby!
Do I hear you saying,
    "What's going on here? Why me?"
The answer's simple: You're guilty,
    hugely guilty.
Your guilt has your life endangered,
    your guilt has you writhing in pain.

Can an African change skin?
    Can a leopard get rid of its spots?

So what are the odds on you doing good,
    you who are so long-practiced in evil?

"I'll blow these people away—
    like wind-blown leaves.
You have it coming to you.
    I've measured it out precisely."
        GOD's Decree.
"It's because you forgot me
    and embraced the Big Lie,
    that so-called god Baal.
I'm the one who will rip off your clothes,
    expose and shame you before the watching world.
Your obsessions with gods, gods, and more gods,
    your goddess affairs, your god-adulteries.
Gods on the hills, gods in the fields—
    every time I look you're off with another god.
Oh Jerusalem, what a sordid life!
    Is there any hope for you!"

14

TIME AND AGAIN WE'VE BETRAYED GOD

GOD's Message that came to Jeremiah regarding the drought:

"Judah weeps,
    her cities mourn.
The people fall to the ground, moaning,
    while sounds of Jerusalem's sobs rise up, up.
The rich people sent their servants for water.
    They went to the cisterns, but the cisterns were dry.
They came back with empty buckets,
    wringing their hands, shaking their heads.
All the farm work has stopped.
    Not a drop of rain has fallen.
The farmers don't know what to do.
    They wring their hands, they shake their heads.
Even the doe abandons her fawn in the field
    because there is no grass—

Eyes glazed over, on her last legs,
  nothing but skin and bones."

We know we're guilty. We've lived bad lives—
  but do something, GOD. Do it for *your* sake!
Time and time again we've betrayed you.
  No doubt about it—we've sinned against you.
Hope of Israel! Our only hope!
  Israel's last chance in this trouble!
Why are you acting like a tourist,
  taking in the sights, here today and gone tomorrow?
Why do you just stand there and stare,
  like someone who doesn't know what to do in a crisis?
But GOD, you are, in fact, *here,* here *with us*!
  You know who we are—you named us!
  Don't leave us in the lurch.

Then GOD said of these people:

"Since they loved to wander this way and that,
  never giving a thought to where they were going,
I will now have nothing more to do with them—
  except to note their guilt and punish their sins."

THE KILLING FIELDS

GOD said to me, "Don't pray that everything will turn out all right for this people. When they skip their meals in order to pray, I won't listen to a thing they say. When they redouble their prayers, bringing all kinds of offerings from their herds and crops, I'll not accept them. I'm finishing them off with war and famine and disease."

I said, "But Master, GOD! Their preachers have been telling them that everything is going to be all right—no war and no famine—that there's nothing to worry about."

Then GOD said, "These preachers are liars, and they use my name to cover their lies. I never sent them, I never commanded them, and I don't talk with them. The sermons they've been handing out are sheer illusion, tissues of lies, whistlings in the dark.

"So this is my verdict on them: All the preachers who preach using my name as their text, preachers I never sent in the first place, preachers who say, 'War and famine will never come here'—these preachers will die in war and by starvation. And the people to whom they've been preaching will end up as corpses, victims of war and starvation, thrown out in the streets of Jerusalem unburied—no funerals for them or their wives or their children! I'll make sure they get the full brunt of all their evil.

"And you, Jeremiah, will say this to them:

"'My eyes pour out tears.
　　Day and night, the tears never quit.
My dear, dear people are battered and bruised,
　　hopelessly and cruelly wounded.
I walk out into the fields,
　　shocked by the killing fields strewn with corpses.
I walk into the city,
　　shocked by the sight of starving bodies.
And I watch the preachers and priests
　　going about their business as if nothing's happened!'"

God, have you said your final No to Judah?
　　Can you simply not stand Zion any longer?
If not, why have you treated us like this,
　　beaten us nearly to death?
We hoped for peace—
　　nothing good came from it;
We looked for healing—
　　and got kicked in the stomach.
We admit, oh GOD, how bad we've lived,
　　and our ancestors, how bad they were.
We've sinned, they've sinned,
　　we've all sinned against you!
Your reputation is at stake! Don't quit on us!
　　Don't walk out and abandon your glorious Temple!
Remember your covenant.
　　Don't break faith with us!
Can the no-gods of the godless nations cause rain?
　　Can the sky water the earth by itself?
You're the one, oh GOD, who does this.
　　So you're the one for whom we wait.
You made it all,
　　you do it all.

15

Then GOD said to me: "Jeremiah, even if Moses and Samuel stood here and made their case, I wouldn't feel a thing for this people. Get them out of here. Tell them to get lost! And if they ask you, 'So where do we go?' tell them GOD says,

"'If you're assigned to die, go and die;
    if assigned to war, go and get killed;
If assigned to starve, go starve;
    if assigned to exile, off to exile you go!'

"I've arranged for four kinds of punishment: death in battle, the corpses dropped off by killer dogs, the rest picked clean by vultures, the bones gnawed by hyenas. They'll be a sight to see, a sight to shock the whole world—and all because of Manasseh son of Hezekiah and all he did in Jerusalem.

"Who do you think will feel sorry for you, Jerusalem?
    Who do you think will waste tears on you?
Who will bother to take the time to ask,
    'So, how are things going?'

"*You* left *me*, remember?" GOD's Decree.
    "You turned your back and walked out.
So I will grab you and hit you hard.
    I'm tired of letting you off the hook.
I threw you to the four winds
    and let the winds scatter you like leaves.
I made sure you'll lose everything,
    since nothing makes you change.
I created more widows among you
    than grains of sand on the ocean beaches.
At noon mothers will get the news
    of their sons killed in action.
Sudden anguish for the mothers—
    all those terrible deaths.
A mother of seven falls to the ground,
    gasping for breath,
Robbed of her children in their prime.

Her sun sets at high noon!
Then I'll round up any of you that are left alive
    and see that you're killed by your enemies."
        GOD's Decree.

GIVING EVERYTHING AWAY FOR NOTHING

Unlucky mother—that you had me as a son,
    given the unhappy job of indicting the whole country!
I've never hurt or harmed a soul,
    and yet everyone is out to get me.
But, GOD knows, I've done everything I could to help them,
    prayed for them and against their enemies.
I've always been on their side, trying to stave off disaster.
    God knows how I've tried!

✝

"Oh Israel, oh Judah, what are your chances
    against the iron juggernaut from the north?
In punishment for your sins, I'm giving away
    everything you've got, giving it away for nothing.
I'll make you slaves to your enemies
    in a strange and faroff land.
My anger is blazing and fierce,
    burning in hot judgment against you."

✝

You know where I am, GOD! Remember what I'm doing here!
    Take my side against my detractors.
Don't stand back while they ruin me.
    Just look at the abuse I'm taking!
When your words showed up, I ate them—
    swallowed them whole. What a feast!
What delight I took in being yours,
    oh GOD, God-of-the-Angel-Armies!
I never joined the party crowd
    in their laughter and their fun.
Led by you, I went off by myself.

You'd filled me with indignation. Their sin had me seething.
But why, why this chronic pain,
    this ever worsening wound and no healing in sight?
You're nothing, GOD, but a mirage,
    a lovely oasis in the distance—and then nothing!

☩

This is how GOD answered me:

"Take back those words, and I'll take you back.
    Then you'll stand tall before me.
Use words truly and well. Don't stoop to cheap whining.
    Then, but only then, you'll speak for me.
Let your words change *them*.
    Don't change your words to suit them.
I'll turn you into a steel wall,
    a thick steel wall, impregnable.
They'll attack you but won't put a dent in you
    because I'm at your side, defending and delivering."
        GOD's Decree.
"I'll deliver you from the grip of the wicked.
    I'll get you out of the clutch of the ruthless."

16

CAN MORTALS MANUFACTURE GODS?

GOD's Message to me:

"Jeremiah, don't get married. Don't raise a family here. I have signed the death warrant on all the children born in this country, the mothers who bear them and the fathers who beget them—an epidemic of death. Death unlamented, the dead unburied, dead bodies decomposing and stinking like dung, all the killed and starved corpses served up as meals for carrion crows and mongrel dogs!"

GOD continued: "Don't enter a house where there's mourning. Don't go to the funeral. Don't sympathize. I've quit caring about what happens to this people." GOD's Decree. "No more loyal love on my part, no more compassion. The famous and obscure will die alike here, unlamented and unburied. No funerals will be conducted, no one will give them a second thought, no one will care, no one will say, 'I'm sorry,' no one will so much as offer a cup of tea, not even for the mother or father.

"And if there happens to be a feast celebrated, don't go there either to enjoy the festivities."

GOD-of-the-Angel-Armies, the God of Israel, says, "Watch this! I'm about to banish smiles and laughter from this place. No more brides and bridegrooms celebrating. And I'm doing it in your lifetime, before your very eyes.

"When you tell this to the people and they ask, 'Why is GOD talking this way, threatening us with all these calamities? We're not criminals, after all. What have we done to our GOD to be treated like this?' tell them this: 'It's because your ancestors left me, walked off and never looked back. They took up with the no-gods, worshiped and doted on them, and ignored me and wouldn't do a thing I told them. And *you're* even *worse*! Take a good look in the mirror—each of you doing whatever you want, whenever you want, refusing to pay attention to me. And for this I'm getting rid of you, throwing you out in the cold, into a far and strange country. You can worship your precious no-gods there to your heart's content. Rest assured, I won't bother you anymore.'

✠

"On the other hand, don't miss this: The time is coming when no one will say any longer, 'As sure as GOD lives, the God who delivered Israel from Egypt.' What they'll say is, 'As sure as GOD lives, the God who brought Israel back from the land of the north, brought them back from all the places where he'd scattered them.' That's right, I'm going to bring them back to the land I first gave to their ancestors.

✠

"Now, watch for what comes next: I'm going to assemble a bunch of fishermen." GOD's Decree! "They'll go fishing for my people and pull them in for judgment. Then I'll send out a party of hunters, and they'll hunt them out in all the mountains, hills, and caves. I'm watching their every move. I haven't lost track of a single one of them, neither them nor their sins.

"They won't get by with a thing. They'll pay double for everything they did wrong. They've made a complete mess of things, littering their lives with their obscene no-gods, leaving piles of stinking god-junk all over the place."

GOD, my strength, my stronghold,
    my safe retreat when trouble descends:
The godless nations will come
    from earth's four corners, saying,
"Our ancestors lived on lies,
    useless illusions, all smoke."
Can mortals manufacture gods?
    Their factories turn out no-gods!

"Watch closely now. I'm going to teach these wrongheaded people.
    Starting right now, I'm going to teach them
Who I am and what I do,
    teach them the meaning of my name, GOD—'I AM.'

17

THE HEART IS HOPELESSLY DARK AND DECEITFUL

"Judah's sin is engraved
    with a steel chisel,
A steel chisel with a diamond point—
    engraved on their granite hearts,
    engraved on the stone corners of their altars.
The evidence against them is plain to see:
    sex-and-religion altars and sacred sex shrines
Anywhere there's a grove of trees,
    anywhere there's an available hill.

"I'll use your mountains as roadside stands
    for giving away everything you have.
All your 'things' will serve as reparations
    for your sins all over the country.
You'll lose your gift of land,
    The inheritance I gave you.
I'll make you slaves of your enemies
    in a faroff and strange land.
My anger is hot and blazing and fierce,
    and no one will put it out."

✝

GOD'S Message:

"Cursed is the strong one
    who depends on mere humans,
Who thinks he can make it on muscle alone
    and sets GOD aside as dead weight.
He's like a tumbleweed on the prairie,
    out of touch with the good earth.
He lives rootless and aimless
    in a land where nothing grows.

"But blessed is the man who trusts me, GOD,
    the woman who sticks with GOD.
They're like trees replanted in Eden,
    putting down roots near the rivers—
Never a worry through the hottest of summers,
    never dropping a leaf,
Serene and calm through droughts,
    bearing fresh fruit every season.

☩

"The heart is hopelessly dark and deceitful,
    a puzzle that no one can figure out.
But I, GOD, search the heart
    and examine the mind.
I get to the heart of the human.
    I get to the root of things.
I treat them as they really are,
    not as they pretend to be."

☩

Like a cowbird that cheats by laying its eggs
    in another bird's nest
Is the person who gets rich by cheating.
    When the eggs hatch, the deceit is exposed.
What a fool he'll look like then!

☩

From early on your Sanctuary was set high,
    a throne of glory, exalted!
Oh GOD, you're the hope of Israel.
    All who leave you end up as fools,
Deserters with nothing to show for their lives,
    who walk off from GOD, fountain of living waters—
    and wind up dead!

⁘

GOD, pick up the pieces.
    Put me back together again.
    You are my praise!
Listen to how they talk about me:
    "So where's this 'Word of GOD'?
    We'd like to see something happen!"
But it wasn't my idea to call for Doomsday.
    I never wanted trouble.
You know what I've said.
    It's all out in the open before you.
Don't add to my troubles.
    Give me some relief!
Let those who harass me be harassed, not me.
    Let *them* be disgraced, not me.
Bring down upon them the day of doom.
    Lower the boom. *Boom!*

KEEP THE SABBATH DAY HOLY

GOD's Message to me: "Go stand in the People's Gate, the one used by Judah's kings as they come and go, and then proceed in turn to all the gates of Jerusalem. Tell them: 'Listen, you kings of Judah, listen to GOD's Message—and all you people who go in and out of these gates, you listen!

"'This is GOD's Message. Be careful, if you care about your lives, not to desecrate the Sabbath by turning it into just another workday, lugging stuff here and there. Don't use the Sabbath to do business as usual. Keep the Sabbath day holy, as I commanded your ancestors. They never did it, as you know. They paid no attention to what I said and went about their own business, refusing to be guided or instructed by me.

"'But now, take seriously what I tell you. Quit desecrating the Sabbath by busily going about your own work, and keep the Sabbath day holy by not doing business as usual. Then kings from the time of David and their officials will continue to ride through these gates on horses or in chariots. The people of Judah and citizens of Jerusalem will continue to pass through them, too. Jerusalem will always be filled with people. People will stream in from all over Judah, from the province of Benjamin, from the Jerusalem suburbs, from foothills and mountains and deserts. They'll come to worship, bringing all kinds of offerings—animals, grains, incense, expressions of thanks—into the Sanctuary of GOD.

"'But if you won't listen to me, won't keep the Sabbath holy, won't quit using the Sabbath for doing your own work, busily going in and out of the city gates on your self-important business, then I'll burn the gates down. In fact, I'll burn the whole city down, palaces and all, with a fire nobody will be able to put out!'"

18

TO WORSHIP THE BIG LIE

GOD told Jeremiah, "Up on your feet! Go to the potter's house. When you get there, I'll tell you what I have to say."

So I went to the potter's house, and sure enough, the potter was there, working away at his wheel. Whenever the pot the potter was working on turned out badly, as sometimes happens when you are working with clay, the potter would simply start over and use the same clay to make another pot.

Then GOD's Message came to me: "Can't I do just as this potter does, people of Israel?" GOD's Decree! "Watch this potter. In the same way that this potter works his clay, I work on you, people of Israel. At any moment I may decide to pull up a people or a country by the roots and get rid of them. But if they repent of their wicked lives, I will think twice and start over with them. At another time I might decide to plant a people or country, but if they don't cooperate and won't listen to me, I will think again and give up on the plans I had for them.

"So, tell the people of Judah and citizens of Jerusalem my Message: 'Danger! I'm shaping doom against you, laying plans against you. Turn back from your doomed way of life. Straighten out your lives.'

"But they'll just say, 'Why should we? What's the point? We'll live just the way we've always lived, doom or no doom.'"

✝

God's Message:

"Ask around.
    Survey the godless nations.
Has anyone heard the likes of this?
    Virgin Israel has become a slut!
Does snow disappear from the Lebanon peaks? ·
    Do alpine streams run dry?
But my people have left me
    to worship the Big Lie.
They've gotten off the track,
    the old, well-worn trail,
And now bushwhack through underbrush
    in a tangle of roots and vines.
Their land's going to end up a mess—
    a fool's memorial to be spit on.
Travelers passing through
    will shake their heads in disbelief.
I'll scatter my people before their enemies,
    like autumn leaves in a high wind.
On their day of doom, they'll stare at my back as I walk away,
    catching not so much as a glimpse of my face."

✝

Some of the people said, "Come on, let's cook up a plot against Jeremiah. We'll still have the priests to teach us the law, wise counselors to give us advice, and prophets to tell us what God has to say. Come on, let's discredit him so we don't have to put up with him any longer."

    And I said to God:

"God, listen to me!
    Just listen to what my enemies are saying.
Should I get paid evil for good?
    That's what they're doing. They've made plans to kill me!
Remember all the times I stood up for them before you,

speaking up for them,
trying to soften your anger?
But enough! Let their children starve!
Let them be massacred in battle!
Let their wives be childless and widowed,
their friends die and their proud young men be killed.
Let cries of panic sound from their homes
as you surprise them with war parties!
They're all set to lynch me.
The noose is practically around my neck!
But you know all this, GOD.
You know they're determined to kill me.
Don't whitewash their crimes,
don't overlook a single sin!
Round the bunch of them up before you.
Strike while the iron of your anger is hot!"

19

SMASHING THE CLAY POT

GOD said to me, "Go, buy a clay pot. Then get a few leaders from the people and a few of the leading priests and go out to the Valley of Ben-hinnom, just outside the Potsherd Gate, and preach there what I tell you.

"Say, 'Listen to GOD's Word, you kings of Judah and people of Jerusalem! This is the Message from GOD-of-the-Angel-Armies, the God of Israel. I'm about to bring doom crashing down on this place. Oh, and will ears ever ring! Doom—because they've walked off and left me, and made this place strange by worshiping strange gods, gods never heard of by them, their parents, or the old kings of Judah. Doom—because they have massacred innocent people. Doom—because they've built altars to that no-god Baal, and burned their own children alive in the fire as offerings to Baal, an atrocity I never ordered, never so much as hinted at!

"'And so it's pay day, and soon'—GOD's Decree!—'this place will no longer be known as Topheth or Valley of Ben-hinnom, but Massacre Meadows. I'm canceling all the plans Judah and Jerusalem had for this place, and I'll have them killed by their enemies. I'll stack their dead bodies to be eaten by carrion crows and wild dogs. I'll turn this city into such a museum of atrocities that anyone coming near will be shocked speechless by the savage brutality. The people will turn into cannibals. Dehumanized by the pressure of the enemy siege, they'll eat their own children! Yes, they'll eat one another, family and friends alike.'

"Say all this, and then smash the pot in front of the men who have come with you. Then say, 'This is what GOD-of-the-Angel-Armies says: I'll smash this people and this city like a man who smashes a clay pot into so many pieces it can never be put together again. They'll bury bodies here in Topheth until there's no more room. And the whole city will become a Topheth. The city will be turned by people and kings alike into a center for worshiping the star gods and goddesses, turned into an open grave, the whole city an open grave, stinking like a sewer, like Topheth.'"

Then Jeremiah left Topheth, where GOD had sent him to preach the sermon, and took his stand in the court of GOD's Temple and said to the people, "This is the Message from GOD-of-the-Angel-Armies to you: 'Warning! Danger! I'm bringing down on this city and all the surrounding towns the doom that I have pronounced. They're set in their ways and won't budge. They refuse to do a thing I say.'"

20

LIFE'S BEEN NOTHING BUT TROUBLE AND TEARS

The priest Pashur son of Immer was the senior priest in GOD's Temple. He heard Jeremiah preach this sermon. He whipped Jeremiah the prophet and put him in the stocks at the Upper Benjamin Gate of GOD's Temple. The next day Pashur came and let him go. Jeremiah told him, "GOD has a new name for you: not Pashur but Danger-Everywhere, because GOD says, 'You're a danger to yourself and everyone around you. All your friends are going to get killed in battle while you stand there and watch. What's more, I'm turning all of Judah over to the king of Babylon to do whatever he likes with them—haul them off into exile, kill them at whim. Everything worth anything in this city, property and possessions along with everything in the royal treasury—I'm handing it all over to the enemy. They'll rummage through it and take what they want back to Babylon.

"'And you, Pashur, you and everyone in your family will be taken prisoner into exile—that's right, exile in Babylon. You'll die and be buried there, you and all your cronies to whom you preached your lies.'"

✠

You pushed me into this, GOD, and I let you do it.
    You were too much for me.
And now I'm a public joke.
    They all poke fun at me.
Every time I open my mouth
    I'm shouting, "Murder!" or "Rape!"
And all I get for my GOD-warnings
    are insults and contempt.
But if I say, "Forget it!
    No more GOD-Messages from me!"
The words are fire in my belly,
    a burning in my bones.
I'm worn out trying to hold it in.
    I can't do it any longer!
Then I hear whispering behind my back:
    "There goes old 'Danger-Everywhere.' Shut him up! Report
        him!"
Old friends watch, hoping I'll fall flat on my face:
    "One misstep and we'll have him. We'll get rid of him for good!"

But GOD, a most fierce warrior, is at my side.
    Those who are after me will be sent sprawling—
Slapstick buffoons falling all over themselves,
    a spectacle of humiliation no one will ever forget.

Oh, GOD-of-the-Angel-Armies, no one fools you.
    You see through everyone, everything.
I want to see you pay them back for what they've done.
    I rest my case with you.

Sing to GOD! All praise to GOD!
    He saves the weak from the grip of the wicked.

✠

Curse the day
    I was born!

The day my mother bore me—
    a curse on it, I say!
And curse the man who delivered
    the news to my father:
"You've got a new baby—a boy baby!"
    (How happy it made him.)
Let that birth notice be blacked out,
    deleted from the records,
And the man who brought it haunted to his death
    with the bad news he brought.
He should have killed me before I was born,
    with that womb as my tomb,
My mother pregnant for the rest of her life
    with a baby dead in her womb.
Why, oh why, did I ever leave that womb?
    Life's been nothing but trouble and tears,
    and what's coming is more of the same.

21

START EACH DAY WITH A SENSE OF JUSTICE

GOD's Message to Jeremiah when King Zedekiah sent Pashur son of Malkijah and the priest Zephaniah son of Maaseiah to him with this request: "Nebuchadnezzar, king of Babylon, has waged war against us. Pray to GOD for us. Ask him for help. Maybe GOD will intervene with one of his famous miracles and make him leave."

But Jeremiah said, "Tell Zedekiah: 'This is the GOD of Israel's Message to you: You can say goodbye to your army, watch morale and weapons flushed down the drain. I'm going to personally lead the king of Babylon and the Chaldeans, against whom you're fighting so hard, right into the city itself. I'm joining *their* side and fighting against *you*, fighting all-out, holding nothing back. And in fierce anger. I'm prepared to wipe out the population of this city, people and animals alike, in a raging epidemic. And then I will personally deliver Zedekiah king of Judah, his princes, and any survivors left in the city who haven't died from disease, been killed, or starved. I'll deliver them to Nebuchadnezzar, king of Babylon—yes, hand them over to their enemies, who have come to kill them. He'll kill them ruthlessly, showing no mercy.'

"And then tell the people at large, 'GOD's Message to you is this: Listen carefully. I'm giving you a choice: life or death. Whoever stays in this city will die—either in battle or by starvation or disease. But whoever goes out and surrenders to the Chaldeans who have surrounded the city will live. You'll lose everything—but not your life. I'm determined to see this city destroyed. I'm that angry with this place! GOD's Decree. I'm going to give it to the king of Babylon, and he's going to burn it to the ground.'

✠

"To the royal house of Judah, listen to GOD's Message!
    House of David, listen—GOD's Message to you:
'Start each day by dealing with justice.
    Rescue victims from their exploiters.
Prevent fire—the fire of my anger—
    for once it starts, it can't be put out.
Your evil regime
    is fuel for my anger.
Don't you realize that I'm against you,
    yes, *against* you.
You think you've got it made,
    all snug and secure.
You say, "Who can possibly get to us?
    Who can crash our party?"
Well, I can—and will!
    I'll punish your evil regime.
I'll start a fire that will rage unchecked,
    burn everything in sight to cinders.'"

22

WALKING OUT ON THE COVENANT OF GOD

GOD's orders: "Go to the royal palace and deliver this Message. Say, 'Listen to what GOD says, oh King of Judah, you who sit on David's throne—you and your officials and all the people who go in and out of these palace gates. This is GOD's Message: Attend to matters of justice. Set things right between people. Rescue victims from their exploiters. Don't take advantage of the homeless, the orphans, the widows. Stop the murdering!

"'If you obey these commands, then kings who follow in the line of David will continue to go in and out of these palace gates mounted on horses and riding in chariots—they and their officials and the citizens of Judah. But if you don't obey these commands, then I swear—GOD's Decree!—this palace will end up a heap of rubble.'"

✠

This is GOD's verdict on Judah's royal palace:

"I number you among my favorite places—
    like the lovely hills of Gilead,
    like the soaring peaks of Lebanon.
Yet I swear I'll turn you into a wasteland,
    as empty as a ghost town.
I'll hire a demolition crew,
    well-equipped with sledgehammers and wrecking bars,
Pound the country to a pulp
    and burn it all up.

"Travelers from all over will come through here and say to one another, 'Why would GOD do such a thing to this wonderful city?' They'll be told, 'Because they walked out on the covenant of their GOD, took up with other gods and worshiped them.'"

BUILDING A FINE HOUSE BUT DESTROYING LIVES

Don't weep over dead King Josiah.
    Don't waste your tears.
Weep for his exiled son:
    He's gone for good.
    He'll never see home again.
    For this is GOD's Word on Shallum son of Josiah, who succeeded his father as king of Judah: "He's gone from here, gone for good. He'll die in the place they've taken him to. He'll never see home again."

✠

"Doom to him who builds palaces but bullies people,
    who makes a fine house but destroys lives,

Who cheats his workers
    and won't pay them for their work,
Who says, 'I'll build me an elaborate mansion
    with spacious rooms and fancy windows.
I'll bring in rare and expensive woods
    and the latest in interior decor.'
So, that makes you a king—
    living in a fancy palace?
Your father got along just fine, didn't he?
    He did what was right and treated people fairly,
And things went well with him.
    He stuck up for the down-and-out,
And things went well for Judah.
    Isn't this what it means to know me?"
        GOD's Decree!
"But you're blind and brainless.
    All you think about is yourself,
Taking advantage of the weak,
    bulldozing your way, bullying victims."

This is God's epitaph on Jehoiakim son of Josiah king of Judah:
    "Doom to this man!
Nobody will shed tears over him,
    'Poor, poor brother!'
Nobody will shed tears over him,
    'Poor, poor master!'
They'll give him a donkey's funeral,
    drag him out of the city and dump him.

YOU'VE MADE A TOTAL MESS OF YOUR LIFE

"People of Jerusalem, climb a Lebanon peak and weep,
    climb a Bashan mountain and wail,
Climb the Abarim ridge and cry—
    you've made a total mess of your life.
I spoke to you when everything was going your way.
    You said, 'I'm not interested.'
You've been that way as long as I've known you,
    never listened to a thing I said.

All your leaders will be blown away,
    all your friends end up in exile,
And you'll find yourself in the gutter,
    disgraced by your evil life.
You big-city people thought you were so important,
    thought you were 'king of the mountain'!
You're soon going to be doubled up in pain,
    pain worse than the pangs of childbirth.

☩

"As sure as I am the living God"—GOD's Decree—"even if you, Jehoiachin son of Jehoiakim king of Judah, were the signet ring on my right hand, I'd pull you off and give you to those who are out to kill you, to Nebuchadnezzar king of Babylon and the Chaldeans, and then throw you, both you and your mother, into a foreign country, far from your place of birth. There you'll both die.

"You'll be homesick, desperately homesick, but you'll never get home again."

Is Jehoiachin a leaky bucket,
    a rusted-out pail good for nothing?
Why else would he be thrown away, he and his children,
    thrown away to a foreign place?
Oh land, land, land,
    listen to GOD's Message!
This is GOD's verdict:
"Write this man off as if he were childless,
    a man who will never amount to anything.
Nothing will ever come of his life.
    He's the end of the line, the last of the kings."

23

AN AUTHENTIC DAVID-BRANCH

"Doom to the shepherd-leaders who butcher and scatter my sheep!" GOD's Decree. "So here is what I, GOD, Israel's God, say to the shepherd-leaders who misled my people: 'You've scattered my sheep. You've driven them off. You haven't kept your eye on them. Well, let me tell you, I'm keeping my eye on *you*, keeping track of your criminal behavior. I'll take over and gather what's left of my sheep, gather them in from all the lands where I've driven them. I'll bring them back where they belong, and they'll recover and flourish. I'll set shepherd-leaders over them who will take good care of them. They won't live in fear or panic anymore. All the lost sheep rounded up!' GOD's Decree."

"Time's coming"—GOD's Decree—
    "when I'll establish a truly righteous David-Branch,
A ruler who knows how to rule justly.
    He'll make sure of justice and keep people united.
In his time Judah will be secure again
    and Israel will live in safety.
This is the name they'll give him:
    'GOD-Who-Puts-Everything-Right.'

"So watch for this. The time's coming"—GOD's Decree—"when no one will say, 'As sure as GOD lives, the God who brought the Israelites out of Egypt,' but, 'As sure as GOD lives, the God who brought the descendants of Israel back from the north country and from the other countries where he'd driven them, so that they can live on their own good earth.'"

THE "EVERYTHING WILL TURN OUT FINE" SERMON

My head is reeling,
    my limbs are limp,
I'm staggering like a drunk,
    seeing double from too much wine—
And all because of GOD,
    because of his holy words.

Now for what GOD says regarding the lying prophets:

"Can you believe it? A country teeming with adulterers!
    faithless, promiscuous idolater-adulterers!
They're a curse on the land.
    The land's a wasteland.
Their unfaithfulness
    is turning the country into a cesspool,

Prophets and priests devoted to desecration.
    They have nothing to do with me as their God.
My very own Temple, mind you—
    mud-spattered with their crimes." GOD's Decree.
"But they won't get by with it.
    They'll find themselves on a slippery slope,
Careening into the darkness,
    somersaulting into the pitch-black dark.
I'll make them pay for their crimes.
    It will be the Year of Doom." GOD's Decree.

✢

"Over in Samaria I saw prophets
    acting like silly fools—shocking!
They preached using that no-god Baal for a text,
    messing with the minds of my people.
And the Jerusalem prophets are even worse—horrible!—
    sex-driven, living a lie,
Subsidizing a culture of wickedness,
    and never giving it a second thought.
They're as bad as those wretches in old Sodom,
    the degenerates of old Gomorrah."

    So here's the Message to the prophets from GOD-of-the-Angel-Armies:

"I'll cook them a supper of maggoty meat
    with after-dinner drinks of strychnine.
The Jerusalem prophets are behind all this.
    They're the cause of the godlessness polluting this country."

✢

A Message from GOD-of-the-Angel-Armies:

"Don't listen to the sermons of the prophets.
    It's all hot air. Lies, lies, and more lies.
They make it all up.
    Not a word they speak comes from me.

They preach their 'Everything Will Turn Out Fine' sermon
    to congregations with no taste for God,
Their 'Nothing Bad Will Ever Happen to You' sermon
    to people who are set in their own ways.

"Have any of these prophets bothered to meet with me,
      the true GOD?
    bothered to take in what *I* have to say?
    listened to and then *lived out* my Word?
Look out! GOD's hurricane will be let loose—
    my hurricane blast,
Spinning the heads of the wicked like tops!
    God's raging anger won't let up
Until I've made a clean sweep,
    completing the job I began.
When the job's done,
    you'll see that it's been well done.

QUIT THE "GOD TOLD ME THIS" KIND OF TALK

"I never sent these prophets,
    but they ran anyway.
I never spoke to them,
    but they preached away.
If they'd have bothered to sit down and meet with me,
    they'd have preached my Message to my people.
They'd have gotten them back on the right track,
    gotten them out of their evil ruts.

☩

"Am I not a God near at hand"—GOD's Decree—
    "and not a God far off?
Can anyone hide out in a corner
    where I can't see him?"
      GOD's Decree.
"Am I not present everywhere,
    whether seen or unseen?"
      GOD's Decree.

⊹

"I know what they're saying, all these prophets who preach lies using me as their text, saying 'I had this dream! I had this dream!' How long do I have to put up with this? Do these prophets give two cents about me as they preach their lies and spew out their grandiose delusions? They swap dreams with one another, feed on each other's delusive dreams, trying to distract my people from me just as their ancestors were distracted by the no-god Baal.

"You prophets who do nothing but dream—
    go ahead and tell your silly dreams.
But you prophets who have a message from me—
    tell it truly and faithfully.
What does straw have in common with wheat?
    Nothing else is like GOD's Decree.
Isn't my Message like fire?" GOD's Decree.
    "Isn't it like a sledgehammer busting a rock?

"I've had it with the 'prophets' who get all their sermons second-hand from each other. Yes, I've had it with them. They make up stuff and then pretend it's a real sermon.

"Oh yes, I've had it with the prophets who preach the lies they dream up, spreading them all over the country, ruining the lives of my people with their cheap and reckless lies.

"I never sent these prophets, never authorized a single one of them. They do nothing for this people—*nothing*!" GOD's Decree.

"And anyone, including prophets and priests, who asks, 'What's GOD got to say about all this, what's troubling him?' tell him, 'You, you're the trouble, and I'm getting rid of you.'" GOD's Decree.

"And if anyone, including prophets and priests, goes around saying glibly 'GOD's Message! GOD's Message!' I'll punish him and his family.

"Instead of claiming to know what GOD says, ask questions of one another, such as 'How do we understand GOD in this?' But don't go around pretending to know it all, saying 'God told me this . . . God told me that. . . .' I don't want to hear it anymore. Only the person I authorize speaks for me. Otherwise, my Message gets twisted, the Message of the living GOD-of-the-Angel-Armies.

"You can ask the prophets, 'How did GOD answer you? What did he tell you?' But don't pretend that you know all the answers yourselves and talk like you know it all. I'm telling you: Quit the 'God told me this . . . God told me that . . .' kind of talk.

"Are you paying attention? You'd better, because I'm about to take you in hand and throw you to the ground, you and this entire city that I gave to your ancestors. I've had it with the lot of you. You're never going to live this down. You're going down in history as a disgrace."

24

TWO BASKETS OF FIGS

GOD showed me two baskets of figs placed in front of the Temple of GOD. This was after Nebuchadnezzar king of Babylon had taken Jehoiachin son of Jehoiakim king of Judah from Jerusalem into exile in Babylon, along with the leaders of Judah, the craftsmen, and the skilled laborers. In one basket the figs were of the finest quality, ripe and ready to eat. In the other basket the figs were rotten, so rotten they couldn't be eaten.

GOD said to me, "Jeremiah, what do you see?"

"Figs," I said. "Excellent figs of the finest quality, and also rotten figs, so rotten they can't be eaten."

Then GOD told me, "This is the Message from the GOD of Israel: The exiles from here that I've sent off to the land of the Babylonians are like the good figs, and I'll make sure they get good treatment. I'll keep my eye on them so that their lives are good, and I'll bring them back to this land. I'll build them up, not tear them down; I'll plant them, not uproot them.

"And I'll give them a heart to know me, GOD. They'll be my people and I'll be their God, for they'll have returned to me with all their hearts.

"But like the rotten figs, so rotten they can't be eaten, is Zedekiah king of Judah. Rotten figs—that's how I'll treat him and his leaders, along with the survivors here and those down in Egypt. I'll make them something that the whole world will look on as disgusting—repugnant outcasts, their names used as curse words wherever in the world I drive them. And I'll make sure they die like flies—from war, starvation, disease, whatever—until the land I once gave to them and their ancestors is completely rid of them."

25

DON'T FOLLOW THE GOD-FADS OF THE DAY

This is the Message given to Jeremiah for all the people of Judah. It came in the fourth year of Jehoiakim son of Josiah king of Judah. It was the first year of Nebuchadnezzar king of Babylon.

Jeremiah the prophet delivered the Message to all the people of Judah and citizens of Jerusalem:

From the thirteenth year of Josiah son of Amon king of Judah right up to the present day—twenty-three years it's been!—GOD's Word has come to me, and from early each morning to late every night I've passed it on to you. And you haven't listened to a word of it!

Not only that, but GOD also sent a steady stream of prophets to you who were just as persistent as me, and you never listened. They told you, "Turn back—right now, each one of you!—from your evil way of life and bad behavior, and live in the land GOD gave you and your ancestors, the land he intended to give you forever. Don't follow the god-fads of the day, taking up and worshiping these no-gods. Don't make me angry with your god-businesses, making and selling gods—a dangerous business!

"You refused to listen to any of this, and now I am really angry. These god-making businesses of yours are your doom."

The verdict of GOD-of-the-Angel-Armies on all this: "Because you have refused to listen to what I've said, I'm stepping in. I'm sending for the armies out of the north headed by Nebuchadnezzar king of Babylon, my servant in this, and I'm setting them on this land and people and even the surrounding countries. I'm devoting the whole works to total destruction—a horror to top all the horrors in history. And I'll banish every sound of joy—singing, laughter, marriage festivities, genial workmen, candlelit suppers. The whole landscape will be one vast wasteland. These countries will be in subjection to the king of Babylon for seventy years.

"Once the seventy years is up, I'll punish the king of Babylon and the whole nation of Babylon for their sin. Then *they'll* be the wasteland. Everything that I said I'd do to that country, I'll do—everything that's written in this book, everything Jeremiah preached against all the godless nations. Many nations and great kings will make slaves of the Babylonians, paying them back for everything they've done to others. They won't get by with anything." GOD's Decree.

GOD PUTS THE HUMAN RACE ON TRIAL

This is a Message that the GOD of Israel gave me: "Take this cup filled with the wine of my wrath that I'm handing to you. Make all the nations where I send you drink it down. They'll drink it and get drunk, staggering in delirium because of the killing that I'm going to unleash among them."

I took the cup from GOD's hand and made them drink it, all the nations to which he sent me:

Jerusalem and the towns of Judah, along with their kings and leaders, turning them into a vast wasteland, a horror to look at, a cuss word— which, in fact, they now are;

Pharaoh king of Egypt with his attendants and leaders, plus all his people and the melting pot of foreigners collected there;

All the kings of Uz;

All the kings of the Philistines from Ashkelon, Gaza, Ekron, and what's left of Ashdod;

Edom, Moab, and the Ammonites;

All the kings of Tyre, Sidon, and the coastlands across the sea;

Dedan, Tema, Buz, and the nomads on the fringe of the desert;

All the kings of Arabia and the various Bedouin sheiks and chieftains wandering about in the desert;

All the kings of Zimri, Elam, and the Medes;

All the kings from the north countries near and far, one by one;

All the kingdoms on planet Earth . . .

And the king of Sheshak (that is, Babylon) will be the last to drink.

"Tell them, 'These are orders from GOD-of-the-Angel-Armies, the God of Israel: "Drink and get drunk and vomit. Fall on your faces and don't get up again. You're slated for a massacre."'

"If any of them refuse to take the cup from you and drink it, say to them, 'GOD-of-the-Angel-Armies has ordered you to drink. So drink!

"'Prepare for the worst! I'm starting off the catastrophe in the city that I claim as my own, so don't think you are going to get out of it. No, you're not getting out of anything. It's the sword and nothing but the sword against everyone everywhere!'" The GOD-of-the-Angel-Armies' Decree.

"Preach it all, Jeremiah. Preach the entire Message to them. Say:

"'GOD roars like a lion from high heaven;

thunder rolls out from his holy dwelling—
Ear-splitting bellows against his people,
    shouting hurrahs like workers in harvest.
The noise reverberates all over the earth;
    everyone everywhere hears it.
GOD makes his case against the godless nations.
    He's about to put the human race on trial.
For the wicked the verdict is clear-cut:
    death by the sword.'" GOD's Decree.

✝

A Message from GOD-of-the-Angel-Armies:

"Prepare for the worst! Doomsday!
    Disaster is spreading from nation to nation.
A huge storm is about to rage
    all across planet Earth."

✝

Laid end to end, those killed in GOD's judgment that day will stretch
from one end of the earth to the other. No tears will be shed and no
burials conducted. The bodies will be left where they fall, like so much
horse dung fertilizing the fields.

✝

Wail, shepherds! Cry out for help!
    Grovel in the dirt, you masters of flocks!
Time's up—you're slated for the slaughterhouse,
    like a choice ram with its throat cut.
There's no way out for the rulers,
    no escape for those shepherds.
Hear that? Rulers crying for help,
    shepherds of the flock wailing!
GOD is about to ravage their fine pastures.
    The peaceful sheepfolds will be silent with death,
    silenced by GOD's deadly anger.

God will come out into the open
　　like a lion leaping from its cover,
And the country will be torn to pieces,
　　ripped and ravaged by his anger.

26

Change the Way You're Living

At the beginning of the reign of Jehoiakim son of Josiah king of Judah, this Message came from GOD to Jeremiah:

"GOD's Message: Stand in the court of GOD's Temple and preach to the people who come from all over Judah to worship in GOD's Temple. Say everything I tell you to say to them. Don't hold anything back. Just maybe they'll listen and turn back from their bad lives. Then I'll reconsider the disaster that I'm planning to bring on them because of their evil behavior.

"Say to them, 'This is GOD's Message: If you refuse to listen to me and live by my teaching that I've revealed so plainly to you, and if you continue to refuse to listen to my servants the prophets that I tirelessly keep on sending to you—but you've never listened! Why would you start now?— then I'll make this Temple a pile of ruins like Shiloh, and I'll make this city nothing but a bad joke worldwide.'"

Everybody there—priests, prophets, and people—heard Jeremiah preaching this Message in the Temple of GOD. When Jeremiah had finished his sermon, saying everything God had commanded him to say, the priests and prophets and people all grabbed him, yelling, "Death! You're going to die for this! How dare you preach—and using GOD's name!—saying that this Temple will become a heap of rubble like Shiloh and this city be wiped out without a soul left in it!"

All the people mobbed Jeremiah right in the Temple itself.

✝

Officials from the royal court of Judah were told of this. They left the palace immediately and came to GOD's Temple to investigate. They held court on the spot, at the New Gate entrance to GOD's Temple.

The prophets and priests spoke first, addressing the officials, but also the people: "Death to this man! He deserves nothing less than death! He has preached against this city—you've heard the evidence with your own ears."

Jeremiah spoke next, publicly addressing the officials before the crowd: "GOD sent me to preach against both this Temple and city everything that's been reported to you. So do something about it! Change the way you're living, change your behavior. Listen obediently to the Message of your GOD. Maybe GOD will reconsider the disaster he has threatened.

"As for me, I'm at your mercy—do whatever you think is best. But take warning: If you kill me, you're killing an innocent man, and you and the city and the people in it will be liable. I didn't say any of this on my own. GOD sent me and told me what to say. You've been listening to *GOD* speak, not Jeremiah."

The court officials, backed by the people, then handed down their ruling to the priests and prophets: "Acquittal. No death sentence for this man. He has spoken to us with the authority of our GOD."

Then some of the respected leaders stood up and addressed the crowd: "In the reign of Hezekiah king of Judah, Micah of Moresheth preached to the people of Judah this sermon: This is GOD-of-the-Angel-Armies' Message for you:

"'Because of people like you,
    Zion will be turned back into farmland,
Jerusalem end up as a pile of rubble,
    and instead of the Temple on the mountain,
    a few scraggly scrub pines.'

"Did King Hezekiah or anyone else in Judah kill Micah of Moresheth because of that sermon? Didn't Hezekiah honor him and pray for mercy from GOD? And then didn't GOD call off the disaster he had threatened?

"Friends, we're at the brink of bringing a terrible calamity upon ourselves."

✝

(At another time there had been a man, Uriah son of Shemaiah from Kiriath-jearim, who had preached similarly in the name of GOD. He preached against this same city and country just as Jeremiah did. When King Jehoiakim and his royal court heard his sermon, they determined to kill him. Uriah, afraid for his life, went into hiding in Egypt. King Jehoiakim sent Elnathan son of Achbor with a posse of men after him. They brought him back from Egypt and presented him to the king. And the king had him killed. They dumped his body unceremoniously outside the city.

But in Jeremiah's case, Ahikam son of Shaphan stepped forward and took his side, preventing the mob from lynching him.)

27

HARNESS YOURSELVES UP TO THE YOKE

Early in the reign of Zedekiah son of Josiah king of Judah, Jeremiah received this Message from GOD: "Make a harness and a yoke and then harness yourself up. Send a message to the kings of Edom, Moab, Ammon, Tyre, and Sidon. Send it through their ambassadors who have come to Jerusalem to see Zedekiah king of Judah. Give them this charge to take back to their masters: 'This is a Message from GOD-of-the-Angel-Armies, the God of Israel. Tell your masters:

""'I'm the one who made the earth, man and woman, and all the animals in the world. I did it on my own without asking anyone's help and I hand it out to whomever I will. Here and now I give all these lands over to my servant Nebuchadnezzar king of Babylon. I have made even the wild animals subject to him. All nations will be under him, then his son, and then his grandson. Then his country's time will be up and the tables will be turned: *Babylon* will be the underdog servant. But until then, any nation or kingdom that won't submit to Nebuchadnezzar king of Babylon must take the yoke of the king of Babylon and harness up. I'll punish that nation with war and starvation and disease until I've got them where I want them.

""'So don't for a minute listen to all your prophets and spiritualists and fortunetellers, who claim to know the future and who tell you not to give in to the king of Babylon. They're handing you a line of lies, barefaced lies, that will end up putting you in exile far from home. I myself will drive you out of your lands, and that'll be the end of you. But the nation that accepts the yoke of the king of Babylon and does what he says, I'll let that nation stay right where it is, minding its own business."""

Then I gave this same message to Zedekiah king of Judah: "Harness yourself up to the yoke of the king of Babylon. Serve him and his people. Live a long life! Why choose to get killed or starve to death or get sick and die, which is what GOD has threatened to any nation that won't throw its lot in with Babylon? Don't listen to the prophets who are telling you not to submit to the king of Babylon. They're telling you lies, *preaching* lies. GOD's Word on this is, 'I didn't send those prophets, but they keep preaching lies, claiming I sent them. If you listen to them, I'll end up driving you out of here and that will be the end of you, both you and the lying prophets.'"

And finally I spoke to the priests and the people at large: "This is GOD's Message: Don't listen to the preaching of the prophets who keep telling you, 'Trust us: The furnishings, plundered from GOD's Temple, are going to be returned from Babylon any day now.' That's a lie. Don't listen to them. Submit to the king of Babylon and live a long life. Why do something that will destroy this city and leave it a heap of rubble? If they are real prophets and have a Message from GOD, let them come to GOD-of-the-Angel-Armies in prayer so that the furnishings that are still left in GOD's Temple, the king's palace, and Jerusalem aren't also lost to Babylon. That's because GOD-of-the-Angel-Armies has already spoken about the Temple furnishings that remain—the pillars, the great bronze basin, the stands, and all the other bowls and chalices that Nebuchadnezzar king of Babylon didn't take when he took Jehoiachin son of Jehoiakim off to Babylonian exile along with all the leaders of Judah and Jerusalem. He said that the furnishings left behind in the Temple of GOD and in the royal palace and in Jerusalem will be taken off to Babylon and stay there until, in GOD's words, 'I take the matter up again and bring them back where they belong.'"

28

FROM A WOODEN TO AN IRON YOKE

Later that same year (it was in the fifth month of King Zedekiah's fourth year) Hananiah son of Azzur, a prophet from Gibeon, confronted Jeremiah in the Temple of GOD in front of the priests and all the people who were there. Hananiah said:

"This Message is straight from GOD-of-the-Angel-Armies, the God of Israel: 'I will most certainly break the yoke of the king of Babylon. Before two years are out I'll have all the furnishings of GOD's Temple back here, all the things that Nebuchadnezzar king of Babylon plundered and hauled off to Babylon. I'll also bring back Jehoiachin son of Jehoiakim king of Judah and all the exiles who were taken off to Babylon.' GOD's Decree. 'Yes, I will break the king of Babylon's yoke. You'll no longer be in harness to him.'"

Prophet Jeremiah stood up to Prophet Hananiah in front of the priests and all the people who were in GOD's Temple that day. Prophet Jeremiah said, "Wonderful! Would that it were true—that GOD would validate your preaching by bringing the Temple furnishings and all the exiles back from Babylon. But listen to me, listen closely. Listen to what I tell both you and all the people here today: The old prophets, the ones before our time, preached judgment against many countries and kingdoms, warning of war and disaster and plague. So any prophet who preaches that everything is just fine and there's nothing to worry about stands out like a sore thumb. We'll wait and see. If it happens, it happens—and then we'll know that GOD sent him."

At that, Hananiah grabbed the yoke from Jeremiah's shoulders and smashed it. And then he addressed the people: "This is GOD's Message: In just this way I will smash the yoke of the king of Babylon and get him off the neck of all the nations—and within two years."

Jeremiah walked out.

Later, sometime after Hananiah had smashed the yoke from off his shoulders, Jeremiah received this Message from GOD: "Go back to Hananiah and tell him, 'This is GOD's Message: You smashed the wooden yoke-bars; now you've got iron yoke-bars. This is a Message from GOD-of-the-Angel-Armies, Israel's own God: I've put an iron yoke on all these nations. They're harnessed to Nebuchadnezzar king of Babylon. They'll do just what he tells them. Why, I'm even putting him in charge of the wild animals.'"

So prophet Jeremiah told prophet Hananiah, "Hold it, Hananiah! GOD never sent you. You've talked the whole country into believing a pack of lies! And so GOD says, 'You claim to be sent? I'll send you all right—right off the face of the earth! Before the year is out, you'll be dead because you fomented sedition against GOD.'"

Prophet Hananiah died that very year, in the seventh month.

29

PLANS TO GIVE YOU THE FUTURE YOU HOPE FOR

This is the letter that the prophet Jeremiah sent from Jerusalem to what was left of the elders among the exiles, to the priests and prophets and all the exiles whom Nebuchadnezzar had taken to Babylon from Jerusalem, including King Jehoiachin, the queen mother, the government leaders, and all the skilled laborers and craftsmen.

The letter was carried by Elasah son of Shaphan and Gemariah son of Hilkiah, whom Zedekiah king of Judah had sent to Nebuchadnezzar king of Babylon. The letter said:

This is the Message from GOD-of-the-Angel-Armies, Israel's God, to all the exiles I've taken from Jerusalem to Babylon:

"Build houses and make yourselves at home.

"Put in gardens and eat what grows in that country.

"Marry and have children. Encourage your children to marry and have children so that you'll thrive in that country and not waste away.

"Make yourselves at home there and work for the country's welfare.

"Pray for Babylon's well-being. If things go well for Babylon, things will go well for you."

Yes. Believe it or not, this is the Message from GOD-of-the-Angel-Armies, Israel's God: "Don't let all those so-called preachers and know-it-alls who are all over the place there take you in with their lies. Don't pay any attention to the fantasies they keep coming up with to please you. They're a bunch of liars preaching lies—and claiming I sent them! I never sent them, believe me." GOD's Decree!

This is GOD's Word on the subject: "As soon as Babylon's seventy years are up and not a day before, I'll show up and take care of you as I promised and bring you back home. I know what I'm doing. I have it all planned out—plans to take care of you, not abandon you, plans to give you the future you hope for.

"When you call on me, when you come and pray to me, I'll listen.

"When you come looking for me, you'll find me.

"Yes, when you get serious about finding me and want it more than anything else, I'll make sure you won't be disappointed." GOD's Decree.

"I'll turn things around for you. I'll bring you back from all the countries into which I drove you"—GOD's Decree— "bring you home to the place from which I sent you off into exile. You can count on it.

"But for right now, because you've taken up with these newfangled prophets who set themselves up as 'Babylonian specialists,' spreading the word 'GOD sent them just for us!' GOD is setting the record straight: As for the king still sitting on David's throne and all the people left in Jerusalem who didn't go into exile with you, they're facing bad times. GOD-of-the-Angel-Armies says, 'Watch this! Catastrophe is on the way: war, hunger, disease! They're a barrel of rotten apples. I'll rid the country of them through war and hunger and disease. The whole world is going to hold its nose at the smell, shut its eyes at the horrible sight. They'll end up in slum ghettos because they wouldn't listen to a thing I said when I sent my servant-prophets preaching tirelessly and urgently. No, they wouldn't listen to a word I said.'" GOD's Decree.

"And you—you exiles whom I sent out of Jerusalem to Babylon—listen to GOD's Message to you. As far as Ahab son of Kolaiah and Zedekiah son of Maaseiah are concerned, the 'Babylonian specialists' who are preaching lies in my name, I will turn them over to Nebuchadnezzar king of Babylon, who will kill them while you watch. The exiles from Judah will take what they see at the execution and use it as a curse: 'GOD fry you to a crisp like the king of Babylon fried Zedekiah and Ahab in the fire!' Those two men, sex predators and prophet-impostors, got what they deserved. They pulled every woman they got their hands on into bed—their neighbors' wives, no less—and preached lies claiming it was my Message. I never sent those men. I've never had anything to do with them." GOD's Decree.

"They won't get away with a thing. I've witnessed it all."

And this is the Message for Shemaiah the Nehelamite: "GOD-of-the-Angel-Armies, the God of Israel, says: You took it on yourself to send letters to all the people in Jerusalem and to the priest Zephaniah son of Maaseiah and the company of priests. In your letter you told Zephaniah that GOD set you up as priest replacing priest Jehoiadah. He's put you in charge of GOD's Temple and made you responsible for locking up any crazy fellow off the street who takes it into his head to be a prophet.

"So why haven't you done anything about muzzling Jeremiah of Anathoth, who's going around posing as a prophet? He's gone so far as to write to us in Babylon, 'It's going to be a long exile, so build houses and make yourselves at home. Plant gardens and prepare Babylonian recipes.'"

The priest Zephaniah read that letter to the prophet Jeremiah.

✝

Then GOD told Jeremiah, "Send this Message to the exiles. Tell them what GOD says about Shemaiah the Nehelamite: Shemaiah is preaching lies to you. I didn't send him. He is seducing you into believing lies. So this is GOD's verdict: I will punish Shemaiah the Nehelamite and his whole family. He's going to end up with nothing and no one. No one from his family will be around to see any of the good that I am going to do for my people because he has preached rebellion against me." GOD's Decree.

30

DON'T DESPAIR, ISRAEL

This is the Message Jeremiah received from GOD: "GOD's Message, the God of Israel: 'Write everything I tell you in a book.

"'Look. The time is coming when I will turn everything around for my people, both Israel and Judah. I, GOD, say so. I'll bring them back to the land I gave their ancestors, and they'll take up ownership again.'"

This is the way GOD put it to Israel and Judah:

"GOD's Message:

"'Cries of panic are being heard.
  The peace has been shattered.
Ask around! Look around!
  Can men bear babies?
So why do I see all these he-men
  holding their bellies like women in labor,
Faces contorted,
  pale as death?
The blackest of days,
  no day like it ever!
A time of deep trouble for Jacob—
  but he'll come out of it alive.

"'And then I'll enter the darkness.
  I'll break the yoke from their necks,
Cut them loose from the harness.
  No more slave labor to foreigners!

232

They'll serve their GOD
  and the David-King I'll establish for them.

"'So fear no more, Jacob, dear servant.
  Don't despair, Israel.
Look up! I'll save you out of faraway places,
  I'll bring your children back from exile.
Jacob will come back and find life good,
  safe and secure.
I'll be with you. I'll save you.
  I'll finish off all the godless nations
Among which I've scattered you,
  but I won't finish you off.
I'll punish you, but fairly.
  I won't send you off with just a slap on the wrist.'

  "This is GOD's Message:

"'You're a burned-out case,
  as good as dead.
Everyone has given up on you.
  You're hopeless.
All your fair-weather friends have skipped town
  without giving you a second thought.
But I delivered the knockout blow,
  a punishment you will never forget,
Because of the enormity of your guilt,
  the endless list of your sins.
So why all this self-pity, licking your wounds?
  You deserve all this, and more.
Because of the enormity of your guilt,
  the endless list of your sins,
I've done all this to you.

"'Everyone who hurt you will be hurt;
  your enemies will end up as slaves.
Your plunderers will be plundered;
  your looters will become loot.
As for you, I'll come with healing,
  curing the incurable,

Because they all gave up on you
    and dismissed you as hopeless—
    "that good-for-nothing Zion.'"

    "Again, GOD's Message:

"'I'll turn things around for Jacob.
    I'll compassionately come in and rebuild homes.
The town will be rebuilt on its old foundations;
    the mansions will be splendid again.
Thanksgivings will pour out of the windows;
    laughter will spill through the doors.
Things will get better and better.
    Depression days are over.
They'll thrive, they'll flourish.
    The days of contempt will be over.
They'll look forward to having children again,
    to being a community in which I take pride.
I'll punish anyone who hurts them,
    and their prince will come from their own ranks.
One of their own people shall be their leader.
    Their ruler will come from their own ranks.
I'll grant him free and easy access to me.
    Would anyone dare to do that on his own,
    to enter my presence uninvited?' GOD's Decree.

"'And that's it: You'll be my very own people,
    I'll be your very own God.'"

Look out! GOD's hurricane is let loose,
    his hurricane blast,
Spinning the heads of the wicked like dust devils!
    God's raging anger won't let up
Until he's made a clean sweep
    completing the job he began.
When the job's done
    you'll see it's been well done.

☦

31

"And when that happens"—GOD's Decree—
   "it will be plain as the sun at high noon:
I'll be the God of every man, woman, and child in Israel
   and they shall be my very own people."

☩

This is the way GOD put it:

"They found grace out in the desert,
   these people who survived the killing.
Israel, out looking for a place to rest,
   met God out looking for them!"
GOD told them, "I've never quit loving you and never will.
   Expect love, love, and more love!
And so now I'll start over with you and build you up again,
   dear virgin Israel.
You'll resume your singing,
   grabbing tambourines and joining the dance.
You'll go back to your old work of planting vineyards
   on the Samaritan hillsides,
And sit back and enjoy the fruit—
   oh, how you'll enjoy those harvests!
The time's coming when watchmen will call out
   from the hilltops of Ephraim:
'On your feet! Let's go to Zion,
   go to meet our GOD!'"

☩

Oh yes, GOD says so:

"Shout for joy at the top of your lungs for Jacob!
   Announce the good news to the number-one nation!
Raise cheers! Sing praises. Say,
   'GOD has saved his people,
   saved the core of Israel.'

"Watch what comes next:

"I'll bring my people back
    from the north country
And gather them up from the ends of the earth,
    gather those who've gone blind
And those who are lame and limping,
    gather pregnant women,
Even the mothers whose birth pangs have started,
    bring them all back, a huge crowd!

"Watch them come! They'll come weeping for joy
    as I take their hands and lead them,
Lead them to fresh flowing brooks,
    lead them along smooth, uncluttered paths.
Yes, it's because I'm Israel's Father
    and Ephraim's my firstborn son!

"Hear this, nations! GOD's Message!
    Broadcast this all over the world!
Tell them, 'The One who scattered Israel
    will gather them together again.
From now on he'll keep a careful eye on them,
    like a shepherd with his flock.'
I, GOD, will pay a stiff ransom price for Jacob;
    I'll free him from the grip of the Babylonian bully.
The people will climb up Zion's slopes shouting with joy,
    their faces beaming because of GOD's bounty—
Grain and wine and oil,
    flocks of sheep, herds of cattle.
Their lives will be like a well-watered garden,
    never again left to dry up.
Young women will dance and be happy,
    young men and old men will join in.
I'll convert their weeping into laughter,
    lavishing comfort, invading their grief with joy.
I'll make sure that their priests get three square meals a day
    and that my people have more than enough.'" GOD's Decree.

✠

Again, GOD's Message:

"Listen to this! Laments coming out of Ramah,
    wild and bitter weeping.
It's Rachel weeping for her children,
    Rachel refusing all solace.
Her children are gone,
    gone—long gone into exile."
But GOD says, "Stop your incessant weeping,
    hold back your tears.
Collect wages from your grief work." GOD's Decree.
    "They'll be coming back home!
There's hope for your children." GOD's Decree.

"I've heard the contrition of Ephraim.
    Yes, I've heard it clearly, saying,
'You trained me well.
    You broke me, a wild yearling horse, to the saddle.
Now put me, trained and obedient, to use.
    You are my GOD.
After those years of running loose, I repented.
    After you trained me to obedience,
I was ashamed of my past, my wild, unruly past.
    Humiliated, I beat on my chest.
Will I ever live this down?'

"Oh! Ephraim is my dear, dear son,
    my child in whom I take pleasure!
Every time I mention his name,
    my heart bursts with longing for him!
Everything in me cries out for him.
    Softly and tenderly I wait for him." GOD's Decree.

"Set up signposts to mark your trip home.
    Get a good map.
Study the road conditions.
    The road out is the road back.
Come back, dear virgin Israel,
    come back to your hometowns.
How long will you flit here and there, indecisive?
    How long before you make up your fickle mind?

GOD will create a new thing in this land:
A transformed woman will embrace the transforming GOD!"

✛

A Message from Israel's GOD-of-the-Angel-Armies: "When I've turned everything around and brought my people back, the old expressions will be heard on the streets: 'GOD bless you!' . . . 'Oh True Home!' . . . 'Oh Holy Mountain!' All Judah's people, whether in town or country, will get along just fine with each other.

"I'll refresh tired bodies;
I'll restore tired souls."

Just then I woke up and looked around—what a pleasant and satisfying sleep!

✛

"Be ready. The time's coming"—GOD's Decree—"when I will plant people and animals in Israel and Judah, just as a farmer plants seed. And in the same way that earlier I relentlessly pulled up and tore down, took apart and demolished, so now I am sticking with them as they start over, building and planting.
"When that time comes you won't hear the old proverb anymore,

'Parents ate the green apples,
their children got the stomachache.'

No, each person will pay for his own sin. You eat green apples, you're the one who gets sick.

✛

"That's right. The time is coming when I will make a brand-new covenant with Israel and Judah. It won't be a repeat of the covenant I made with their ancestors when I took their hand to lead them out of the land of Egypt. They broke that covenant even though I did my part as their Master." GOD's Decree.
"This is the brand-new covenant that I will make with Israel when the time comes. I will put my law within them—write it on their

238

hearts!—and be their God. And they will be my people. They will no longer go around setting up schools to teach each other about GOD. They'll know me firsthand, the dull and the bright, the smart and the slow. I'll wipe the slate clean for each of them. I'll forget they ever sinned!" GOD's Decree.

IF THIS ORDERED COSMOS EVER FELL TO PIECES

GOD's Message, from the God who lights up the day with sun and
    brightens the night with moon and stars,
Who whips the ocean into a billowy froth,
    whose name is GOD-of-the-Angel-Armies:

"If this ordered cosmos ever fell to pieces,
    fell into chaos before me"—GOD's Decree—
"Then and only then might Israel fall apart
    and disappear as a nation before me."

✠

GOD's Message:

"If the skies could be measured with a yardstick
    and the earth explored to its core,
Then and only then would I turn my back on Israel,
    disgusted with all they've done." GOD's Decree.

✠

"The time is coming"—it's GOD's Decree—"when GOD's city will be rebuilt, rebuilt all the way from the Citadel of Hanamel to the Corner Gate. The master plan will extend west to Gareb Hill and then around to Goath. The whole valley to the south where incinerated corpses are dumped—a death valley if there ever was one!—and all the terraced fields out to the Brook Kidron on the east as far north as the Horse Gate will be consecrated to me as a holy place.

    "This city will never again be torn down or destroyed."

32

KILLING AND DISEASE ARE ON OUR DOORSTEP

The Message Jeremiah received from GOD in the tenth year of Zedekiah king of Judah. It was the eighteenth year of Nebuchadnezzar. At that time the army of the king of Babylon was holding Jerusalem under siege. Jeremiah was shut up in jail in the royal palace. Zedekiah, king of Judah, had locked him up, complaining, "How dare you preach, saying, 'GOD says, "I'm warning you: I will hand this city over to the king of Babylon and he will take it over. Zedekiah king of Judah will be handed over to the Chaldeans right along with the city. He will be handed over to the king of Babylon and forced to face the music. He'll be hauled off to Babylon where he'll stay until I deal with him." GOD's Decree. "Fight against the Babylonians all you want—it won't get you anywhere."'"

Jeremiah said, "GOD's Message came to me like this: 'Prepare yourself! Hanamel, your uncle Shallum's son, is on his way to see you. He is going to say, "Buy my field in Anathoth. You have the legal right to buy it."'

"And sure enough, just as GOD had said, my cousin Hanamel came to me while I was in jail and said, 'Buy my field in Anathoth in the territory of Benjamin, for you have the legal right to keep it in the family. Buy it. Take it over.'

"That did it. I knew it was GOD's Message.

"So I bought the field at Anathoth from my cousin Hanamel. I paid him seventeen silver shekels. I followed all the proper procedures: In the presence of witnesses I wrote out the bill of sale, sealed it, and weighed out the money on the scales. Then I took the deed of purchase—the sealed copy that contained the contract and its conditions and also the open copy—and gave them to Baruch son of Neriah, the son of Mahseiah. All this took place in the presence of my cousin Hanamel and the witnesses who had signed the deed, as the Jews who were at the jail that day looked on.

"Then, in front of all of them, I told Baruch, 'These are orders from GOD-of-the-Angel-Armies, the God of Israel: Take these documents— both the sealed and the open deeds—and put them for safekeeping in a pottery jar. For GOD-of-the-Angel-Armies, the God of Israel, says, "Life is going to return to normal. Homes and fields and vineyards are again going to be bought in this country."'

"And then, having handed over the legal documents to Baruch son of Neriah, I prayed to GOD, 'Dear GOD, my Master, you created earth and sky by your great power—by merely stretching out your arm! There is nothing you can't do. You're loyal in your steadfast love to thousands upon thousands—but you also make children live with the fallout from their parents' sins. Great and powerful God, named GOD-of-the-Angel-Armies, determined in purpose and relentless in following through, you see everything that men and women do and respond appropriately to the way they live, to the things they do.

"'You performed signs and wonders in the country of Egypt and continue to do so right into the present, right here in Israel and everywhere else, too. You've made a reputation for yourself that doesn't diminish. You brought your people Israel out of Egypt with signs and wonders—a powerful deliverance!—by merely stretching out your arm. You gave them this land and solemnly promised to their ancestors a bountiful and fertile land. But when they entered the land and took it over, they didn't listen to you. They didn't do what you commanded. They wouldn't listen to a thing you told them. And so you brought this disaster on them.

"'Oh, look at the siege ramps already set in place to take the city. Killing and starvation and disease are on our doorstep. The Babylonians are attacking! The Word you spoke is coming to pass—it's daily news! And yet you, GOD, the Master, even though it is certain that the city will be turned over to the Babylonians, also told me, "Buy the field. Pay for it in cash. And make sure there are witnesses."'"

☩

Then GOD's Message came again to Jeremiah: "Stay alert! I am GOD, the God of everything living. Is there anything I can't do? So listen to GOD's Message: No doubt about it, I'm handing this city over to the Babylonians and Nebuchadnezzar king of Babylon. He'll take it. The attacking Chaldeans will break through and burn the city down: All those houses whose roofs were used as altars for offerings to Baal and the worship of who knows how many other gods provoked me. It isn't as if this were the first time they had provoked me. The people of Israel and Judah have been doing this for a long time—doing what I hate, making me angry by the way they live." GOD's Decree.

"This city has made me angry from the day they built it, and now I've had my fill. I'm destroying it. I can't stand to look any longer at the wicked lives of the people of Israel and Judah, deliberately making me angry, the whole lot of them—kings and leaders and priests and preachers, in the country and in the city. They've turned their backs on me—won't even look me in the face!—even though I took great pains to teach them how to live. They refused to listen, refused to be taught. Why, they even set up obscene god and goddess statues in the Temple built in my honor—an outrageous desecration! And then they went out and built shrines to the god Baal in the valley of Hinnom, where they burned their children in sacrifice to the god Molech—I can hardly conceive of such evil!—turning the whole country into one huge act of sin.

✝

"But there is also this Message from me, the GOD of Israel, to this city of which you have said, 'In killing and starvation and disease this city will be delivered up to the king of Babylon':

"'Watch for this! I will collect them from all the countries to which I will have driven them in my anger and rage and indignation. Yes, I'll bring them all back to this place and let them live here in peace. They will be my people, I will be their God. I'll make them of one mind and heart, always honoring me, so that they can live good and whole lives, they and their children after them. What's more, I'll make a covenant with them that will last forever, a covenant to stick with them no matter what, and work for their good. I'll fill their hearts with a deep respect for me so they'll not even *think* of turning away from me.

"'Oh how I'll rejoice in them! Oh how I'll delight in doing good things for them! Heart and soul, I'll plant them in this country and keep them here!'

"Yes, this is GOD's Message: 'I will certainly bring this huge catastrophe on this people, but I will also usher in a wonderful life of prosperity. I promise. Fields are going to be bought here again, yes, in this very country that you assume is going to end up desolate—gone to the dogs, unlivable, wrecked by the Babylonians. Yes, people will buy farms again, and legally, with deeds of purchase, sealed documents, proper witnesses—and right here in the territory of Benjamin, and in the area around Jerusalem, around the villages of Judah and the hill country, the Shephelah and the Negev. I will restore everything that was lost.' GOD's Decree."

33

Things You Could Never Figure Out on Your Own

While Jeremiah was still locked up in jail, a second Message from God was given to him:

"This is God's Message, the God who made earth, made it livable and lasting, known everywhere as God: 'Call to me and I will answer you. I'll tell you marvelous and wondrous things that you could never figure out on your own.'

"This is what God, the God of Israel, has to say about what's going on in this city, about the homes of both people and kings that have been demolished, about all the ravages of war and the killing by the Chaldeans, and about the streets littered with the dead bodies of those killed because of my raging anger—about all that's happened because the evil actions in this city have turned my stomach in disgust.

"But now take another look. I'm going to give this city a thorough renovation, working a true healing inside and out. I'm going to show them life whole, life brimming with blessings. I'll restore everything that was lost to Judah and Jerusalem. I'll build everything back as good as new. I'll scrub them clean from the dirt they've done against me. I'll forgive everything they've done wrong, forgive all their rebellions. And Jerusalem will be a center of joy and praise and glory for all the countries on earth. They'll get reports on all the good I'm doing for her. They'll be in awe of the blessings I am pouring on her.

"Yes, God's Message: 'You're going to look at this place, these empty and desolate towns of Judah and streets of Jerusalem, and say, "A wasteland. Unlivable. Not even a dog could live here." But the time is coming when you're going to hear laughter and celebration, marriage festivities, people exclaiming, "Thank God-of-the-Angel-Armies. He's so good! His love never quits," as they bring thank offerings into God's Temple. I'll restore everything that was lost in this land. I'll make everything as good as new.' I, God, say so.

"God-of-the-Angel-Armies says: 'This coming desolation, unfit for even a stray dog, is once again going to become a pasture for shepherds who care for their flocks. You'll see flocks everywhere—in the mountains around the towns of the Shephelah and Negev, all over the territory of Benjamin, around Jerusalem and the towns of Judah—flocks under the care of shepherds who keep track of each sheep.' God says so.

A Fresh and True Shoot From the David-Tree

"'Watch for this: The time is coming'—God's Decree—'when I will keep the promise I made to the families of Israel and Judah. When that time comes, I will make a fresh and true shoot sprout from the David-Tree. He will run this country honestly and fairly. He will set things right. That's when Judah will be secure and Jerusalem live in safety. The motto for the city will be, "God Has Set Things Right for Us." God has made it clear that there will always be a descendant of David ruling the people of Israel and that there will always be Levitical priests on hand to offer burnt offerings, present grain offerings, and carry on the sacrificial worship in my honor.'"

✝

God's Message to Jeremiah: "God says, 'If my covenant with day and my covenant with night ever fell apart so that day and night became haphazard and you never knew which was coming and when, then and only then would my covenant with my servant David fall apart and his descendants no longer rule. The same goes for the Levitical priests who serve me. Just as you can't number the stars in the sky nor measure the sand on the seashore, neither will you be able to account for the descendants of David my servant and the Levites who serve me.'"

✝

God's Message to Jeremiah: "Have you heard the saying that's making the rounds: 'The two families God chose, Israel and Judah, he disowned'? And have you noticed that my people are treated with contempt, with rumors afoot that there's nothing to them anymore?

"Well, here's God's response: 'If my covenant with day and night wasn't in working order, if sky and earth weren't functioning the way I set them going, then, but only then, you might think I had disowned the descendants of Jacob and of my servant David, and that I wouldn't set up any of David's descendants over the descendants of Abraham, Isaac, and Jacob. But as it is, I will give them back everything they've lost. The last word is, I will have mercy on them.'"

34

FREEDOM TO THE SLAVES

GOD's Message to Jeremiah at the time King Nebuchadnezzar of Babylon mounted an all-out attack on Jerusalem and all the towns around it with his armies and allies and everyone he could muster:

"I, GOD, the God of Israel, direct you to go and tell Zedekiah king of Judah: 'This is GOD's Message. Listen to me. I am going to hand this city over to the king of Babylon, and he is going to burn it to the ground. And don't think you'll get away. You'll be captured and be his prisoner. You will have a personal confrontation with the king of Babylon and be taken off with him, captive, to Babylon.

"'But listen, oh Zedekiah king of Judah, to the rest of the Message of GOD. You won't be killed. You'll die a peaceful death. They will honor you with funeral rites as they honored your ancestors, the kings who preceded you. They will properly mourn your death, weeping, "Master, master!" This is a solemn promise. GOD's Decree.'"

The prophet Jeremiah gave this Message to Zedekiah king of Judah in Jerusalem, gave it to him word for word. It was at the very time that the king of Babylon was mounting his all-out attack on Jerusalem and whatever cities in Judah that were still standing—only Lachish and Azekah, as it turned out (they were the only fortified cities left in Judah).

✝

GOD delivered a Message to Jeremiah after King Zedekiah made a covenant with the people of Jerusalem to decree freedom to the slaves who were Hebrews, both men and women. The covenant stipulated that no one in Judah would own a fellow Jew as a slave. All the leaders and people who had signed the covenant set free the slaves, men and women alike.

But a little while later, they reneged on the covenant, broke their promise and forced their former slaves to become slaves again.

Then Jeremiah received this Message from GOD: "GOD, the God of Israel, says, 'I made a covenant with your ancestors when I delivered them out of their slavery in Egypt. At the time I made it clear: "At the end of seven years, each of you must free any fellow Hebrew who has had to sell himself to you. After he has served six years, set him free." But your ancestors totally ignored me.

245

"'And now, *you*—what have you done? First you turned back to the right way and did the right thing, decreeing freedom for your brothers and sisters—and you made it official in a solemn covenant in my Temple. And then you turned right around and broke your word, making a mockery of both me and the covenant, and made them all slaves again, these men and women you'd just set free. You forced them back into slavery.

"'So here is what I, GOD, have to say: You have not obeyed me and set your brothers and sisters free. Here is what I'm going to do: I'm going to set *you* free—GOD's Decree—free to get killed in war or by disease or by starvation. I'll make you a spectacle of horror. People all over the world will take one look at you and shudder. Everyone who violated my covenant, who didn't do what was solemnly promised in the covenant ceremony when they split the young bull into two halves and walked between them, all those people that day who walked between the two halves of the bull—leaders of Judah and Jerusalem, palace officials, priests, and all the rest of the people—I'm handing the lot of them over to their enemies who are out to kill them. Their dead bodies will be carrion food for vultures and stray dogs.

"'As for Zedekiah king of Judah and his palace staff, I'll also hand them over to their enemies, who are out to kill them. The army of the king of Babylon has pulled back for a time, but not for long, for I'm going to issue orders that will bring them back to this city. They'll attack and take it and burn it to the ground. The surrounding cities of Judah will fare no better. I'll turn them into ghost towns, unlivable and unlived in.'" GOD's Decree.

35

MEETING IN GOD'S TEMPLE

The Message that Jeremiah received from GOD ten years earlier, during the time of Jehoiakim son of Josiah king of Israel:

"Go visit the Rechabite community. Invite them to meet with you in one of the rooms in GOD's Temple. And serve them wine."

So I went and got Jaazaniah son of Jeremiah, son of Habazziniah, along with all his brothers and sons—the whole community of the Rechabites as it turned out—and brought them to GOD's Temple and to the meeting room of Hanan son of Igdaliah, a man of God. It was next to the meeting room of the Temple officials and just over the apartment of Maaseiah son of Shallum, who was in charge of Temple affairs.

Then I set out chalices and pitchers of wine for the Rechabites and said, "A toast! Drink up!"

But they wouldn't do it. "We don't drink wine," they said. "Our ancestor Jonadab son of Rechab commanded us, 'You are not to drink wine, you or your children, ever. Neither shall you build houses or settle down, planting fields and gardens and vineyards. Don't own property. Live in tents as nomads so that you will live well and prosper in a wandering life.'

"And we've done it, done everything Jonadab son of Rechab commanded. We and our wives, our sons and daughters, drink no wine at all. We don't build houses. We don't have vineyards or fields or gardens. We live in tents as nomads. We've listened to our ancestor Jonadab and we've done everything he commanded us.

"But when Nebuchadnezzar king of Babylon invaded our land, we said, 'Let's go to Jerusalem and get out of the path of the Chaldean and Aramean armies, find ourselves a safe place.' That's why we're living in Jerusalem right now."

WHY WON'T YOU LEARN YOUR LESSON?

Then Jeremiah received this Message from GOD: "GOD-of-the-Angel-Armies, the God of Israel, wants you to go tell the people of Judah and the citizens of Jerusalem that I say, 'Why won't you learn your lesson and do what I tell you?' GOD's Decree. 'The commands of Jonadab son of Rechab to his sons have been carried out to the letter. He told them not to drink wine, and they haven't touched a drop to this very day. They honored and obeyed their ancestor's command. But look at you! I have gone to a lot of trouble to get your attention, and you've ignored me. I sent prophet after prophet to you, all of them my servants, to tell you from early morning to late at night to change your life, make a clean break with your evil past and do what is right, to not take up with every Tom, Dick, and Harry of a god that comes down the pike, but settle down and be faithful in this country I gave your ancestors.

"'And what do I get from you? Deaf ears. The descendants of Jonadab son of Rechab carried out to the letter what their ancestor commanded them, but this people ignores me.'

"So here's what is going to happen. GOD-of-the-Angel-Armies, the God of Israel, says, 'I will bring calamity down on the heads of the people of Judah and Jerusalem—the very calamity I warned you was coming—because you turned a deaf ear when I spoke, turned your backs when I called.'"

Then, turning to the Rechabite community, Jeremiah said, "And this is what GOD-of-the-Angel-Armies, the God of Israel, says to you: 'Because you have done what Jonadab your ancestor told you, obeyed his commands and followed through on his instructions, receive this Message from GOD-of-the-Angel-Armies, the God of Israel: "There will always be a descendant of Jonadab son of Rechab at my service! Always!"'"

36

READING GOD'S MESSAGE

In the fourth year of Jehoiakim son of Josiah king of Judah, Jeremiah received this Message from GOD:

"Get a scroll and write down everything I've told you regarding Israel and Judah and all the other nations from the time I first started speaking to you in Josiah's reign right up to the present day.

"Maybe the community of Judah will finally get it, finally understand the catastrophe that I'm planning for them, turn back from their bad lives, and let me forgive their perversity and sin."

So Jeremiah called in Baruch son of Neriah. Jeremiah dictated and Baruch wrote down on a scroll everything that GOD had said to him.

Then Jeremiah told Baruch, "I'm blacklisted. I can't go into GOD's Temple, so you'll have to go in my place. Go into the Temple and read everything you've written at my dictation. Wait for a day of fasting when everyone is there to hear you. And make sure that all the people who come from the Judean villages hear you.

"Maybe, just maybe, they'll start praying and GOD will hear their prayers. Maybe they'll turn back from their bad lives. This is no light matter. GOD has certainly let them know how angry he is!"

Baruch son of Neriah did everything Jeremiah the prophet told him to do. In the Temple of GOD he read the Message of GOD from the scroll.

It came about in December of the fifth year of Jehoiakim son of Josiah king of Judah that all the people of Jerusalem, along with all the people from the Judean villages, were there in Jerusalem to observe a fast to GOD.

Baruch took the scroll to the Temple and read out publicly the words of Jeremiah. He read from the meeting room of Gemariah son of

Shaphan the secretary of state, which was in the upper court right next to the New Gate of GOD's Temple. Everyone could hear him.

The moment Micaiah the son of Gemariah heard what was being read from the scroll—GOD's Message!—he went straight to the palace and to the chambers of the secretary of state where all the government officials were holding a meeting: Elishama the secretary, Delaiah son of Shemaiah, Elnathan son of Achbor, Gemariah son of Shaphan, Zedekiah son of Hananiah, and all the other government officials.

Micaiah reported everything he had heard Baruch read from the scroll as the officials listened.

Immediately they dispatched Jehudi son of Nethaniah, son of Semaiah, son of Cushi, to Baruch, ordering him, "Take the scroll that you have read to the people and bring it here." So Baruch went and retrieved the scroll.

The officials told him, "Sit down. Read it to us, please." Baruch read it.

When they had heard it all, they were upset. They talked it over. "We've got to tell the king all this."

They asked Baruch, "Tell us, how did you come to write all this? Was it at Jeremiah's dictation?"

Baruch said, "That's right. Every word right from his own mouth. And I wrote it down, word for word, with pen and ink."

The government officials told Baruch, "You need to get out of here. Go into hiding, you and Jeremiah. Don't let anyone know where you are!"

The officials went to the court of the palace to report to the king, having put the scroll for safekeeping in the office of Elishama the secretary of state. The king sent Jehudi to get the scroll. He brought it from the office of Elishama the secretary. Jehudi then read it to the king and the officials who were in the king's service.

It was December. The king was sitting in his winter quarters in front of a charcoal fire. After Jehudi would read three or four columns, the king would cut them off the scroll with his pocketknife and throw them in the fire. He continued in this way until the entire scroll had been burned up in the fire.

Neither the king nor any of his officials showed the slightest twinge of conscience as they listened to the messages read. Elnathan, Delaiah, and Gemariah tried to convince the king not to burn the scroll, but he brushed them off. He just plowed ahead and ordered Prince Jerahameel, Seraiah son of Azriel, and Shelemiah son of Abdeel to arrest Jeremiah the prophet and his secretary Baruch. But GOD had hidden them away.

☩

After the king had burned the scroll that Baruch had written at Jeremiah's dictation, Jeremiah received this Message from GOD: "Get another blank scroll and do it all over again. Write out everything that was in that first scroll that Jehoiakim king of Judah burned up.

"And send this personal message to Jehoiakim king of Judah: 'GOD says, You had the gall to burn this scroll and then the nerve to say, "What kind of nonsense is this written here—that the king of Babylon will come and destroy this land and kill everything in it?"

"'Well, do you want to know what GOD says about Jehoiakim king of Judah? This: No descendant of his will ever rule from David's throne. His corpse will be thrown in the street and left unburied, exposed to the hot sun and the freezing night. I will punish him and his children and the officials in his government for their blatant sin. I'll let loose on them and everyone in Jerusalem the doomsday disaster of which I warned them but they spit at.'"

So Jeremiah went and got another scroll and gave it to Baruch son of Neriah, his secretary. At Jeremiah's dictation he again wrote down everything that Jehoiakim king of Judah had burned in the fire. There were also generous additions, but of the same kind of thing.

37

IN AN UNDERGROUND DUNGEON

King Zedekiah son of Josiah, a puppet king set on the throne by Nebuchadnezzar king of Babylon in the land of Judah, was now king in place of Jehoiachin son of Jehoiakim. But neither he nor his officials nor the people themselves paid a bit of attention to the Message GOD gave by Jeremiah the prophet.

However, King Zedekiah sent Jehucal son of Shelemiah, and Zephaniah the priest, son of Maaseiah, to Jeremiah the prophet, saying, "Pray for us—pray hard!—to the Master, our GOD."

Jeremiah was still moving about freely among the people in those days. This was before he had been put in jail. Pharaoh's army was marching up from Egypt. The Chaldeans fighting against Jerusalem heard that the Egyptians were coming and pulled back.

Then Jeremiah the prophet received this Message from GOD: "I, the

God of Israel, want you to give this Message to the king of Judah, who has just sent you to me to find out what he should do. Tell him, 'Get this: Pharaoh's army, which is on its way to help you, isn't going to stick it out. No sooner will they get here than they'll leave and go home to Egypt. And then the Babylonians will come back and resume their attack, capture this city and burn it to the ground. I, God, am telling you: Don't kid yourselves, reassuring one another, "The Babylonians will leave in a few days." I tell you, they aren't leaving. Why, even if you defeated the entire attacking Chaldean army and all that was left were a few wounded soldiers in their tents, the wounded would still do the job and burn this city to the ground.'"

✢

When the Chaldean army pulled back from Jerusalem, Jeremiah left Jerusalem to go over to the territory of Benjamin to take care of some personal business. When he got to the Benjamin Gate, the officer on guard there, Irijah son of Shelemiah, son of Hananiah, grabbed Jeremiah the prophet, accusing him, "You're deserting to the Chaldeans!"

"That's a lie," protested Jeremiah. "I wouldn't think of deserting to the Chaldeans."

But Irijah wouldn't listen to him. He arrested him and took him to the police. The police were furious with Jeremiah. They beat him up and threw him into jail in the house of Jonathan the secretary of state. (They were using the house for a prison cell.) So Jeremiah entered an underground cell in a cistern turned into a dungeon. He stayed there a long time.

Later King Zedekiah had Jeremiah brought to him. The king questioned him privately, "Is there a Message from God?"

"There certainly is," said Jeremiah. "You're going to be turned over to the king of Babylon."

Jeremiah continued speaking to King Zedekiah: "Can you tell me why you threw me into prison? What crime did I commit against you or your officials or this people? And tell me, whatever has become of your prophets who preached all those sermons saying that the king of Babylon would never attack you or this land? Listen to me, please, my master—my king! Please don't send me back to that dungeon in the house of Jonathan the secretary. I'll die there!"

So King Zedekiah ordered that Jeremiah be assigned to the courtyard of the palace guards. He was given a loaf of bread from Bakers' Alley every day until all the bread in the city was gone. And that's where Jeremiah remained—in the courtyard of the palace guards.

38

<small>From the Dungeon to the Palace</small>

Shaphatiah son of Mattan, Gedaliah son of Pashur, Jehucal son of Shelemiah, and Pashur son of Malkijah heard what Jeremiah was telling the people, namely:

"This is God's Message: 'Whoever stays in this town will die—will be killed or starve to death or get sick and die. But those who go over to the Babylonians will save their necks and live.'

"And, God's sure Word: 'This city is destined to fall to the army of the king of Babylon. He's going to take it over.'"

These officials told the king, "Please, kill this man. He's got to go! He's ruining the resolve of the soldiers who are still left in the city, as well as the people themselves, by spreading these words. This man isn't looking after the good of this people. He's trying to ruin us!"

King Zedekiah caved in: "If you say so. Go ahead, handle it your way. You're too much for me."

So they took Jeremiah and threw him into the cistern of Malkijah the king's son that was in the courtyard of the palace guard. They lowered him down with ropes. There wasn't any water in the cistern, only mud. Jeremiah sank into the mud.

Ebed-melek the Ethiopian, a court official assigned to the royal palace, heard that they had thrown Jeremiah into the cistern. While the king was holding court in the Benjamin Gate, Ebed-melek went immediately from the palace to the king and said, "My master, oh king—these men are committing a great crime in what they're doing, throwing Jeremiah the prophet into the cistern and leaving him there to starve. He's as good as dead. There isn't a scrap of bread left in the city."

So the king ordered Ebed-melek the Ethiopian, "Get three men and pull Jeremiah the prophet out of the cistern before he dies."

Ebed-melek got three men and went to the palace wardrobe and got some scraps of old clothing, which they tied together and lowered down with ropes to Jeremiah in the cistern. Ebed-melek the Ethiopian called down to Jeremiah, "Put these scraps of old clothing under your armpits and around the ropes."

Jeremiah did what he said.

And so they pulled Jeremiah up out of the cistern by the ropes. But he was still confined in the courtyard of the palace guard.

Later, King Zedekiah sent for Jeremiah the prophet and had him brought to the third entrance of the Temple of GOD. The king said to Jeremiah, "I'm going to ask you something. Don't hold anything back from me."

Jeremiah said, "If I told you the whole truth, you'd kill me. And no matter what I said, you wouldn't pay any attention anyway."

Zedekiah swore to Jeremiah right there, but in secret, "As sure as GOD lives, who gives *us* life, I won't kill you, nor will I turn you over to the men who are trying to kill you."

So Jeremiah told Zedekiah, "This is the Message from GOD, God-of-the-Angel-Armies, the God of Israel: 'If you will turn yourself over to the generals of the king of Babylon, you will live, this city won't be burned down, and your family will live. But if you don't turn yourself over to the generals of the king of Babylon, this city will go into the hands of the Chaldeans and they'll burn it down. And don't for a minute think there's any escape for you.'"

King Zedekiah said to Jeremiah, "But I'm afraid of the Judeans who have already deserted to the Chaldeans. If they get hold of me, they'll rough me up good."

Jeremiah assured him, "They won't get hold of you. Listen, please. Listen to GOD's voice. I'm telling you this for your own good so that you'll live. But if you refuse to turn yourself over, this is what GOD has shown me will happen: Picture this in your mind—all the women still left in the palace of the king of Judah, led out to the officers of the king of Babylon, and as they're led out they are saying:

"'They lied to you and did you in,
    those so-called friends of yours;
And now you're stuck, about knee-deep in mud,
    and your "friends," where are they now?'

"They'll take all your wives and children and give them to the Chaldeans. And you, don't think you'll get out of this—the king of Babylon will seize you and then burn this city to the ground."

Zedekiah said to Jeremiah, "Don't let anyone know of this conversation, if you know what's good for you. If the government officials get wind that I've been talking with you, they may come and say, 'Tell us what went on between you and the king, what you said and what he said. Hold nothing back and we won't kill you.' If this happens, tell them, 'I presented my case to the king so that he wouldn't send me back to the dungeon of Jonathan to die there.'"

And sure enough, all the officials came to Jeremiah and asked him. He responded as the king had instructed. So they quit asking. No one had overheard the conversation.

Jeremiah lived in the courtyard of the palace guards until the day that Jerusalem was captured.

39

BAD NEWS, NOT GOOD NEWS

In the ninth year and tenth month of Zedekiah king of Judah, Nebuchadnezzar king of Babylon came with his entire army and laid siege to Jerusalem. In the eleventh year and fourth month, on the ninth day of Zedekiah's reign, they broke through into the city.

All the officers of the king of Babylon came and set themselves up as a ruling council from the Middle Gate: Nergal-sharezer of Simmagar, Nebushazban the Rabsaris, Nergal-sharezer the Rabmag, along with all the other officials of the king of Babylon.

When Zedekiah king of Judah and his remaining soldiers saw this, they ran for their lives. They slipped out at night on a path in the king's garden through the gate between two walls and headed for the wilderness, toward the Jordan Valley. The Babylonian army chased them and caught Zedekiah in the wilderness of Jericho. They seized him and took him to Nebuchadnezzar king of Babylon at Riblah in the country of Hamath. Nebuchadnezzar decided his fate. The king of Babylon killed all the sons of Zedekiah in Riblah right before his eyes and then killed all the nobles of Judah. After Zedekiah had seen the slaughter, Nebuchadnezzar blinded him, chained him up, and then took him off to Babylon.

Meanwhile, the Babylonians burned down the royal palace, the Temple, and all the homes of the people. They leveled the walls of Jerusalem. Nebuzaradan, commander of the king's bodyguard, rounded up everyone left in the city, along with those who had surrendered to him, and herded them off to exile in Babylon. He didn't bother taking the few poor people who had nothing. He left them in the land of Judah to eke out a living as best they could in the vineyards and fields.

✜

Nebuchadnezzar king of Babylon gave Nebuzaradan captain of the king's bodyguard special orders regarding Jeremiah: "Look out for him. Make sure nothing bad happens to him. Give him anything he wants."

So Nebuzaradan, chief of the king's bodyguard, along with Neb-ushazban the Rabsaris, Nergal-sharezer the Rabmag, and all the chief officers of the king of Babylon, sent for Jeremiah, taking him from the courtyard of the royal guards and putting him under the care of Gedaliah son of Ahikam, the son of Shaphan, to be taken home. And so he was able to live with the people.

✜

Earlier, while Jeremiah was still in custody in the courtyard of the royal guards, GOD's Message came to him: "Go and speak with Ebed-melek the Ethiopian. Tell him, 'GOD-of-the-Angel-Armies, the God of Israel, says, "Listen carefully: I will do exactly what I said I would do to this city—bad news, not good news. When it happens, you will be there to see it. But I'll deliver you on that doomsday. You won't be handed over to those men whom you have good reason to fear. Yes, I'll most certainly save you. You won't be killed. You'll walk out of there safe and sound because you trusted me."'" GOD's Decree.

40

GO AND LIVE WHEREVER YOU WISH

GOD's Message to Jeremiah after Nebuzaradan captain of the bodyguard set him free at Ramah. When Nebuzaradan came upon him, he was in chains, along with all the other captives from Jerusalem and Judah who were being herded off to exile in Babylon.

The captain of the bodyguard singled out Jeremiah and said to him, "Your GOD pronounced doom on this place. GOD came and did what he had warned he'd do because you all sinned against GOD and wouldn't do what he told you. So now you're all suffering the consequences.

"But today, Jeremiah, I'm setting you free, taking the chains off your hands. If you'd like to come to Babylon with me, come along. I'll take good care of you. But if you don't want to come to Babylon with me, that's just fine, too. Look, the whole land stretches out before you. Do what you like. Go and live wherever you wish. If you want to stay home, go back to Gedaliah son of Ahikam son of Shaphan. The king of Babylon made him governor of the cities of Judah. Stay with him and your people. Or go wherever you'd like. It's up to you."

The captain of the bodyguard gave him food for the journey and a parting gift, and sent him off.

Jeremiah went to Gedaliah son of Ahikam at Mizpah and made his home with him and the people who were left behind in the land.

TAKE CARE OF THE LAND

When the army leaders and their men, who had been hiding out in the fields, heard that the king of Babylon had appointed Gedaliah son of Ahikam as governor of the land, putting him in charge of the men, women, and children of the poorest of the poor who hadn't been taken off to exile in Babylon, they came to Gedaliah at Mizpah: Ishmael son of Nethaniah, Johanan and Jonathan the sons of Kareah, Seraiah son of Tanhumeth, the sons of Ephai the Netophathite, and Jaazaniah son of the Maacathite, accompanied by their men.

Gedaliah son of Ahikam, the son of Shaphan, promised them and their men, "You have nothing to fear from the Chaldean officials. Stay here on the land. Be subject to the king of Babylon. You'll get along just fine.

"My job is to stay here in Mizpah and be your advocate before the Chaldeans when they show up. Your job is take care of the land: Make wine, harvest the summer fruits, press olive oil. Store it all in pottery jugs and settle into the towns that you have taken over."

The Judeans who had escaped to Moab, Ammon, Edom, and other countries heard that the king of Babylon had left a few survivors in Judah and made Gedaliah son of Ahikam, son of Shaphan, governor over them. They all started coming back to Judah from all the places where they'd been scattered. They came to Judah and to Gedaliah at Mizpah and went to work gathering in a huge supply of wine and summer fruits.

☩

One day Johanan son of Kareah and all the officers of the army who had been hiding out in the back country came to Gedaliah at Mizpah and told him, "You know, don't you, that Baaliss king of Ammon has sent Ishmael son of Nethaniah to kill you?" But Gedaliah son of Ahikam didn't believe them.

Then Johanan son of Kareah took Gedaliah aside privately in Mizpah: "Let me go and kill Ishmael son of Nethaniah. No one needs to know about it. Why should we let him kill you and plunge the land into anarchy? Why let everyone you've taken care of be scattered and what's left of Judah destroyed?"

But Gedaliah son of Ahikam told Johanan son of Kareah, "Don't do it. I forbid it. You're spreading a false rumor about Ishmael."

41
MURDER

But in the seventh month, Ishmael son of Nethaniah, son of Elishama, came. He had royal blood in his veins and had been one of the king's high-ranking officers. He paid a visit to Gedaliah son of Ahikam at Mizpah with ten of his men. As they were eating together, Ishmael and his ten men jumped to their feet and knocked Gedaliah down and killed him, killed the man the king of Babylon had appointed governor of the land. Ishmael also killed all the Judeans who were with Gedaliah in Mizpah, as well as the Chaldean soldiers who were stationed there.

On the second day after the murder of Gedaliah—no one yet knew of it—men arrived from Shechem, Shiloh, and Samaria, eighty of them, with their beards shaved, their clothing ripped, and gashes on their bodies. They were pilgrims carrying grain offerings and incense on their way to worship at the Temple in Jerusalem.

Ishmael son of Nethaniah went out from Mizpah to welcome them, weeping ostentatiously. When he greeted them he invited them in: "Come and meet Gedaliah son of Ahikam."

But as soon as they were inside the city, Ishmael son of Nethaniah and his henchmen slaughtered the pilgrims and dumped the bodies in a cistern. Ten of the men talked their way out of the massacre. They bargained with Ishmael, "Don't kill us. We have a hidden store of wheat, barley, olive oil, and honey out in the fields." So he held back and didn't kill them with their fellow pilgrims.

Ishmael's reason for dumping the bodies into a cistern was to cover up the earlier murder of Gedaliah. The cistern had been built by king

Asa as a defense against Baasha king of Israel. This was the cistern that Ishmael son of Nethaniah filled with the slaughtered men.

Ishmael then took everyone else in Mizpah, including the king's daughters entrusted to the care of Gedaliah son of Ahikam by Nebuzaradan the captain of the bodyguard, as prisoners. Rounding up the prisoners, Ishmael son of Nethaniah proceeded to take them over into the country of Ammon.

Johanan son of Kareah and all the army officers with him heard about the atrocities committed by Ishmael son of Nethaniah. They set off at once after Ishmael son of Nethaniah. They found him at the large pool at Gibeon.

When all the prisoners from Mizpah who had been taken by Ishmael saw Johanan son of Kareah and the army officers with him, they couldn't believe their eyes. They were so happy! They all rallied around Johanan son of Kareah and headed back home. But Ishmael son of Nethaniah got away, escaping from Johanan with eight men into the land of Ammon.

Then Johanan son of Kareah and the army officers with him gathered together what was left of the people whom Ishmael son of Nethaniah had taken prisoner from Mizpah after the murder of Gedaliah son of Ahikam—men, women, children, eunuchs—and brought them back from Gibeon.

They set out at once for Egypt to get away from the Chaldeans, stopping on the way at Geruth-kimham near Bethlehem. They were afraid of what the Chaldeans might do in retaliation of Ishmael son of Nethaniah's murder of Gedaliah son of Ahikam, whom the king of Babylon had appointed as governor of the country.

42

What You Fear Will Catch Up With You

All the army officers, led by Johanan son of Kareah and Jezaniah son of Hoshaiah, accompanied by all the people, small and great, came to Jeremiah the prophet and said, "We have a request. Please listen. Pray to your GOD for us, what's left of us. You can see for yourself how few we are! Pray that your GOD will tell us the way we should go and what we should do."

Jeremiah the prophet said, "I hear your request. And I will pray to your GOD as you have asked. Whatever GOD says, I'll pass on to you.

I'll tell you everything, holding nothing back."

They said to Jeremiah, "Let GOD be our witness, a true and faithful witness against us, if we don't do everything that your GOD directs you to tell us. Whether we like it or not, we'll do it. We'll obey whatever our GOD tells us. Yes, count on us. We'll do it."

Ten days later GOD's Message came to Jeremiah. He called together Johanan son of Kareah and all the army officers with him, including all the people, regardless of how much clout they had.

He then spoke: "This is the Message from GOD, the God of Israel, to whom you sent me to present your prayer. He says, 'If you are ready to stick it out in this land, I will build you up and not drag you down, I will plant you and not pull you up like a weed. I feel deep compassion on account of the doom I have visited on you. You don't have to fear the king of Babylon. Your fears are for nothing. I'm on your side, ready to save and deliver you from anything he might do. I'll pour mercy on you. What's more, *he* will show you mercy! He'll let you come back to your very own land.'

"But do not say, 'We're not staying around this place,' refusing to obey the command of your GOD and saying instead, 'No! We're off to Egypt, where things are peaceful—no wars, no attacking armies, plenty of food. We're going to live there.' If what's left of Judah is headed down that road, then listen to GOD's Message. This is what GOD-of-the-Angel-Armies says: 'If you have determined to go to Egypt and make that your home, then the very wars you fear will catch up with you in Egypt and the starvation you dread will track you down in Egypt. You'll die there! Every last one of you who is determined to go to Egypt and make it your home will either be killed, starve, or get sick and die. No survivors, not one! No one will escape the doom that I'll bring upon you.'

"This is the Message from GOD-of-the-Angel-Armies, the God of Israel: 'In the same way that I swept the citizens of Jerusalem away with my anger and wrath, I'll do the same thing all over again in Egypt. You'll end up being cursed, reviled, ridiculed, and mocked. And you'll never see your homeland again.'

"GOD has plainly told you, you leftovers from Judah, 'Don't go to Egypt.' Could anything be plainer? I warn you this day that you are living out a fantasy. You're making a fatal mistake.

"Didn't you just now send me to your GOD, saying, 'Pray for us to our GOD. Tell us everything that GOD says and we'll do it all'?

"Well, now I've told you, told you everything he said, and you haven't obeyed a word of it, not a single word of what your GOD sent me to tell you. So now let me tell you what will happen next: You'll be killed, you'll starve to death, you'll get sick and die in the wonderful country where you've determined to go and live."

43

DEATH! EXILE! SLAUGHTER!

When Jeremiah finished telling all the people the whole Message that their GOD had sent him to give them—all these words—Azariah son of Hoshaiah and Johanan son of Kareah, backed by all the self-important men, said to Jeremiah, "Liar! Our GOD never sent you with this message telling us not to go to Egypt and live there. Baruch son of Neriah is behind this. He has turned you against us. He's playing into the hands of the Babylonians so we'll either end up being killed or taken off to exile in Babylon."

Johanan son of Kareah and the army officers, and the people along with them, wouldn't listen to GOD's Message that they stay in the land of Judah and live there.

Johanan son of Kareah and the army officers gathered up everyone who was left from Judah, who had come back after being scattered all over the place—the men, women, and children, the king's daughters, all the people that Nebuzaradan captain of the bodyguard had left in the care of Gedaliah son of Ahikam, the son of Shaphan, and last but not least, Jeremiah the prophet and Baruch son of Neriah. They entered the land of Egypt in total disobedience of GOD's Message and arrived at the city of Tahpanhes.

While in Tahpanhes, GOD's Word came to Jeremiah: "Pick up some large stones and cover them with mortar in the vicinity of the pavement that leads up to the building set aside for Pharaoh's use in Tahpanhes. Make sure some of the men of Judah are watching.

"Then address them: 'This is what GOD-of-the-Angel-Armies says: "Be on the lookout! I'm sending for and bringing Nebuchadnezzar the king of Babylon—my servant, mind you!—and he'll set up his throne on these stones that I've had buried here and he'll spread out his canopy over them. He'll come and absolutely smash Egypt, sending each to his assigned fate: death, exile, slaughter. He'll burn down the temples of Egypt's gods. He'll either burn up the gods or haul them off as booty. Like a shepherd who picks lice from his robes, he'll pick Egypt clean. And then he'll walk away without a hand being laid on him. He'll shatter the sacred obelisks at Egypt's House of the Sun and make a huge bonfire of the temples of Egypt's gods.""

44

THE SAME FATE WILL FALL UPON ALL

The Message that Jeremiah received for all the Judeans who lived in the land of Egypt, who had their homes in Migdol, Tahpanhes, Noph, and the land of Pathros: "This is what GOD-of-the-Angel-Armies, the God of Israel, says: 'You saw with your own eyes the terrible doom that I brought down on Jerusalem and the Judean cities. Look at what's left: ghost towns of rubble and smoking ruins, and all because they took up with evil ways, making me angry by going off to offer sacrifices and worship the latest in gods—no-gods that neither they nor you nor your ancestors knew the first thing about. Morning after morning and long into the night I kept after you, sending you all those prophets, my servants, begging you, "Please, please—don't do this, don't fool around in this loathsome gutter of gods that I hate with a passion." But do you think anyone paid the least bit of attention or repented of evil or quit offering sacrifices to the no-gods? Not one. So I let loose with my anger, a firestorm of wrath in the cities of Judah and the streets of Jerusalem, and left them in ruins and wasted. And they're *still* in ruins and wasted.'

"This is the Message of GOD, God-of-the-Angel-Armies, the God of Israel: 'So why are you ruining your lives by amputating yourselves—man, woman, child, and baby—from the life of Judah, leaving yourselves isolated, unconnected? And why do you deliberately make me angry by what you do, offering sacrifices to these no-gods in the land of Egypt where you've come to live? You'll only destroy yourselves and make yourselves an example used in curses and an object of ridicule among all the nations of the earth.

"'Have you so soon forgotten the evil lives of your ancestors, the evil lives of the kings of Judah and their wives, to say nothing of your own evil lives, you and your wives, the evil you flaunted in the land of Judah and the streets of Jerusalem? And to this day, there's not a trace of remorse, not a sign of reverence, nobody caring about living by what I tell them or following my instructions that I've set out so plainly before you and your parents! So this is what GOD-of-the-Angel-Armies decrees:

"'Watch out! I've decided to bring doom on you and get rid of everyone connected with Judah. I'm going to take what's left of Judah, those who have decided to go to Egypt and live there, and finish them off. In Egypt they will either be killed or starve to death. The same fate will fall upon both the obscure and the important. Regardless of their status, they will either be killed or starve. You'll end up cursed, reviled, ridiculed, and mocked. I'll give those who are in Egypt the same medicine I gave those in Jerusalem: massacre, starvation, and disease. None of those who managed to get out of Judah alive and get away to Egypt are going to make it back to the Judah for which they're so homesick. None will make it back, except maybe a few fugitives.'"

MAKING GODDESS COOKIES

The men who knew that their wives had been burning sacrifices to the no-gods, joined by a large crowd of women, along with virtually everyone living in Pathros of Egypt, answered Jeremiah: "We're having nothing to do with what you tell us is GOD's Message. We're going to go right on offering sacrifices to the Queen of Heaven and pouring out drink offerings to her, keeping up the traditions set by our ancestors, our kings and government leaders in the cities of Judah and the streets of Jerusalem in the good old days. We had a good life then—lots of food, rising standard of living, and no bad luck. But the moment we quit sacrificing to the Queen of Heaven and pouring out offerings to her, everything fell apart. We've had nothing but massacres and starvation ever since."

And then the women chimed in: "Yes! Absolutely! We're going to keep at it, offering sacrifices to the Queen of Heaven and pouring out offerings to her. Aren't our husbands behind us? They like it that we make goddess cookies and pour out our offerings to her."

✦

Then Jeremiah spoke up, confronting the men and the women, all the people who had answered so insolently. He said, "The sacrifices that you and your parents, your kings, your government officials, and the common people of the land offered up in the cities of Judah and the streets of Jerusalem—don't you think GOD noticed? He noticed, all right. And he got fed up. Finally, he couldn't take your evil behavior and your disgusting acts any longer. Your land became a wasteland, a death valley, a horror story, a ghost town. And it continues to be just that. This doom has come upon you because you kept offering all those sacrifices, and you sinned against GOD! You refused to listen to him, wouldn't live the way he directed, ignored the covenant conditions."

Jeremiah kept going, but now zeroed in on the women: "Listen, all you who are from Judah and living in Egypt—please, listen to GOD's Word. GOD-of-the-Angel-Armies, the God of Israel, says: 'You women! You said it and then you did it. You said, "We're going to keep the vows we made to sacrifice to the Queen of Heaven and pour out offerings to her, and nobody's going to stop us!"'

"Well, go ahead. Keep your vows. Do it up big. But also listen to what GOD has to say about it, all you who are from Judah but live in Egypt: 'I swear by my great name, backed by everything I am—this is GOD speaking!—that never again shall my name be used in vows, such as "As sure as the Master, GOD, lives!" by anyone in the whole country of Egypt. I've targeted each one of you for doom. The good is gone for good.

"'All the Judeans in Egypt will die off by massacre or starvation until they're wiped out. The few who get out of Egypt alive and back to Judah will be *very* few, hardly worth counting. Then that ragtag bunch that left Judah to live in Egypt will know who had the last word.

"'And this will be the evidence: I will bring punishment right here, and by this you'll know that the decrees of doom against you are the real thing. Watch for this sign of doom: I will give Pharaoh Hophra king of Egypt over to his enemies, those who are out to kill him, exactly as I gave Zedekiah king of Judah to his enemy Nebuchadnezzar, who was after him.'"

45

GOD'S PILING ON THE PAIN

This is what Jeremiah told Baruch one day in the fourth year of Jehoiakim's reign as he was taking dictation from the prophet:

"These are the words of GOD, the God of Israel, to you, Baruch. You say, 'These are bad times for me! It's one thing after another. GOD is piling on the pain. I'm worn out and there's no end in sight.'

"But GOD says, 'Look around. What I've built I'm about to wreck, and what I've planted I'm about to rip up. And I'm doing it everywhere—all over the whole earth! So forget about making any big plans for yourself. Things are going to get worse before they get better. But don't worry. I'll keep you alive through the whole business.'"

46

You Vainly Collect Medicines

God's Messages through the prophet Jeremiah regarding the godless nations.

The Message to Egypt and the army of Pharaoh Neco king of Egypt at the time it was defeated by Nebuchadnezzar king of Babylon while camped at Carchemish on the Euphrates River in the fourth year of the reign of Jehoiakim king of Judah:

"'Present arms!
    March to the front!
Harness the horses!
    Up in the saddles!
Battle formation! Helmets on,
    spears sharpened, armor in place!'
But what's this I see?
    They're scared out of their wits!
They break ranks and run for cover.
    Their soldiers panic.
They run this way and that,
    stampeding blindly.
It's total chaos, total confusion, danger everywhere!"
    God's Decree.

"The swiftest runners won't get away,
    the strongest soldiers won't escape.
In the north country, along the river Euphrates,
    they'll stagger, stumble, and fall.

"Who is this like the Nile in flood?
    like its streams torrential?
Why, it's Egypt like the Nile in flood,
    like its streams torrential,
Saying, 'I'll take over the world.
    I'll wipe out cities and peoples.'

Run, horses!
Roll, chariots!
Advance, soldiers
from Cush and Put with your shields,
Soldiers from Lud,
experts with bow and arrow.

"But it's not your day. It's the Master's, me, GOD-of-the-Angel-
Armies—
the day when I have it out with my enemies,
The day when Sword puts an end to my enemies,
when Sword exacts vengeance.
I, the Master, GOD-of-the-Angel-Armies,
will pile them on an altar—a huge sacrifice!—
In the great north country,
along the mighty Euphrates.

"Oh, virgin Daughter Egypt,
climb into the mountains of Gilead, get healing balm.
You will vainly collect medicines,
for nothing will be able to cure what ails you.
The whole world will hear your anguished cries.
Your wails fill the earth,
As soldier falls against soldier
and they all go down in a heap."

EGYPT'S ARMY SLITHERS LIKE A SNAKE

The Message that GOD gave to the prophet Jeremiah when Nebuchadnezzar king of Babylon was on his way to attack Egypt:

"Tell Egypt, alert Migdol,
post warnings in Noph and Tahpanhes:
'Wake up! Be prepared!
War's coming!'

"Why will your bull-god Apis run off?
Because GOD will drive him off.
Your ragtag army will fall to pieces.
The word is passing through the ranks,

'Let's get out of here while we still can.
    Let's head for home and save our skins.'
When they get home they'll nickname Pharaoh
    'Big-Talk-Bad-Luck.'
As sure as I am the living God"
    —the King's Decree, GOD-of-the-Angel-Armies is his name—
"A conqueror is coming: like Tabor, singular among mountains;
    like Carmel, jutting up from the sea!
So pack your bags for exile,
    you coddled daughters of Egypt,
For Memphis will soon be nothing,
    a vacant lot grown over with weeds.

"Too bad, Egypt, a beautiful sleek heifer
    attacked by a horsefly from the north!
All her hired soldiers are stationed to defend her—
    like well-fed calves they are.
But when their lives are on the line, they'll run off,
    cowards every one.
When the going gets tough,
    they'll take the easy way out.

"Egypt will slither and hiss like a snake
    as the enemy army comes in force.
They will rush in, swinging axes
    like lumberjacks cutting down trees.
They'll level the country"—GOD's Decree—"nothing
    and no one standing for as far as you can see.
The invaders will be a swarm of locusts,
    innumerable, past counting.
Daughter Egypt will be ravished,
    raped by vandals from the north."

GOD-of-the-Angel-Armies, the God of Israel, says, "Watch out when I visit doom on the god Amon of Thebes, Egypt and its gods and kings, Pharaoh and those who trust in him. I'll turn them over to those who are out to kill them, to Nebuchadnezzar and his military. Egypt will be set back a thousand years. Eventually people will live there again." GOD's Decree.

✠

"But you, dear Jacob my servant, you have nothing to fear.
      Israel, there's no need to worry.
Look up! I'll save you from that far country,
      I'll get your children out of the land of exile.
Things are going to be normal again for Jacob,
      safe and secure, smooth sailing.
Yes, dear Jacob my servant, you have nothing to fear.
      Depend on it, I'm on your side.
I'll finish off all the godless nations
      among which I've scattered you,
But I won't finish you off.
      I have more work left to do on you.
I'll punish you, but fairly.
      No, I'm not finished with you yet."

47

IT'S DOOMSDAY FOR PHILISTINES

GOD's Message to the prophet Jeremiah regarding the Philistines just before Pharaoh attacked Gaza. This is what GOD says:

"Look out! Water will rise in the north country,
      swelling like a river in flood.
The torrent will flood the land,
      washing away city and citizen.
Men and women will scream in terror,
      wails from every door and window,
As the thunder from the hooves of the horses will be heard,
      the clatter of chariots, the banging of wheels.
Fathers, paralyzed by fear,
      won't even grab up their babies
Because it will be doomsday for Philistines, one and all,
      no hope of help for Tyre and Sidon.
GOD will finish off the Philistines,
      what's left of those from the island of Crete.
Gaza will be shaved bald as an egg,
      Ashkelon struck dumb as a post.

You're on your last legs.
    How long will you keep flailing?

"Oh, Sword of GOD,
    how long will you keep this up?
Return to your scabbard.
    Haven't you had enough? Can't you call it quits?

"But how can it quit
    when I, GOD, command the action?
I've ordered it to cut down
    Ashkelon and the seacoast."

48

GET OUT WHILE YOU CAN!

The Message on Moab from GOD-of-the-Angel-Armies, the God of Israel:

"Doom to Nebo! Leveled to the ground!
    Kiriathaim demeaned and defeated,
The mighty fortress reduced to a molehill,
    Moab's glory—dust and ashes.
Conspirators plot Heshbon's doom:
    'Come, let's wipe Moab off the map.'
Dungface Dimon will loudly lament,
    as killing follows killing.
Listen! A cry out of Horonaim:
    'Disaster—doom and more doom!'
Moab will be shattered.
    Her cries will be heard clear down in Zoar.
Up the ascent of Luhith
    climbers weep,
And down the descent from Horonaim,
    cries of loss and devastation.
Oh, run for your lives! Get out while you can!
    Survive by your wits in the wild!
You trusted in thick walls and big money, yes?
    But it won't help you now.
Your big god Chemosh will be hauled off,

268

his priests and managers with him.
A wrecker will wreck every city.
    Not a city will survive.
The valley fields will be ruined,
    the plateau pastures destroyed, just as I told you.
Cover the land of Moab with salt.
    Make sure nothing ever grows here again.
Her towns will all be ghost towns.
    Nobody will ever live here again.
Sloppy work in GOD's name is cursed,
    and cursed all halfhearted use of the sword.

"Moab has always taken it easy—
    lazy as a dog in the sun,
Never had to work for a living,
    never faced any trouble,
Never had to grow up,
    never once worked up a sweat.
But those days are a thing of the past.
    I'll put him to work at hard labor.
That will wake him up to the world of hard knocks.
    That will smash his illusions.
Moab will be as ashamed of god Chemosh
    as Israel was ashamed of her Bethel calf-gods,
    the calf-gods she thought were so great.
For how long do you think you'll be saying, 'We're tough.
    We can beat anyone anywhere'?
The destruction of Moab has already begun.
    Her choice young soldiers are lying dead right now."
The King's Decree—
    his full name, GOD-of-the-Angel-Armies.
"Yes. Moab's doom is on countdown,
    disaster targeted and launched.
Weep for Moab, friends and neighbors,
    all who know how famous he's been.
Lament, 'His mighty scepter snapped in two like a toothpick,
    that magnificent royal staff!'

"Come down from your high horse, pampered beauty of Dibon.
    Sit in dog dung.

The destroyer of Moab will come against you.
> He'll wreck your safe, secure houses.
Stand on the roadside,
> pampered women of Aroer.
Interview the refugees who are running away.
> Ask them 'What's happened? And why?'
Moab will be an embarrassing memory, nothing left of the place.
> Wail and weep your eyes out!
Tell the bad news along the Arnon river.
> Tell the world that Moab is no more.

"My judgment will come to the plateau cities: on Holon, Jahzah, and Mephaath; on Dibon, Nebo, and Beth-diblathaim; on Kiriathaim, Beth-gamul, and Beth-meon; on Kerioth, Bozrah, and all the cities of Moab, far and near.

"Moab's link to power is severed.
> Moab's arm is broken." GOD's Decree.

THE SHEER NOTHINGNESS OF MOAB

"Turn Moab into a drunken sot, drunk on the wine of my wrath, a dung-faced drunk, filling the country with vomit—Moab a falling-down drunk, a joke in bad taste. Wasn't it you, Moab, who made crude jokes over Israel? And when they were caught in bad company, didn't you cluck and gossip and snicker?

"Leave town! Leave! Look for a home in the cliffs,
> you who grew up in Moab.
Try living like a dove
> who nests high in the river gorge.

"We've all heard of Moab's pride,
> that legendary pride,
The strutting, bullying, puffed-up pride,
> the insufferable arrogance.
I know"—GOD's Decree—"his rooster-crowing pride,
> the inflated claims, the sheer nothingness of Moab.
But I will weep for Moab,
> yes, I will mourn for the people of Moab.
> I will even mourn for the people of Kir-heres.

270

I'll weep for the grapevines of Sibmah
    and join Jazer in her weeping—
Grapevines that once reached the Dead Sea
    with tendrils as far as Jazer.
Your summer fruit and your bursting grapes
    will be looted by brutal plunderers,
Lush Moab stripped
    of song and laughter.
And yes, I'll shut down the winepresses,
    stop all the shouts and hurrahs of harvest.

"Heshbon and Elealeh will cry out, and the people in Jahaz will hear the cries. They will hear them all the way from Zoar to Horonaim and Eglath-shelishiyah. Even the waters of Nimrim will be dried up.

"I will put a stop in Moab"— God's Decree— "to all hiking to the high places to offer burnt sacrifices to the gods.

"My heart moans for Moab, for the men of Kir-heres, like soft flute sounds carried by the wind. They've lost it all. They've got nothing.

"Everywhere you look are signs of mourning:
    heads shaved, beards cut,
Hands scratched and bleeding,
    clothes ripped and torn.

"In every house in Moab there'll be loud lamentation, on every street in Moab, loud lamentation. As with a pottery jug that no one wants, I'll smash Moab to bits." God's Decree.

"Moab ruined!
    Moab shamed and ashamed to be seen!
Moab a cruel joke!
    The stark horror of Moab!"

☩

God's verdict on Moab. Indeed!

"Look! An eagle is about to swoop down
    and spread its wings over Moab.

The towns will be captured,
    the fortresses taken.
Brave warriors will double up in pain, helpless to fight,
    like a woman giving birth to a baby.
There'll be nothing left of Moab, nothing at all,
    because of his defiant arrogance against me.

"Terror and pit and trap
    are what you have facing you, Moab." GOD's Decree.
"A man running in terror
    will fall into a trap.
A man climbing out of a pit
    will be caught in a trap.
This is my agenda for Moab
    on doomsday." GOD's Decree.

"On the outskirts of Heshbon,
    refugees will pull up short, worn out.
Fire will flame high from Heshbon,
    a firestorm raging from the capital of Sihon's kingdom.
It will burn off Moab's eyebrows,
    will scorch the skull of the braggarts.
That's all for you, Moab!
    You worshipers of Chemosh will be finished off!
Your sons will be trucked off to prison camps;
    your daughters will be herded into exile.
But yet there's a day that's coming
    when I'll put things right in Moab.

    "For now, that's the judgment on Moab."

49

YOU'RE A BROKEN-DOWN HAS-BEEN

GOD's Message on the Ammonites:

"Doesn't Israel have any children,
    no one to step into her inheritance?
So why is the god Milcom taking over Gad's land,

his followers moving into its towns?
But not for long! The time's coming"
   —GOD's Decree—
"When I'll fill the ears of Rabbah, Ammon's big city,
   with battle cries.
She'll end up a pile of rubble,
   all her towns burned to the ground.
Then Israel will kick out the invaders.
   I, GOD, say so, and it will *be* so.
Wail Heshbon, Ai is in ruins.
   Villages of Rabbah, wring your hands!
Dress in mourning, weep buckets of tears.
   Go into hysterics, run around in circles!
Your god Milcom will be hauled off to exile,
   and all his priests and managers right with him.
Why do you brag of your once-famous strength?
   You're a broken-down has-been, a cast-off
Who fondles his trophies and dreams of glory days
   and vainly thinks, 'No one can lay a hand on me.'
Well, think again. I'll face you with terror from all sides."
   Word of the Master, GOD-of-the-Angel-Armies.
"You'll be stampeded headlong,
   with no one to round up the runaways.
Still, the time will come
   when I will make things right with Ammon." GOD's Decree.

STRUTTING ACROSS THE STAGE OF HISTORY

The Message of GOD-of-the-Angel-Armies on Edom:

"Is there nobody wise left in famous Teman?
   no one with a sense of reality?
Has their wisdom gone wormy and rotten?
   Run for your lives! Get out while you can!
Find a good place to hide,
   you who live in Dedan!
I'm bringing doom to Esau.
   It's time to settle accounts.
When harvesters work your fields,
   don't they leave gleanings?

When burglars break into your house,
    don't they take only what they want?
But I'll strip Esau clean.
    I'll search out every nook and cranny.
I'll destroy everything connected with him,
    children and relatives and neighbors.
There'll be no one left who will be able to say,
    'I'll take care of your orphans.
    Your widows can depend on me.'"

Indeed. GOD says, "I tell you, if there are people who have to drink
the cup of God's wrath even though they don't deserve it, why would
you think you'd get off? You won't get off. You'll drink it. Oh yes, you'll
drink every drop. And as for Bozrah, your capital, I swear by all that I
am"—GOD's Decree—"that that city will end up a pile of charred ruins,
a stinking garbage dump, an obscenity—and all her daughter-cities
with her."

I've just heard the latest from GOD.
    He's sent an envoy to the nations:
"Muster your troops and attack Edom.
    Present arms! Go to war!"

"Ah, Edom, I'm dropping you to last place among nations,
    the bottom of the heap, kicked around.
You think you're so great—
    strutting across the stage of history,
Living high in the impregnable rocks,
    acting like king of the mountain.
You think you're above it all, don't you,
    like an eagle in its aerie?
Well, you're headed for a fall.
    I'll bring you crashing to the ground." GOD's Decree.

"Edom will end up trash. Stinking, despicable trash. A wonder of
the world in reverse. She'll join Sodom and Gomorrah and their neighbors in the sewers of history." GOD says so.

"No one will live there,
    no mortal soul move in there.

"Watch this: Like a lion coming up
    from the thick jungle of the Jordan
Looking for prey in the mountain pastures,
    I will come upon Edom and pounce.
I'll take my pick of the flock—and who's to stop me?
    The shepherds of Edom are helpless before me."

So, listen to this plan that GOD has worked out against Edom, the
blueprint of what he's prepared for those who live in Teman:

"Believe it or not, the young, the vulnerable—
    mere lambs and kids—will be dragged off.
Believe it or not, the flock
    in shock, helpless to help, will watch it happen.
The very earth will shudder because of their cries,
    cries of anguish heard at the distant Red Sea.
Look! An eagle soars, swoops down,
    spreads its wings over Bozrah.
Brave warriors will double up in pain, helpless to fight,
    like a woman giving birth to a baby."

THE BLOOD WILL DRAIN FROM THE FACE OF DAMASCUS

The Message on Damascus:

"Hamath and Arpad will be in shock
    when they hear the bad news.
Their hearts will melt in fear
    as they pace back and forth in worry.
The blood will drain from the face of Damascus
    as she turns to flee.
Hysterical, she'll fall to pieces,
    disabled, like a woman in childbirth.
And now how lonely—bereft, abandoned!
    The once famous city, the once happy city.
Her bright young men dead in the streets,
    her brave warriors silent as death.
On that day"—Decree of GOD-of-the-Angel-Armies—
    "I'll start a fire at the wall of Damascus
    that will burn down all of Ben-hadad's forts."

FIND A SAFE PLACE TO HIDE

The Message on Kedar and the sheikdoms of Hazor who were attacked
by Nebuchadnezzar king of Babylon. This is GOD's Message:

"On your feet! Attack Kedar!
    Plunder the Bedouin nomads from the east.
    Grab their blankets and pots and pans.
Steal their camels.
    Traumatize them, shouting, 'Terror! Death! Doom!
Danger everywhere!'
    Oh, run for your lives,
You nomads from Hazor." GOD's Decree.
    "Find a safe place to hide.
Nebuchadnezzar king of Babylon
    has plans to wipe you out,
    to go after you with a vengeance:
'After them,' he says. 'Go after these relaxed nomads
    who live free and easy in the desert,
Who live in the open with no doors to lock,
    who live off by themselves.'
Their camels are there for the taking,
    their herds and flocks, easy picking.
I'll scatter them to the four winds,
    these defenseless nomads on the fringes of the desert.
I'll bring terror from every direction.
    They won't know what hit them." GOD's Decree.
"Jackals will take over the camps of Hazor,
    camps abandoned to wind and sand.
No one will live there,
    no mortal soul move in there."

THE WINDS WILL BLOW AWAY ELAM

GOD's Message to the prophet Jeremiah on Elam at the outset of the reign
of Zedekiah king of Judah. This is what GOD-of-the-Angel-Armies says:

"Watch this! I'll break Elam's bow,
    her weapon of choice, across my knee.
Then I'll let four winds loose on Elam,
    winds from the four corners of earth.

I'll blow them away in all directions,
  landing homeless Elamites in every country on earth.
They'll live in constant fear and terror
  among enemies who want to kill them.
I'll bring doom on them,
  my anger-fueled doom.
I'll set murderous hounds on their heels
  until there's nothing left of them.
And then I'll set up my throne in Elam,
  having thrown out the king and his henchmen.
But the time will come when I make
  everything right for Elam again." GOD's Decree.

50

GET OUT OF BABYLON AS FAST AS YOU CAN

The Message of GOD through the prophet Jeremiah on Babylon, land
of the Chaldeans:

"Get the word out to the nations! Preach it!
  Go public with this, broadcast it far and wide:
Babylon taken, god-Bel hanging his head in shame,
  god-Marduk exposed as a fraud.
All her god-idols shuffling in shame,
  all her play-gods exposed as cheap frauds.
For a nation will come out of the north to attack her,
  reduce her cities to rubble.
Empty of life—no animals, no people—
  not a sound, not a movement, not a breath.

"In those days, at that time"—GOD's Decree—
  "the people of Israel will come,
And the people of Judah with them.
  Walking and weeping, they'll seek me, their GOD.
They'll ask directions to Zion
  and set their faces toward Zion.
They'll come and hold tight to GOD,
  bound in a covenant eternal they'll never forget.

"My people were lost sheep.
    Their shepherds led them astray.
They abandoned them in the mountains
    where they wandered aimless through the hills.
They lost track of home,
    couldn't remember where they came from.
Everyone who met them took advantage of them.
    Their enemies had no qualms:
'Fair game' they said. 'They walked out on GOD.
    They abandoned the True Pasture, the hope of their parents.'

"But now, get out of Babylon as fast as you can.
    Be rid of that Babylonian country.
On your way. Good sheepdogs lead, but don't you be led.
    Lead the way home!
Do you see what I'm doing?
    I'm rallying a host of nations against Babylon.
They'll come out of the north,
    attack and take her.
Oh, they know how to fight, these armies.
    They never come home empty-handed.
Babylon is ripe for picking!
    All her plunderers will fill their bellies!" GOD's Decree.

"You Babylonians had a good time while it lasted, didn't you?
    You lived it up, exploiting and using my people,
Frisky calves romping in lush pastures,
    wild stallions out having a good time!
Well, your mother would hardly be proud of you.
    The woman who bore you wouldn't be pleased.
Look at what's come of you! A nothing nation!
    Rubble and garbage and weeds!
Emptied of life by my holy anger,
    a desert of death and emptiness.
Travelers who pass by Babylon will gasp, appalled,
    shaking their heads at such a comedown.
Gang up on Babylon! Pin her down!
    Throw everything you have against her.
Hold nothing back. Knock her flat.
    She's sinned—oh, how she's sinned, against me!

278

Shout battle cries from every direction.
    All the fight has gone out of her.
Her defenses have been flattened,
    her walls smashed.
'Operation God's Vengeance.'
    Pile on the vengeance!
Do to her as she has done.
    Give her a good dose of her own medicine!
Destroy her farms and farmers,
    ravage her fields, empty her barns.
And you captives, while the destruction rages,
    get out while the getting's good,
    get out fast and run for home.

✠

"Israel is a scattered flock,
    hunted down by lions.
The king of Assyria started the carnage.
    The king of Babylon, Nebuchadnezzar,
Has completed the job,
    gnawing the bones clean."

And now this is what God-of-the-Angel-Armies,
    the God of Israel, has to say:
"Just watch! I'm bringing doom on the king of Babylon and his land,
    the same doom I brought on the king of Assyria.
But Israel I'll bring home to good pastures.
    He'll graze on the hills of Carmel and Bashan,
On the slopes of Ephraim and Gilead.
    He will eat to his heart's content.
In those days and at that time"—God's Decree—
    "they'll look high and low for a sign of Israel's guilt—nothing;
Search nook and cranny for a trace of Judah's sin—nothing.
    These people that I've saved will start out with a clean slate.

✠

"Attack Merathaim, land of rebels!
    Go after Pekod, country of doom!
Hunt them down. Make a clean sweep." God's Decree.

"These are my orders. Do what I tell you.

"The thunderclap of battle
    shakes the foundations!
The Hammer has been hammered,
    smashed and splintered,
Babylon pummeled
    beyond recognition.
I set out a trap and you were caught in it.
    Oh Babylon, you never knew what hit you,
Caught and held in the steel grip of that trap!
    That's what you get for taking on GOD.

"I, GOD, opened my arsenal.
    I brought out my weapons of wrath.
The Master, GOD-of-the-Angel-Armies,
    has a job to do in Babylon.
Come at her from all sides!
    Break into her granaries!
Shovel her into piles and burn her up.
    Leave nothing! Leave no one!
Kill all her young turks.
    Send them to their doom!
Doom to them! Yes, Doomsday!
    The clock has finally run out on them.
And here's a surprise:
    Runaways and escapees from Babylon
Show up in Zion reporting the news of GOD's vengeance,
    taking vengeance for my own Temple.

"Call in the troops against Babylon,
    anyone who can shoot straight!
Tighten the noose!
    Leave no loopholes!
Give her back as good as she gave,
    a dose of her own medicine!
Her brazen insolence is an outrage
    against GOD, the Holy of Israel.
And now she pays: her young strewn dead in the streets,
    her soldiers dead, silent forever." GOD's Decree.

"Do you get it, Mister Pride? I'm your enemy!"
    Decree of the Master, GOD-of-the-Angel-Armies.
"Time's run out on you:
    That's right: It's Doomsday.
Mister Pride will fall flat on his face.
    No one will offer him a hand.
I'll set his towns on fire.
    The fire will spread wild through the country."

✠

And here's more from GOD-of-the-Angel-Armies:

"The people of Israel are beaten down,
    the people of Judah along with them.
Their oppressors have them in a grip of steel.
    They won't let go.
But the Rescuer is strong:
    GOD-of-the-Angel-Armies.
Yes, I will take their side,
    I'll come to their rescue.
I'll soothe their land,
    but rough up the people of Babylon.

"It's all-out war in Babylon"—GOD's Decree—
    "total war against people, leaders, and the wise!
War to the death on her boasting pretenders, fools one and all!
    War to the death on her soldiers, cowards to a man!
War to the death on her hired killers, gutless wonders!
    War to the death on her banks—looted!
War to the death on her water supply—drained dry!
    A land of make-believe gods gone crazy—hobgoblins!
The place will be haunted with jackals and scorpions,
    night-owls and vampire bats.
No one will ever live there again.
    The land will reek with the stench of death.
It will join Sodom and Gomorrah and their neighbors,
    the cities I did away with." GOD's Decree.
"No one will live there again.
    No one will again draw breath in that land, ever.

⊹

"And now, watch this! People pouring
    out of the north, hordes of people,
A mob of kings stirred up
    from faroff places.
Flourishing deadly weapons,
    barbarians they are, cruel and pitiless.
Roaring and relentless, like ocean breakers,
    they come riding fierce stallions,
In battle formation, ready to fight
    you, Daughter Babylon!
Babylon's king hears them coming.
    He goes white as a ghost, limp as a dishrag.
Terror-stricken, he doubles up in pain, helpless to fight,
    like a woman giving birth to a baby.

"And now watch this: Like a lion coming up
    from the thick jungle of the Jordan,
Looking for prey in the mountain pastures,
    I'll take over and pounce.
I'll take my pick of the flock—and who's to stop me?
    All the so-called shepherds are helpless before me."

So, listen to this plan that GOD has worked out against Babylon, the
blueprint of what he's prepared for dealing with Chaldea:

Believe it or not, the young,
    the vulnerable—mere lambs and kids—will be dragged off.
Believe it or not, the flock
    in shock, helpless to help, watches it happen.
When the shout goes up, "Babylon's down!"
    the very earth will shudder at the sound.
    The news will be heard all over the world.

51

HURRICANE PERSIA

There's more. GOD says more:

"Watch this:

I'm whipping up
A death-dealing hurricane against Babylon—'Hurricane Persia'—
    against all who live in that perverse land.
I'm sending a cleanup crew into Babylon.
    They'll clean the place out from top to bottom.
When they get through there'll be nothing left of her
    worth taking or talking about.
They won't miss a thing.
    A total and final Doomsday!
Fighters will fight with everything they've got.
    It's no holds barred.
They will spare nothing and no one.
    It's final and wholesale destruction—the end!
Babylon littered with the wounded,
    streets piled with corpses.
It turns out that Israel and Judah
    are not widowed after all.
As their God, GOD-of-the-Angel-Armies, I am still alive and well,
    committed to them even though
They filled their land with sin
    against Israel's most Holy God.

"Get out of Babylon as fast as you can.
    Run for your lives! Save your necks!
Don't linger and lose your lives to my vengeance on her
    as I pay her back for her sins.
Babylon was a fancy gold chalice
    held in my hand,
Filled with the wine of my anger
    to make the whole world drunk.
The nations drank the wine
    and they've all gone crazy.
Babylon herself will stagger and crash,
    senseless in a drunken stupor—tragic!
Get anointing balm for her wound.
    Maybe she can be cured."

✝

"We did our best, but she can't be helped.
    Babylon is past fixing.
Give her up to her fate.
    Go home.

The judgment on her will be vast,
    a skyscraper-memorial of vengeance.

YOUR LIFELINE IS CUT

"GOD has set everything right for us.
    Come! Let's tell the good news
Back home in Zion.
    Let's tell what our GOD did to set things right.

"Sharpen the arrows!
    Fill the quivers!
GOD has stirred up the kings of the Medes,
    infecting them with war fever: 'Destroy Babylon!'
GOD's on the warpath.
    He's out to avenge his Temple.
Give the signal to attack Babylon's walls.
    Station guards around the clock.
Bring in reinforcements.
    Set men in ambush.
GOD will do what he planned,
    what he said he'd do to the people of Babylon.
You have more water than you need,
    you have more money than you need—
But your life is over,
    your lifeline cut."

☩

GOD-of-the-Angel-Armies has solemnly sworn:
    "I'll fill this place with soldiers.
They'll swarm through here like locusts
    chanting victory songs over you."

☩

By his power he made earth.
    His wisdom gave shape to the world.
    He crafted the cosmos.
He thunders and rain pours down.
    He sends the clouds soaring.
He embellishes the storm with lightnings,

launches the wind from his warehouse.
Stick-god worshipers look mighty foolish!
  god-makers embarrassed by their handmade gods!
Their gods are frauds, dead sticks—
  deadwood gods, tasteless jokes.
They're nothing but stale smoke.
  When the smoke clears, they're gone.
But the Portion-of-Jacob is the real thing;
  he put the whole universe together,
With special attention to Israel.
  His name? GOD-of-the-Angel-Armies!

THEY'LL SLEEP AND NEVER WAKE UP

God says, "You, Babylon, are my hammer,
  my weapon of war.
I'll use you to smash godless nations,
  use you to knock kingdoms to bits.
I'll use you to smash horse and rider,
  use you to smash chariot and driver.
I'll use you to smash man and woman,
  use you to smash the old man and the boy.
I'll use you to smash the young man and young woman,
  use you to smash shepherd and sheep.
I'll use you to smash farmer and yoked oxen,
  use you to smash governors and senators.

"Judeans, you'll see it with your own eyes. I'll pay Babylon and all
the Chaldeans back for all the evil they did in Zion." GOD's Decree.

"I'm your enemy, Babylon, Mount Destroyer,
  you ravager of the whole earth.
I'll reach out, I'll take you in my hand,
  and I'll crush you till there's no mountain left.
I'll turn you into a gravel pit—
  no more cornerstones cut from you,
No more foundation stones quarried from you!
  Nothing left of you but gravel." GOD's Decree.

✠

285

"Raise the signal in the land,
    blow the shofar-trumpet for the nations.
Consecrate the nations for holy work against her.
    Call kingdoms into service against her.
    Enlist Ararat, Minni, and Ashkenaz.
Appoint a field marshal against her,
    and round up horses, locust hordes of horses!
Consecrate the nations for holy work against her—
    the king of the Medes, his leaders and people.

"The very land trembles in terror, writhes in pain,
    terrorized by my plans against Babylon,
Plans to turn the country of Babylon
    into a lifeless moonscape—a wasteland.
Babylon's soldiers have quit fighting.
    They hide out in ruins and caves—
Cowards who've given up without a fight,
    exposed as cowering milksops.
Babylon's houses are going up in flames,
    the city gates torn off their hinges.
Runner after runner comes racing in,
    each on the heels of the last,
Bringing reports to the king of Babylon
    that his city is a lost cause.
The fords of the rivers are all taken.
    Wildfire rages through the swamp grass.
Soldiers desert left and right.
    I, GOD-of-the-Angel-Armies, said it would happen:
'Daughter Babylon is a threshing floor
    at threshing time.
Soon, oh very soon, her harvest will come
    and then the chaff will fly!'

✝

"Nebuchadnezzar king of Babylon
    chewed up my people and spit out the bones.
He wiped his dish clean, pushed back his chair,
    and belched—a huge gluttonous belch.
Lady Zion says,

'The brutality done to me be done to Babylon!'
And Jerusalem says,
    'The blood spilled from me be charged to the Chaldeans!'
Then I, GOD, step in and say,
    'I'm on your side, taking up your cause.
I'm your Avenger. You'll get your revenge.
    I'll dry up her rivers, plug up her springs.
Babylon will be a pile of rubble,
    scavenged by stray dogs and cats,
A dumping ground for garbage,
    a godforsaken ghost town.'

✠

"The Babylonians will be like lions and their cubs,
    ravenous, roaring for food.
I'll fix them a meal, all right—a banquet, in fact.
    They'll drink themselves falling-down drunk.
Dead drunk, they'll sleep—and sleep, and sleep . . .
    and they'll never wake up." GOD's Decree.
"I'll haul these 'lions' off to the slaughterhouse
    like the lambs, rams, and goats,
    never to be heard of again.

✠

"Babylon is finished—
    the pride of the whole earth is flat on her face.
What a comedown for Babylon,
    to end up inglorious in the sewer!
Babylon drowned in chaos,
    battered by waves of enemy soldiers.
Her towns stink with decay and rot,
    the land empty and bare and sterile.
No one lives in these towns anymore.
    Travelers give them a wide berth.
I'll bring doom on the glutton god-Bel in Babylon.
    I'll make him vomit up all he gulped down.
No more visitors stream into this place,
    admiring and gawking at the wonders of Babylon.

The wonders of Babylon are no more.
Run for your lives, my dear people!
    Run, and don't look back!
Get out of this place while you can,
    this place torched by GOD's raging anger.
Don't lose hope. Don't ever give up
    when the rumors pour in hot and heavy.
One year it's this, the next year it's that—
    rumors of violence, rumors of war.
Trust me, the time is coming
    when I'll put the no-gods of Babylon in their place.
I'll show up the whole country as a sickening fraud,
    with dead bodies strewn all over the place.
Heaven and earth, angels and people,
    will throw a victory party over Babylon
When the avenging armies from the north
    descend on her." GOD's Decree!

REMEMBER GOD IN YOUR LONG AND DISTANT EXILE

"Babylon must fall—
    compensation for the war dead in Israel.
Babylonians will be killed
    because of all that Babylonian killing.
But you exiles who have escaped a Babylonian death,
    get out! And fast!
Remember GOD in your long and distant exile.
    Keep Jerusalem alive in your memory."

How we've been humiliated, taunted and abused,
    kicked around for so long that we hardly know who we are!
And we hardly know what to think—
    our old Sanctuary, GOD's house, desecrated by strangers.

"I know, but trust me: The time is coming"
    —GOD's Decree—
"When I will bring doom on her no-god idols,
    and all over this land her wounded will groan.
Even if Babylon climbed a ladder to the moon
    and pulled up the ladder so that no one could get to her,

That wouldn't stop me.
    I'd make sure my avengers would reach her."
    GOD's Decree.

"But now listen! Do you hear it? A cry out of Babylon!
    An unearthly wail out of Chaldea!
GOD is taking his wrecking bar to Babylon.
    We'll be hearing the last of her noise—
Death throes like the crashing of waves,
    death rattles like the roar of cataracts.
The avenging destroyer is about to enter Babylon:
    Her soldiers are taken, her weapons are trashed.
Indeed, GOD is a God who evens things out.
    All end up with their just deserts.

"I'll get them drunk, the whole lot of them—
    princes, sages, governors, soldiers.
Dead drunk, they'll sleep—and sleep and sleep . . .
    and never wake up." The King's Decree.
His name? GOD-of-the-Angel-Armies!

    GOD-of-the-Angel-Armies speaks:

"The city walls of Babylon—those massive walls!—
    will be flattened.
And those city gates—huge gates!—
    will be set on fire.
The harder you work at this empty life,
    the less you are.
Nothing comes of ambition like this
    but ashes."

☩

Jeremiah the prophet gave a job to Seraiah son of Neriah, son of Mahseiah, when Seraiah went with Zedekiah king of Judah to Babylon. It was in the fourth year of Zedekiah's reign. Seraiah was in charge of travel arrangements.

    Jeremiah had written down in a little booklet all the bad things that would come down on Babylon. He told Seraiah, "When you get to

Babylon, read this out in public. Read, 'You, oh GOD, said that you would destroy this place so that nothing could live here, neither human nor animal—a wasteland to top all wastelands, an eternal nothing.'

"When you've finished reading the page, tie a stone to it, throw it into the River Euphrates, and watch it sink. Then say, 'That's how Babylon will sink to the bottom and stay there after the disaster I'm going to bring upon her.'"

52

THE DESTRUCTION OF JERUSALEM AND EXILE OF JUDAH

Zedekiah was twenty-one years old when he started out as king. He was king in Jerusalem for eleven years. His mother's name was Hamutal, the daughter of Jeremiah. Her hometown was Libnah.

As far as GOD was concerned, Zedekiah was just one more evil king, a carbon copy of Jehoiakim.

The source of all this doom to Jerusalem and Judah was GOD's anger. GOD turned his back on them as an act of judgment.

Zedekiah revolted against the king of Babylon. Nebuchadnezzar set out for Jerusalem with a full army. He set up camp and sealed off the city by building siege mounds around it. He arrived on the ninth year and tenth month of Zedekiah's reign. The city was under siege for nineteen months (until the eleventh year of Zedekiah).

By the fourth month of Zedekiah's eleventh year, on the ninth day of the month, the famine was so bad that there wasn't so much as a crumb of bread for anyone. Then the Babylonians broke through the city walls. Under cover of the night darkness, the entire Judean army fled through an opening in the wall (it was the gate between the two walls above the King's Garden). They slipped through the lines of the Babylonians who surrounded the city and headed for the Jordan into the Arabah Valley, but the Babylonians were in full pursuit. They caught up with them in the Plains of Jericho. But by then Zedekiah's army had deserted and was scattered.

The Babylonians captured Zedekiah and marched him off to the king of Babylon at Riblah in Hamath, who tried and sentenced him on the spot. The king of Babylon then killed Zedekiah's sons right before his eyes. The summary murder of his sons was the last thing Zedekiah saw, for they then blinded him. The king of Babylon followed that up by killing all the officials of Judah. Securely handcuffed, Zedekiah was hauled off to Babylon. The king of Babylon threw him in prison, where he stayed until the day he died.

In the nineteenth year of Nebuchadnezzar king of Babylon on the seventh day of the fifth month, Nebuzaradan, the king of Babylon's chief deputy, arrived in Jerusalem. He burned the Temple of GOD to the ground, went on to the royal palace, and then finished off the city. He burned the whole place down. He put the Babylonian troops he had with him to work knocking down the city walls. Finally, he rounded up everyone left in the city, including those who had earlier deserted to the king of Babylon, and took them off into exile. He left a few poor dirt farmers behind to tend the vineyards and what was left of the fields.

The Babylonians broke up the bronze pillars, the bronze washstands, and the huge bronze basin (the "Sea") that were in the Temple of GOD, and hauled the bronze off to Babylon. They also took the various bronze-crafted liturgical accessories, as well as the gold and silver censers and sprinkling bowls, used in the services of Temple worship. The king's deputy didn't miss a thing. He took every scrap of precious metal he could find.

The amount of bronze they got from the two pillars, the "Sea," the twelve bronze bulls that supported the "Sea," and the ten washstands that Solomon had made for the Temple of GOD was enormous. They couldn't weigh it all! Each pillar stood twenty-seven feet high with a circumference of eighteen feet. The pillars were hollow, the bronze a little less than an inch thick. Each pillar was topped with an ornate capital of bronze pomegranates and filigree, which added another seven and a half feet to its height. There were ninety-six pomegranates evenly spaced—in all, a hundred pomegranates worked into the filigree.

The king's deputy took a number of special prisoners: Seraiah the chief priest, Zephaniah the associate priest, three wardens, the chief remaining army officer, seven of the king's counselors who happened to be in the city, the chief recruiting officer for the army, and sixty men of standing from among the people who were still there. Nebuzaradan the king's deputy marched them all off to the king of Babylon at Riblah. And there at Riblah, in the land of Hamath, the king of Babylon killed the lot of them in cold blood.

Judah went into exile, orphaned from her land.

✠

3,023 men of Judah were taken into exile by Nebuchadnezzar in the seventh year of his reign.

832 from Jerusalem were taken in the eighteenth year of his reign.

745 men from Judah were taken off by Nebuzaradan, the king's chief deputy, in Nebuchadnezzar's twenty-third year.

The total number of exiles was 4,600.

✠

When Jehoiachin king of Judah had been in exile for thirty-seven years, Evil-Merodach became king in Babylon and let Jehoiachin out of prison. This release took place on the twenty-fifth day of the twelfth month. The king treated him most courteously and gave him preferential treatment beyond anything experienced by the political prisoners held in Babylon. Jehoiachin took off his prison garb and from then on ate his meals in company with the king. The king provided everything he needed to live comfortably for the rest of his life.

LAMENTATIONS

L amentations is a concentrated and intense biblical witness to suffering. Suffering is a huge, unavoidable element in the human condition. To be human is to suffer. No one gets an exemption. It comes as no surprise then to find that our Holy Scriptures, immersed as they are in the human condition, provide extensive witness to suffering.

There are two polar events in the history of the Hebrew people: the Exodus from Egypt and the Exile into Babylon. Exodus is the definitive story of salvation into a free life. God delivered his people from Egyptian slavery (in about 1200 B.C.). It is a story of freedom. It's accompanied by singing and dancing—an exuberant experience. Exile is the definitive story of judgment accompanied by immense suffering. God's people are taken into Babylonian slavery (the fall of Jerusalem in 587 B.C. marks the event). It is a time of devastation and lament. It is a terrible experience. The two events, Exodus and Exile, are bookends holding together the wide-ranging experiences of God's people that fall between the exuberance that accompanies salvation and the suffering associated with judgment.

Lamentations, written out of the Exile experience, provides the community of faith with a form and vocabulary for dealing with loss and pain. The precipitating event, the fall of Jerusalem, is told in 2 Kings 25 and Jeremiah 52. It is impossible to overstate either the intensity or the complexity of the suffering that came to a head in the devastation of Jerusalem and then continued on into the seventy years of exile in Babylon. Loss was total. Carnage was rampant. Cannibalism and sacrilege were twin horrors stalking the streets of destroyed Jerusalem. The desperate slaying of innocent children showed complete loss of respect for human worth, and the angry murder of priests showed absolute loss of respect for divine will. The worst that can happen to body and spirit, to person and nation, happened here—a nadir of suffering. And throughout the world the suffering continues, both in large-scale horrors and in personal agonies.

Neither explaining suffering nor offering a program for the elimination of suffering, Lamentations keeps company with the extensive biblical witness that gives dignity to suffering by insisting that God enters our suffering and is companion to our suffering.

LAMENTATIONS

1

WORTHLESS, CHEAP, ABJECT!
Oh, oh, oh . . .
How empty the city, once teeming with people.
    A widow, this city, once in the front rank of nations,
    once queen of the ball, she's now a drudge in the kitchen.

She cries herself to sleep each night, tears soaking her pillow.
    No one's left among her lovers to sit and hold her hand.
    Her friends have all dumped her.

After years of pain and hard labor, Judah has gone into exile.
    She camps out among the nations, never feels at home.
    Hunted by all, she's stuck between a rock and a hard place.

Zion's roads weep, empty of pilgrims headed to the feasts.
    All her city gates are deserted, her priests in despair.
    Her virgins are sad. How bitter her fate.

Her enemies have become her masters. Her foes are living it up
    because GOD laid her low, punishing her repeated rebellions.
    Her children, prisoners of the enemy, trudge into exile.

All beauty has drained from Daughter Zion's face.
    Her princes are like deer famished for food,
    chased to exhaustion by hunters.

Jerusalem remembers the day she lost everything,
    when her people fell into enemy hands, and not a soul there
        to help.
    Enemies looked on and laughed, laughed at her helpless silence.

Jerusalem, who outsinned the whole world, is an outcast.
    All who admired her despise her now that they see beneath the
        surface.
    Miserable, she groans and turns away in shame.

She played fast and loose with life, she never considered tomorrow,
    and now she's crashed royally, with no one to hold her hand:
    "Look at my pain, oh GOD! And how the enemy cruelly struts."

The enemy reached out to take all her favorite things. She watched
    as pagans barged into her Sanctuary, those very people for whom
    you posted orders: KEEP OUT: THIS ASSEMBLY OFF-LIMITS.

All the people groaned, so desperate for food, so desperate to
        stay alive
    that they bartered their favorite things for a bit of breakfast:
    "Oh GOD, look at me! Worthless, cheap, abject!

"And you passersby, look at me! Have you ever seen anything
        like this?
    Ever seen pain like my pain, seen what he did to me,
    what GOD did to me in his rage?

"He struck me with lightning, skewered me from head to foot,
    then he set traps all around so I could hardly move.
    He left me with nothing—left me sick, and sick of living.

"He wove my sins into a rope
    and harnessed me to captivity's yoke.
    I'm goaded by cruel taskmasters.

"The Master piled up my best soldiers in a heap,
    then called in thugs to break their fine young necks.
    The Master crushed the life out of fair virgin Judah.

"For all this I weep, weep buckets of tears,
    and not a soul within miles around cares for my soul.
    My children are wasted, my enemy got his way."

Zion reached out for help, but no one helped.
    GOD ordered Jacob's enemies to surround him,
    and now no one wants anything to do with Jerusalem.

"GOD has right on his side. I'm the one who did wrong.
    Listen everybody! Look at what I'm going through!
    My fair young women, my fine young men, all herded into exile!

"I called to my friends; they betrayed me.
My priests and my leaders only looked after themselves,
trying but failing to save their own skins.

"Oh God, look at the trouble I'm in! My stomach in knots,
my heart wrecked by a life of rebellion.
Massacres in the streets, starvation in the houses.

"Oh, listen to my groans. No one listens, no one cares.
When my enemies heard of the trouble you gave me,
they cheered.
Bring on judgment day! Let them get what I got!

"Take a good look at their evil ways and give it to them!
Give them what you gave me for my sins.
Groaning in pain, body and soul, I've had all I can take."

2

GOD WALKED AWAY FROM HIS HOLY TEMPLE

Oh, oh, oh . . .
How the Master has cut down Daughter Zion
from the skies, dashed Israel's glorious city to earth,
in his anger treated his favorite as throwaway junk.

The Master, without a second thought, took Israel in one gulp.
Raging, he smashed Judah's defenses,
made hash of her king and princes.

His anger blazing, he knocked Israel flat,
broke Israel's arm and turned his back just as the enemy
approached,
came on Jacob like a wildfire from every direction.

Like an enemy, he aimed his bow, bared his sword,
and killed our young men, our pride and joy.
His anger, like fire, burned down the homes in Zion.

The Master became the enemy. He had Israel for supper.
    He chewed up and spit out all the defenses.
    He left Daughter Judah moaning and groaning.

He plowed up his old trysting place, trashed his favorite rendezvous.
    GOD wiped out Zion's memories of feast days and sabbaths,
    angrily sacked king and priest alike.

GOD abandoned his altar, walked away from his holy Temple
    and turned the fortifications over to the enemy.
    As they cheered in GOD's Temple, you'd have thought it was
        a feast day!

GOD drew up plans to tear down the walls of Daughter Zion.
    He assembled his crew, set to work and went at it.
    Total demolition! The stones wept!

Her city gates, iron bars and all, disappeared in the rubble:
    her kings and princes off to exile—no one left to instruct
        or lead;
    her prophets useless—they neither saw nor heard anything
        from GOD.

The elders of Daughter Zion sit silent on the ground.
    They throw dust on their heads, dress in rough penitential
        burlap—
    the young virgins of Jerusalem, their faces creased with the dirt.

My eyes are blind with tears, my stomach in a knot.
    My insides have turned to jelly over my people's fate.
    Babies and children are fainting all over the place,

Calling to their mothers, "I'm hungry! I'm thirsty!"
    then fainting like dying soldiers in the streets,
    breathing their last in their mothers' laps.

How can I understand your plight, dear Jerusalem?
    What can I say to give you comfort, dear Zion?
    Who can put you together again? This bust-up is past
        understanding.

Your prophets courted you with sweet talk.
> They didn't face you with your sin so that you could repent.
> Their sermons were all wishful thinking, deceptive illusions.

Astonished, passersby can't believe what they see.
> They rub their eyes, they shake their heads over Jerusalem.
> Is this the city voted "Most Beautiful" and "Best Place to Live"?

But now your enemies gape, slack-jawed.
> Then they rub their hands in glee: "We've got them!
> We've been waiting for this! Here it is!"

GOD did carry out, item by item, exactly what he said he'd do.
> He always said he'd do this. Now he's done it—torn the place
>> down.
> He's let your enemies walk all over you, declared them world
>> champions!

Give out heart-cries to the Master, dear repentant Zion.
> Let the tears roll like a river, day and night,
> and keep at it—no time-outs. Keep those tears flowing!

As each night watch begins, get up and cry out in prayer.
> Pour your heart out face to face with the Master.
> Lift high your hands. Beg for the lives of your children
> who are starving to death out on the streets.

"Look at us, GOD. Think it over. Have you ever treated *anyone*
>> like this?
> Should women eat their own babies, the very children they
>> raised?
> Should priests and prophets be murdered in the Master's own
>> Sanctuary?

"Boys and old men lie in the gutters of the streets,
> my young men and women killed in their prime.
> Angry, you killed them in cold blood, cut them down without
>> mercy.

"You invited, like friends to a party, men to swoop down in attack
    so that on the big day of God's wrath no one would get away.
    The children I loved and reared—gone, gone, gone."

3

God Locked Me Up in Deep Darkness

I'm the man who has seen trouble,
    trouble coming from the lash of God's anger.
He took me by the hand and walked me
    into pitch-black darkness.
Yes, he's given me the back of his hand
    over and over and over again.

He turned me into a scarecrow
    of skin and bones, then broke the bones.
He hemmed me in, ganged up on me,
    poured on the trouble and hard times.
He locked me up in deep darkness,
    like a corpse nailed inside a coffin.

He shuts me in so I'll never get out,
    manacles my hands, shackles my feet.
Even when I cry out and plead for help,
    he locks up my prayers and throws away the key.
He sets up blockades with quarried limestone.
    He's got me cornered.

He's a prowling bear tracking me down,
    a lion in hiding ready to pounce.
He knocked me from the path and ripped me to pieces.
    When he finished, there was nothing left of me.
He took out his bow and arrows
    and used me for target practice.

He shot me in the stomach
    with arrows from his quiver.
Everyone took me for a joke,
    made me the butt of their mocking ballads.

He forced rotten, stinking food down my throat,
    bloated me with vile drinks.

He ground my face into the gravel.
    He pounded me into the mud.
I gave up on life altogether.
    I've forgotten what the good life is like.
I said to myself, "This is it. I'm finished.
    GOD is a lost cause."

IT'S A GOOD THING TO HOPE FOR HELP FROM GOD

I'll never forget the trouble, the utter lostness,
    the taste of ashes, the poison I've swallowed.
I remember it all—oh, how well I remember—
    the feeling of hitting the bottom.
But there's one other thing I remember,
    and remembering, I keep a grip on hope:

GOD's loyal love couldn't have run out,
    his merciful love couldn't have dried up.
They're created new every morning.
    How great your faithfulness!
I'm sticking with GOD (I say it over and over).
    He's all I've got left.

GOD proves to be good to the man who passionately waits,
    to the woman who diligently seeks.
It's a good thing to quietly hope,
    quietly hope for help from GOD.
It's a good thing when you're young
    to stick it out through the hard times.

When life is heavy and hard to take,
    go off by yourself. Enter the silence.
Bow in prayer. Don't ask questions:
    Wait for hope to appear.
Don't run from trouble. Take it full-face.
    The "worst" is never the worst.

Why? Because the Master won't ever
    walk out and fail to return.

If he works severely, he also works tenderly.
His stockpiles of loyal love are immense.
He takes no pleasure in making life hard,
in throwing roadblocks in the way:

Stomping down hard
on luckless prisoners,
Refusing justice to victims
in the court of High God,
Tampering with evidence—
the Master does not approve of such things.

GOD SPEAKS BOTH GOOD THINGS AND HARD THINGS INTO BEING

Who do you think "spoke and it happened"?
It's the Master who gives such orders.
Doesn't the High God speak everything,
good things and hard things alike, into being?
And why would anyone gifted with life
complain when punished for sin?

Let's take a good look at the way we're living
and reorder our lives under GOD.
Let's lift our hearts and hands at one and the same time,
praying to God in heaven:
"We've been contrary and willful,
and you haven't forgiven.

"You lost your temper with us, holding nothing back.
You chased us and cut us down without mercy.
You wrapped yourself in thick blankets of clouds
so no prayers could get through.
You treated us like dirty dishwater,
threw us out in the backyard of the nations.

"Our enemies shout abuse,
their mouths full of derision, spitting invective.
We've been to hell and back.
We've nowhere to turn, nowhere to go.
Rivers of tears pour from my eyes
at the smash-up of my dear people.

"The tears stream from my eyes,
    an artesian well of tears,
Until you, GOD, look down from on high,
    look and see my tears.
When I see what's happened to the young women in the city,
    the pain breaks my heart.

"Enemies with no reason to be enemies
    hunted me down like a bird.
They threw me into a pit,
    then pelted me with stones.
Then the rains came and filled the pit.
    The water rose over my head. I said, 'It's all over.'

"I called out your name, oh GOD,
    called from the bottom of the pit.
You listened when I called out, 'Don't shut your ears!
    Get me out of here! Save me!'
You came close when I called out.
    You said, 'It's going to be all right.'

"You took my side, Master;
    you brought me back alive!
GOD, you saw the wrongs heaped on me.
    Give me my day in court!
Yes, you saw their mean-minded schemes,
    their plots to destroy me.

"You heard, GOD, their vicious gossip,
    their behind-my-back plots to ruin me.
They never quit, these enemies of mine, dreaming up mischief,
    hatching out malice, day after day after day.
Sitting down or standing up—just look at them!—
    they mock me with vulgar doggerel.

"Make them pay for what they've done, GOD.
    Give them their just deserts.
Break their miserable hearts!
    Damn their eyes!

Get good and angry. Hunt them down.
    Make a total demolition here under your heaven!"

4

Waking Up With Nothing

Oh, oh, oh . . .
How gold is treated like dirt,
    the finest gold thrown out with the garbage,
Priceless jewels scattered all over,
    jewels loose in the gutters.

And the people of Zion, once prized,
    far surpassing their weight in gold,
Are now treated like cheap pottery,
    like everyday pots and bowls mass-produced by a potter.

Even wild jackals nurture their babies,
    give them their breasts to suckle.
But my people have turned cruel to their babies,
    like an ostrich in the wilderness.

Babies have nothing to drink.
    Their tongues stick to the roofs of their mouths.
Little children ask for bread
    but no one gives them so much as a crust.

People used to the finest cuisine
    forage for food in the streets.
People used to the latest in fashions
    pick through the trash for something to wear.

The evil guilt of my dear people
    was worse than the sin of Sodom—
The city was destroyed in a flash,
    and no one around to help.

The splendid and sacred nobles
    once glowed with health.
Their bodies were robust and ruddy,
    their beards like carved stone.

305

But now they are smeared with soot,
    unrecognizable in the street,
Their bones sticking out,
    their skin dried out like old leather.

Better to have been killed in battle
    than killed by starvation.
Better to have died of battle wounds
    than to slowly starve to death.

Nice and kindly women
    boiled their own children for supper.
This was the only food in town
    when my dear people were broken.

GOD let all his anger loose, held nothing back.
    He poured out his raging wrath.
He set a fire in Zion
    that burned it to the ground.

The kings of the earth couldn't believe it.
    World rulers were in shock,
Watching old enemies march in big as you please,
    right through Jerusalem's gates.

Because of the sins of her prophets
    and the evil of her priests,
Who exploited good and trusting people,
    robbing them of their lives,

These prophets and priests blindly grope their way through
    the streets,
    grimy and stained from their dirty lives,
Wasted by their wasted lives,
    shuffling from fatigue, dressed in rags.

People yell at them, "Get out of here, dirty old men!
    Get lost, don't touch us, don't infect us!"
They have to leave town. They wander off.
    Nobody wants them to stay here.

Everyone knows, wherever they wander,
    that they've been kicked out of their own hometown.

GOD himself scattered them.
    No longer does he look out for them.
He has nothing to do with the priests;
    he cares nothing for the elders.

We watched and watched,
    wore our eyes out looking for help. And nothing.
We mounted our lookouts and looked
    for the help that never showed up.

They tracked us down, those hunters.
    It wasn't safe to go out in the street.
Our end was near, our days numbered.
    We were doomed.

They came after us faster than eagles in flight,
    pressed us hard in the mountains, ambushed us in the desert.

Our king, our life's breath, the anointed of GOD,
    was caught in their traps—
Our king under whose protection
    we always said we'd live.

Celebrate while you can, oh Edom!
    Live it up in Uz!
For it won't be long before you drink this cup, too.
    You'll find out what it's like to drink God's wrath,
Get drunk on God's wrath
    and wake up with nothing, stripped naked.

And that's it for you, Zion. The punishment's complete.
    You won't have to go through this exile again.
But Edom, your time is coming:
    He'll punish your evil life, put all your sins on display.

5

GIVE US A FRESH START

"Remember, GOD, all we've been through.
  Study our plight, the black mark we've made in history.
Our precious land has been given to outsiders,
  our homes to strangers.
Orphans we are, not a father in sight,
  and our mothers no better than widows.
We have to pay to drink our own water.
  Even our firewood comes at a price.
We're nothing but slaves, bullied and bowed,
  worn out and without any rest.
We sold ourselves to Assyria and Egypt
  just to get something to eat.
Our parents sinned and are no more,
  and now we're paying for the wrongs they did.
Slaves rule over us;
  there's no escape from their grip.
We risk our lives to gather food
  in the bandit-infested desert.
Our skin has turned black as an oven,
  dried out like old leather from the famine.
Our wives were raped in the streets in Zion,
  and our virgins in the cities of Judah.
They hanged our princes by their hands,
  dishonored our elders.
Strapping young men were put to women's work,
  mere boys forced to do men's work.
The city gate is empty of wise elders.
  Music from the young is heard no more.
All the joy is gone from our hearts.
  Our dances have turned into dirges.
The crown of glory has toppled from our head.
  Woe! Woe! Would that we'd never sinned!
Because of all this we're heartsick;
  we can't see through the tears.
On Mount Zion, wrecked and ruined,
  jackals pace and prowl.

And yet, GOD, you're sovereign still,
    your throne intact and eternal.
So why do you keep forgetting us?
    Why dump us and leave us like this?
Bring us back to you, GOD—we're ready to come back.
    Give us a fresh start.
As it is, you've cruelly disowned us.
    You've been so very angry with us."

EZEKIEL

Catastrophe strikes and a person's world falls apart. People respond variously, but two of the more common responses are denial and despair. Denial refuses to acknowledge the catastrophe. It shuts its eyes tight or looks the other way; it manages to act as if everything is going to be just fine; it takes refuge in distractions and lies and fantasies. Despair is paralyzed by the catastrophe and accepts it as the end of the world. It is unwilling to do anything, concluding that life for all intents and purposes is over. Despair listlessly closes its eyes to a world in which all the color has drained out, a world gone dead.

Among biblical writers, Ezekiel is our master at dealing with catastrophe. When catastrophe struck—it was the sixth century B.C. invasion of Israel by Babylon—denial was the primary response. Ezekiel found himself living among a people of God who (astonishingly similar to us!) stubbornly refused to see what was right before their eyes (the denial crowd). There were also some who were unwilling to see anything other than what was right before their eyes (the despair crowd).

But Ezekiel saw. He saw what the people with whom he lived either couldn't or wouldn't see. He saw in wild and unforgettable images, elaborated in exuberant detail—God at work in a catastrophic era. The denial people refused to see that the catastrophe was in fact catastrophic. How could it be? God wouldn't let anything that bad happen to them. Ezekiel showed them. He showed them that, yes, there *was* catastrophe, but God was at work in the catastrophe, sovereignly *using* the catastrophe. He showed them so that they would be able to embrace God in the worst of times.

The despair people, overwhelmed by the devastation, refused to see that life was worth living. How could it be? They had lost everything, or would soon— country, Temple, freedom, and many, many lives. Ezekiel showed them. He showed them that God was and would be at work in the wreckage and rubble, sovereignly *using* the disaster to create a new people of God.

Whether through denial or despair, the people of God nearly lost their identity as a people of God. But they didn't. God's people emerged from that catastrophic century robust and whole. And the reason, in large part, was Ezekiel.

EZEKIEL

1

WHEELS WITHIN WHEELS, LIKE A GYROSCOPE

When I was thirty years of age, I was living with the exiles on the Chebar River. On the fifth day of the fourth month, the sky opened up and I saw visions of God.

(It was the fifth day of the month in the fifth year of the exile of King Jehoiachin that GOD's Word came to Ezekiel the priest, the son of Buzi, on the banks of the Chebar River in the country of Babylon. GOD's hand came upon him that day.)

✛

I looked: I saw an immense dust storm come from the north, an immense cloud with lightning flashing from it, a huge ball of fire glowing like bronze. Within the fire were what looked like four creatures vibrant with life. Each had the form of a human being, but each also had four faces and four wings. Their legs were as sturdy and straight as columns, but their feet were hoofed like those of a calf and sparkled from the fire like burnished bronze. On all four sides under their wings they had human hands. All four had both faces and wings, with the wings touching one another. They turned neither one way nor the other; they went straight forward.

Their faces looked like this: In front a human face, on the right side the face of a lion, on the left the face of an ox, and in back the face of an eagle. So much for the faces. The wings were spread out with the tips of one pair touching the creature on either side; the other pair of wings covered its body. Each creature went straight ahead. Wherever the spirit went, they went. They didn't turn as they went.

The four creatures looked like a blazing fire, or like fiery torches. Tongues of fire shot back and forth between the creatures, and out of the fire, bolts of lightning. The creatures flashed back and forth like strikes of lightning.

As I watched the four creatures, I saw something that looked like a wheel on the ground beside each of the four-faced creatures. This is what the wheels looked like: They were identical wheels, sparkling like diamonds in the sun. It looked like they were wheels within wheels, like a gyroscope.

313

They went in any one of the four directions they faced, but straight, not veering off. The rims were immense, circled with eyes. When the living creatures went, the wheels went; when the living creatures lifted off, the wheels lifted off. Wherever the spirit went, they went, the wheels sticking right with them, for the spirit of the living creatures was in the wheels. When the creatures went, the wheels went; when the creatures stopped, the wheels stopped; when the creatures lifted off, the wheels lifted off, because the spirit of the living creatures was in the wheels.

Over the heads of the living creatures was something like a dome, shimmering like a sky full of cut glass, vaulted over their heads. Under the dome one set of wings was extended toward the others, with another set of wings covering their bodies. When they moved I heard their wings—it was like the roar of a great waterfall, like the voice of the Strong God, like the noise of a battlefield. When they stopped, they folded their wings.

And then, as they stood with folded wings, there was a voice from above the dome over their heads. Above the dome there was something that looked like a throne, sky-blue like a sapphire, with a humanlike figure towering above the throne. From what I could see, from the waist up he looked like burnished bronze and from the waist down like a blazing fire. Brightness everywhere! The way a rainbow springs out of the sky on a rainy day—that's what it was like. It turned out to be the Glory of GOD!

When I saw all this, I fell to my knees, my face to the ground. Then I heard a voice.

✠

2

It said, "Son of man, stand up. I have something to say to you."

The moment I heard the voice, the Spirit entered me and put me on my feet. As he spoke to me, I listened.

He said, "Son of man, I'm sending you to the family of Israel, a rebellious nation if there ever was one. They and their ancestors have fomented rebellion right up to the present. They're a hard case, these people to whom I'm sending you—hardened in their sin. Tell them, 'This is the Message of GOD, the Master.' They are a defiant bunch. Whether or not they listen, at least they'll know that a prophet's been here. But don't be afraid of them, son of man, and don't be afraid of anything they say. Don't be afraid when living among them is like stepping on thorns or finding scorpions in your bed. Don't be afraid of their mean words or their hard looks. They're a bunch of rebels. Your job is to speak to them. Whether they listen is not your concern. They're hardened rebels.

"Only take care, son of man, that you don't rebel like these rebels. Open your mouth and eat what I give you."

When I looked he had his hand stretched out to me, and in the hand a book, a scroll. He unrolled the scroll. On both sides, front and back, were written lamentations and mourning and doom.

3

WARN THESE PEOPLE

He told me, "Son of man, eat what you see. Eat this book. Then go and speak to the family of Israel."

As I opened my mouth, he gave me the scroll to eat, saying, "Son of man, eat this book that I am giving you. Make a full meal of it!"

So I ate it. It tasted so good—just like honey.

Then he told me, "Son of man, go to the family of Israel and speak my Message. Look, I'm not sending you to a people who speak a hard-to-learn language with words you can hardly pronounce. If I had sent you to such people, their ears would have perked up and they would have listened immediately.

"But it won't work that way with the family of Israel. They won't listen to you because they won't listen to me. They are, as I said, a hard case, hardened in their sin. But I'll make you as hard in your way as they are in theirs. I'll make your face as hard as rock, harder than granite. Don't let them intimidate you. Don't be afraid of them, even though they're a bunch of rebels."

Then he said, "Son of man, get all these words that I'm giving you inside you. Listen to them obediently. Make them your own. And now go. Go to the exiles, your people, and speak. Tell them, 'This is the Message of GOD, the Master.' Speak your piece, whether they listen or not."

Then the Spirit picked me up. Behind me I heard a great commotion— "Blessed be the Glory of GOD in his Sanctuary!"— the wings of the living creatures beating against each other, the whirling wheels, the rumble of a great earthquake.

The Spirit lifted me and took me away. I went bitterly and angrily. I didn't want to go. But GOD had me in his grip. I arrived among the exiles who lived near the Chebar River at Tel Aviv. I came to where they were living and sat there for seven days, appalled.

At the end of the seven days, I received this Message from GOD:

"Son of man, I've made you a watchman for the family of Israel. Whenever you hear me say something, warn them for me. If I say to the wicked, 'You are going to die,' and you don't sound the alarm warning them that it's a matter of life or death, they will die and it will be your fault. I'll hold you responsible. But if you warn the wicked and they keep right on sinning anyway, they'll most certainly die for their sin, but *you* won't die. You'll have saved your life.

"And if the righteous turn back from living righteously and take up with evil when I step in and put them in a hard place, they'll die. If you haven't warned them, they'll die because of their sins, and none of the right things they've done will count for anything—and I'll hold you responsible. But if you warn these righteous people not to sin and they listen to you, they'll live because they took the warning—and again, you'll have saved your life."

GOD grabbed me by the shoulder and said, "Get up. Go out on the plain. I want to talk with you."

So I got up and went out on the plain. I couldn't believe my eyes: the Glory of GOD! Right there! It was like the Glory I had seen at the Chebar River. I fell to the ground, prostrate.

Then the Spirit entered me and put me on my feet. He said, "Go home and shut the door behind you." And then something odd: "Son of man: They'll tie you hand and foot with ropes so you can't leave the house. I'll make your tongue stick to the roof of your mouth so you won't be able to talk and tell the people what they're doing wrong, even though they are a bunch of rebels.

"But then when the time is ripe, I'll free your tongue and you'll say, 'This is what GOD, the Master, says: . . .' From then on it's up to them. They can listen or not listen, whichever they like. They *are* a bunch of rebels!

4

THIS IS WHAT SIN DOES

"Now, Son of man, take a brick and place it before you. Draw a picture of the city Jerusalem on it. Then make a model of a military siege against the brick: Build siege walls, construct a ramp, set up army camps, lay in battering rams around it. Then get an iron skillet and place it upright between you and the city—an iron wall. Face the model: The city shall be under siege and you shall be the besieger. This is a sign to the family of Israel.

"Next lie on your left side and place the sin of the family of Israel on yourself. You will bear their sin for as many days as you lie on your side. The number of days you bear their sin will match the number of years of their sin, namely, 390. For 390 days you will bear the sin of the family of Israel.

"Then, after you have done this, turn over and lie down on your right side and bear the sin of the family of Judah. Your assignment this time is to lie there for forty days, a day for each year of their sin. Look straight at the siege of Jerusalem. Roll up your sleeve, shake your bare arm, and preach against her.

"I will tie you up with ropes, tie you so you can't move or turn over until you have finished the days of the siege.

"Next I want you to take wheat and barley, beans and lentils, dried millet and spelt, and mix them in a bowl to make a flat bread. This is your food ration for the 390 days you lie on your side. Measure out about half a pound for each day and eat it on schedule. Also measure out your daily ration of about a pint of water and drink it on schedule. Eat the bread as you would a muffin. Bake the muffins out in the open where everyone can see you, using dried human dung for fuel."

GOD said, "This is what the people of Israel are going to do: Among the pagan nations where I will drive them, they will eat foods that are strictly taboo to a holy people."

I said, "GOD, my Master! Never! I've never contaminated myself with food like that. Since my youth I've never eaten anything forbidden by law, nothing found dead or violated by wild animals. I've never taken a single bite of forbidden food."

"All right," he said. "I'll let you bake your bread over cow dung instead of human dung."

Then he said to me, "Son of man, I'm going to cut off all food from Jerusalem. The people will live on starvation rations, worrying where the next meal's coming from, scrounging for the next drink of water. Famine conditions. People will look at one another, see nothing but skin and bones, and shake their heads. This is what sin does."

5

A JEALOUS GOD, NOT TO BE TRIFLED WITH

"Now, son of man, take a sharp sword and use it as a straight razor, shaving your head and your beard. Then, using a set of balancing scales, divide the hair into thirds. When the days of the siege are over, take one-third of the hair and burn it inside the city. Take another third, chop it into bits with the sword and sprinkle it around the city. The final third you'll throw to the wind. Then I'll go after them with a sword.

"Retrieve a few of the hairs and slip them into your pocket. Take some of them and throw them into the fire—burn them up. From them, fire will spread to the whole family of Israel.

"This is what GOD, the Master, says: This means *Jerusalem*. I set her at the center of the world, all the nations ranged around her. But she rebelled against my laws and ordinances, rebelled far worse than the nations ranged around her—sheer wickedness!—refused my guidance, ignored my directions.

"Therefore this is what GOD, the Master, says: You've been more headstrong and willful than any of the nations around you, refusing my guidance, ignoring my directions. You've sunk to the gutter level of those around you.

"Therefore this is what GOD, the Master, says: I'm setting myself against you—yes, against you, Jerusalem. I'm going to punish you in full sight of the nations. Because of your disgusting no-god idols, I'm going to do something to you that I've never done before and will never do again: turn families into cannibals—parents eating children, children eating parents! Punishment indeed. And whoever's left over I'll throw to the winds.

"Therefore, as sure as I am the living God—Decree of GOD, the Master—because you've polluted my Sanctuary with your obscenities and disgusting no-god idols, I'm pulling out. Not an ounce of pity will I show you. A third of your people will die of either disease or hunger inside the city, a third will be killed outside the city, and a third will be thrown to the winds and chased by killers.

"Only then will I calm down and let my anger cool. Then you'll know that I was serious about this all along, that I'm a jealous God and not to be trifled with.

"When I get done with you, you'll be a pile of rubble. Nations who walk by will make coarse jokes. When I finish my angry punishment and searing rebukes, you'll be reduced to an object of ridicule and mockery, turned into a horror story circulating among the surrounding nations. I, GOD, have spoken.

"When I shoot my lethal famine arrows at you, I'll shoot to kill. Then I'll step up the famine and cut off food supplies. Famine and more famine—and then I'll send in the wild animals to finish off your children. Epidemic disease, unrestrained murder, death—and I will have sent it! I, GOD, have spoken."

6

TURN ISRAEL INTO WASTELAND

Then the Word of GOD came to me: "Son of man, now turn and face the mountains of Israel and preach against them: 'Oh Mountains of Israel, listen to the Message of GOD, the Master. GOD, the Master, speaks to the mountains and hills, to the ravines and the valleys: I'm about to destroy your sacred god and goddess shrines. I'll level your altars, bust up your sun-god pillars, and kill your people as they bow down to your no-god idols. I'll stack the dead bodies of Israelites in front of your idols and then scatter your bones around your shrines. Every place where you've lived, the towns will be torn down and the pagan shrines demolished—altars busted up, idols smashed, all your custom-made sun-god pillars in ruins. Corpses everywhere you look! Then you'll know that I am GOD.

"'But I'll let a few escape the killing as you are scattered through other lands and nations. In the foreign countries where they're taken as prisoners of war, they'll remember me. They'll realize how devastated I was by their betrayals, by their voracious lust for gratifying themselves in their idolatries. They'll be disgusted with their evil ways, disgusting to God in the way they've lived. They'll know that I am GOD. They'll know that my judgment against them was no empty threat.

"'This is what GOD, the Master, says: "Clap your hands, stamp your feet, yell out, 'No, no, no!' because of all the evil obscenities rife in Israel. They're going to be killed, dying of hunger, dying of disease—death everywhere you look, people dropping like flies, people far away dying, people nearby dying, and whoever's left in the city starving to death. Why? Because I'm angry, furiously angry. They'll realize that I am GOD when they see their people's corpses strewn over and around all their ruined sex-and-religion shrines on the bare hills and in the lush fertility groves, in all the places where they indulged their sensual rites. I'll bring my hand down hard on them, demolish the country wherever they live, turn it into wasteland from one end to the other, from the wilderness to Riblah. Then they'll know that I am GOD!""'

7

FATE HAS CAUGHT UP WITH YOU

GOD's Word came to me, saying, "You, son of man—GOD, the Master, has this Message for the land of Israel:

"'Endtime.
    The end of business as usual for everyone.
It's all over. The end is upon you.
    I've launched my anger against you.
I've issued my verdict on the way you live.
    I'll make you pay for your disgusting obscenities.
I won't look the other way,
    I won't feel sorry for you.
I'll make you pay for the way you've lived:
    Your disgusting obscenities will boomerang on you,
    and you'll realize that I am GOD.'

"I, GOD, the Master, say:
    'Disaster after disaster! Look, it comes!
Endtime—
    the end comes.
The end is ripe. Watch out, it's coming!
    This is your fate, you who live in this land.
Time's up.
    It's zero hour.
No dragging of feet now,
    no bargaining for more time.
Soon now I'll pour my wrath on you,
    pay out my anger against you,
Render my verdict on the way you've lived,
    make you pay for your disgusting obscenities.
I won't look the other way,
    I won't feel sorry for you.
I'll make you pay for the way you've lived.
    Your disgusting obscenities will boomerang on you.
Then you'll realize
    that it is I, GOD, who has hit you.

320

"'Judgment Day!
    Fate has caught up with you.
The scepter outsized and pretentious,
    pride bursting all bounds,
Violence strutting,
    brandishing the evil scepter.
But there's nothing to them,
    and nothing will be left of them.
Time's up.
    Countdown: five, four, three, two . . .
Buyer, don't crow; seller, don't worry:
    Judgment wrath has turned the world topsy-turvy.
The bottom has dropped out of buying and selling.
    It will never be the same again.
But don't fantasize an upturn in the market.
    The country is bankrupt because of its sins,
    and it's not going to get any better.

"'The trumpet signals the call to battle:
    "Present arms!"
But no one marches into battle.
    My wrath has them paralyzed!
On the open roads you're killed,
    or else you go home and die of hunger and disease.
Either get murdered out in the country
    or die of sickness or hunger in town.
Survivors run for the hills.
    They moan like doves in the valleys,
Each one moaning
    for his own sins.

"'Every hand hangs limp,
    every knee turns to rubber.
They dress in rough burlap—
    sorry scarecrows,
Shifty and shamefaced,
    with their heads shaved bald.

"'They throw their money into the gutters.
    Their hard-earned cash stinks like garbage.

321

They find that it won't buy a thing
    they either want or need on Judgment Day.
They tripped on money
    and fell into sin.
Proud and pretentious with their jewels,
    they deck out their vile and vulgar no-gods in finery.
    I'll make those god-obscenities a stench in their nostrils.
I'll give away their religious junk—
    strangers will pick it up for free,
    the godless spit on it and make jokes.
I'll turn my face so I won't have to look
    as my treasured place and people are violated,
As violent strangers walk in
    and desecrate place and people—
A bloody massacre,
    as crime and violence fill the city.
I'll bring in the dregs of humanity
    to move into their houses.
I'll put a stop to the boasting and strutting
    of the high-and-mighty,
And see to it that there'll be nothing holy
    left in their holy places.
Catastrophe descends. They look for peace,
    but there's no peace to be found—
Disaster on the heels of disaster,
    one rumor after another.
They clamor for the prophet to tell them what's up,
    but nobody knows anything.
Priests don't have a clue;
    the elders don't know what to say.
The king holds his head in despair;
    the prince is devastated.
The common people are paralyzed.
    Gripped by fear, they can't move.
I'll deal with them where they are,
    judge them on their terms.
        They'll know that I am GOD.'"

8

THE SPIRIT CARRIED ME IN VISIONS

In the sixth year, in the sixth month and the fifth day, while I was sitting at home meeting with the leaders of Judah, it happened that the hand of my Master, GOD, gripped me. When I looked, I was astonished. What I saw looked like a man—from the waist down like fire and from the waist up like highly burnished bronze. He reached out what looked like a hand and grabbed me by the hair. The Spirit swept me high in the air and carried me in visions of God to Jerusalem, to the entrance of the north gate of the Temple's inside court where the image of the sex goddess that makes God so angry had been set up. Right before me was the Glory of the God of Israel, exactly like the vision I had seen out on the plain.

He said to me, "Son of man, look north." I looked north and saw it: Just north of the entrance loomed the altar of the sex goddess, Asherah, that makes God so angry.

Then he said, "Son of man, do you see what they're doing? Outrageous obscenities! And doing them right here! It's enough to drive me right out of my own Temple. But you're going to see worse yet."

✝

He brought me to the door of the Temple court. I looked and saw a gaping hole in the wall.

He said, "Son of man, dig through the wall."

I dug through the wall and came upon a door.

He said, "Now walk through the door and take a look at the obscenities they're engaging in."

I entered and looked. I couldn't believe my eyes: Painted all over the walls were pictures of reptiles and animals and monsters—the whole pantheon of Egyptian gods and goddesses—being worshiped by Israel. In the middle of the room were seventy of the leaders of Israel, with Jaazaniah son of Shaphan standing in the middle. Each held his censer with the incense rising in a fragrant cloud.

He said, "Son of man, do you see what the elders are doing here in the dark, each one before his favorite god-picture? They tell themselves, 'GOD doesn't see us. GOD has forsaken the country.'"

Then he said, "You're going to see worse yet."

✠

He took me to the entrance at the north gate of the Temple of GOD. I saw women sitting there, weeping for Tammuz, the Babylonian fertility god. He said, "Have you gotten an eyeful, son of man? You're going to see worse yet."

✠

Finally, he took me to the inside court of the Temple of GOD. There between the porch and the altar were about twenty-five men. Their backs were to GOD's Temple. They were facing east, bowing in worship to the sun.

He said, "Have you seen enough, son of man? Isn't it bad enough that Judah engages in these outrageous obscenities? They fill the country with violence and now provoke me even further with their obscene gestures. That's it. They have an angry God on their hands! From now on, no mercy. They can shout all they want, but I'm not listening."

9

A MARK ON THE FOREHEAD

Then I heard him call out loudly, "Executioners, come! And bring your deadly weapons with you."

Six men came down the road from the upper gate that faces north, each carrying his lethal weapon. With them was a man dressed in linen with a writing case slung from his shoulder. They entered and stood by the bronze altar.

The Glory of the God of Israel ascended from his usual place above the cherubim-angels, moved to the threshold of the Temple, and called to the man with the writing case who was dressed in linen: "Go through the streets of Jerusalem and put a mark on the forehead of everyone who is in anguish over the outrageous obscenities being done in the city."

I listened as he went on to address the executioners: "Follow him through the city and kill. Feel sorry for no one. Show no compassion. Kill old men and women, young men and women, mothers and children. But don't lay a hand on anyone with the mark. Start at my Temple."

They started with the leaders in front of the Temple.

He told the executioners, "Desecrate the Temple. Fill it with corpses. Then go out and continue the killing." So they went out and struck the city.

While the massacre went forward, I was left alone. I fell on my face in prayer: "Oh, oh, GOD, my Master! Are you going to kill everyone left in Israel in this pouring out of your anger on Jerusalem?"

He said, "The guilt of Israel and Judah is enormous. The land is swollen with murder. The city is bloated with injustice. They all say, 'GOD has forsaken the country. He doesn't see anything we do.' Well, I do see, and I'm not feeling sorry for any of them. They're going to pay for what they've done."

Just then, the man dressed in linen and carrying the writing case came back and reported, "I've done what you told me."

10

THE TEMPLE, FILLED WITH THE PRESENCE OF GOD

When I next looked, oh! Above the dome over the heads of the cherubim-angels was what looked like a throne, sky-blue, like a sapphire!

GOD said to the man dressed in linen, "Enter the place of the wheels under the cherubim-angels. Fill your hands with burning coals from beneath the cherubim and scatter them over the city."

I watched as he entered. The cherubim were standing on the south side of the Temple when the man entered. A cloud filled the inside courtyard. Then the Glory of GOD ascended from the cherubim and moved to the threshold of the Temple. The cloud filled the Temple. Court and Temple were both filled with the blazing presence of the Glory of GOD. And the sound! The wings of the cherubim were audible all the way to the outer court—the sound of the voice was like The Strong God in thunder.

When GOD commanded the man dressed in linen, "Take fire from among the wheels, from between the cherubim," he went in and stood beside a wheel. One of the cherubim reached into the fire, took some coals, and put them in the hands of the man dressed in linen. He took them and went out. Something that looked like a human hand could be seen under the wings of the cherubim.

And then I saw four wheels beside the cherubim, one beside each cherub. The wheels radiating were sparkling like diamonds in the sun.

All four wheels looked alike, each like a wheel within a wheel. When they moved, they went in any of the four directions but in a perfectly straight line. Where the cherubim went, the wheels went straight ahead. The cherubim were full of eyes in their backs, hands, and wings. The wheels likewise were full of eyes. I heard the wheels called "wheels within wheels."

Each of the cherubim had four faces: the first, of an angel; the second, a human; the third, a lion; the fourth, an eagle.

Then the cherubim ascended. They were the same living creatures I had seen at the Chebar River. When the cherubim moved, the wheels beside them moved. When the cherubim spread their wings to take off from the ground, the wheels stayed right with them. When the cherubim stopped, the wheels stopped. When the cherubim rose, the wheels rose, because the spirit of the living creatures was also in the wheels.

Then the Glory of GOD left the Temple entrance and hovered over the cherubim. I watched as the cherubim spread their wings and left the ground, the wheels right with them. They stopped at the entrance of the east gate of the Temple. The Glory of the God of Israel was above them.

These were the same living creatures I had seen previously beneath the God of Israel at the Chebar River. I recognized them as cherubim. Each had four faces and four wings. Under their wings was what looked like human hands. Their faces looked exactly like those I had seen at the Chebar River. Each went straight ahead.

11

A NEW HEART AND A NEW SPIRIT

Then the Spirit picked me up and took me to the gate of the Temple that faces east. There were twenty-five men standing at the gate. I recognized the leaders, Jaazaniah son of Azzur and Pelatiah son of Benaiah.

GOD said, "Son of man, these are the men who draw up blueprints for sin, who think up new programs for evil in this city. They say, 'We can make anything happen here. We're the best. We're the choice pieces of meat in the soup pot.'

"Oppose them, son of man. Preach against them."

Then the Spirit of GOD came upon me and told me what to say: "This is what GOD says: 'That's a fine public speech, Israel, but I know what you are thinking. You've murdered a lot of people in this city. The streets are piled high with corpses.'

"Therefore this is what GOD, the Master, says: 'The corpses that you've piled in the streets are the meat and this city is the soup pot, and *you're* not even in the pot! I'm throwing you out! You fear war, but war is what you're going to get. I'm bringing war against you. I'm throwing you out of this city, giving you over to foreigners, and punishing you good. You'll be killed in battle. I'll carry out judgment on you at the borders of Israel. Then you'll realize that I am GOD. This city will not be your soup pot and you won't be the choice pieces of meat in it either. Hardly. I will carry out judgment on you at the borders of Israel and you'll realize that I am GOD, for you haven't followed my statutes and ordinances. Instead of following my ways, you've sunk to the level of the laws of the nations around you.'"

Even while I was preaching, Pelatiah son of Benaiah died. I fell down, face to the ground, and prayed loudly, "Oh Master, GOD! Will you completely wipe out what's left of Israel?"

The answer from GOD came back: "Son of man, your brothers—I mean the whole people of Israel who are in exile with you—are the people of whom the citizens of Jerusalem are saying, 'They're in the far country, far from GOD. This land has been given to us to own.'

"Well, tell them this: 'This is your Message from GOD, the Master. True, I sent you to the far country and scattered you through other lands. All the same, I've provided you a temporary sanctuary in the countries where you've gone. I will gather you back from those countries and lands where you've been scattered and give you back the land of Israel. You'll come back and clean house, throw out all the rotten images and obscene idols. I'll give you a new heart. I'll put a new spirit in you. I'll cut out your stone heart and replace it with a red-blooded, firm-muscled heart. Then you'll obey my statutes and be careful to obey my commands. You'll be my people! I'll be your God!

"'But not those who are self-willed and addicted to their rotten images and obscene idols! I'll see that they're paid in full for what they've done.' Decree of GOD, the Master."

Then the cherubim spread their wings, with the wheels beside them and the Glory of the God of Israel hovering over them. The Glory of GOD ascended from within the city and rested on the mountain to the east of the city.

✤

Then, still in the vision given me by the Spirit of God, the Spirit took me and carried me back to the exiles in Babylon. And then the vision left me. I told the exiles everything that GOD had shown me.

12

PUT THE BUNDLE ON YOUR SHOULDER AND WALK INTO THE NIGHT

GOD's Message came to me: "Son of man, you're living with a bunch of rebellious people. They have eyes but don't see a thing, they have ears but don't hear a thing. They're rebels all. So, son of man, pack up your exile duffel bags. Leave in broad daylight with everyone watching and go off, as if into exile. Maybe then they'll understand what's going on, rebels though they are. You'll take up your baggage while they watch, a bundle of the bare necessities of someone going into exile, and toward evening leave, just like a person going off into exile. As they watch, dig through the wall of the house and carry your bundle through it. In full sight of the people, put the bundle on your shoulder and walk out into the night. Cover your face so you won't have to look at what you'll never see again. I'm using you as a sign for the family of Israel."

I did exactly as he commanded me. I got my stuff together and brought it out in the street where everyone could see me, bundled it up the way someone being taken off into exile would, and then, as the sun went down, made a hole in the wall of the house with my hands. As it grew dark and as they watched, I left, throwing my bundle across my shoulders.

The next morning GOD spoke to me: "Son of man, when anyone in Israel, that bunch of rebels, asks you, 'What are you doing?' Tell them, 'GOD, the Master, says that this Message especially concerns the prince in Jerusalem—Zedekiah—but includes all the people of Israel.'

"Also tell them, 'I am drawing a picture for you. As I am now doing, it will be done to all the people of Israel. They will go into exile as captives.'

"The prince will put his bundle on his shoulders in the dark and leave. He'll dig through the wall of the house, covering his face so he won't have to look at the land he'll never see again. But I'll make sure he gets caught and is taken to Babylon. Blinded, he'll never see that land in which he'll die. I'll scatter to the four winds those who helped him escape, along with his troops, and many will die in battle. They'll realize that I am GOD when I scatter them among foreign countries.

"I'll permit a few of them to escape the killing, starvation, and deadly sickness so that they can confess among the foreign countries all the disgusting obscenities they've been involved in. They will realize that I am GOD."

✝

GOD's Message came to me: "Son of man, eat your meals shaking in your boots, drink your water trembling with fear. Tell the people of this land, everyone living in Jerusalem and Israel, GOD's Message: 'You'll eat your meals shaking in your boots and drink your water in terror because your land is going to be stripped bare as punishment for the brutality rampant in it. All the cities and villages will be emptied out and the fields destroyed. Then you'll realize that I am GOD.'"

✝

GOD's Message came to me: "Son of man, what's this proverb making the rounds in the land of Israel that says, 'Everything goes on the same as ever; all the prophetic warnings are false alarms'?

"Tell them, 'GOD, the Master, says, This proverb's going to have a short life!'

"Tell them, 'Time's about up. Every warning is about to come true. False alarms and easygoing preaching are a thing of the past in the life of Israel. I, GOD, am doing the speaking. What I say happens. None of what I say is on hold. What I say, I'll do—and soon, you rebels!' Decree of God the Master."

✝

GOD's Message came to me: "Son of man, do you hear what Israel is saying: that the alarm the prophet raises is for a long time off, that he's preaching about the faroff future? Well, tell them, 'GOD, the Master, says, "Nothing of what I say is on hold. What I say happens."' Decree of GOD, the Master."

13

PEOPLE WHO LOVE LISTENING TO LIES

GOD's Message came to me: "Son of man, preach against the prophets of Israel who are making things up out of their own heads and calling it 'prophesying.'

"Preach to them the real thing. Tell them, 'Listen to GOD's Message!'

GOD, the Master, pronounces doom on the empty-headed prophets who do their own thing and know nothing of what's going on! Your prophets, Israel, are like jackals scavenging through the ruins. They haven't lifted a finger to repair the defenses of the city and have risked nothing to help Israel stand on GOD's Day of Judgment. All they do is fantasize comforting illusions and preach lying sermons. They say 'GOD says . . .' when GOD hasn't so much as breathed in their direction. And yet they stand around thinking that something they said is going to happen.

"Haven't you fantasized sheer nonsense? Aren't your sermons tissues of lies, saying 'GOD says . . .' when I've done nothing of the kind? Therefore—and this is Message of GOD, the Master, remember—I'm dead set against prophets who substitute illusions for visions and use sermons to tell lies. I'm going to ban them from the council of my people, remove them from membership in Israel, and outlaw them from the land of Israel. Then you'll realize that I am GOD, the Master.

"The fact is that they've lied to my people. They've said, 'No problem; everything's just fine,' when things are not at all fine. When people build a wall, they're right behind them slapping on whitewash. Tell those who are slapping on the whitewash, 'When a torrent of rain comes and the hailstones crash down and the hurricane sweeps in and the wall collapses, what's the good of the whitewash that you slapped on so liberally, making it look so good?'

"And that's exactly what will happen. I, GOD, the Master, say so: 'I'll let the hurricane of my wrath loose, a torrent of my hailstone-anger. I'll make that wall you've slapped with whitewash collapse. I'll level it to the ground so that only the foundation stones will be left. And in the ruin you'll all die. You'll realize then that I am GOD.

"'I'll dump my wrath on that wall, all of it, and on those who plastered it with whitewash. I will say to them, "There is no wall, and those who did such a good job of whitewashing it wasted their time, those prophets of Israel who preached to Jerusalem and announced all their visions telling us things were just fine when they weren't at all fine. Decree of GOD, the Master."'

"And the women prophets—son of man, take your stand against the women prophets who make up stuff out of their own minds. Oppose them. Say 'Doom' to the women who sew magic bracelets and head scarves to suit every taste, devices to trap souls. Say, 'Will you kill the souls of my people, use living souls to make yourselves rich and popular? You have profaned me among my people just to get ahead yourselves, used me to make yourselves look good—killing souls who should never have died and coddling souls who shouldn't live. You've lied to people who love listening to lies.'

"Therefore GOD says, 'I am against all the devices and techniques you use to hunt down souls. I'll rip them out of your hands. I'll free the souls you're trying to catch. I'll rip your magic bracelets and scarves to shreds and deliver my people from your influence so they'll no longer be victimized by you. That's how you'll come to realize that I am GOD.

"'Because you've confounded and confused good people, unsuspecting and innocent people, with your lies, and because you've made it easy for others to persist in evil so that it wouldn't even dawn on them to turn to me so I could save them, as of now you're finished. No more delusion-mongering from you, no more sermonic lies. I'm going to rescue my people from your clutches. And you'll realize that I am GOD.'"

14

IDOLS IN THEIR HEARTS

Some of the leaders of Israel approached me and sat down with me. GOD's Message came to me: "Son of Man, these people have installed idols in their hearts. They have embraced the wickedness that will ruin them. Why should I even bother with their prayers? Therefore tell them, 'The Message of GOD, the Master: All in Israel who install idols in their hearts and embrace the wickedness that will ruin them and still have the gall to come to a prophet, be on notice: I, GOD, will step in and personally answer them as they come dragging along their mob of idols. I am ready to go to work on the hearts of the house of Israel, all of whom have left me for their idols.'

"Therefore, say to the house of Israel: 'GOD, the Master, says, Repent! Turn your backs on your no-god idols. Turn your backs on all your outrageous obscenities. To every last person from the house of Israel, including any of the resident aliens who live in Israel—all who turn their backs on me and embrace idols, who install the wickedness that will ruin them at the center of their lives and then have the gall to go to the prophet to ask me questions—I, GOD, will step in and give the answer myself. I'll oppose those people to their faces, make an example of them—a warning lesson—and get rid of them so you will realize that I am GOD.

"'If a prophet is deceived and tells these idolaters the lies they want to hear, I, GOD, get blamed for those lies. He won't get by with it. I'll grab him by the scruff of the neck and get him out of there. They'll be equally guilty, the prophet and the one who goes to the prophet, so that the house of Israel will never again wander off my paths and make themselves filthy in their rebellions, but will rather be my people, just as I am their God. Decree of GOD, the Master.'"

✝

GOD's Message came to me: "Son of man, when a country sins against me by living faithlessly and I reach out and destroy its food supply by bringing on a famine, wiping out humans and animals alike, even if Noah, Daniel, and Job—the Big Three—were alive at the time, it wouldn't do the population any good. Their righteousness would only save their own lives." Decree of GOD, the Master.

"Or, if I make wild animals go through the country so that everyone has to leave and the country becomes wilderness and no one dares enter it anymore because of the wild animals, even if these three men were living there, as sure as I am the living God, neither their sons nor daughters would be rescued, but only those three, and the country would revert to wilderness.

"Or, if I bring war on that country and give the order, 'Let the killing begin!' leaving both people and animals dead, even if those three men were alive at the time, as sure as I am the living God, neither sons nor daughters would be rescued, but only these three.

"Or, if I visit a deadly disease on that country, pouring out my lethal anger, killing both people and animals, and Noah, Daniel, and Job happened to be alive at the time, as sure as I am the living God, not a son, not a daughter, would be rescued. Only these three would be delivered because of their righteousness.

"Now then, that's the picture," says GOD, the Master, "once I've sent my four catastrophic judgments on Jerusalem—war, famine, wild animals, disease—to kill off people and animals alike. But look! Believe it or not, there'll be survivors. Some of their sons and daughters will be brought out. When they come out to you and their salvation is right in your face, you'll see for yourself the life they've been saved from. You'll know that this severe judgment I brought on Jerusalem was worth it, that it had to be. Yes, when you see in detail the kind of lives they've been living, you'll feel much better. You'll see the reason behind all that I've done in Jerusalem." Decree of GOD, the Master.

15

Used as Fuel for the Fire

God's Message came to me: "Son of man, how would you compare the wood of a vine with the branches of any tree you'd find in the forest? Is vine wood ever used to make anything? Is it used to make pegs to hang things from?

"I don't think so. At best it's good for fuel. Look at it: a flimsy piece of vine, thrown in the fire and then rescued—the ends burned off and the middle charred. Now is it good for anything?

"Hardly. When it was whole it wasn't good for anything. Half-burned is no improvement. What's it good for?

"So here's the Message of God, the Master: Like the wood of the vine I selected from among of the trees of the forest and used as fuel for the fire, just so I'll treat those who live in Jerusalem. I am dead set against them. Even though at one time they got out of the fire charred, the fire's going to burn them up. When I take my stand against them, you'll realize that I am God. I'll turn this country into a wilderness because they've been faithless." Decree of God, the Master.

16

Your Beauty Went to Your Head

God's Message came to me: "Son of man, confront Jerusalem with her outrageous violations. Say this: 'The Message of God, the Master, to Jerusalem: You were born and bred among Canaanites. Your father was an Amorite and your mother a Hittite.

"'On the day you were born your umbilical cord was not cut, you weren't bathed and cleaned up, you weren't rubbed with salt, you weren't wrapped in a baby blanket. No one cared a fig for you. No one did one thing to care for you tenderly in these ways. You were thrown out into a vacant lot and left there, dirty and unwashed—a newborn nobody wanted.

"'And then I came by. I saw you all miserable and bloody. Yes, I said to you, lying there helpless and filthy, "Live! Grow up like a plant in the field!" And you did. You grew up. You grew tall and matured as a woman, full-breasted, with flowing hair. But you were naked and vulnerable, fragile and exposed.

"'I came by again and saw you, saw that you were ready for love and a lover. I took care of you, dressed you and protected you. I promised you my love and entered the covenant of marriage with you. I, GOD, the Master, gave my word. You became mine. I gave you a good bath, washing off all that old blood, and anointed you with aromatic oils. I dressed you in a colorful gown and put leather sandals on your feet. I gave you linen blouses and a fashionable wardrobe of expensive clothing. I adorned you with jewelry: I placed bracelets on your wrists, fitted you out with a necklace, emerald rings, sapphire earrings, and a diamond tiara. You were provided with everything precious and beautiful: with exquisite clothes and elegant food, garnished with honey and oil. You were absolutely stunning. You were a queen! You became world-famous, a legendary beauty brought to perfection by my adornments. Decree of GOD, the Master.

"But your beauty went to your head and you became a common whore, grabbing anyone coming down the street and taking him into your bed. You took your fine dresses and made "tents" of them, using them as brothels in which you practiced your trade. This kind of thing should never happen, never.

WHAT A SICK SOUL!

"And then you took all that fine jewelry I gave you, my gold and my silver, and made pornographic images of them for your brothels. You decorated your beds with fashionable silks and cottons, and perfumed them with my aromatic oils and incense. And then you set out the wonderful foods I provided — the fresh breads and fruits, with fine herbs and spices, which were my gifts to you — and you served them as delicacies in your whorehouses. That's what happened, says GOD, the Master.

"And then you took your sons and your daughters, whom you had given birth to as my children, and you killed them, sacrificing them to idols. Wasn't it bad enough that you had become a whore? And now you're a murderer, killing my children and sacrificing them to idols.

"Not once during these years of outrageous obscenities and whorings did you remember your infancy, when you were naked and exposed, a blood-smeared newborn.

"And then to top off all your evil acts, you built your bold brothels in every town square. Doom! Doom to you, says GOD, the Master! At every major intersection you built your bold brothels and exposed your sluttish sex, spreading your legs for everyone who passed by.

"And then you went international with your whoring. You fornicated with the Egyptians, seeking them out in their sex orgies. The more promiscuous you became, the angrier I got. Finally, I intervened, reduced your borders and turned you over to the rapacity of your enemies. Even the Philistine women—can you believe it?—were shocked at your sluttish life.

"'You went on to fornicate with the Assyrians. Your appetite was insatiable. But still you weren't satisfied. You took on the Babylonians, a country of businessmen, and *still* you weren't satisfied.

"'What a sick soul! Doing all this stuff—the champion whore! You built your bold brothels at every major intersection, opened up your whorehouses in every neighborhood, but you were different from regular whores in that you wouldn't accept a fee.

"'Wives who are unfaithful to their husbands accept gifts from their lovers. And men commonly pay their whores. But you pay your lovers! You bribe men from all over to come to bed with you! You're just the opposite of the regular whores who get paid for sex. Instead, you pay men for *their* favors! You even pervert whoredom!

"'Therefore, whore, listen to GOD's Message: I, GOD, the Master, say, Because you've been unrestrained in your promiscuity, stripped down for every lover, flaunting your sex, and because of your pornographic idols and all the slaughtered children you offered to them, therefore, because of all this, I'm going to get all your lovers together, all those you've used for your own pleasure, the ones you loved and the ones you loathed. I'll assemble them as a courtroom of spectators around you. In broad daylight I'll strip you naked before them—they'll see what you *really* look like. Then I'll sentence you to the punishment for an adulterous woman and a murderous woman. I'll give you a taste of my wrath!

"'I'll gather all your lovers around you and turn you over to them. They'll tear down your bold brothels and sex shrines. They'll rip off your clothes, take your jewels, and leave you naked and exposed. Then they'll call for a mass meeting. The mob will stone you and hack you to pieces with their swords. They'll burn down your houses. A massive judgment—with all the women watching!

"'I'll have put a full stop to your whoring life—no more paying lovers to come to your bed! By then my anger will be played out. My jealousy will subside.

"'Because you didn't remember what happened when you were young but made me angry with all this behavior, I'll make you pay for your waywardness. Didn't you just exponentially compound your outrageous obscenities with all your sluttish ways?

"'Everyone who likes to use proverbs will use this one: "Like mother, like daughter." You're the daughter of your mother, who couldn't stand her husband and children. And you're a true sister of your sisters, who couldn't stand their husbands and children. Your mother was a Hittite and your father an Amorite.

"'Your older sister is Samaria. She lived to the north of you with her daughters. Your younger sister is Sodom, who lived to the south of you with her daughters. Haven't you lived just like they did? Haven't you engaged in outrageous obscenities just like they did? In fact, it didn't take you long to catch up and pass them! As sure as I am the living God!—Decree of God, the Master—your sister Sodom and her daughters never even came close to what you and your daughters have done.

"'The sin of your sister Sodom was this: She lived with her daughters in the lap of luxury—proud, gluttonous, and lazy. They ignored the oppressed and the poor. They put on airs and lived obscene lives. And you know what happened: I did away with them.

"'And Samaria. Samaria didn't sin half as much as you. You've committed far more obscenities than she ever did. Why, you make your two sisters look good in comparison with what you've done! Face it, your sisters look mighty good compared with you. Because you've outsinned them so completely, you've actually made them look righteous. Aren't you ashamed? But you're going to have to live with it. What a reputation to carry into history: outsinning your two sisters!

"'But I'm going to reverse their fortunes, the fortunes of Sodom and her daughters and the fortunes of Samaria and her daughters. And—get this—*your* fortunes right along with them! Still, you're going to have to live with your shame. And by facing and accepting your shame, you're going to provide some comfort to your two sisters. Your sisters, Sodom with her daughters and Samaria with her daughters, will become what they were before, and you will become what you were before. Remember the days when you were putting on airs, acting so high and mighty, looking down on sister Sodom? That was before your evil ways were exposed. And now *you're* the butt of contempt, despised by the Edomite women, the Philistine women, and everybody else around. But you have to face it, to accept the shame of your obscene and vile life. Decree of God, the Master.

"'God, the Master, says, I'll do to you just as you have already done, you who have treated my oath with contempt and broken the covenant. All the same, I'll remember the covenant I made with you when you were young and I'll make a new covenant with you that will last forever. You'll remember your sorry past and be properly contrite when you receive back your sisters, both the older and the younger. I'll give them to you as daughters, but not as participants in your covenant. I'll firmly establish my covenant with you and you'll know that I am GOD. You'll remember your past life and face the shame of it, but when I make atonement for you, make everything right after all you've done, it will leave you speechless.'" Decree of GOD, the Master.

17

THE GREAT TREE IS MADE SMALL AND THE SMALL TREE GREAT

GOD's Message came to me: "Son of man, make a riddle for the house of Israel. Tell them a story. Say, 'GOD, the Master, says:

"'A great eagle
    with a huge wingspan and long feathers,
In full plumage and bright colors,
    came to Lebanon
And took the top off a cedar,
    broke off the top branch,
Took it to a land of traders,
    and set it down in a city of shopkeepers.
Then he took a cutting from the land
    and planted it in good, well-watered soil,
    like a willow on a riverbank.
It sprouted into a flourishing vine,
    low to the ground.
Its branches grew toward the eagle
    and the roots became established—
A vine putting out shoots,
    developing branches.

"'There was another great eagle
    with a huge wingspan and thickly feathered.
This vine sent out its roots toward him
    from the place where it was planted.
Its branches reached out to him
    so he could water it
    from a long distance.

It had been planted
    in good, well-watered soil,
And it put out branches and bore fruit,
    and became a noble vine.

"'GOD, the Master, says,
    Will it thrive?
Won't he just pull it up by the roots
    and leave the grapes to rot
And the branches to shrivel up,
    a withered, dead vine?
It won't take much strength
    or many hands to pull it up.
Even if it's transplanted,
    will it thrive?
When the hot east wind strikes it,
    won't it shrivel up?
Won't it dry up and blow away
    from the place where it was planted?'"

☩

GOD's Message came to me: "Tell this house of rebels, 'Do you get it? Do you know what this means?'

"Tell them, 'The king of Babylon came to Jerusalem and took its king and its leaders back to Babylon. He took one of the royal family and made a covenant with him, making him swear his loyalty. The king of Babylon took all the top leaders into exile to make sure that this kingdom stayed weak—didn't get any big ideas of itself—and kept the covenant with him so that it would have a future.

"But he rebelled and sent emissaries to Egypt to recruit horses and a big army. Do you think that's going to work? Are they going to get by with this? Does anyone break a covenant and get off scot-free?

"'As sure as I am the living God, this king who broke his pledge of loyalty and his covenant will die in that country, in Babylon. Pharaoh with his big army—all those soldiers!—won't lift a finger to fight for him when Babylon sets siege to the city and kills everyone inside. Because he broke his word and broke the covenant, even though he gave his solemn promise, because he went ahead and did all these things anyway, he won't escape.

"'Therefore, GOD, the Master, says, As sure as I am the living God, because the king despised my oath and broke my covenant, I'll bring the consequences crashing down on his head. I'll send out a search party and catch him. I'll take him to Babylon and have him brought to trial because of his total disregard for me. All his elite soldiers, along with the rest of the army, will be killed in battle, and whoever is left will be scattered to the four winds. Then you'll realize that I, GOD, have spoken.

"'GOD, the Master, says, I personally will take a shoot from the top of the towering cedar, a cutting from the crown of the tree, and plant it on a high and towering mountain, on the high mountain of Israel. It will grow, putting out branches and fruit—a majestic cedar. Birds of every sort and kind will live under it. They'll build nests in the shade of its branches. All the trees of the field will recognize that I, GOD, made the great tree small and the small tree great, made the green tree turn dry and the dry tree sprout green branches. I, GOD, said it—and I did it.'"

18

JUDGED ACCORDING TO THE WAY YOU LIVE

GOD's Message to me: "What do you people mean by going around the country repeating the saying,

'The parents ate green apples,
The children got stomachache'?

"As sure as I'm the living God, you're not going to repeat this saying in Israel any longer. Every soul—man, woman, child—belongs to me, parent and child alike. You die for your own sin, not another's.

"Imagine a person who lives well, treating others fairly, keeping good relationships—

doesn't eat at the pagan shrines,
doesn't worship the idols so popular in Israel,
doesn't seduce a neighbor's spouse,
doesn't indulge in casual sex,
doesn't bully anyone,
doesn't pile up bad debts,
doesn't steal,
doesn't refuse food to the hungry,

doesn't refuse clothing to the ill-clad,
doesn't exploit the poor,
doesn't live by impulse and greed,
doesn't treat one person better than another,
But lives by my statutes and faithfully
    honors and obeys my laws.
This person who lives upright and well
    shall live a full and true life.
        Decree of GOD, the Master.

"But if this person has a child who turns violent and murders and goes off and does any of these things, even though the parent has done none of them—

eats at the pagan shrines,
seduces his neighbor's spouse,
bullies the weak,
steals,
piles up bad debts,
admires idols,
commits outrageous obscenities,
exploits the poor—

do you think this person, the child, will live? Not a chance! Because he's done all these vile things, he'll die. And his death will be his own fault.

"Now look: Suppose that this child has a child who sees all the sins done by his parent. The child sees them, but doesn't follow in the parent's footsteps—

doesn't eat at the pagan shrines,
doesn't worship the popular idols of Israel,
doesn't seduce his neighbor's spouse,
doesn't bully anyone,
doesn't refuse to loan money,
doesn't steal,
doesn't refuse food to the hungry
doesn't refuse to give clothes to the ill-clad,
doesn't live by impulse and greed,
doesn't exploit the poor.

He does what I say;
    he performs my laws and lives by my statutes.

"This person will not die for the sins of the parent; he will live truly and well. But the parent will die for what the parent did, for the sins of—

    oppressing the weak,
    robbing brothers and sisters,
    doing what is dead wrong in the community.

"Do you need to ask, 'So why does the child not share the guilt of the parent?'

"Isn't it plain? It's because the child did what is fair and right. Since the child was careful to do what is lawful and right, the child will live truly and well. The soul that sins is the soul that dies. The child does not share the guilt of the parent, nor the parent the guilt of the child. If you live upright and well, you get the credit; if you live a wicked life, you're guilty as charged.

"But a wicked person who turns his back on that life of sin and keeps all my statutes, living a just and righteous life, he'll live, really live. He won't die. I won't keep a list of all the things he did wrong. He will live. Do you think I take any pleasure in the death of wicked men and women? Isn't it my pleasure that they turn around, no longer living wrong but living right—really living?

"The same thing goes for a good person who turns his back on an upright life and starts sinning, plunging into the same vile obscenities that the wicked person practices. Will this person live? I don't keep a list of all the things this person did right, like money in the bank he can draw on. Because of his defection, because he accumulates sin, he'll die.

"Do I hear you saying, 'That's not fair! God's not fair!'?

"Listen, Israel. I'm not fair? You're the ones who aren't fair! If a good person turns away from his good life and takes up sinning, he'll die for it. He'll die for his own sin. Likewise, if a bad person turns away from his bad life and starts living a good life, a fair life, he will save his life. Because he faces up to all the wrongs he's committed and puts them behind him, he will live, really live. He won't die.

"And yet Israel keeps on whining, 'That's not fair! God's not fair.'

"I'm not fair, Israel? You're the ones who aren't fair.

"The upshot is this, Israel: I'll judge each of you according to the way you live. So turn around! Turn your backs on your rebellious living so that sin won't drag you down. Clean house. No more rebel-lions, please. Get a new heart! Get a new spirit! Why would you choose to die, Israel? I take no pleasure in anyone's death. Decree of GOD, the Master.

"Make a clean break! Live!"

19

A STORY OF TWO LIONS

Sing the blues over the princes of Israel. Say:

What a lioness was your mother
    among lions!
She crouched in a pride of young lions.
    Her cubs grew large.
She reared one of her cubs to maturity,
    a robust young lion.
He learned to hunt.
    He ate men.
Nations sounded the alarm.
    He was caught in a trap.
They took him with hooks
    and dragged him to Egypt.

When the lioness saw she was luckless,
    that her hope for that cub was gone,
She took her other cub
    and made him a strong young lion.
He prowled with the lions,
    a robust young lion.
He learned to hunt.
    He ate men.
He rampaged through their defenses,
    left their cities in ruins.
The country and everyone in it
    was terrorized by the roars of the lion.
The nations got together to hunt him.
    Everyone joined the hunt.
They set out their traps
    and caught him.

They put a wooden collar on him
    and took him to the king of Babylon.
No more would that voice be heard
    disturbing the peace in the mountains of Israel!

Here's another way to put it:
    Your mother was like a vine in a vineyard,
    transplanted alongside streams of water,
Luxurious in branches and grapes
    because of the ample water.
It grew sturdy branches
    fit to be carved into a royal scepter.
It grew high, reaching into the clouds.
    Its branches filled the horizon,
    and everyone could see it.
Then it was ripped up in a rage
    and thrown to the ground.
The hot east wind shriveled it up
    and stripped its fruit.
The sturdy branches dried out,
    fit for nothing but kindling.
Now it's a stick stuck out in the desert,
    a bare stick in a desert of death,
Good for nothing but making fires,
    campfires in the desert.
Not a hint now of those sturdy branches
    fit for use as a royal scepter!

(This is a sad song, a text for singing the blues.)

20

GET RID OF ALL THE THINGS YOU'VE BECOME ADDICTED TO

In the seventh year, the fifth month, on the tenth day of the month, some of the leaders of Israel came to ask for guidance from GOD. They sat down before me.

Then GOD's Message came to me: "Son of man, talk with the leaders of Israel. Tell them, 'GOD, the Master, says, "Have you come to ask me questions? As sure as I am the living God, I'll not put up with questions from you. Decree of GOD, the Master."'"

"Son of man, why don't *you* do it? Yes, go ahead. Hold them accountable. Confront them with the outrageous obscenities of their parents. Tell them that GOD, the Master, says:

"'On the day I chose Israel, I revealed myself to them in the country of Egypt, raising my hand in a solemn oath to the people of Jacob, in which I said, "I am GOD, your personal God." On the same day that I raised my hand in the solemn oath, I promised them that I would take them out of the country of Egypt and bring them into a country that I had searched out just for them, a country flowing with milk and honey, a jewel of a country.

"'At that time I told them, "Get rid of all the vile things that you've become addicted to. Don't make yourselves filthy with the Egyptian no-god idols. *I alone* am GOD, your God."

"'But they rebelled against me, wouldn't listen to a word I said. None got rid of the vile things they were addicted to. They held on to the no-gods of Egypt as if for dear life. I seriously considered inflicting my anger on them in force right there in Egypt. Then I thought better of it. I acted out of who I was, not by how I felt. And I acted in a way that would evoke honor, not blasphemy, from the nations around them, nations who had seen me reveal myself by promising to lead my people out of Egypt. And then I did it: I led them out of Egypt into the desert.

"'I gave them laws for living, showed them how to live well and obediently before me. I also gave them my weekly holy rest days, my "sabbaths," a kind of signpost erected between me and them to show them that I, GOD, am in the business of making them holy.

"'But Israel rebelled against me in the desert. They didn't follow my statutes. They despised my laws for living well and obediently in the ways I had set out. And they totally desecrated my holy sabbaths. I seriously considered unleashing my anger on them right there in the desert. But I thought better of it and acted out of who I was, not by what I felt, so that I might be honored and not blasphemed by the nations who had seen me bring them out. But I did lift my hand in a solemn oath there in the desert and promise them that I would not bring them into the country flowing with milk and honey that I had chosen for them, that jewel among all lands. I canceled my promise because they despised my laws for living obediently, wouldn't follow my statutes, and went ahead and desecrated my holy sabbaths. They preferred living by their no-god idols. But I didn't go all the way: I didn't wipe them out, didn't finish them off in the desert.

"'Then I addressed myself to their children in the desert: "Don't do what your parents did. Don't take up their practices. Don't make yourselves filthy with their no-god idols. I myself am GOD, your God: Keep my statutes and live by my laws. Keep my sabbaths as holy rest days, signposts between me and you, signaling that I am GOD, *your* God."

"'But the children also rebelled against me. They neither followed my statutes nor kept my laws for living upright and well. And they desecrated my sabbaths. I seriously considered dumping my anger on them, right there in the desert. But I thought better of it and acted out of who I was, not by what I felt, so that I might be honored and not blasphemed by the nations who had seen me bring them out.

"'But I did lift my hand in solemn oath there in the desert, and swore that I would scatter them all over the world, disperse them every which way because they didn't keep my laws nor live by my statutes. They desecrated my sabbaths and remained addicted to the no-god idols of their parents. Since they were determined to live bad lives, I myself gave them statutes that could not produce goodness and laws that did not produce life. I abandoned them. Filthy in the gutter, they perversely sacrificed their firstborn children in the fire. The very horror should have shocked them into recognizing that I am GOD.'

"Therefore, speak to Israel, son of man. Tell them that GOD says, 'As if that wasn't enough, your parents further insulted me by betraying me. When I brought them into that land that I had solemnly promised with my upraised hand to give them, every time they saw a hill with a sex-and-religion shrine on it or a grove of trees where the sacred whores practiced, they were there, buying into the whole pagan system. I said to them, "What hill do you go to?"' (It's still called "Whore Hills.")

"Therefore, say to Israel, 'The Message of GOD, the Master: You're making your lives filthy by copying the ways of your parents. In repeating their vile practices, you've become whores yourselves. In burning your children as sacrifices, you've become as filthy as your no-god idols—as recently as today!

"'Am I going to put up with questions from people like you, Israel? As sure as I am the living God, I, GOD, the Master, refuse to be called into question by you!

"'What you're secretly thinking is never going to happen. You're thinking, "We're going to be like everybody else, just like the other nations. We're going to worship gods we can make and control."

"'As sure as I am the living God, says GOD, the Master, think again! With a mighty show of strength and a terrifying rush of anger, I will be King over you! I'll bring you back from the nations, collect you out of the countries to which you've been scattered, with a mighty show of strength and a terrifying rush of anger. I'll bring you to the desert of nations and haul you into court, where you'll be face to face with judgment.

"'As I faced your parents with judgment in the desert of Egypt, so I'll face you with judgment. I'll scrutinize and search every person as you arrive, and I'll bring you under the bond of the covenant. I'll cull out the rebels and traitors. I'll lead them out of their exile, but I won't bring them back to Israel.

"'Then you'll realize that I am GOD.

"'But you, people of Israel, this is the Message of GOD, the Master, to you: Go ahead, serve your no-god idols! But later, you'll think better of it and quit throwing filth and mud on me with your pagan offerings and no-god idols. For on my holy mountain, the high mountain of Israel, I, GOD, the Master, tell you that the entire people of Israel will worship me. I'll receive them there with open arms. I'll demand your best gifts and offerings, all your holy sacrifices. What's more, I'll receive you as the best kind of offerings when I bring you back from all the lands and countries in which you've been scattered. I'll demonstrate in the eyes of the world that I am The Holy. When I return you to the land of Israel, the land that I solemnly promised with upraised arm to give to your parents, you'll realize that I am GOD. Then and there you'll remember all that you've done, the way you've lived that has made you so filthy—and you'll loathe yourselves.

"'But, dear Israel, you'll also realize that I am GOD when I respond to you out of who I am, not by what I feel about the evil lives you've lived, the corrupt history you've compiled. Decree of GOD, the Master.'"

NOBODY WILL PUT OUT THE FIRE

GOD's Message came to me: "Son of man, face south. Let the Message roll out against the south. Prophesy against the wilderness forest of the south.

"Tell the forest of the south, 'Listen to the Message of GOD! GOD, the Master, says, I'll set a fire in you that will burn up every tree, dead trees and live trees alike. Nobody will put out the fire. The whole country from south to north will be blackened by it. Everyone is going to see that I, GOD, started the fire and that it's not going to be put out.'"

And I said, "Oh GOD, everyone is saying of me, 'He just makes up stories.'"

21

A SWORD! A SWORD!

GOD's Message came to me: "Son of man, now face Jerusalem and let the Message roll out against the Sanctuary. Prophesy against the land of Israel. Say, 'GOD's Message: I'm against you. I'm pulling my sword from its sheath and killing both the wicked and the righteous. Because I'm treating everyone the same, good and bad, everyone from south to north is going to feel my sword! Everyone will know that I mean business.'

"So, son of man, groan! Double up in pain. Make a scene!

"When they ask you, 'Why all this groaning, this carrying on?' say, 'Because of the news that's coming. It'll knock the breath out of everyone. Hearts will stop cold, knees turn to rubber. Yes, it's coming. No stopping it. Decree of GOD, the Master.'"

⊹

GOD's Message to me: "Son of man, prophesy. Tell them, 'The Master says:

"'A sword! A sword!
    razor-sharp and polished,
Sharpened to kill,
    polished to flash like lightning!

"'My child, you've despised the scepter of Judah
    by worshiping every tree-idol.

"'The sword is made to glisten,
    to be held and brandished.
It's sharpened and polished,
    ready to be brandished by the killer.'

"Yell out and wail, son of man.
    The sword is against my people!

347

The princes of Israel
     and my people—abandoned to the sword!
Wring your hands!
     Tear out your hair!

"'Testing comes.
     Why have you despised discipline?
You can't get around it.
     Decree of GOD, the Master.'

"So, prophesy, son of man!
     Clap your hands. Get their attention.
Tell them that the sword's coming down
     once, twice, three times.
It's a sword to kill,
     a sword for a massacre,
A sword relentless,
     a sword inescapable—
People collapsing right and left,
     going down like dominoes.
I've stationed a murderous sword
     at every gate in the city,
Flashing like lightning,
     brandished murderously.
Cut to the right, thrust to the left,
     murderous, sharp-edged sword!
Then I'll clap my hands,
     a signal that my anger is spent.
          I, GOD, have spoken."

☩

GOD's Message came to me: "Son of man, lay out two roads for the sword of the king of Babylon to take. Start them from the same place. Place a signpost at the beginning of each road. Post one sign to mark the road of the sword to Rabbah of the Ammonites. Post the other to mark the road to Judah and Fort Jerusalem. The king of Babylon stands at the fork in the road and he decides by divination which of the two roads to take.

He draws straws, he throws god-dice, he examines a goat liver. He opens his right hand: The omen says, 'Head for Jerusalem!' So he's on his way with battering rams, roused to kill, sounding the battle cry, pounding down city gates, building siege works.

"To the Judah leaders, who themselves have sworn oaths, it will seem like a false divination, but he will remind them of their guilt, and so they'll be captured.

"So this is what GOD, the Master, says: 'Because your sin is now out in the open so everyone can see what you've been doing, you'll be taken captive.

"'Oh Zedekiah, blasphemous and evil prince of Israel: Time's up. It's "punishment payday." GOD says, Take your royal crown off your head. No more "business as usual." The underdog will be promoted and the top dog will be demoted. Ruins, ruins, ruins! I'll turn the whole place into ruins. And ruins it will remain until the one comes who has a right to it. Then I'll give it to him.'

"But, son of man, your job is to prophesy. Tell them, 'This is the Message from GOD, the Master, against the Ammonites and against their cruel taunts:

"'A sword! A sword!
    Bared to kill,
Sharp as a razor,
    flashing like lightning.
Despite false sword propaganda
    circulated in Ammon,
The sword will sever Ammonite necks,
    for whom it's punishment payday.
Return the sword to the sheath! I'll judge you in your home country,
    in the land where you grew up.
I'll empty out my wrath on you,
    breathe hot anger down your neck.
I'll give you to vicious men
    skilled in torture.
You'll end up as stove-wood.
    Corpses will litter your land.
Not so much as a memory will be left of you.
    I, GOD, have said so.'"

22

THE SCARECROW OF THE NATIONS

GOD's Message came to me: "Son of man, are you going to judge this bloody city or not? Come now, are you going to judge her? Do it! Face her with all her outrageous obscenities. Tell her, 'This is what GOD, the Master, says: You're a city murderous at the core, just asking for punishment. You're a city obsessed with no-god idols, making yourself filthy. In all your killing, you've piled up guilt. In all your idol-making, you've become filthy. You've forced a premature end to your existence. I'll put you on exhibit as the scarecrow of the nations, the world's worst joke. From far and near they'll deride you as infamous in filth, notorious for chaos.

"'Your leaders, the princes of Israel among you, compete in crime. You're a community that's insolent to parents, abusive to outsiders, oppressive against orphans and widows. You treat my holy things with contempt and desecrate my sabbaths. You have people spreading lies and spilling blood, flocking to the hills to the sex shrines and fornicating unrestrained. Incest is common. Men force themselves on women regardless of whether they're ready or willing. Sex is now anarchy. Anyone is fair game: neighbor, daughter-in-law, sister. Murder is for hire, usury is rampant, extortion is commonplace.

"'And you've forgotten *me*. Decree of GOD, the Master.

"'Now look! I've clapped my hands, calling everyone's attention to your rapacious greed and your bloody brutalities. Can you stick with it? Will you be able to keep at this once I start dealing with you?

"'I, GOD, have spoken. I'll put an end to this. I'll throw you to the four winds. I'll scatter you all over the world. I'll put a full stop to your filthy living. You will be defiled, spattered with your own mud in the eyes of the nations. And you'll recognize that I am GOD.'"

GOD's Message came to me: "Son of man, the people of Israel are slag to me, the useless byproduct of refined copper, tin, iron, and lead left at the smelter—a worthless slag heap. So tell them, 'GOD, the Master, has spoken: Because you've all become worthless slag, you're on notice: I'll assemble you in Jerusalem. As men gather silver, copper, iron, lead, and tin into a furnace and blow fire on it to melt it down, so in my wrath I'll gather you and melt you down. I'll blow on you with the fire of my wrath to melt you down in the furnace. As silver is melted down, you'll be melted down. That should get through to you. Then you'll recognize that I, GOD, have let my wrath loose on you.'"

GOD's Message came to me: "Son of man, tell her, 'You're a land that during the time I was angry with you got no rain, not so much as a spring shower. The leaders among you became desperate, like roaring, ravaging lions killing indiscriminately. They grabbed and looted, leaving widows in their wake.

"'Your priests violated my law and desecrated my holy things. They can't tell the difference between sacred and secular. They tell people there's no difference between right and wrong. They're contemptuous of my holy sabbaths, profaning me by trying to pull me down to their level. Your politicians are like wolves prowling and killing and rapaciously taking whatever they want. Your preachers cover up for the politicians by pretending to have received visions and special revelations. They say, "This is what GOD, the Master, says . . ." when GOD hasn't said so much as one word. Extortion is rife, robbery is epidemic, the poor and needy are abused, outsiders are kicked around at will, with no access to justice.'

"I looked for someone to stand up for me against all this, to repair the defenses of the city, to take a stand for me and stand in the gap to protect this land so I wouldn't have to destroy it. I couldn't find anyone. Not one. So I'll empty out my wrath on them, burn them to a crisp with my hot anger, serve them with the consequences of all they've done. Decree of GOD, the Master."

23

WILD WITH LUST

GOD's Message came to me: "Son of man, there were two women, daughters of the same mother. They became whores in Egypt, whores from a young age. Their breasts were fondled, their young bosoms caressed. The older sister was named Oholah, the younger was Oholibah. They were my daughters, and they gave birth to sons and daughters.

"Oholah is Samaria and Oholibah is Jerusalem.

"Oholah started whoring while she was still mine. She lusted after Assyrians as lovers: military men smartly uniformed in blue, ambassadors and governors, good-looking young men mounted on fine horses. Her lust was unrestrained. She was a whore to the Assyrian elite. She compounded her filth with the idols of those to whom she gave herself in lust. She never slowed down. The whoring she began while young in Egypt she continued, sleeping with men who played with her breasts and spent their lust on her.

"So I left her to her Assyrian lovers, for whom she was so obsessed with lust. They ripped off her clothes, took away her children, and then, the final indignity, killed her. Among women her name became Shame— history's judgment on her.

"Her sister Oholibah saw all this, but she became even worse than her sister in lust and whoring, if you can believe it. She also went crazy with lust for Assyrians: ambassadors and governors, military men smartly dressed and mounted on fine horses—the Assyrian elite. And I saw that she also had become incredibly filthy. Both women followed the same path. But Oholibah surpassed her sister. When she saw figures of Babylonians carved in relief on the walls and painted red, fancy belts around their waists, elaborate turbans on their heads, all of them looking important—famous Babylonians!—she went wild with lust and sent invitations to them in Babylon. The Babylonians came on the run, fornicated with her, made her dirty inside and out. When they had thoroughly debased her, she lost interest in them. Then she went public with her fornication. She exhibited her sex to the world.

"I turned my back on her just as I had on her sister. But that didn't slow her down. She went at her whoring harder than ever. She remembered when she was young, just starting out as a whore in Egypt. That whetted her appetite for more virile, vulgar, and violent lovers—stallions obsessive in their lust. She longed for the sexual prowess of her youth back in Egypt, where her firm young breasts were caressed and fondled.

"'Therefore, Oholibah, this is the Message from GOD, the Master: I will incite your old lovers against you, lovers you got tired of and left in disgust. I'll bring them against you from every direction, Babylonians and all the Chaldeans, Pekod, Shoa, and Koa, and all Assyrians—good-looking young men, ambassadors and governors, elite officers and celebrities—all of them mounted on fine, spirited horses. They'll come down on you out of the north, armed to the teeth, bringing chariots and troops from all sides. I'll turn over the task of judgment to them. They'll punish you according to their rules. I'll stand totally and relentlessly against you as they rip into you furiously. They'll mutilate you, cutting off your ears and nose, killing at random. They'll enslave your children—and anybody left over will be burned. They'll rip off your clothes and steal your jewelry. I'll put a stop to your sluttish sex, the whoring life you began in Egypt. You won't look on whoring with fondness anymore. You won't think back on Egypt with stars in your eyes.

"'A Message from GOD, the Master: I'm at the point of abandoning you to those you hate, to those by whom you're repulsed. They'll treat you hatefully, leave you publicly naked, your whore's body exposed in the cruel glare of the sun. Your sluttish lust will be exposed. Your lust has brought you to this condition because you whored with pagan nations and made yourself filthy with their no-god idols.

"'You copied the life of your sister. Now I'll let you drink the cup she drank.

"'This is the Message of GOD, the Master:

"'You'll drink your sister's cup,
    a cup canyon-deep and ocean-wide.
You'll be shunned and taunted
    as you drink from that cup, full to the brim.
You'll be falling-down-drunk and the tears will flow
    as you drink from that cup titanic with terror:
    It's the cup of your sister Samaria.
You'll drink it dry,
    then smash it to bits and eat the pieces,
    and end up tearing at your breasts.
I've given the word—
    Decree of GOD, the Master.

"'Therefore GOD, the Master, says, Because you've forgotten all about me, pushing me into the background, you now must pay for what you've done—pay for your sluttish sex and whoring life.'"

Then GOD said to me, "Son of man, will you confront Oholah and Oholibah with what they've done? Make them face their outrageous obscenities, obscenities ranging from adultery to murder. They committed adultery with their no-god idols, sacrificed the children they bore me in order to feed their idols! And there is also this: They've defiled my holy Sanctuary and desecrated my holy sabbaths. The same day that they sacrificed their children to their idols, they walked into my Sanctuary and defiled it. That's what they did—in *my* house!

"Furthermore, they even sent out invitations by special messenger to men far away—and, sure enough, they came. They bathed themselves, put on makeup and provocative lingerie. They reclined on a sumptuous bed, aromatic with incense and oils—*my* incense and oils! The crowd gathered, jostling and pushing, a drunken rabble. They adorned the sisters with bracelets on their arms and tiaras on their heads.

"I said, 'She's burned out on sex!' but that didn't stop them. They kept banging on her doors night and day as men do when they're after a whore. That's how they used Oholah and Oholibah, the worn-out whores.

"Righteous men will pronounce judgment on them, giving out sentences for adultery and murder. That was their lifework: adultery and murder."

"GOD says, 'Let a mob loose on them: Terror! Plunder! Let the mob stone them and hack them to pieces—kill all their children, burn down their houses!

"'I'll put an end to sluttish sex in this country so that all women will be well warned and not copy you. You'll pay the price for all your obsessive sex. You'll pay in full for your promiscuous affairs with idols. And you'll realize that I am GOD, the Master.'"

24

BRING THE POT TO A BOIL

The Message of GOD came to me in the ninth year, the tenth month, and the tenth day of the month: "Son of man, write down this date. The king of Babylon has laid siege to Jerusalem this very day. Tell this company of rebels a story:

"'Put on the soup pot.
    Fill it with water.
Put chunks of meat into it,
    all the choice pieces—loin and brisket.
Pick out the best soup bones
    from the best of the sheep in the flock.
Pile wood beneath the pot.
    Bring it to a boil
    and cook the soup.

"'GOD, the Master, says:

"'Doom to the city of murder,

to the pot thick with scum,
    thick with a filth that can't be scoured.
Empty the pot piece by piece;
    don't bother who gets what.

"'The blood from murders
    has stained the whole city;
Blood runs bold on the street stones,
    with no one bothering to wash it off—
Blood out in the open to public view
    to provoke my wrath,
        to trigger my vengeance.

"'Therefore, this is what GOD, the Master, says:

"'Doom to the city of murder!
    I, too, will pile on the wood.
Stack the wood high,
    light the match,
Cook the meat, spice it well, pour out the broth,
    and then burn the bones.
Then I'll set the empty pot on the coals
    and heat it red-hot so the bronze glows,
So the germs are killed
    and the corruption is burned off.
But it's hopeless. It's too far gone.
    The filth is too thick.

"'Your encrusted filth is your filthy sex. I wanted to clean you up, but you wouldn't let me. I'll make no more attempts at cleaning you up until my anger quiets down. I, GOD, have said it, and I'll do it. I'm not holding back. I've run out of compassion. I'm not changing my mind. You're getting exactly what's coming to you. Decree of GOD, the Master.'"

NO TEARS

GOD's Message came to me: "Son of man, I'm about to take from you the delight of your life—a real blow, I know. But, please, no tears. Keep your grief to yourself. No public mourning. Get dressed as usual and go about your work—none of the usual funeral rituals."

I preached to the people in the morning. That evening my wife died. The next morning I did as I'd been told.

The people came to me, saying, "Tell us why you're acting like this. What does it mean, anyway?"

So I told them, "GOD's Word came to me, saying, 'Tell the family of Israel, "This is what GOD, the Master, says: I will desecrate my Sanctuary, your proud impregnable fort, the delight of your life, your heart's desire. The children you left behind will be killed.

""Then you'll do exactly as I've done. You'll perform none of the usual funeral rituals. You'll get dressed as usual and go about your work. No tears. But your sins will eat away at you from within and you'll groan among yourselves. Ezekiel will be your example. The way he did it is the way you'll do it.

""When this happens you'll recognize that I am GOD, the Master.""

"And you, son of man: The day I take away the people's refuge, their great joy, the delight of their life, what they've most longed for, along with all their children—on that very day a survivor will arrive and tell you what happened to the city. You'll break your silence and start talking again, talking to the survivor. Again, you'll be an example for them. And they'll recognize that I am GOD."

25

ACTS OF VENGEANCE

GOD's Message came to me:

"Son of man, face Ammon and preach against the people: Listen to the Message of GOD, the Master. This is what GOD has to say: Because you cheered when my Sanctuary was desecrated and the land of Judah was devastated and the people of Israel were taken into exile, I'm giving you over to the people of the east. They'll move in and make themselves at home, eating the food right off your tables and drinking your milk. I'll turn your capital, Rabbah, into pasture for camels and all your villages into corrals for flocks. Then you'll realize that I am GOD.

"GOD, the Master, says, Because you clapped and cheered, venting all your malicious contempt against the land of Israel, I'll step in and hand you out as loot—first come, first served. I'll cross you off the roster of nations. There'll be nothing left of you. And you'll realize that I am GOD."

✠

"GOD, the Master, says: Because Moab said, 'Look, Judah's nothing special,' I'll lay wide open the flank of Moab by exposing its lovely frontier villages to attack: Beth-jeshimoth, Baal-meon, and Kiriathaim. I'll lump Moab in with Ammon and give them to the people of the east for the taking. Ammon won't be heard from again. I'll punish Moab severely. And they'll realize that I am GOD."

✠

"GOD, the Master, says: Because Edom reacted against the people of Judah in spiteful revenge and was so criminally vengeful against them, therefore I, GOD, the Master, will oppose Edom and kill the lot of them, people and animals both. I'll waste it—corpses stretched from Teman to Dedan. I'll use my people Israel to bring my vengeance down on Edom. My wrath will fuel their action. And they'll realize it's *my* vengeance. Decree of God the Master."

✠

"GOD, the Master, says: Because the Philistines were so spitefully vengeful—all those centuries of stored up malice!—and did their best to destroy Judah, therefore I, GOD, the Master, will oppose the Philistines and cut down the Cretans and anybody else left along the seacoast. Huge acts of vengeance, massive punishments! When I bring vengeance, they'll realize that I am GOD."

26

As the Waves of the Sea, Surging Against the Shore

In the eleventh year, on the first day of the month, GOD's Message came to me: "Son of man, Tyre cheered when they got the news of Jerusalem, exclaiming,

"'Good! The gateway city is smashed!
    Now all her business comes my way.

357

She's in ruins
 and I'm in clover.'

"Therefore, GOD, the Master, has this to say:

"'I'm against you, Tyre,
 and I'll bring many nations surging against you,
 as the waves of the sea surging against the shore.
They'll smash the city walls of Tyre
 and break down her towers.
I'll wash away the soil
 and leave nothing but bare rock.
She'll be an island of bare rock in the ocean,
 good for nothing but drying fishnets.
Yes, I've said so.' Decree of GOD, the Master.
 'She'll be loot, free pickings for the nations!
Her surrounding villages will be butchered.
 Then they'll realize that I am GOD.'

"GOD, the Master, says: Look! Out of the north I'm bringing Nebuchadnezzar king of Babylon, a king's king, down on Tyre. He'll come with chariots and horses and riders—a huge army. He'll massacre your surrounding villages and lay siege to you. He'll build siege ramps against your walls. A forest of shields will advance against you! He'll pummel your walls with his battering rams and shatter your towers with his iron weapons. You'll be covered with dust from his horde of horses—a thundering herd of war horses pouring through the breaches, pulling chariots. Oh, it will be an earthquake of an army and a city in shock! Horses will stampede through the streets. Your people will be slaughtered and your huge pillars strewn like matchsticks. The invaders will steal and loot—all that wealth, all that stuff! They'll knock down your fine houses and dump the stone and timber rubble into the sea. And your parties, your famous good-time parties, will be no more. No more songs, no more lutes. I'll reduce you to an island of bare rock, good for nothing but drying fishnets. You'll never be rebuilt. I, GOD, have said so. Decree of GOD, the Master.

INTRODUCED TO THE TERRORS OF DEATH

"This is the Message of GOD, the Master, to Tyre: Won't the ocean islands shake at the crash of your collapse, at the groans of your wounded, at your mayhem and massacre?

"All up and down the coast, the princes will come down from their thrones, take off their royal robes and fancy clothes, and wrap themselves in sheer terror. They'll sit on the ground, shaken to the core, horrified at you. Then they'll begin chanting a funeral song over you:

"'Sunk! Sunk to the bottom of the sea,
    famous city on the sea!
Power of the seas,
    you and your people,
Intimidating everyone
    who lived in your shadows.
But now the islands are shaking
    at the sound of your crash,
Ocean islands in tremors
    from the impact of your fall.'

"The Message of GOD, the Master: 'When I turn you into a wasted city, a city empty of people, a ghost town, and when I bring up the great ocean deeps and cover you, then I'll push you down among those who go to the grave, the long, long dead. I'll make you live there, in the grave in old ruins, with the buried dead. You'll never see the land of the living again. I'll introduce you to the terrors of death and that'll be the end of you. They'll send out search parties for you, but you'll never be found. Decree of GOD, the Master.'"

27

TYRE, GATEWAY TO THE SEA

GOD's Message came to me: "You, son of man, raise a funeral song over Tyre. Tell Tyre, gateway to the sea, merchant to the world, trader among the faroff islands, 'This is what GOD, the Master, says:

"'You boast, Tyre:
    "I'm the perfect ship—stately, handsome."
You ruled the high seas from
    a real beauty, crafted to perfection.
Your planking came from
    Mount Hermon junipers.

A Lebanon cedar
supplied your mast.
They made your oars
from sturdy Bashan oaks.
Cypress from Cyprus inlaid with ivory
was used for the decks.
Your sail and flag were of colorful
embroidered linen from Egypt.
Your purple deck awnings
also came from Cyprus.
Men of Sidon and Arvad pulled the oars.
Your seasoned seamen, oh Tyre, were the crew.
Ship's carpenters
were old salts from Byblos.
All the ships of the sea and their sailors
clustered around you to barter for your goods.

"'Your army was composed of soldiers
from Paras, Lud, and Put,
Elite troops in uniformed splendor.
They put you on the map!
Your city police were imported from
Arvad, Helech, and Gammad.
They hung their shields from the city walls,
a final, perfect touch to your beauty.

"'Tarshish carried on business with you because of your great wealth. They worked for you, trading in silver, iron, tin, and lead for your products.

"'Greece, Tubal, and Meshech did business with you, trading slaves and bronze for your products.

"'Beth-togarmah traded work horses, war horses, and mules for your products.

"'The people of Rhodes did business with you. Many faroff islands traded with you in ivory and ebony.

"'Edom did business with you because of all your goods. They traded for your products with agate, purple textiles, embroidered cloth, fine linen, coral, and rubies.

"'Judah and Israel did business with you. They traded for your products with premium wheat, millet, honey, oil, and balm.

"'Damascus, attracted by your vast array of products and well-stocked warehouses, carried on business with you, trading in wine from Helbon and wool from Zahar.

"'Danites and Greeks from Uzal traded with you, using wrought iron, cinnamon, and spices.

"'Dedan traded with you for saddle blankets.

"'Arabia and all the Bedouin sheiks of Kedar traded lambs, rams, and goats with you.

"'Traders from Sheba and Raamah in South Arabia carried on business with you in premium spices, precious stones, and gold.

"'Haran, Canneh, and Eden from the east in Assyria and Media traded with you, bringing elegant clothes, dyed textiles, and elaborate carpets to your bazaars.

"'The great Tarshish ships were your freighters, importing and exporting. Oh, it was big business for you, trafficking the seaways!

"'Your sailors row mightily,
    taking you into the high seas.
Then a storm out of the east
    shatters your ship in the ocean deep.
Everything sinks—your rich goods and products,
    sailors and crew, ship's carpenters and soldiers,
Sink to the bottom of the sea.
    Total shipwreck.
The cries of your sailors
    reverberate on shore.
Sailors everywhere abandon ship.
    Veteran seamen swim for dry land.
They cry out in grief,
    a choir of bitter lament over you.
They smear their faces with ashes,
    shave their heads,
Wear rough burlap,
    wildly keening their loss.
They raise their funeral song:
    "Who on the high seas is like Tyre!"

"'As you crisscrossed the seas with your products,
    you satisfied many peoples.
Your worldwide trade

made earth's kings rich.
And now you're battered to bits by the waves,
    sunk to the bottom of the sea,
And everything you've bought and sold
    has sunk to the bottom with you.
Everyone on shore looks on in terror.
    The hair of kings stands on end,
    their faces drawn and haggard!
The buyers and sellers of the world
    throw up their hands:
"This horror can't happen!
    Oh, this *has* happened!"'"

28

THE MONEY HAS GONE TO YOUR HEAD

GOD's Message came to me, "Son of man, tell the prince of Tyre, 'This is what GOD, the Master, says:

"'Your heart is proud,
    going around saying, "I'm a god.
I sit on God's divine throne,
    ruling the sea"—
You, a mere mortal,
    not even close to being a god,
A mere mortal
    trying to be a god.
Look, you think you're smarter than Daniel.
    No enigmas can stump you.
Your sharp intelligence
    made you world-wealthy.
You piled up gold and silver
    in your banks.
You used your head well,
    worked good deals, made a lot of money.
But the money has gone to your head,
    swelled your head—what a big head!

"'Therefore, GOD, the Master, says:

"'Because you're acting like a god,
    pretending to *be* a god,
I'm giving fair warning: I'm bringing strangers down on you,
    the most vicious of all nations.
They'll pull their swords and make hash
    of your reputation for knowing it all.
They'll puncture the balloon
    of your god-pretensions.
They'll bring you down from your self-made pedestal
    and bury you in the deep blue sea.
Will you protest to your assassins,
    "You can't do that! I'm a god"?
To them you're a mere mortal.
    They're killing a man, not a god.
You'll die like a stray dog,
    killed by strangers—
Because I said so.
    Decree of GOD, the Master.'"

GOD's Message came to me: "Son of man, raise a funeral song over the king of Tyre. Tell him, 'A Message from GOD, the Master:

"'You had everything going for you.
    You were in Eden, God's garden.
You were dressed in splendor,
    your robe studded with jewels:
Carnelian, peridot, and moonstone,
    beryl, onyx, and jasper,
Sapphire, turquoise, and emerald,
    all in settings of engraved gold.
A robe was prepared for you
    the same day you were created.
You were the anointed cherub.
    I placed you on the mountain of God.
You strolled in magnificence
    among the stones of fire.
From the day of your creation
    you were sheer perfection . . .
    and then imperfection—evil!—was detected in you.

In much buying and selling
    you turned violent, you sinned!
I threw you, disgraced, off the mountain of God.
    I threw you out—you, the anointed angel-cherub.
    No more strolling among the gems of fire for you!
Your beauty went to your head.
    You corrupted wisdom
    by using it to get worldly fame.
I threw you to the ground,
    sent you sprawling before an audience of kings
    and let them gloat over your demise.
By sin after sin after sin,
    by your corrupt ways of doing business,
    you defiled your holy places of worship.
So I set a fire around and within you.
    It burned you up. I reduced you to ashes.
All anyone sees now
    when they look for you is ashes,
    a pitiful mound of ashes.
All who once knew you
    now throw up their hands:
"This can't have happened!
    This *has* happened!"'"

✠

GOD's Message came to me: "Son of man, confront Sidon. Preach against it. Say, 'Message from GOD, the Master:

"'Look! I'm against you, Sidon.
    I intend to be known for who I truly am among you.'
They'll know that I am GOD
    when I set things right
    and reveal my holy presence.
I'll order an epidemic of disease there,
    along with murder and mayhem in the streets.
People will drop dead right and left,
    as war presses in from every side.
Then they'll realize that I mean business,
    that I am GOD.

"No longer will Israel have to put up with
    their thistle-and-thorn neighbors
Who have treated them so contemptuously.
    And they also will realize that I am GOD."

GOD, the Master, says, "When I gather Israel from the peoples among whom they've been scattered and put my holiness on display among them with all the nations looking on, then they'll live in their own land that I gave to my servant Jacob. They'll live there in safety. They'll build houses. They'll plant vineyards, living in safety. Meanwhile, I'll bring judgment on all the neighbors who have treated them with such contempt. And they'll realize that I am GOD."

29

NEVER A WORLD POWER AGAIN

In the tenth year, in the tenth month, on the twelfth day, GOD's Message came to me: "Son of man, confront Pharaoh king of Egypt. Preach against him and all the Egyptians. Tell him, 'GOD, the Master, says:

"'Watch yourself, Pharaoh, king of Egypt.
    I'm dead set against you,
You lumbering old dragon,
    lolling and flaccid in the Nile,
Saying, "It's my Nile.
    I made it. It's mine."
I'll set hooks in your jaw;
    I'll make the fish of the Nile stick to your scales.
I'll pull you out of the Nile,
    with all the fish stuck to your scales.
Then I'll drag you out into the desert,
    you and all the Nile fish sticking to your scales.
You'll lie there in the open, rotting in the sun,
    meat to the wild animals and carrion birds.
Everybody living in Egypt
    will realize that I am GOD.

"'Because you've been a flimsy reed crutch to Israel so that when they gripped you, you splintered and cut their hand, and when they leaned on you, you broke and sent them sprawling—Message of GOD, the Master—I'll bring war against you, do away with people and animals alike, and turn the country into an empty desert so they'll realize that I am GOD.

"'Because you said, "It's my Nile. I made it. It's all mine," therefore I am against you and your rivers. I'll reduce Egypt to an empty, desolate wasteland all the way from Migdol in the north to Syene and the border of Ethiopia in the south. Not a human will be seen in it, nor will an animal move through it. It'll be just empty desert, empty for forty years.

"'I'll make Egypt the most desolate of all desolations. For forty years I'll make her cities the most wasted of all wasted cities. I'll scatter Egyptians to the four winds, send them off every which way into exile.

"'But,' says GOD, the Master, 'that's not the end of it. After the forty years, I'll gather up the Egyptians from all the places where they've been scattered. I'll put things back together again for Egypt. I'll bring her back to Pathros where she got her start long ago. There she'll start over again from scratch. She'll take her place at the bottom of the ladder and there she'll stay, never to climb that ladder again, never to be a world power again. Never again will Israel be tempted to rely on Egypt. All she'll be to Israel is a reminder of old sin. Then Egypt will realize that I am GOD, the Master.'"

✠

In the twenty-seventh year, in the first month, on the first day of the month, GOD's Message came to me: "Son of man, Nebuchadnezzar, king of Babylon, has worn out his army against Tyre. They've worked their fingers to the bone and have nothing to show for it.

"Therefore, GOD, the Master, says, 'I'm giving Egypt to Nebuchadnezzar king of Babylon. He'll haul away its wealth, pick the place clean. He'll pay his army with Egyptian plunder. He's been working for me all these years without pay. This is his pay: Egypt. Decree of GOD, the Master.

"'And then I'll stir up fresh hope in Israel—the dawn of deliverance!—and I'll give you, Ezekiel, bold and confident words to speak. And they'll realize that I am GOD.'"

30

EGYPT ON FIRE

GOD, the Master, spoke to me: "Son of man, preach. Give them the Message of GOD, the Master. Wail:

"'Doomsday!'
Time's up!
GOD's big day of judgment is near.
Thick clouds are rolling in.
It's doomsday for the nations.
Death will rain down on Egypt.
Terror will paralyze Ethiopia
When they see the Egyptians killed,
their wealth hauled off,
their foundations demolished,
And Ethiopia, Put, Lud, Arabia, Libya
—all of Egypt's old allies—
killed right along with them.

"'GOD says:

"'Egypt's allies will fall
and her proud strength will collapse—
From Migdol in the north to Syene in the south,
a great slaughter in Egypt!
Decree of GOD, the Master.
Egypt, most desolate of the desolate,
her cities wasted beyond wasting,
Will realize that I am GOD
when I burn her down
and her helpers are knocked flat.

"'When that happens, I'll send out messengers by ship to sound the alarm among the easygoing Ethiopians. They'll be terrorized. Egypt's doomed! Judgment's coming!

"'GOD, the Master, says:

"'I'll put a stop to Egypt's arrogance.
I'll use Nebuchadnezzar king of Babylon to do it.

He and his army, the most brutal of nations,
    shall be used to destroy the country.
They'll brandish their swords
    and fill Egypt with corpses.
I'll dry up the Nile
    and sell off the land to a bunch of crooks.
I'll hire outsiders to come in
    and waste the country, strip it clean.
    I, GOD, have said so.

"'And now this is what GOD, the Master, says:

"'I'll smash all the no-god idols;
    I'll topple all those huge statues in Memphis.
The prince of Egypt will be gone for good,
    and in his place I'll put *fear*—fear throughout Egypt!
I'll demolish Pathros,
    burn Zoan to the ground, and punish Thebes,
Pour my wrath on Pelusium, Egypt's fort,
    and knock Thebes off its proud pedestal.
I'll set Egypt on fire:
    Pelusium will writhe in pain,
Thebes blown away,
    Memphis raped.
The young warriors of On and Pi-beseth
    will be killed and the cities exiled.
A dark day for Tahpanhes
    when I shatter Egypt,
When I break Egyptian power
    and put an end to her arrogant oppression!
She'll disappear in a cloud of dust,
    her cities hauled off as exiles.
That's how I'll punish Egypt,
    and that's how she'll realize that I am GOD.'"

✝

In the eleventh year, on the seventh day of the first month, GOD's Message came to me:

"Son of man, I've broken the arm of Pharaoh king of Egypt. And look! It hasn't been set. No splint has been put on it so the bones can knit and heal, so he can use a sword again.

"Therefore, GOD, the Master, says, I am dead set against Pharaoh king of Egypt and will go ahead and break his other arm—both arms broken! There's no way he'll ever swing a sword again. I'll scatter Egyptians all over the world. I'll make the arms of the king of Babylon strong and put my sword in his hand, but I'll break the arms of Pharaoh and he'll groan like one who is mortally wounded. I'll make the arms of the king of Babylon strong, but the arms of Pharaoh shall go limp. The Egyptians will realize that I am GOD when I place my sword in the hand of the king of Babylon. He'll wield it against Egypt and I'll scatter Egyptians all over the world. Then they'll realize that I am GOD."

31

THE FUNERAL OF THE BIG TREE

In the eleventh year, on the first day of the third month, GOD's Message came to me: "Son of man, tell Pharaoh king of Egypt, that pompous old goat:

"'Who do you, astride the world,
      think you really are?
Look! Assyria was a Big Tree, huge as a Lebanon cedar,
      beautiful limbs offering cool shade,
Skyscraper high,
      piercing the clouds.
The waters gave it drink,
      the primordial deep lifted it high,
Gushing out rivers around
      the place where it was planted,
And then branching out in streams
      to all the trees in the forest.
It was immense,
      dwarfing all the trees in the forest—
Thick boughs, long limbs,
      roots delving deep into earth's waters.
All the birds of the air
      nested in its boughs.
All the wild animals

gave birth under its branches.
All the mighty nations
    lived in its shade.
It was stunning in its majesty—
    the reach of its branches!
    the depth of its water-seeking roots!
Not a cedar in God's garden came close to it.
    No pine tree was anything like it.
Mighty oaks looked like bushes
    growing alongside it.
Not a tree in God's garden
    was in the same class of beauty.
I made it beautiful,
    a work of art in limbs and leaves,
The envy of every tree in Eden,
    every last tree in God's garden.'"

Therefore, God, the Master, says, "'Because it skyscrapered upwards, piercing the clouds, swaggering and proud of its stature, I turned it over to a world-famous leader to call its evil to account. I'd had enough. Outsiders, unbelievably brutal, felled it across the mountain ranges. Its branches were strewn through all the valleys, its leafy boughs clogging all the streams and rivers. Because its shade was gone, everybody walked off. No longer a tree—just a log. On that dead log birds perch. Wild animals burrow under it.

"'That marks the end of the "big tree" nations. No more trees nourished from the great deep, no more cloud-piercing trees, no more earthborn trees taking over. They're all slated for death—back to earth, right along with men and women, for whom it's "dust to dust."

"'The Message of God, the Master: On the day of the funeral of the Big Tree, I threw the great deep into mourning. I stopped the flow of its rivers, held back great seas, and wrapped the Lebanon mountains in black. All the trees of the forest fainted and fell. I made the whole world quake when it crashed, and threw it into the underworld to take its place with all else that gets buried. All the trees of Eden and the finest and best trees of Lebanon, well-watered, were relieved—they had descended to the underworld with it—along with everyone who had lived in its shade and all who had been killed.

"'Which of the trees of Eden came anywhere close to you in splendor and size? But you're slated to be cut down to take your place in the underworld with the trees of Eden, to be a dead log stacked with all the other dead logs, among the other uncircumcised who are dead and buried.

"'This means Pharaoh, the pompous old goat.

"'Decree of GOD, the Master.'"

32

A CLOUD ACROSS THE SUN

In the twelfth year, on the first day of the twelfth month, GOD's Message came to me: "Son of man, sing a funeral lament over Pharaoh king of Egypt. Tell him:

> "'You think you're a young lion
> > prowling through the nations.
> You're more like a dragon in the ocean,
> > snorting and thrashing about.

> "'GOD, the Master, says:

> "'I'm going to throw my net over you
> > —many nations will get in on this operation—
> > and haul you out with my dragnet.
> I'll dump you on the ground
> > out in an open field
> And bring in all the crows and vultures
> > for a sumptuous carrion lunch.
> I'll invite wild animals from all over the world
> > to gorge on your guts.
> I'll scatter hunks of your meat in the mountains
> > and strew your bones in the valleys.
> The country, right up to the mountains,
> > will be drenched with your blood,
> > your blood filling every ditch and channel.
> When I blot you out,
> > I'll pull the curtain on the skies
> > and shut out the stars.
> I'll throw a cloud across the sun
> > and turn off the moonlight.

I'll turn out every light in the sky above you
>and put your land in the dark.
>>Decree of GOD, the Master.
I'll shake up everyone worldwide
>when I take you off captive to strange and faroff countries.
I'll shock people with you.
>Kings will take one look and shudder.
I'll shake my sword
>and they'll shake in their boots.
On the day you crash, they'll tremble,
>thinking, "That could be me!"

TO LAY YOUR PRIDE LOW

"'GOD, the Master, says:

"'The sword of the king of Babylon
>is coming against you.
I'll use the swords of champions
>to lay your pride low,
Use the most brutal of nations
>to knock Egypt off her high horse,
>>to puncture that hot-air pomposity.
I'll destroy all their livestock
>that graze along the river.
Neither human foot nor animal hoof
>will muddy those waters anymore.
I'll clear their springs and streams,
>make their rivers flow clean and smooth.
>>Decree of GOD, the Master.
When I turn Egypt back to the wild
>and strip her clean of all her abundant produce,
When I strike dead all who live there,
>then they'll realize that I am GOD.'

"This is a funeral song. Chant it.
>Daughters of the nations, chant it.
Chant it over Egypt for the death of its pomp."
>Decree of GOD, the Master.

In the twelfth year, on the fifteenth day of the first month, God's Message came to me:

"Son of man, lament over Egypt's pompous ways.
    Send her on her way.
Dispatch Egypt
    and her proud daughter nations
To the underworld,
    down to the country of the dead and buried.
Say, 'You think you're so high and mighty?
    Down! Take your place with the heathen in that unhallowed
        grave!'

"She'll be dumped in with those killed in battle. The sword is bared. Drag her off in all her proud pomp! All the big men and their helpers down among the dead and buried will greet them: 'Welcome to the grave of the heathen! Join the ranks of the victims of war!'

"Assyria is there and its congregation, the whole nation a cemetery. Their graves are in the deepest part of the underworld, a congregation of graves, all killed in battle, these people who terrorized the land of the living.

"Elam is there in all her pride, a cemetery—all killed in battle, dumped in her heathen grave with the dead and buried, these people who terrorized the land of the living. They carry their shame with them, along with the others in the grave. They turned Elam into a resort for the pompous dead, landscaped with heathen graves, slaughtered in battle. They once terrorized the land of the living. Now they carry their shame down with the others in deep earth. They're in the section set aside for the slain in battle.

"Meshech-tubal is there in all her pride, a cemetery in uncircumcised ground, dumped in with those slaughtered in battle—just deserts for terrorizing the land of the living. Now they carry their shame down with the others in deep earth. They're in the section set aside for the slain. They're segregated from the heroes, the old-time giants who entered the grave in full battle dress, their swords placed under their heads and their shields covering their bones, those heroes who spread terror through the land of the living.

"And you, Egypt, will be dumped in a heathen grave, along with all the rest, in the section set aside for the slain.

"Edom is there, with her kings and princes. In spite of her vaunted greatness, she is dumped in a heathen grave with the others headed for the grave.

"The princes of the north are there, the whole lot of them, and all the Sidonians who carry their shame to their graves—all that terror they spread with their brute power!—dumped in unhallowed ground with those killed in battle, carrying their shame with the others headed for deep earth.

"Pharaoh will see them all and, pompous old goat that he is, take comfort in the company he'll keep—Pharaoh and his slaughtered army. Decree of GOD, the Master.

"I used him to spread terror in the land of the living and now I'm dumping him in heathen ground with those killed by the sword—Pharaoh and all his pomp. Decree of GOD, the Master."

33

YOU ARE THE WATCHMAN

GOD's Message came to me: "Son of man, speak to your people. Tell them: 'If I bring war on this land and the people take one of their citizens and make him their watchman, and if the watchman sees war coming and blows the trumpet, warning the people, then if anyone hears the sound of the trumpet and ignores it and war comes and takes him off, it's his own fault. He heard the alarm, he ignored it—it's his own fault. If he had listened, he would have saved his life.

"'But if the watchman sees war coming and doesn't blow the trumpet, warning the people, and war comes and takes anyone off, I'll hold the watchman responsible for the bloodshed of any unwarned sinner.'

"You, son of man, are the watchman. I've made you a watchman for Israel. The minute you hear a message from me, warn them. If I say to the wicked, 'Wicked man, wicked woman, you're on the fast track to death!' and you don't speak up and warn the wicked to change their ways, the wicked will die unwarned in their sins and I'll hold you responsible for their bloodshed. But if you warn the wicked to change their ways and they don't do it, they'll die in their sins well-warned and at least you will have saved your own life.

"Son of man, speak to Israel. Tell them: 'You've said, "Our rebellions and sins are weighing us down. We're wasting away. How can we go on living?"'

"Tell them, 'As sure as I am the living God, I take no pleasure from the death of the wicked. I want the wicked to change their ways and live. Turn your life around! Reverse your evil ways! Why *die*, Israel?'

"There's more, son of man. Tell your people: 'A good person's good life won't save him when he decides to rebel, and a bad person's bad life won't prevent him from repenting of his rebellion. A good person who sins can't expect to live when he chooses to sin. It's true that I tell good people, "Live! Be alive!" But if they trust in their good deeds and turn to evil, that good life won't amount to a hill of beans. They'll die for their evil life.

"'On the other hand, if I tell a wicked person, "You'll die for your wicked life," and he repents of his sin and starts living a righteous and just life—being generous to the down-and-out, restoring what he had stolen, cultivating life-nourishing ways that don't hurt others—he'll live. He won't die. None of his sins will be kept on the books. He's doing what's right, living a good life. He'll live.

"'Your people say, "The Master's way isn't fair." But it's the way *they're* living that isn't fair. When good people turn back from living good lives and plunge into sin, they'll die for it. And when a wicked person turns away from his wicked life and starts living a just and righteous life, he'll come alive.

"'Still, you keep on saying, "The Master's way isn't fair." We'll see, Israel. I'll decide on each of you exactly according to how you live.'"

☩

In the twelfth year of our exile, on the fifth day of the tenth month, a survivor from Jerusalem came to me and said, "The city's fallen."

The evening before the survivor arrived, the hand of GOD had been on me and restored my speech. By the time he arrived in the morning I was able to speak. I could talk again.

GOD's Message came to me: "Son of man, those who are living in the ruins back in Israel are saying, 'Abraham was only one man and he owned the whole country. But there are *lots* of us. Our ownership is even more certain.'

"So tell them, 'GOD the Master says, You eat flesh that contains blood, you worship no-god idols, you murder at will—and you expect to own this land? You rely on the sword, you engage in obscenities, you indulge in sex at random—anyone, anytime. And you still expect to own this land?'

"Tell them this, Ezekiel: 'The Message of GOD, the Master. As sure as I am the living God, those who are still alive in the ruins will be killed. Anyone out in the field I'll give to wild animals for food. Anyone hiding out in mountain forts and caves will die of disease. I'll make this country an empty wasteland—no more arrogant bullying! Israel's mountains will become dangerously desolate. No one will dare pass through them.'

"They'll realize that I am GOD when I devastate the country because of all the obscenities they've practiced.

"As for you, son of man, you've become quite the talk of the town. Your people meet on street corners and in front of their houses and say, 'Let's go hear the latest news from GOD.' They show up, as people tend to do, and sit in your company. They listen to you speak, but don't do a thing you say. They flatter you with compliments, but all they care about is making money and getting ahead. To them you're merely entertainment—a country singer of sad love songs, playing a guitar. They love to hear you talk, but nothing comes of it.

"But when all this happens—and it is going to happen!—they'll realize that a prophet was among them."

34

WHEN THE SHEEP GET SCATTERED

GOD's Message came to me: "Son of man, prophesy against the shepherd-leaders of Israel. Yes, prophesy! Tell those shepherds, 'GOD, the Master, says: Doom to you shepherds of Israel, feeding your own mouths! Aren't shepherds supposed to feed sheep? You drink the milk, you make clothes from the wool, you roast the lambs, but you don't feed the sheep. You don't build up the weak ones, don't heal the sick, don't doctor the injured, don't go after the strays, don't look for the lost. You bully and badger them. And now they're scattered every which way because there was no shepherd—scattered and easy pickings for wolves and coyotes. Scattered—*my sheep!*—exposed and vulnerable across mountains and hills. My sheep scattered all over the world, and no one out looking for them!

"'Therefore, shepherds, listen to the Message of GOD: As sure as I am the living God—Decree of GOD, the Master—because my sheep have been turned into mere prey, into easy meals for wolves because you shepherds ignored them and only fed yourselves, listen to what GOD has to say:

"'Watch out! I'm coming down on the shepherds and taking my sheep back. They're fired as shepherds of my sheep. No more shepherds who just feed themselves! I'll rescue my sheep from their greed. They're not going to feed off my sheep any longer!

"'GOD, the Master, says: From now on, *I myself* am the shepherd. I'm going looking for them. As shepherds go after their flocks when they get scattered, I'm going after my sheep. I'll rescue them from all the places they've been scattered to in the storms. I'll bring them back from foreign peoples, gather them from foreign countries, and bring them back to their home country. I'll feed them on the mountains of Israel, along the streams, among their own people. I'll lead them into lush pasture so they can roam the mountain pastures of Israel, graze at leisure, feed in the rich pastures on the mountains of Israel. And I myself will be the shepherd of my sheep. I myself will make sure they get plenty of rest. I'll go after the lost, I'll collect the strays, I'll doctor the injured, I'll build up the weak ones and oversee the strong ones so they're not exploited.

"'And as for you, my dear flock, I'm stepping in and judging between one sheep and another, between rams and goats. Aren't you satisfied to feed in good pasture without taking over the whole place? Can't you be satisfied to drink from the clear stream without muddying the water with your feet? Why do the rest of my sheep have to make do with grass that's trampled down and water that's been muddied?

"'Therefore, GOD, the Master, says: I myself am stepping in and making things right between the plump sheep and the skinny sheep. Because you forced your way with shoulder and rump and butted at all the weaker animals with your horns till you scattered them all over the hills, I'll come in and save my dear flock, no longer let them be pushed around. I'll step in and set things right between one sheep and another.

"'I'll appoint one shepherd over them all: my servant David. He'll feed them. He'll be their shepherd. And I, GOD, will be their God. My servant David will be their prince. I, GOD, have spoken.

"'I'll make a covenant of peace with them. I'll banish fierce animals from the country so the sheep can live safely in the wilderness and sleep in the forest. I'll make them and everything around my hill a blessing. I'll send down plenty of rain in season—showers of blessing! The trees in the orchards will bear fruit, the ground will produce, they'll feel content and safe on their land, and they'll realize that I am GOD when I break them out of their slavery and rescue them from their slave masters.

"'No longer will they be exploited by outsiders and ravaged by fierce beasts. They'll live safe and sound, fearless and free. I'll give them rich gardens, lavish in vegetables—no more living half-starved, no longer taunted by outsiders.

"'They'll know, beyond doubting, that I, GOD, am their God, that I'm with them and that they, the people Israel, are my people. Decree of GOD, the Master:

"'You are my dear flock,
    the flock of my pasture, my human flock,
And I am your God.
    Decree of GOD, the Master.'"

35

A PILE OF RUBBLE

GOD's Message came to me: "Son of man, confront Mount Seir. Prophesy against it! Tell them, 'GOD, the Master, says:

"'I'm coming down hard on you, Mount Seir.
    I'm stepping in and turning you to a pile of rubble.
I'll reduce your towns to piles of rocks.
    There'll be nothing left of you.
    Then you'll realize that I am GOD.

"'I'm doing this because you've kept this age-old grudge going against Israel: You viciously attacked them when they were already down, looking their final punishment in the face. Therefore, as sure as I am the living God, I'm lining you up for a real bloodbath. Since you loved blood so much, you'll be chased by rivers of blood. I'll reduce Mount Seir to a heap of rubble. No one will either come or go from that place! I'll blanket your mountains with corpses. Massacred bodies will cover your hills and fill up your valleys and ditches. I'll reduce you to ruins and all your towns will be ghost towns—population zero. Then you'll realize that I am GOD.

"'Because you said, "These two nations, these two countries, are mine. I'm taking over" (even though GOD is right there watching, right there listening), I'll turn your hate-bloated anger and rage right back on you. You'll know I mean business when I bring judgment on you. You'll realize then that I, GOD, have overheard all the vile abuse you've poured out against the mountains of Israel, saying, "They're road-kill and we're going to eat them up." You've strutted around, talking so big, insolently pitting yourselves against me. And I've heard it all.

"'This is the verdict of GOD, the Master: With the whole earth applauding, I'll demolish you. Since you danced in the streets, thinking it was so wonderful when Israel's inheritance was demolished, I'll give you the same treatment: demolition. Mount Seir demolished—yes, every square inch of Edom. Then they'll realize that I am GOD!'

36

BACK TO YOUR OWN LAND

"And now, son of man, prophesy to the mountains of Israel. Say, 'Mountains of Israel, listen to GOD's Message. GOD, the Master, says, Because the enemy crowed over you, "Good! Those old hills are now ours!" now here is a prophecy in the name of GOD, the Master: Because nations came at you from all sides, ripping and plundering, hauling pieces of you off every which way, and you've become the butt of cheap gossip and jokes, therefore, Mountains of Israel, listen to the Message of GOD, the Master. My Message to mountains and hills, to ditches and valleys, to the heaps of rubble and the emptied towns that are looted for plunder and turned into jokes by all the surrounding nations: Therefore, says GOD, the Master, now I'm speaking in a fiery rage against the rest of the nations, but especially against Edom, who in an orgy of violence and shameless insolence robbed me of my land, grabbed it for themselves.'

"Therefore prophesy over the land of Israel, preach to the mountains and hills, to every ditch and valley: 'The Message of GOD, the Master: Look! Listen! I'm angry—and I care. I'm speaking to you because you've been humiliated among the nations. Therefore I, GOD, the Master, am telling you that I've solemnly sworn that the nations around you are next. It's their turn to be humiliated.

"'But you, Mountains of Israel, will burst with new growth, putting out branches and bearing fruit for my people Israel. My people are coming home! Do you see? I'm back again. I'm on your side. You'll be plowed and planted as before! I'll see to it that your population grows all over Israel, that the towns fill up with people, that the ruins are rebuilt. I'll make this place teem with life—human and animal. The country will burst into life, life, and more life, your towns and villages full of people just as in the old days. I'll treat you better than I ever have. And you'll realize that I am GOD. I'll put people over you—my own people Israel! They'll take care of you and you'll be their inheritance. Never again will you be a harsh and unforgiving land to them.

"'GOD, the Master, says: Because you have a reputation of being a land that eats people alive and makes women barren, I'm now telling you that you'll never eat people alive again nor make women barren. Decree of GOD, the Master. And I'll never again let the taunts of outsiders be heard over you nor permit nations to look down on you. You'll no longer be a land that makes women barren. Decree of GOD, the Master.'"

GOD's Message came to me: "Son of man, when the people of Israel lived in their land, they polluted it by the way they lived. I poured out my anger on them because of the polluted blood they poured out on the ground. And so I got thoroughly angry with them polluting the country with their wanton murders and dirty gods. I kicked them out, exiled them to other countries. I sentenced them according to how they had lived. Wherever they went, they gave me a bad name. People said, 'These are GOD's people, but they got kicked off his land.' I suffered much pain over my holy reputation, which the people of Israel blackened in every country they entered.

"Therefore, tell Israel, 'Message of GOD, the Master: I'm not doing this for you, Israel. I'm doing it for me, to save my character, my holy name, which you've blackened in every country where you've gone. I'm going to put my great and holy name on display, the name that has been ruined in so many countries, the name that you blackened wherever you went. Then the nations will realize who I really am, that I am GOD, when I show my holiness through you so that they can see it with their own eyes.

"'For here's what I'm going to do: I'm going to take you out of these countries, gather you from all over, and bring you back to your own land. I'll pour pure water over you and scrub you clean. I'll give you a new heart, put a new spirit in you. I'll remove the stone heart from your body and replace it with a heart that's God-willed, not self-willed. I'll put my Spirit in you and make it possible for you to do what I tell you and live by my commands. You'll once again live in the land I gave your ancestors. You'll be my people! I'll be your God!

"'I'll pull you out of that stinking pollution. I'll give personal orders to the wheat fields, telling them to grow bumper crops. I'll send no more famines. I'll make sure your fruit trees and field crops flourish. Other nations won't be able to hold you in contempt again because of famine.

"'And then you'll think back over your terrible lives—the evil, the shame—and be thoroughly disgusted with yourselves, realizing how badly you've lived—all those obscenities you've carried out.

"'I'm not doing this for you. Get this through your thick heads! Shame on you. What a mess you made of things, Israel!

"'Message of GOD, the Master: On the day I scrub you clean from all your filthy living, I'll also make your cities livable. The ruins will be rebuilt. The neglected land will be worked again, no longer overgrown with weeds and thistles, worthless in the eyes of passersby. People will exclaim, "Why, this weed patch has been turned into a Garden of Eden! And the ruined cities, smashed into oblivion, are now thriving!" The nations around you that are still in existence will realize that I, GOD, rebuild ruins and replant empty waste places. I, GOD, said so, and I'll do it.

"'Message of GOD, the Master: Yet again I'm going to do what Israel asks. I'll increase their population as with a flock of sheep. Like the milling flocks of sheep brought for sacrifices in Jerusalem during the appointed feasts, the ruined cities will be filled with flocks of people. And they'll realize that I am GOD.'"

37

BREATH OF LIFE

GOD grabbed me. GOD's Spirit took me up and sat me down in the middle of an open plain strewn with bones. He led me around and among them—a lot of bones! There were bones all over the plain—dry bones, bleached by the sun.

He said to me, "Son of man, can these bones live?"

I said, "Master GOD, only you know that."

He said to me, "Prophesy over these bones: 'Dry bones, listen to the Message of GOD!'"

GOD, the Master, told the dry bones, "Watch this: I'm bringing the breath of life to you and you'll come to life. I'll attach sinews to you, put meat on your bones, cover you with skin, and breathe life into you. You'll come alive and you'll realize that I am GOD!"

I prophesied just as I'd been commanded. As I prophesied, there was a sound and, oh, rustling! The bones moved and came together, bone to bone. I kept watching. Sinews formed, then muscles on the bones, then skin stretched over them. But they had no breath in them.

He said to me, "Prophesy to the breath. Prophesy, son of man. Tell the breath, 'GOD, the Master, says, Come from the four winds. Come, breath. Breathe on these slain bodies. Breathe life!'"

So I prophesied, just as he commanded me. The breath entered them and they came alive! They stood up on their feet, a huge army.

Then God said to me, "Son of man, these bones are the whole house of Israel. Listen to what they're saying: 'Our bones are dried up, our hope is gone, there's nothing left of us.'

"Therefore, prophesy. Tell them, 'GOD, the Master, says: I'll dig up your graves and bring you out alive—oh my people! Then I'll take you straight to the land of Israel. When I dig up graves and bring you out as my people, you'll realize that I am GOD. I'll breathe my life into you and you'll live. Then I'll lead you straight back to your land and you'll realize that I am GOD. I've said it and I'll do it. GOD's Decree.'"

✢

GOD's Message came to me: "You, son of man: Take a stick and write on it, 'For Judah, with his Israelite companions.' Then take another stick and write on it, 'For Joseph—Ephraim's stick, together with all his Israelite companions.' Then tie the two sticks together so that you're holding one stick.

"When your people ask you, 'Are you going to tell us what you're doing?' tell them, 'GOD, the Master, says, Watch me! I'll take the Joseph stick that is in Ephraim's hand, with the tribes of Israel connected with him, and lay the Judah stick on it. I'll make them into one stick. I'm holding one stick.'

"Then take the sticks you've inscribed and hold them up so the people can see them. Tell them, 'GOD, the Master, says, Watch me! I'm taking the Israelites out of the nations in which they've been exiled. I'll gather them in from all directions and bring them back home. I'll make them one nation in the land, on the mountains of Israel, and give them one king—one king over all of them. Never again will they be divided into two nations, two kingdoms. Never again will they pollute their lives with their no-god idols and all those vile obscenities and rebellions. I'll save them out of all their old sinful haunts. I'll clean them up. They'll be my people! I'll be their God! My servant David will be king over them. They'll all be under one shepherd.

"'They'll follow my laws and keep my statutes. They'll live in the same land I gave my servant Jacob, the land where your ancestors lived. They and their children and their grandchildren will live there forever, and my servant David will be their prince forever. I'll make a covenant of peace with them that will hold everything together, an everlasting covenant. I'll make them secure and place my holy place of worship at the center of their lives forever. I'll live right there with them. I'll be their God! They'll be my people!

"'The nations will realize that I, GOD, make Israel holy when my holy place of worship is established at the center of their lives forever.'"

38

GOD AGAINST GOG

GOD'S Message came to me: "Son of man, confront Gog from the country of Magog, head of Meshech and Tubal. Prophesy against him. Say, 'GOD, the Master, says: Be warned, Gog. I am against you, head of Meshech and Tubal. I'm going to turn you around, put hooks in your jaws, and drag you off with your whole army, your horses and riders in full armor—all those shields and bucklers and swords—fighting men armed to the teeth! Persia and Cush and Put will be in the ranks, also well-armed, as will Gomer and its army and Beth-togarmah out of the north with its army. Many nations will be with you!

"'Get ready to fight, you and the whole company that's been called out. Take charge and wait for orders. After a long time, you'll be given your orders. In the distant future you'll arrive at a country that has recovered from a devastating war. People from many nations will be gathered there on the mountains of Israel, for a long time now a wasteland. These people have been brought back from many countries and now live safe and secure. You'll rise like a thunderstorm and roll in like clouds and cover the land, you and the massed troops with you.

"'Message of GOD, the Master: At that time you'll start thinking things over and cook up an evil plot. You'll say, "I'm going to invade a country without defenses, attack an unsuspecting, carefree people going about their business—no gates to their cities, no locks on their doors. And I'm going to plunder the place, march right in and clean them out, this rebuilt country risen from the ashes, these returned exiles and their booming economy centered down at the navel of the earth."

"'Sheba and Dedan and Tarshish, traders all out to make a fast buck, will say, "So! You've opened a new market for plunder! You've brought in your troops to get rich quick!"'

"Therefore, son of man, prophesy! Tell Gog, 'A Message from GOD, the Master: When my people Israel are established securely, will you make your move? Will you come down out of the far north, you and that mob of armies, charging out on your horses like a tidal wave across the land, and invade my people Israel, covering the country like a cloud? When the time's ripe, I'll unleash you against my land in such a way that the nations will recognize me, realize that through you, Gog, in full view of the nations, I am putting my holiness on display.

"'A Message of GOD, the Master: Years ago when I spoke through my servants, the prophets of Israel, wasn't it you I was talking about? Year after year they prophesied that I would bring you against them. And when the day comes, Gog, you will attack that land of Israel. Decree of GOD, the Master. My raging anger will erupt. Fueled by blazing jealousy, I tell you that then there will be an earthquake that rocks the land of Israel. Fish and birds and wild animals—even ants and beetles!—and every human being will tremble and shake before me. Mountains will disintegrate, terraces will crumble. I'll order all-out war against you, Gog—Decree of GOD, the Master—Gog killing Gog on all the mountains of Israel. I'll deluge Gog with judgment: disease and massacre, torrential rain and hail, volcanic lava pouring down on you and your mobs of troops and people.

"'I'll show you how great I am, how holy I am. I'll make myself known all over the world. Then you'll realize that I am GOD.'

39

CALL THE WILD ANIMALS!

"Son of man, prophesy against Gog. Say, 'A Message of GOD, the Master: I'm against you, Gog, head of Meshech and Tubal. I'm going to turn you around and drag you out, drag you out of the far north and down on the mountains of Israel. Then I'll knock your bow out of your left hand and your arrows from your right hand. On the mountains of Israel you'll be slaughtered, you and all your troops and the people with you. I'll serve you up as a meal to carrion birds and scavenging animals. You'll be killed in the open field. I've given my word. Decree of GOD, the Master.'

"I'll set fire to Magog and the faroff islands, where people are so seemingly secure. And they'll realize that I am GOD.

"I'll reveal my holy name among my people Israel. Never again will I let my holy name be dragged in the mud. Then the nations will realize that I, GOD, am The Holy in Israel.

"It's coming! Yes, it will happen! This is the day I've been telling you about.

"People will come out of the cities of Israel and make a huge bonfire of the weapons of war, piling on shields large and small, bows and arrows, clubs and spears, a fire they'll keep going for seven years. They won't need to go into the woods to get fuel for the fire. There'll be plenty of weapons to keep it going. They'll strip those who stripped them. They'll rob those who robbed them. Decree of GOD, the Master.

"At that time I'll set aside a burial ground for Gog in Israel at Traveler's Rest, just east of the sea. It will obstruct the route of travelers, blocking their way, the mass grave of Gog and his mob of an army. They'll call the place Gog's Mob.

"Israel will bury the corpses in order to clean up the land. It will take them seven months. All the people will turn out to help with the burials. It will be a big day for the people when it's all done and I'm given my due. Men will be hired full-time for the cleanup burial operation and will go through the country looking for defiling, decomposing corpses. At the end of seven months, there'll be an all-out final search. Anyone who sees a bone will mark the place with a stick so the buriers can get it and bury it in the mass burial site, Gog's Mob. (A town nearby is called Mobville, or Hamonah.) That's how they'll clean up the land.

"Son of man, GOD, the Master, says: Call the birds! Call the wild animals! Call out, 'Gather and come, gather around my sacrificial meal that I'm preparing for you on the mountains of Israel. You'll eat meat and drink blood. You'll eat off the bodies of great heroes and drink the blood of famous princes as if they were so many rams and lambs, goats and bulls, the choicest grain-fed animals of Bashan. At the sacrificial meal I'm fixing for you, you'll eat fat till you're stuffed and drink blood till you're drunk. At the table I set for you, you'll stuff yourselves with horses and riders, heroes and fighters of every kind.' Decree of GOD, the Master.

"I'll put my glory on display among the nations and they'll all see the judgment I execute, see me at work handing out judgment. From that day on, Israel will realize that I am their GOD. And the nations will get the message that it was because of their sins that Israel went into exile. They were disloyal to me and I turned away from them. I turned them over to their enemies and they were all killed. I treated them as their polluted and sin-sated lives deservèd. I turned away from them, refused to look at them.

"But now I will return Jacob back from exile, I'll be compassionate with all the people of Israel, and I'll be zealous for my holy name. Eventually the memory will fade, the memory of their shame over their betrayals of me when they lived securely in their own land, safe and unafraid. Once I've brought them back from foreign parts, gathered them in from enemy territories, I'll use them to demonstrate my holiness with all the nations watching. Then they'll realize for sure that I am their GOD, for even though I sent them off into exile, I will gather them back to their own land, leaving not one soul behind. After I've poured my Spirit on Israel, filled them with my life, I'll no longer turn away. I'll look them full in the face. Decree of GOD, the Master."

40

MEASURING THE TEMPLE COMPLEX

In the twenty-fifth year of our exile, at the beginning of the year on the tenth of the month—it was the fourteenth year after the city fell—GOD touched me and brought me here. He brought me in divine vision to the land of Israel and set me down on a high mountain. To the south there were buildings that looked like a city. He took me there and I met a man deeply tanned, like bronze. He stood at the entrance holding a linen cord and a measuring stick

The man said to me, "Son of man, look and listen carefully. Pay close attention to everything I'm going to show you. That's why you've been brought here. And then tell Israel everything you see."

✠

First I saw a wall around the outside of the Temple complex. The measuring stick in the man's hand was ten feet long. He measured the thickness of the wall: twenty-one inches. The height was also twenty-one inches.

✠

He went into the gate complex that faced the east and went up the seven steps. He measured the depth of the outside threshold of the gate complex: ten feet. There were alcoves flanking the gate corridor, each ten feet square, each separated by a wall seven and a half feet thick. The inside threshold of the gate complex that led to the porch facing into the Temple courtyard was ten feet deep.

He measured the inside porch of the gate complex: twelve feet deep, flanked by pillars three feet thick. The porch opened onto the Temple courtyard.

Inside this east gate complex were three alcoves on each side. Each room was the same size and the separating walls were identical.

He measured the outside entrance to the gate complex: fifteen feet wide and nineteen and a half feet deep.

In front of each alcove was a low wall eighteen inches high. The alcoves were ten feet square.

He measured the width of the gate complex from the outside edge of the alcove roof on one side to the outside edge of the alcove roof on the other: thirty-seven and a half feet from one top edge to the other.

He measured the inside walls of the gate complex: ninety feet to the porch leading into the courtyard.

The distance from the entrance of the gate complex to the far end of the porch was seventy-five feet.

The alcoves and their connecting walls inside the gate complex were topped by narrow windows all the way around. The porch also. All the windows faced inward. The doorjambs between the alcoves were decorated with palm trees.

✠

The man then led me to the outside courtyard and all its rooms. A paved walkway had been built connecting the courtyard gates. Thirty rooms lined the courtyard. The walkway was the same length as the gateways. It flanked them and ran their entire length. This was the walkway for the outside courtyard. He measured the distance from the front of the entrance gateway across to the entrance of the inner court: one hundred fifty feet.

✠

Then he took me to the north side. Here was another gate complex facing north, exiting the outside courtyard. He measured its length and width. It had three alcoves on each side. Its gateposts and porch were the same as in the first gate: eighty-seven and a half feet by forty-three and three-quarters feet. The windows and palm trees were identical to the east gateway. Seven steps led up to it, and its porch faced inward. Opposite this gate complex was a gate complex to the inside courtyard, on the north as on the east. The distance between the two was one hundred seventy-five feet.

Then he took me to the south side, to the south gate complex. He measured its gateposts and its porch. It was the same size as the others. The porch with its windows was the same size as those previously mentioned. It also had seven steps up to it. Its porch opened onto the outside courtyard, with palm trees decorating its gateposts on both sides. Opposite to it, the gate complex for the inner court faced south. He measured the distance across the courtyard from gate to gate: one hundred seventy-five feet.

✠

He led me into the inside courtyard through the south gate complex. He measured it and found it the same as the outside ones. Its alcoves, connecting walls, and vestibule were the same. The gate complex and porch, windowed all around, measured eighty-seven and a half by forty-three and three-quarters feet. The vestibule of each of the gate complexes leading to the inside courtyard was forty-three and three-quarters by eight and three-quarters feet. Each vestibule faced the outside courtyard. Palm trees were carved on its doorposts. Eight steps led up to it.

He then took me to the inside courtyard on the east and measured the gate complex. It was identical to the others—alcoves, connecting walls, and vestibule all the same. The gate complex and vestibule had windows all around. It measured eighty-seven and a half by forty-three and three-quarters feet. Its porch faced the outside courtyard. There were palm trees on the doorposts on both sides. And it had eight steps.

He brought me to the gate complex to the north and measured it: same measurements. The alcoves, connecting walls, and vestibule with its windows: eighty-seven and a half by forty-three and three-quarters feet. Its porch faced the outside courtyard. There were palm trees on its doorposts on both sides. And it had eight steps.

✠

There was a room with a door at the vestibule of the gate complex where the burnt offerings were cleaned. Two tables were placed within the vestibule, one on either side, on which the animals for burnt offerings, sin offerings, and guilt offerings were slaughtered. Two tables were also placed against both outside walls of the vestibule—four tables inside and four tables outside, eight tables in all for slaughtering the sacrificial animals. The four tables used for the burnt offerings were thirty-one and a half inches square and twenty-one inches high. The tools for slaughtering the sacrificial animals and other sacrifices were kept there. Meat hooks, three inches long, were fastened to the walls. The tables were for the sacrificial animals.

✠

Right where the inside gate complex opened onto the inside courtyard there were two rooms, one at the north gate facing south and the one at the south gate facing north. The man told me, "The room facing south is for the priests who are in charge of the Temple. And the room facing north is for the priests who are in charge of the altar. These priests are the sons of Zadok, the only sons of Levi permitted to come near to GOD to serve him."

He measured the inside courtyard: a hundred seventy-five feet square. The altar was in front of the Temple.

✠

He led me to the porch of the Temple and measured the gateposts of the porch: eight and three-quarters feet high on both sides. The entrance to the gate complex was twenty-one feet wide and its connecting walls were four and a half feet thick. The vestibule itself was thirty-five feet wide and twenty-one feet deep. Ten steps led up to the porch. Columns flanked the gateposts.

✠

41

He brought me into the Temple itself and measured the doorposts on each side. Each was ten and a half feet thick. The entrance was seventeen and a half feet wide. The walls on each side were eight and three-quarters feet thick.

He also measured the Temple Sanctuary: seventy feet by thirty-five feet.

He went further in and measured the doorposts at the entrance: Each was three and a half feet thick. The entrance itself was ten and a half feet wide, and the entrance walls were twelve and a quarter feet thick. He measured the inside Sanctuary, thirty-five feet square, set at the end of the main Sanctuary. He told me, "This is The Holy of Holies."

He measured the wall of the Temple. It was ten and a half feet thick. The side rooms around the Temple were seven feet wide. There were three floors of these side rooms, thirty rooms on each of the three floors. There were supporting beams around the Temple wall to hold up the side rooms, but they were freestanding, not attached to the wall itself. The side rooms around the Temple became wider from first floor to second floor to third floor. A staircase went from the bottom floor, through the middle, and then to the top floor.

I observed that the Temple had a ten-and-a-half-foot-thick raised base around it, which provided a foundation for the side rooms. The outside walls of the side rooms were eight and three-quarters feet thick. The open area between the side rooms of the Temple and the priests' rooms was a thirty-five-foot-wide strip all around the Temple. There were two entrances to the side rooms from the open area, one placed on the north side, the other on the south. There were eight and three-quarters feet of open space all around.

The house that faced the Temple courtyard to the west was one hundred twenty-two and a half feet wide, with eight-and-three-quarters-foot-thick walls. The length of the wall and building was one hundred fifty-seven and a half feet.

He measured the Temple: one hundred seventy-five feet long. The Temple courtyard and the house, including its walls, measured a hundred seventy-five feet. The breadth of the front of the Temple and the open area to the east was a hundred seventy-five feet.

He measured the length of the house facing the courtyard at the back of the Temple, including the shelters on each side: one hundred seventy-five feet. The main Sanctuary, the inner Sanctuary, and the vestibule facing the courtyard were paneled with wood, and had window frames and door frames in all three sections. From floor to windows the walls were paneled. Above the outside entrance to the inner Sanctuary and on the walls at regular intervals all around the inner Sanctuary and the main Sanctuary, angel-cherubim and palm trees were carved in alternating sequence.

Each angel-cherub had two faces: a human face toward the palm tree on the right and the face of a lion toward the palm tree on the left.

They were carved around the entire Temple. The cherubim–palm tree motif was carved from floor to door height on the wall of the main Sanctuary.

The main Sanctuary had a rectangular doorframe. In front of the Holy Place was something that looked like an altar of wood, five and a quarter feet high and three and a half feet square. Its corners, base, and sides were of wood. The man said to me, "This is the table that stands before GOD."

Both the main Sanctuary and the Holy Place had double doors. Each door had two leaves: two hinged leaves for each door, one set swinging inward and the other set outward. The doors of the main Sanctuary were carved with angel-cherubim and palm trees. There was a canopy of wood in front of the vestibule outside. There were narrow windows alternating with carved palm trees on both sides of the porch.

✠

42

The man led me north into the outside courtyard and brought me to the rooms that are in front of the open space and the house facing north. The length of the house on the north was one hundred seventy-five feet, and its width eighty-seven and a half feet. Across the thirty-five feet that separated the inside courtyard from the paved walkway at the edge of the outside courtyard, the rooms rose level by level for three stories. In front of the rooms on the inside was a hallway seventeen and a half feet wide and one hundred seventy-five feet long. Its entrances were from the north. The upper rooms themselves were narrower, their galleries being wider than on the first and second floors of the building. The rooms on the third floor had no pillars like the pillars in the outside courtyard and were smaller than the rooms on the first and second floors. There was an outside wall parallel to the rooms and the outside courtyard. It fronted the rooms for eighty-seven and a half feet. The row of rooms facing the outside courtyard was eighty-seven and a half feet long. The row on the side nearest the Sanctuary was one hundred seventy-five feet long. The first-floor rooms had their entrance from the east, coming in from the outside courtyard.

On the south side along the length of the courtyard's outside wall and fronting on the Temple courtyard were rooms with a walkway in front of them. These were just like the rooms on the north—same exits and dimensions—with the main entrance from the east leading to the hallway and the doors to the rooms the same as those on the north side. The design on the south was a mirror image of that on the north.

Then he said to me, "The north and south rooms adjacent to the open area are holy rooms where the priests who come before GOD eat the holy offerings. There they place the holy offerings—grain offerings, sin offerings, and guilt offerings. These are set-apart rooms, holy space. After the priests have entered the Sanctuary, they must not return to the outside courtyard and mingle among the people until they change the sacred garments in which they minister and put on their regular clothes."

After he had finished measuring what was inside the Temple area, he took me out the east gate and measured it from the outside. Using his measuring stick, he measured the east side: eight hundred seventy-five feet.

He measured the north side: eight hundred seventy-five feet.

He measured the south side: eight hundred seventy-five feet.

Last of all he went to the west side and measured it: eight hundred seventy-five feet.

He measured the wall on all four sides. Each wall was eight hundred seventy-five feet. The walls separated the holy from the ordinary.

43

THE MEANING OF THE TEMPLE

The man brought me to the east gate. Oh! The bright Glory of the God of Israel rivered out of the east sounding like the roar of floodwaters, and the earth itself glowed with the bright Glory. It looked just like what I had seen when he came to destroy the city, exactly like what I had seen earlier at the Kebar River. And again I fell, face to the ground.

The bright Glory of GOD poured into the Temple through the east gate. The Spirit put me on my feet and led me to the inside courtyard and—oh! the bright Glory of GOD filled the Temple!

I heard someone speaking to me from inside the Temple while the man stood beside me. He said, "Son of man, this is the place for my throne, the place I'll plant my feet. This is the place where I'll live with the Israelites forever. Neither the people of Israel nor their kings will ever again drag my holy name through the mud with their whoring and the no-god idols their kings set up at all the wayside shrines. When they set up their worship shrines right alongside mine with only a thin wall between them, they dragged my holy name through the mud with their obscene and vile worship. Is it any wonder that I destroyed them in anger? So let them get rid of their whoring ways and the stinking no-god idols introduced by their kings and I'll move in and live with them forever.

"Son of man, tell the people of Israel all about the Temple so they'll be dismayed by their wayward lives. Get them to go over the layout. That will bring them up short. Show them the whole plan of the Temple, its ins and outs, the proportions, the regulations, and the laws. Draw a picture so they can see the design and meaning and live by its design and intent.

"This is the law of the Temple: As it radiates from the top of the mountain, everything around it becomes holy ground. Yes, this is law, the meaning, of the Temple.

✠

"These are the dimensions of the altar, using the long (twenty-one-inch) ruler. The gutter at its base is twenty-one inches deep and twenty-one inches wide, with a four-inch lip around its edge.

"The height of the altar is three and a half feet from the base to the first ledge and twenty inches wide. From the first ledge to the second ledge it is seven feet high and twenty-one inches wide. The altar hearth is another seven feet high. Four horns stick upward from the hearth twenty-one inches high.

"The top of the altar, the hearth, is square, twenty-one by twenty-one feet. The upper ledge is also square, twenty-four and a half feet on each side, with a ten-and-a-half-inch lip and a twenty-one-inch-wide gutter all the way around.

"The steps of the altar ascend from the east."

Then the man said to me, "Son of man, GOD, the Master, says: 'These are the ordinances for conduct at the altar when it is built, for sacrificing burnt offerings and sprinkling blood on it.

"'For a sin offering, give a bull to the priests, the Levitical priests who are from the family of Zadok who come into my presence to serve me. Take some of its blood and smear it on the four horns of the altar that project from the four corners of the top ledge and all around the lip. That's to purify the altar and make it fit for the sacrifice. Then take the bull for the sin offerings and burn it in the place set aside for this in the courtyard outside the Sanctuary.

"'On the second day, offer a male goat without blemish for a sin offering. Purify the altar the same as you purified it for the bull. Then, when you have purified it, offer a bull without blemish and a ram without blemish from the flock. Present them before GOD. Sprinkle salt on them and offer them as a burnt offering to GOD.

"'For seven days, prepare a goat for a sin offering daily, and also a bull and a ram from the flock, animals without blemish. For seven days the priests are to get the altar ready for its work, purifying it. This is how you dedicate it.

"'After these seven days of dedication, from the eighth day on, the priests will present your burnt offerings and your peace offerings. And I'll accept you with pleasure, with delight! Decree of GOD, the Master.'"

44

SANCTUARY RULES

Then the man brought me back to the outside gate complex of the Sanctuary that faces east. But it was shut.

GOD spoke to me: "This gate is shut and it's to stay shut. No one is to go through it because GOD, the God of Israel, has gone through it. It stays shut. Only the prince, because he's the prince, may sit there to eat in the presence of GOD. He is to enter the gate complex through the porch and leave by the same way."

The man led me through the north gate to the front of the Temple. I looked, and—oh!—the bright Glory of GOD filling the Temple of GOD! I fell on my face in worship.

GOD said to me, "Son of man, get a grip on yourself. Use your eyes, use your ears, pay careful attention to everything I tell you about the ordinances of this Temple of GOD, the way all the laws work, instructions regarding it and all the entrances and exits of the Sanctuary.

"Tell this bunch of rebels, this family Israel, 'Message of GOD, the Master: No more of these vile obscenities, Israel, dragging irreverent and unrepentant outsiders, uncircumcised in heart and flesh, into my Sanctuary, feeding them the sacrificial offerings as if it were the food for a neighborhood picnic. With all your vile obscenities, you've broken trust with me, the solemn covenant I made with you. You haven't taken care of my holy things. You've hired out the work to foreigners who care nothing for this place, my Sanctuary. No irreverent and unrepentant aliens, uncircumcised in heart or flesh, not even the ones who live among Israelites, are to enter my Sanctuary.'

"The Levites who walked off and left me, along with everyone else—all Israel—who took up with all the no-god idols, will pay for everything they did wrong. From now on they'll do only the menial work in the Sanctuary: guard the gates and help out with the Temple chores—and also kill the sacrificial animals for the people and serve them. Because they acted as priests to the no-god idols and made my people Israel stumble and fall, I've taken an oath to punish them. Decree of GOD, the Master. Yes, they'll pay for what they've done. They're fired from the priesthood. No longer will they come into my presence and take care of my holy things. No more access to The Holy Place! They'll have to live with what they've done, carry the shame of their vile and obscene lives. From now on, their job is to sweep up and run errands. That's it.

"But the Levitical priests who descend from Zadok, who faithfully took care of my Sanctuary when everyone else went off and left me, are going to come into my presence and serve me. They are going to carry out the priestly work of offering the solemn sacrifices of worship. Decree of GOD, the Master. They're the only ones permitted to enter my Sanctuary. They're the only ones to approach my table and serve me, accompanying me in my work.

"When they enter the gate complex of the inside courtyard, they are to dress in linen. No woolens are to be worn while serving at the gate complex of the inside courtyard or inside the Temple itself. They're to wear linen turbans on their heads and linen underclothes—nothing that makes them sweat. When they go out into the outside courtyard where the people gather, they must first change out of the clothes they have been serving in, leaving them in the sacred rooms where they change to their everyday clothes, so that they don't trivialize their holy work by the way they dress.

"They are to neither shave their heads nor let their hair become unkempt, but must keep their hair trimmed and neat.

"No priest is to drink on the job—no wine while in the inside courtyard.

"Priests are not to marry widows or divorcees, but only Israelite virgins or widows of priests.

"Their job is to teach my people the difference between the holy and the common, to show them how to discern between unclean and clean.

"When there's a difference of opinion, the priests will arbitrate. They'll decide on the basis of my judgments, laws, and statutes. They are in charge of making sure the appointed feasts are honored and my Sabbaths kept holy in the ways I've commanded.

"A priest must not contaminate himself by going near a corpse. But when the dead person is his father or mother, son or daughter, brother or unmarried sister, he can approach the dead. But after he has been purified, he must wait another seven days. Then, when he returns to the inside courtyard of the Sanctuary to do his priestly work in the Sanctuary, he must first offer a sin offering for himself. Decree of GOD, the Master.

"As to priests owning land, I am their inheritance. Don't give any land in Israel to them. *I* am their 'land,' their inheritance. They'll take their meals from the grain offerings, the sin offerings, and the guilt offerings. Everything in Israel offered to GOD in worship is theirs. The best of everything grown, plus all special gifts, comes to the priests. All that is given in worship to GOD goes to them. Serve them first. Serve from your best and your home will be blessed.

"Priests are not to eat any meat from bird or animal unfit for ordinary human consumption, such as carcasses found dead on the road or in the field.

45

SACRED SPACE FOR GOD

"When you divide up the inheritance of the land, you must set aside part of the land as sacred space for GOD: approximately seven miles long by six miles wide, all of it holy ground. Within this rectangle, reserve a seven-hundred-fifty-foot square for the Sanctuary with a seventy-five-foot buffer zone surrounding it. Mark off within the sacred reserve a section seven miles long by three miles wide. The Sanctuary with its Holy of Holies will be placed there. This is where the priests will live, those who lead worship in the Sanctuary and serve GOD there. Their houses will be there along with The Holy Place.

"To the north of the sacred reserve, an area roughly seven miles long and two and a quarter miles wide will be set aside as land for the villages of the Levites who administer the affairs of worship in the Sanctuary.

"To the south of the sacred reserve, measure off a section seven miles long and about a mile and a half wide for the city itself, an area held in common by the whole family of Israel.

"The prince gets the land abutting the seven-mile east and west borders of the central sacred square, extending eastward toward the Jordan and westward toward the Mediterranean. This is the prince's possession in Israel. My princes will no longer bully my people, running roughshod over them. They'll respect the land as it has been allotted to the tribes.

"This is the Message of GOD, the Master: I've put up with you long enough, princes of Israel! Quit bullying and taking advantage of my people. Do what's just and right for a change. Use honest scales—honest weights and honest measures. Every pound must have sixteen ounces. Every gallon must measure four quarts. The ounce is the basic measure for both. And your coins must be honest—no wooden nickels!

EVERYONE IN THE LAND MUST CONTRIBUTE

"'These are the prescribed offerings you are to supply: one-sixtieth part of your wheat, one-sixtieth part of your barley, one-hundredth part of your oil, one sheep out of every two hundred from the lush pastures of Israel. These will be used for the grain offerings, burnt offerings, and peace offerings for making the atonement sacrifices for the people. Decree of GOD, the Master.

"'Everyone in the land must contribute to these special offerings that the prince in Israel will administer. It's the prince's job to provide the burnt offerings, grain offerings, and drink offerings at the Holy Festivals, the New Moons, and the Sabbaths—all the commanded feasts among the people of Israel. Sin offerings, grain offerings, burnt offerings, and peace offerings for making atonement for the people of Israel are his responsibility.

"'This is the Message from GOD, the Master: On the first day of the first month, take an unblemished bull calf and purify the Sanctuary. The priest is to take blood from the sin offerings and rub it on the doorposts of the Temple, on the four corners of the ledge of the altar, and on the gate entrance to the inside courtyard. Repeat this ritual on the seventh day of the month for anyone who sins without knowing it. In this way you make atonement for the Temple.

"'On the fourteenth day of the first month, you will observe the

Passover, a feast of seven days. During the feast you will eat bread made without yeast.

"'On Passover, the prince supplies a bull as a sin offering for himself and all the people of the country. Each day for each of the seven days of the feast, he will supply seven bulls and seven rams unblemished as a burnt offering to GOD, and also each day a male goat.

"'He will supply about five and a half gallons of grain offering and a gallon of oil for each bull and each ram.

"'On the fifteenth day of the seventh month, and on each of the seven days of the feast, he is to supply the same materials for sin offerings, burnt offerings, grain offerings, and oil.

✛

46

"'Message from GOD, the Master: The gate of the inside courtyard on the east is to be shut on the six working days, but open on the Sabbath. It is also to be open on the New Moon. The prince will enter through the entrance area of the gate complex and stand at the gateposts as the priests present his burnt offerings and peace offerings while he worships there on the porch. He will then leave, but the gate won't be shut until evening. On Sabbaths and New Moons, the people are to worship before GOD at the outside entrance to that gate complex.

"'The prince supplies for GOD the burnt offering for the Sabbath—six unblemished lambs and an unblemished ram. The grain offering to go with the ram is about five and a half gallons plus a gallon of oil, and a handful of grain for each lamb.

"'At the New Moon he is to supply a bull calf, six lambs, and a ram, all without blemish. He will also supply five and a half gallons of grain offering and a gallon of oil for both ram and bull, and a handful of grain offering for each lamb.

"'When the prince enters, he will go through the entrance vestibule of the gate complex and leave the same way.

"'But when the people of the land come to worship GOD at the commanded feasts, those who enter through the north gate will exit from the south gate, and those who enter though the south gate will exit from the north gate. You don't exit the gate through which you enter, but through the opposite gate. The prince is to be there, mingling with them, going in and out with them.

"'At the festivals and the commanded feasts, the appropriate grain offering is five and a half gallons, with a gallon of oil for the bull and ram and a handful of grain for each lamb.

"'When the prince brings a freewill offering to GOD, whether a burnt offering or a peace offering, the east gate is to be opened for him. He offers his burnt or peace offering the same as he does on the Sabbath. Then he leaves, and after he is out, the gate is shut.

"'Every morning you are to bring a yearling lamb unblemished for a burnt offering to GOD. Also, every morning bring a grain offering of about a gallon of grain with a quart or so of oil to moisten it. Presenting this grain offering to GOD is standard procedure. The lamb, the grain offering, and the oil for the burnt offering are a regular daily ritual.

"'A Message from GOD, the Master: If the prince deeds a gift from his inheritance to one of his sons, it stays in the family. But if he deeds a gift from his inheritance to a servant, the servant keeps it only until the year of liberation (the Jubilee year). After that, it comes back to the prince. His inheritance is only for his sons. It stays in the family. The prince must not take the inheritance from any of the people, dispossessing them of their land. He can give his sons only what he himself owns. None of my people are to be run off their land.'"

Then the man brought me through the north gate into the holy chambers assigned to the priests and showed me a back room to the west. He said, "This is the kitchen where the priests will cook the guilt offering and sin offering and bake the grain offering so that they won't have to do it in the outside courtyard and endanger the unprepared people out there with The Holy."

He proceeded to take me to the outside courtyard and around to each of its four corners. In each corner I observed another court. In each of the four corners of the outside courtyard were smaller courts sixty by forty-five feet, each the same size. On the inside walls of the courts was a stone shelf, and beneath the shelves, hearths for cooking.

He said, "These are the kitchens where those who serve in the Temple will cook the sacrifices of the people."

47

TREES ON BOTH SIDES OF THE RIVER

Now he brought me back to the entrance to the Temple. I saw water pouring out from under the Temple porch to the east (the Temple faced east). The water poured from the south side of the Temple, south of the altar. He then took me out through the north gate and led me around the outside to the gate complex on the east. The water was gushing from under the south front of the Temple.

He walked to the east with a measuring tape and measured off fifteen hundred feet, leading me through water that was ankle-deep. He measured off another fifteen hundred feet, leading me through water that was knee-deep. He measured off another fifteen hundred feet, leading me through water waist-deep. He measured off another fifteen hundred feet. By now it was a river over my head, water to swim in, water no one could possibly walk through.

He said, "Son of man, have you had a good look?"

Then he took me back to the riverbank. While sitting on the bank, I noticed a lot of trees on both sides of the river.

He told me, "This water flows east, descends to the Arabah and then into the sea, the sea of stagnant waters. When it empties into those waters, the sea will become fresh. Wherever the river flows, life will flourish—great schools of fish—because the river is turning the salt sea into fresh water. Where the river flows, life abounds. Fishermen will stand shoulder to shoulder along the shore from En-gedi all the way north to En-eglaim, casting their nets. The sea will teem with fish of all kinds, like the fish of the Great Mediterranean.

"The swamps and marshes won't become fresh. They'll stay salty.

"But the river itself, on both banks, will grow fruit trees of all kinds. Their leaves won't wither, the fruit won't fail. Every month they'll bear fresh fruit because the river from the Sanctuary flows to them. Their fruit will be for food and their leaves for healing."

Divide Up This Land

A Message from God, the Master: "These are the boundaries by which you are to divide up the inheritance of the land for the twelve tribes of Israel, with Joseph getting two parcels. It is to be divided up equally. I swore in a solemn oath to give it to your ancestors, swore that this land would be your inheritance.

"These are the boundaries of the land:

"The northern boundary runs from the Great Mediterranean Sea along the Hethlon road to where you turn off to the entrance of Hamath, Zedad, Berothah, and Sibraim, which lies between the territory of Damascus and the territory of Hamath, and on to Hazor-hatticon on the border of Hauran. The boundary runs from the Sea to Hazor-enon, with the territories of Damascus and Hamath to the north. That is the northern boundary.

"The eastern boundary runs between Damascus and Hauran, down along the Jordan between Gilead and the land of Israel to the Eastern Sea as far as Tamar. This is the eastern boundary.

"The southern boundary runs west from Tamar to the waters of Meribah-kadesh, along the Brook of Egypt, and out to the Great Mediterranean Sea. This is the southern boundary.

"The western boundary is formed by the Great Mediterranean Sea north to where the road turns east toward the entrance to Hamath. This is the western boundary.

"Divide up this land among the twelve tribes of Israel. Divide it up as your inheritance, and include in it the resident aliens who have made themselves at home among you and now have children. Treat them as if they were born there, just like yourselves. They also get an inheritance among the tribes of Israel. In whatever tribe the resident alien lives, there he gets his inheritance. Decree of GOD, the Master.

48

The Sanctuary of God at the Center

"These are the tribes:

"Dan: one portion, along the northern boundary, following the Hethlon road that turns off to the entrance of Hamath as far as Hazor-enon so that the territory of Damascus lies to the north alongside Hamath, the northern border stretching from east to west.

"Asher: one portion, bordering Dan from east to west.

"Naphtali: one portion, bordering Asher from east to west.

"Manasseh: one portion, bordering Naphtali from east to west.

"Ephraim: one portion, bordering Manasseh from east to west.

"Reuben: one portion, bordering Ephraim from east to west.

"Judah: one portion, bordering Reuben from east to west.

"Bordering Judah from east to west is the consecrated area that you will set aside as holy: a square approximately seven by seven miles, with the Sanctuary set at the center. The consecrated area reserved for GOD is to be seven miles long and a little less than three miles wide.

"This is how it will be parceled out. The priest will get the area measuring seven miles on the north and south boundaries, with a width of a little more than three miles at the east and west boundaries. The Sanctuary of GOD will be at the center. This is for the consecrated priests, the Zakokites who stayed true in their service to me and didn't get off track as the Levites did when Israel wandered off the main road. This is their special gift, a gift from the land itself, most holy ground, bordering the section of the Levites.

"The Levites get a section equal in size to that of the priests, roughly seven by three miles. They are not permitted to sell or trade any of it. It's the choice part of the land, to say nothing of being holy to GOD.

"What's left of the 'sacred square'—each side measures out at seven miles by a mile and a half—is for ordinary use: the city and its buildings with open country around it, but the city at the center. The north, south, east, and west sides of the city are each about a mile and a half in length. A strip of pasture, one hundred twenty-five yards wide, will border the city on all sides. The remainder of this portion, three miles of countryside to the east and to the west of the sacred precinct, is for farming. It will supply food for the city. Workers from all the tribes of Israel will serve as field hands to farm the land.

"This dedicated area, set apart for holy purposes, will be a square, seven miles by seven miles, a 'holy square,' which includes the part set aside for the city.

"The rest of this land, the country stretching east to the Jordan and west to the Mediterranean from the seven-mile sides of the 'holy square,' belongs to the prince. His land is sandwiched between the tribal portions north and south, and goes out both east and west from the 'sacred square' with its Temple at the center. The land set aside for the Levites on one side and the city on the other is in the middle of the territory assigned to the prince. The 'sacred square' is flanked east and west by the prince's land and bordered on the north and south by the territories of Judah and Benjamin respectively.

"And then the rest of the tribes:

"Benjamin: one portion, stretching from the eastern to the western boundary.

"Simeon: one portion, bordering Benjamin from east to west.

"Issachar: one portion, bordering Simeon from east to west.

"Zebulun: one portion, bordering Issachar from east to west.

"Gad: one portion, bordering Zebulun from east to west.

"The southern boundary of Gad will run south from Tamar to the waters of Meribah-kadesh, along the Brook of Egypt and then out to the Great Mediterranean Sea.

"This is the land that you are to divide up among the tribes of Israel as their inheritance. These are their portions." Decree of GOD, the Master.

✠

"These are the gates of the city. On the north side, which is 2,250 yards long (the gates of the city are named after the tribes of Israel), three gates: the gate of Reuben, the gate of Judah, the gate of Levi.

"On the east side, measuring 2,250 yards, three gates: the gate of Joseph, the gate of Benjamin, the gate of Dan.

"On the south side, measuring 2,250 yards, three gates: the gate of Simeon, the gate of Issachar, the gate of Zebulun.

"On the west side, measuring 2,250 yards, three gates: the gate of Gad, the gate of Asher, the gate of Naphtali.

"The four sides of the city measure to a total of nearly six miles.

"From now on the name of the city will be YAHWEH-SHAMMAH:

"GOD-IS-THERE."

DANIEL

I mages generated by the book of Daniel have been percolating through the daily experiences of the people of God for well over two thousand years now, producing a richly aromatic brew stimulating God's people to obey and trust their sovereign God.

Obedience to God in the pressures and stresses of day-by-day living and trust in God's ways in the large sweep of history are always at risk, but especially in times of suffering and persecution. Obedience to God is difficult when we are bullied into compliance to the God-ignoring culture out of sheer survival. Trust in God is likewise at risk of being abandoned in favor of the glamorous seductions of might and size.

Daniel was written out of just such times. There was little or no observable evidence in the circumstances to commend against-the-stream obedience or overarching trust. But Daniel's stories and visions have supplied what that society did not—could not—give. Century after century, Daniel has shot adrenaline into the veins of God-obedience and put backbone into God-trust.

Daniel is composed, in approximately equal parts, of stories and visions—six stories (chapters 1–6) and four visions (chapters 7–12). The stories tell of souls living faithfully in obedience to God in a time of adversity. The visions are widescreen renditions of God's sovereignty worked out among nations who couldn't care less about him. Six soul stories; four sovereignty visions.

The six soul-survival stories nourish a commitment to integrity and perseverance right now. Very few of us live in settings congenial to God-loyalty and among people who affirm a costly discipleship. Hardly a day goes by that we do not have to choose between compliance to what is expedient and loyalty to our Lord. The stories keep us alert to what is at stake day by day, hour by hour.

The four visions of God's history-saving ways nourish hope in God during times when world events seem to put God in eclipse. The visions are difficult to understand, written as they are in a deliberately cryptic style (apocalyptic). From time to time they have been subjected to intense study and explanation.

But for a first reading, perhaps it is better simply to let the strange symbolic figures give witness to the large historical truth that eclipses the daily accumulation of historical facts reported by our news media, namely, that God is sovereign. In the course of all the noise and shuffling, strutting and posing, of arrogant rulers and nations that we call history, with the consequent troubles to us all, God is serenely sovereign; we can trust him to bring all things and people under his rule.

There are always some of us who want to concentrate on the soul, and others of us who want to deal with the big issues of history. Daniel is one of our primary documents for keeping it all together—the personal and the political, the present and the future, the soul and society.

DANIEL

1

Daniel Was Gifted by God

It was the third year of King Jehoiakim's reign in Judah when King Nebuchadnezzar of Babylon declared war on Jerusalem and besieged the city. The Master handed King Jehoiakim of Judah over to him, along with some of the furnishings from the Temple of God. Nebuchadnezzar took king and furnishings to the country of Babylon, the ancient Shinar. He put the furnishings in the sacred treasury.

The king told Ashpenaz, head of the palace staff, to get some Israelites from the royal family and nobility—young men who were healthy and handsome, intelligent and well-educated, good prospects for leadership positions in the government, perfect specimens!—and indoctrinate them in the Babylonian language and the lore of magic and fortunetelling. The king then ordered that they be served from the same menu as the royal table—the best food, the finest wine. After three years of training they would be given positions in the king's court.

Four young men from Judah—Daniel, Hananiah, Mishael, and Azariah—were among those selected. The head of the palace staff gave them Babylonian names: Daniel was named Belteshazzar, Hananiah was named Shadrach, Mishael was named Meshach, Azariah was named Abednego.

But Daniel determined that he would not defile himself by eating the king's food or drinking his wine, so he asked the head of the palace staff to exempt him from the royal diet. The head of the palace staff, by God's grace, liked Daniel, but he warned him, "I'm afraid of what my master the king will do. He is the one who assigned this diet and if he sees that you are not as healthy as the rest, he'll have my head!"

But Daniel appealed to a steward who had been assigned by the head of the palace staff to be in charge of Daniel, Hananiah, Mishael, and Azariah: "Try us out for ten days on a simple diet of vegetables and water. Then compare us with the young men who eat from the royal menu. Make your decision on the basis of what you see."

The steward agreed to do it and fed them vegetables and water for ten days. At the end of the ten days they looked better and more robust than all the others who had been eating from the royal menu. So the steward continued to exempt them from the royal menu of food and drink and served them only vegetables.

God gave these four young men knowledge and skill in both books and life. In addition, Daniel was gifted in understanding all sorts of visions and dreams. At the end of the time set by the king for their training, the head of the royal staff brought them in to Nebuchadnezzar. When the king interviewed them, he found them far superior to all the other young men. None were a match for Daniel, Hananiah, Mishael, and Azariah.

And so they took their place in the king's service. Whenever the king consulted them on anything, on books or on life, he found them ten times better than all the magicians and enchanters in his kingdom put together.

Daniel continued in the king's service until the first year in the reign of King Cyrus.

2

KING NEBUCHADNEZZAR'S DREAM

In the second year of his reign, King Nebuchadnezzar started having dreams that disturbed him deeply. He couldn't sleep. He called in all the Babylonian magicians, enchanters, sorcerers, and fortunetellers to interpret his dreams for him. When they came and lined up before the king, he said to them, "I had a dream that I can't get out of my mind. I can't sleep until I know what it means."

The fortunetellers, speaking in the Aramaic language, said, "Long live the king! Tell us the dream and we will interpret it."

The king answered the fortunetellers, "This is my decree: If you can't tell me both the dream itself and its interpretation, I'll have you ripped to pieces, limb from limb, and your homes torn down. But if you tell me both the dream and its interpretation, I'll lavish you with gifts and honors. So go to it: Tell me the dream and its interpretation."

They answered, "If it please your majesty, tell us the dream. We'll give the interpretation."

But the king said, "I know what you're up to—you're just playing for time. You know you're up a tree. You know that if you can't tell me my dream, you're doomed. I see right through you—you're going to cook up some fancy stories and confuse the issue until I change my mind. Nothing doing! First tell me the dream, then I'll know that you're on the up and up with the interpretation and not just blowing smoke in my eyes."

The fortunetellers said, "Nobody anywhere can do what you ask.

And no king, great or small, has ever demanded anything like this from any magician, enchanter, or fortuneteller. What you're asking is impossible unless some god or goddess should reveal it—and they don't hang around with people like us."

That set the king off. He lost his temper and ordered the whole company of Babylonian wise men killed. When the death warrant was issued, Daniel and his companions were included. They also were marked for execution.

When Arioch, chief of the royal guards, was making arrangements for the execution, Daniel wisely took him aside and quietly asked what was going on: "Why this all of a sudden?"

After Arioch filled in the background, Daniel went to the king and asked for a little time so that he could interpret the dream.

Daniel then went home and told his companions Hananiah, Mishael, and Azariah what was going on. He asked them to pray to the God of heaven for mercy in solving this mystery so that the four of them wouldn't be killed along with the whole company of Babylonian wise men.

DREAM INTERPRETATION: A STORY OF FIVE KINGDOMS

That night the answer to the mystery was given to Daniel in a vision. Daniel blessed the God of heaven, saying,

"Blessed be the name of God,
　　forever and ever.
He knows all, does all:
　　He changes the seasons and guides history,
He raises up kings and also brings them down,
　　he provides both intelligence and discernment,
He opens up the depths, tells secrets,
　　sees in the dark—light spills out of him!
God of all my ancestors, all thanks! all praise!
　　You made me wise and strong.
And now you've shown us what we asked for.
　　You've solved the king's mystery."

So Daniel went back to Arioch, who had been put in charge of the execution. He said, "Call off the execution! Take me to the king and I'll interpret his dream."

Arioch didn't lose a minute. He ran to the king, bringing Daniel with him, and said, "I've found a man from the exiles of Judah who can interpret the king's dream!"

The king asked Daniel (renamed in Babylonian, Belteshazzar), "Are you sure you can do this—tell me the dream I had and interpret it for me?"

Daniel answered the king, "No mere human can solve the king's mystery, I don't care who it is—no wise man, enchanter, magician, diviner. But there is a God in heaven who solves mysteries, and he has solved this one. He is letting King Nebuchadnezzar in on what is going to happen in the days ahead. This is the dream you had when you were lying on your bed, the vision that filled your mind:

"While you were stretched out on your bed, oh king, thoughts came to you regarding what is coming in the days ahead. The Revealer of Mysteries showed you what will happen. But the interpretation is given through me, not because I'm any smarter than anyone else in the country, but so that you will know what it means, so that you will understand what you dreamed.

"What you saw, oh king, was a huge statue standing before you, striking in appearance. And terrifying. The head of the statue was pure gold, the chest and arms were silver, the belly and hips were bronze, the legs were iron, and the feet were an iron-ceramic mixture. While you were looking at this statue, a stone cut out of a mountain by an invisible hand hit the statue, smashing its iron-ceramic feet. Then the whole thing fell to pieces— iron, tile, bronze, silver, and gold, smashed to bits. It was like scraps of old newspapers in a vacant lot in a hot dry summer, blown every which way by the wind, scattered to oblivion. But the stone that hit the statue became a huge mountain, dominating the horizon. This was your dream.

"And now we'll interpret it for the king. You, oh king, are the most powerful king on earth. The God of heaven has given you the works: rule, power, strength, and glory. He has put you in charge of men and women, wild animals and birds, all over the world—you're the head ruler, you are the head of gold. But your rule will be taken over by another kingdom, inferior to yours, and that one by a third, a bronze kingdom, but still ruling the whole land, and after that by a fourth kingdom, iron-like in strength. Just as iron smashes things to bits, breaking and pulverizing, it will bust up the previous kingdoms.

"But then the feet and toes that ended up as a mixture of ceramic and iron will deteriorate into a mongrel kingdom with some remains of iron in it. Just as the toes of the feet were part ceramic and part iron, it will end up a mixed bag of the breakable and unbreakable. That kingdom won't bond, won't hold together any more than iron and clay hold together.

"But throughout the history of these kingdoms, the God of heaven will be building a kingdom that will never be destroyed, nor will this kingdom ever fall under the domination of another. In the end it will crush the other kingdoms and finish them off and come through it all standing strong and eternal. It will be like the stone cut from the mountain by the invisible hand that crushed the iron, the bronze, the ceramic, the silver, and the gold.

"The great God has let the king know what will happen in the years to come. This is an accurate telling of the dream, and the interpretation is also accurate."

When Daniel finished, King Nebuchadnezzar fell on his face in awe before Daniel. He ordered the offering of sacrifices and burning of incense in Daniel's honor. He said to Daniel, "Your God is beyond question the God of all gods, the Master of all kings. And he solves all mysteries, I know, because you've solved this mystery."

Then the king promoted Daniel to a high position in the kingdom, lavished him with gifts, and made him governor over the entire province of Babylon and the chief in charge of all the Babylonian wise men. At Daniel's request the king appointed Shadrach, Meshach, and Abednego to administrative posts throughout Babylon, while Daniel governed from the royal headquarters.

3

FOUR MEN IN THE FURNACE

King Nebuchadnezzar built a gold statue, ninety feet high and nine feet thick. He set it up on the Dura plain in the province of Babylon. He then ordered all the important leaders in the province, everybody who was anybody, to the dedication ceremony of the statue. They all came for the dedication, all the important people, and took their places before the statue that Nebuchadnezzar had erected.

A herald then proclaimed in a loud voice: "Attention, everyone! Every race, color, and creed, listen! When you hear the band strike up—all the trumpets and trombones, the tubas and baritones, the drums and cymbals—fall to your knees and worship the gold statue that King Nebuchadnezzar has set up. Anyone who does not kneel and worship shall be thrown immediately into a roaring furnace."

The band started to play, a huge band equipped with all the musical instruments of Babylon, and everyone—every race, color, and creed—fell to their knees and worshiped the gold statue that King Nebuchadnezzar had set up.

Just then, some Babylonian fortunetellers stepped up and accused the Jews. They said to King Nebuchadnezzar, "Long live the king! You gave strict orders, oh king, that when the big band started playing, everyone had to fall to their knees and worship the gold statue, and whoever did not go to their knees and worship it had to be pitched into a roaring furnace. Well, there are some Jews here—Shadrach, Meshach, and Abednego—whom you have placed in high positions in the province of Babylon. These men are ignoring you, oh king. They don't respect your gods and they won't worship the gold statue you set up."

Furious, King Nebuchadnezzar ordered Shadrach, Meshach, and Abednego to be brought in. When the men were brought in, Nebuchadnezzar asked, "Is it true, Shadrach, Meshach, and Abednego, that you don't respect my gods and refuse to worship the gold statue that I have set up? I'm giving you a second chance—but from now on, when the big band strikes up you must go to your knees and worship the statue I have made. If you don't worship it, you will be pitched into a roaring furnace, no questions asked. Who is the god who can rescue you from my power?"

Shadrach, Meshach, and Abednego answered King Nebuchadnezzar, "Your threat means nothing to us. If you throw us in the fire, the God we serve can rescue us from your roaring furnace and anything else you might cook up, oh king. But even if he doesn't, it wouldn't make a bit of difference, oh king. We still wouldn't serve your gods or worship the gold statue you set up."

Nebuchadnezzar, his face purple with anger, cut off Shadrach, Meshach, and Abednego. He ordered the furnace fired up seven times hotter than usual. He ordered some strong men from the army to tie them up, hands and feet, and throw them into the roaring furnace. Shadrach, Meshach, and Abednego, bound hand and foot, fully dressed from head to toe, were pitched into the roaring fire. Because the king was in such a hurry and the furnace was so hot, flames from the furnace killed the men who carried Shadrach, Meshach, and Abednego to it, while the fire raged around Shadrach, Meshach, and Abednego.

Suddenly King Nebuchadnezzar jumped up in alarm and said, "Didn't we throw three men, bound hand and foot, into the fire?"

"That's right, oh king," they said.

"But look!" he said. "I see four men, walking around freely in the fire, completely unharmed! And the fourth man looks like a son of the gods!"

Nebuchadnezzar went to the door of the roaring furnace and called in, "Shadrach, Meshach, and Abednego, servants of the High God, come out here!"

Shadrach, Meshach, and Abednego walked out of the fire.

All the important people, the government leaders and king's counselors, gathered around to examine them and discovered that the fire hadn't so much as touched the three men—not a hair singed, not a scorch mark on their clothes, not even the smell of fire on them!

Nebuchadnezzar said, "Blessed be the God of Shadrach, Meshach, and Abednego! He sent his angel and rescued his servants who trusted in him! They ignored the king's orders and laid their bodies on the line rather than serve or worship any god but their own.

"Therefore I issue this decree: Anyone anywhere, of any race, color, or creed, who says anything against the God of Shadrach, Meshach, and Abednego will be ripped to pieces, limb from limb, and their houses torn down. There has never been a god who can pull off a rescue like this."

Then the king promoted Shadrach, Meshach, and Abednego in the province of Babylon.

4

A Dream of a Chopped-Down Tree

King Nebuchadnezzar to everyone, everywhere—every race, color, and creed: "Peace and prosperity to all! It is my privilege to report to you the gracious miracles that the High God has done for me.

"His miracles are staggering,
    his wonders are surprising.
His kingdom lasts and lasts,
    his sovereign rule goes on forever.

"I, Nebuchadnezzar, was at home taking it easy in my palace, without a care in the world. But as I was stretched out on my bed I had a dream that scared me—a nightmare that shook me. I sent for all the wise men of Babylon so that they could interpret the dream for me. When they were all assembled—magicians, enchanters, fortunetellers, witches—I told them the dream. None could tell me what it meant.

"And then Daniel came in. His Babylonian name is Belteshazzar, named after my god, a man full of the divine Holy Spirit. I told him my dream.

"'Belteshazzar,' I said, 'chief of the magicians, I know that you are a man full of the divine Holy Spirit and that there is no mystery that you can't solve. Listen to this dream that I had and interpret it for me.

"'This is what I saw as I was stretched out on my bed. I saw a big towering tree at the center of the world. As I watched, the tree grew huge and strong. Its top reached the sky and it could be seen from the four corners of the earth. Its leaves were beautiful, its fruit abundant—enough food for everyone! Wild animals found shelter under it, birds nested in its branches, everything living was fed and sheltered by it.

"'And this also is what I saw as I was stretched out on my bed. I saw a holy watchman descend from heaven, and call out:

""Chop down the tree, lop off its branches,
  strip its leaves and scatter its fruit.
Chase the animals from beneath it
  and shoo the birds from its branches.
But leave the stump and roots in the ground,
  belted with a strap of iron and bronze in the grassy meadow.

""Let him be soaked in heaven's dew
  and take his meals with the animals that graze.
Let him lose his mind
  and get an animal's mind in exchange,
And let this go on
  for seven seasons.

""The angels announce this decree,
  the holy watchmen bring this sentence,
So that everyone living will know
  that the High God rules human kingdoms.
He arranges kingdom affairs however he wishes,
  and makes leaders out of losers."

☩

"'This is what I, King Nebuchadnezzar, dreamed. It's your turn, Belteshazzar—interpret it for me. None of the wise men of Babylon could make heads or tails of it, but I'm sure you can do it. You're full of the divine Holy Spirit.'"

"You Will Graze on the Grass Like an Ox"

At first Daniel, who had been renamed Belteshazzar in Babylon, was upset. The thoughts that came swarming into his mind terrified him.

"Belteshazzar," the king said, "stay calm. Don't let the dream and its interpretation scare you."

"My master," said Belteshazzar, "I wish this dream were about your enemies and its interpretation for your foes.

"The tree you saw that grew so large and sturdy with its top touching the sky, visible from the four corners of the world; the tree with the luxuriant foliage and abundant fruit, enough for everyone; the tree under which animals took cover and in which birds built nests—you, oh king, are that tree.

"You have grown great and strong. Your royal majesty reaches sky-high, and your sovereign rule stretches to the four corners of the world.

"But the part about the holy angel descending from heaven and proclaiming, 'Chop down the tree, destroy it, but leave stump and roots in the ground belted with a strap of iron and bronze in the grassy meadow; let him be soaked with heaven's dew and take his meals with the grazing animals for seven seasons'—this, oh king, also refers to you. It means that the High God has sentenced my master the king: You will be driven away from human company and live with the wild animals. You will graze on grass like an ox. You will be soaked in heaven's dew. This will go on for seven seasons, and you will learn that the High God rules over human kingdoms and that he arranges all kingdom affairs.

"The part about the tree stump and roots being left means that your kingdom will still be there for you after you learn that it is heaven that runs things.

"So, king, take my advice: Make a clean break with your sins and start living for others. Quit your wicked life and look after the needs of the down-and-out. Then *you* will continue to have a good life."

The Loss and Regaining of a Mind and a Kingdom

All this happened to King Nebuchadnezzar. Just twelve months later, he was walking on the balcony of the royal palace in Babylon and boasted, "Look at this, Babylon the great! And I built it all by myself, a royal palace adequate to display my honor and glory!"

The words were no sooner out of his mouth than a voice out of heaven spoke, "This is the verdict on you, King Nebuchadnezzar: Your kingdom is taken from you. You will be driven out of human company

416

and live with the wild animals. You will eat grass like an ox. The sentence is for seven seasons, enough time to learn that the High God rules human kingdoms and puts whomever he wishes in charge."

It happened at once. Nebuchadnezzar was driven out of human company, ate grass like an ox, and was soaked in heaven's dew. His hair grew like the feathers of an eagle and his nails like the claws of a hawk.

⊹

"At the end of the seven years, I, Nebuchadnezzar, looked to heaven. I was given my mind back and I blessed the High God, thanking and glorifying God, who lives forever.

"His sovereign rule lasts and lasts,
    his kingdom never declines and falls.
Life on this earth doesn't add up to much,
    but God's heavenly army keeps everything going.
No one can interrupt his work,
    no one can call his rule into question.

"At the same time that I was given back my mind, I was also given back my majesty and splendor, making my kingdom shine. All the leaders and important people came looking for me. I was reestablished as king in my kingdom and became greater than ever. And that's why I'm singing—I, Nebuchadnezzar—singing and praising the King of Heaven:

"Everything he does is right,
    and he does it the right way.
He knows how to turn a proud person
    into a humble man or woman."

5

The Writing of a Disembodied Hand

King Belshazzar held a great feast for his one thousand nobles. The wine flowed freely. Belshazzar, heady with the wine, ordered that the gold and silver chalices his father Nebuchadnezzar had stolen from God's Temple of Jerusalem be brought in so that he and his nobles, his wives and concubines, could drink from them. When the gold and silver chalices were brought in, the king and his nobles, his wives and his concubines, drank wine from them. They drank the wine and drunkenly praised their gods made of gold and silver, bronze and iron, wood and stone.

At that very moment, the fingers of a human hand appeared and began writing on the lamp-illumined, whitewashed wall of the palace. When the king saw the disembodied hand writing away, he went white as a ghost, scared out of his wits. His legs went limp and his knees knocked. He yelled out for the enchanters, the fortunetellers, and the diviners to come. He told these Babylonian magi, "Anyone who can read this writing on the wall and tell me what it means will be famous and rich—purple robe, the great gold chain—and be third in command in the kingdom."

One after the other they tried, but could make no sense of it. They could neither read what was written nor interpret it to the king. So now the king was really frightened. All the blood drained from his face. The nobles were in a panic.

The queen heard of the hysteria among the king and his nobles and came to the banquet hall. She said, "Long live the king! Don't be upset. Don't sit around looking like ghosts. There is a man in your kingdom who is full of the divine Holy Spirit. During your father's time he was well known for his intellectual brilliance and spiritual wisdom. He was so good that your father, King Nebuchadnezzar, made him the head of all the magicians, enchanters, fortunetellers, and diviners. There was no one quite like him. He could do anything—interpret dreams, solve mysteries, explain puzzles. His name is Daniel, but he was renamed Belteshazzar by the king. Have Daniel called in. He'll tell you what is going on here."

So Daniel was called in. The king asked him, "Are you the Daniel who was one of the Jewish exiles my father brought here from Judah? I've heard about you—that you're full of the Holy Spirit, that you've got a brilliant mind, that you are incredibly wise. The wise men and enchanters were brought in here to read this writing on the wall and interpret it for me. They couldn't figure it out—not a word, not a syllable. But I've heard that you interpret dreams and solve mysteries. So—if you can read the writing and interpret it for me, you'll be rich and famous—a purple robe, the great gold chain around your neck—and third-in-command in the kingdom."

Daniel answered the king, "You can keep your gifts, or give them to someone else. But I will read the writing for the king and tell him what it means.

"Listen, oh king! The High God gave your father Nebuchadnezzar a great kingdom and a glorious reputation. Because God made him so famous, people from everywhere, whatever their race, color, and creed, were totally intimidated by him. He killed or spared people on whim. He promoted or humiliated people capriciously. He developed a big head and a hard spirit. Then God knocked him off his high horse and stripped him of his fame. He was thrown out of human company, lost his mind, and lived like a wild animal. He ate grass like an ox and was soaked by heaven's dew until he learned his lesson: that the High God rules human kingdoms and puts anyone he wants in charge.

"You are his son and have known all this, yet you're as arrogant as he ever was. Look at you, setting yourself up in competition against the Master of heaven! You had the sacred chalices from his Temple brought into your drunken party so that you and your nobles, your wives and your concubines, could drink from them. You used the sacred chalices to toast your gods of silver and gold, bronze and iron, wood and stone—blind, deaf, and imbecile gods. But you treat with contempt the living God who holds your entire life from birth to death in his hand.

"God sent the hand that wrote on the wall, and this is what is written: MENE, TEQEL, and PERES. This is what the words mean:

"*Mene*: God has numbered the days of your rule and they don't add up.

"*Teqel*: You have been weighed on the scales and you don't weigh much.

"*Peres*: Your kingdom has been divided up and handed over to the Medes and Persians."

✠

Belshazzar did what he had promised. He robed Daniel in purple, draped the great gold chain around his neck, and promoted him to third-in-charge in the kingdom.

That same night the Babylonian king Belshazzar was murdered. He was sixty-two years old. Darius the Mede succeeded him as king.

6

DANIEL IN THE LIONS' DEN

Darius reorganized his kingdom. He appointed one hundred twenty governors to administer all the parts of his realm. Over them were three vice-regents, one of whom was Daniel. The governors reported to the vice-regents, who made sure that everything was in order for the king. But Daniel, brimming with spirit and intelligence, so completely out-classed the other vice-regents and governors that the king decided to put him in charge of the whole kingdom.

The vice-regents and governors got together to find some old scandal or skeleton in Daniel's life that they could use against him, but they couldn't dig up anything. He was totally exemplary and trustworthy. They could find no evidence of negligence or misconduct. So they finally gave up and said, "We're never going to find anything against this Daniel unless we can cook up something religious."

The vice-regents and governors conspired together and then went to the king and said, "King Darius, live forever! We've convened your vice-regents, governors, and all your leading officials, and have agreed that the king should issue the following decree:

> For the next thirty days no one is to pray to any god or mortal except you, oh king. Anyone who disobeys will be thrown into the lions' den.

"Issue this decree, oh king, and make it unconditional, as if written in stone like all the laws of the Medes and the Persians."

King Darius signed the decree.

When Daniel learned that the decree had been signed and posted, he continued to pray just as he had always done. His house had windows in the upstairs that opened toward Jerusalem. Three times a day he knelt there in prayer, thanking and praising his God.

The conspirators came and found him praying, asking God for help. They went straight to the king and reminded him of the royal decree that he had signed. "Did you not," they said, "sign a decree forbidding anyone to pray to any god or man except you for the next thirty days? And anyone caught doing it would be thrown into the lions' den?"

"Absolutely," said the king. "Written in stone, like all the laws of the Medes and Persians."

Then they said, "Daniel, one of the Jewish exiles, ignores you, oh king, and defies your decree. Three times a day he prays."

At this, the king was very upset and tried his best to get Daniel out of the fix he'd put him in. He worked at it the whole day long.

But then the conspirators were back: "Remember, oh king, it's the law of the Medes and Persians that the king's decree can never be changed."

The king caved in and ordered Daniel brought and thrown into the lions' den. But he said to Daniel, "Your God, to whom you are so loyal, is going to get you out of this."

A stone slab was placed over the opening of the den. The king sealed the cover with his signet ring and the signet rings of all his nobles, fixing Daniel's fate.

The king then went back to his palace. He refused supper. He couldn't sleep. He spent the night fasting.

At daybreak the king got up and hurried to the lions' den. As he approached the den, he called out anxiously, "Daniel, servant of the living God, has your God, whom you serve so loyally, saved you from the lions?"

"Oh king, live forever!" said Daniel. "My God sent his angel, who closed the mouths of the lions so that they would not hurt me. I've been found innocent before God and also before you, oh king. I've done nothing to harm you."

When the king heard these words, he was happy. He ordered Daniel taken up out of the den. When he was hauled up, there wasn't a scratch on him. He had trusted his God.

Then the king commanded that the conspirators who had informed on Daniel be thrown into the lions' den, along with their wives and children. Before they hit the floor, the lions had them in their jaws, tearing them to pieces.

King Darius published this proclamation to every race, color, and creed on earth:

Peace to you! Abundant peace!
     I decree that Daniel's God shall be worshiped and feared
in all parts of my kingdom.
     He is the living God, world without end. His kingdom never
falls.
     His rule continues eternally.
     He is a savior and rescuer.
     He performs astonishing miracles in heaven and on earth.
     He saved Daniel from the power of the lions.

✛

From then on, Daniel was treated well during the reign of Darius, and also in the following reign of Cyrus the Persian.

7

A VISION OF FOUR ANIMALS

In the first year of the reign of King Belshazzar of Babylon, Daniel had a dream. What he saw as he slept in his bed terrified him—a real nightmare. Then he wrote out his dream:

"In my dream that night I saw the four winds of heaven whipping up a great storm on the sea. Four huge animals, each different from the others, ascended out of the sea.

"The first animal looked like a lion, but it had the wings of an eagle. While I watched, its wings were pulled off. It was then pulled erect so that it was standing on two feet like a man. Then a human heart was placed in it.

"Then I saw a second animal that looked like a bear. It lurched from side to side, holding three ribs in its jaws. It was told, 'Attack! Devour! Fill your belly!'

"Next I saw another animal. This one looked like a panther. It had four birdlike wings on its back. This animal had four heads and was made to rule.

"After that, a fourth animal appeared in my dream. This one was a grisly horror—hideous. It had huge iron teeth. It crunched and swallowed its victims. Anything left over, it trampled into the ground. It was different from the other animals—this one was a real monster. It had ten horns.

"As I was staring at the horns and trying to figure out what they meant, another horn sprouted up, a little horn. Three of the original horns were pulled out to make room for it. There were human eyes in this little horn, and a big mouth speaking arrogantly.

"As I was watching all this,

"Thrones were set in place
    and The Old One sat down.
His robes were white as snow,
    his hair was white like wool.
His throne was flaming with fire,
    its wheels blazing.
A river of fire
    poured out of the throne.
Thousands upon thousands served him,

tens of thousands attended him.
The courtroom was called to order,
    and the books were opened.

"I kept watching. The little horn was speaking arrogantly. Then, as
I watched, the monster was killed and its body cremated in a roaring
fire. The other animals lived on for a limited time, but they didn't really
do anything, had no power to rule. My dream continued.

"I saw a human form, a son of man,
    arriving in a whirl of clouds.
He came to The Old One
    and was presented to him.
He was given power to rule—all the glory of royalty.
    Everyone—race, color, and creed—had to serve him.
His rule would be forever, never ending.
    His kingly rule would never be replaced.

"But as for me, Daniel, I was disturbed. All these dream-visions had
me agitated. So I went up to one of those standing by and asked him
the meaning of all this. And he told me, interpreting the dream for me:
"'These four huge animals,' he said, 'mean that four kingdoms will
appear on earth. But eventually the holy people of the High God will
be given the kingdom and have it ever after—yes, forever and ever.'
"But I wanted to know more. I was curious about the fourth animal,
the one so different from the others, the hideous monster with the iron
teeth and the bronze claws, gulping down what it ripped to pieces and
trampling the leftovers into the dirt. And I wanted to know about the ten
horns on its head and the other horn that sprouted up while three of the
original horns were removed. This new horn had eyes and a big mouth
and spoke arrogantly, dominating the other horns. I watched as this horn
was making war on God's holy people and getting the best of them. But
then The Old One intervened and decided things in favor of the people
of the High God. In the end, God's holy people took over the kingdom.
"The bystander continued, telling me this: 'The fourth animal is a
fourth kingdom that will appear on earth. It will be different from the
first three kingdoms, a monster kingdom that will chew up everyone in
sight and spit them out. The ten horns are ten kings, one after another,
that will come from this kingdom. But then another king will arrive. He
will be different from the earlier kings. He will begin by toppling three

kings. Then he will blaspheme the High God, persecute the followers of the High God, and try to get rid of sacred worship and moral practice. God's holy people will be persecuted by him for a time, two times, half a time.

"'But when the court comes to order, the horn will be stripped of its power and totally destroyed. Then the royal rule and the authority and the glory of all the kingdoms under heaven will be handed over to the people of the High God. Their royal rule will last forever. All other rulers will serve and obey them.'

"And there it ended. I, Daniel, was in shock. I was like a man who had seen a ghost. But I kept it all to myself.

8

A Vision of a Ram and a Billy Goat

"In King Belshazzar's third year as king, another vision came to me, Daniel. This was now the second vision.

"In the vision, I saw myself in Susa, the capital city of the province Elam, standing at the Ulai Canal. Looking around, I was surprised to see a ram also standing at the gate. The ram had two huge horns, one bigger than the other, but the bigger horn was the last to appear. I watched as the ram charged: first west, then north, then south. No beast could stand up to him. He did just as he pleased, strutting as if he were king of the beasts.

"While I was watching this, wondering what it all meant, I saw a billy goat with an immense horn in the middle of its forehead come up out of the west and fly across the whole country, not once touching the ground. The billy goat approached the double-horned ram that I had earlier seen standing at the gate and, enraged, charged it viciously. I watched as, mad with rage, it charged the ram and hit it so hard that it broke off its two horns. The ram didn't stand a chance against it. The billy goat knocked the ram to the ground and stomped all over it. Nothing could have saved the ram from the goat.

"Then the billy goat swelled to an enormous size. At the height of its power its immense horn broke off and four other big horns sprouted in its place, pointing to the four points of the compass. And then from one of these big horns another horn sprouted. It started small, but then grew to an enormous size, facing south and east—toward lovely Palestine. The horn grew tall, reaching to the stars, the heavenly army, and threw some of the stars to the earth and stomped on them. It even dared to challenge the power of God, Prince of the Celestial Army! And then it threw out daily worship and desecrated the Sanctuary. As judgment against their sin, the holy people of God got the same treatment as the daily worship. The horn cast God's Truth aside. High-handed, it took over everything and everyone.

"Then I overheard two holy angels talking. One asked, 'How long is what we see here going to last—the abolishing of daily worship, this devastating judgment against sin, the kicking around of God's holy people and the Sanctuary?'

"The other answered, 'Over the course of 2,300 sacrifices, evening and morning. Then the Sanctuary will be set right again.'

✠

"While I, Daniel, was trying to make sense of what I was seeing, suddenly there was a humanlike figure standing before me.

"Then I heard a man's voice from over by the Ulai Canal calling out, 'Gabriel, tell this man what is going on. Explain the vision to him.' He came up to me, but when he got close I became terrified and fell facedown on the ground.

"He said, 'Understand that this vision has to do with the time of the end.' As soon as he spoke, I fainted, my face in the dirt. But he picked me up and put me on my feet.

"And then he continued, 'I want to tell you what is going to happen as the judgment days of wrath wind down, for there is going to be an end to all this.

"'The double-horned ram you saw stands for the two kings of the Medes and Persians. The billy goat stands for the kingdom of the Greeks. The huge horn on its forehead is the first Greek king. The four horns that sprouted after it was broken off are the four kings that come after him, but without his power.

"'As their kingdoms cool down
    and rebellions heat up,
A king will show up,
    hard-faced, a master trickster.
His power will swell enormously.
    He'll talk big, high-handedly,
Doing whatever he pleases,

knocking off heroes and holy ones left and right.
He'll plot and scheme to make crime flourish—
    and oh, how it will flourish!
He'll think he's invincible
    and get rid of anyone who gets in his way.
But when he takes on the Prince of all princes,
    he'll be smashed to bits—
    but not by human hands.
This vision of the 2,300 sacrifices, evening and morning,
    is accurate but confidential.
Keep it to yourself.
    It refers to the far future.'

✠

"I, Daniel, walked around in a daze, unwell for days. Then I got a grip on myself and went back to work taking care of the king's affairs. But I continued to be upset by the vision. I couldn't make sense of it.

9

GOD'S COVENANT COMMITMENT

"Darius, son of Ahasuerus, born a Mede, became king over the land of Babylon. In the first year of his reign, I, Daniel, was meditating on the Scriptures that gave, according to the Word of GOD to the prophet Jeremiah, the number of years that Jerusalem had to lie in ruins, namely, seventy. I turned to the Master God, asking for an answer—praying earnestly, fasting from meals, wearing rough penitential burlap, and kneeling in the ashes. I poured out my heart, baring my soul to GOD, my God:

"'Oh Master, great and august God. You never waver in your covenant commitment, never give up on those who love you and do what you say. Yet we have sinned in every way imaginable. We've done evil things, rebelled, dodged and taken detours around your clearly marked paths. We've turned a deaf ear to your servants the prophets, who preached your Word to our kings and leaders, our parents, and all the people in the land. You have done everything right, Master, but all we have to show for our lives is guilt and shame, the whole lot of us— people of Judah, citizens of Jerusalem, Israel at home and Israel in exile in all the places we've been banished to because of our betrayal of you. Oh yes, GOD, we've been exposed in our shame, all of us — our kings, leaders, parents — before the whole world. And deservedly so, because of our sin.

"'Compassion is our only hope, the compassion of you, the Master, our God, since in our rebellion we've forfeited our rights. We paid no attention to you when you told us how to live, the clear teaching that came through your servants the prophets. All of us in Israel ignored what you said. We defied your instructions and did what we pleased. And now we're paying for it: The solemn curse written out plainly in the revelation to God's servant Moses is now doing its work among us, the wages of our sin against you. You did to us and our rulers what you said you would do: You brought this catastrophic disaster on us, the worst disaster on record — and in Jerusalem!

"'Just as written in God's revelation to Moses, the catastrophe was total. Nothing was held back. We kept at our sinning, never giving you a second thought, oblivious to your clear warning, and so you had no choice but to let the disaster loose on us in full force. You, our GOD, had a perfect right to do this since we persistently and defiantly ignored you.

"'Master, you are our God, for you delivered your people from the land of Egypt in a show of power — people are still talking about it! We confess that we have sinned, that we have lived bad lives. Following the lines of what you have always done in setting things right, setting *people* right, please stop being so angry with Jerusalem, your very own city, your holy mountain. We know it's our fault that this has happened, all because of our sins and our parents' sins, and now we're an embarrassment to everyone around us. We're a blot on the neighborhood. So listen, God, to this determined prayer of your servant. Have mercy on your ruined Sanctuary. Act out of who you are, not out of what we are.

"'Turn your ears our way, God, and listen. Open your eyes and take a long look at our ruined city, this city named after you. We know that we don't deserve a hearing from you. Our appeal is to your compassion. This prayer is our last and only hope:

"'Master, listen to us!
Master, forgive us!
Master, look at us and do something!
Master, don't put us off!
Your city and your people are named after you:
You have a stake in us!'

427

SEVENTY SEVENS

"While I was pouring out my heart, baring my sins and the sins of my people Israel, praying my life out before my GOD, interceding for the holy mountain of my God—while I was absorbed in this praying, the humanlike Gabriel, the one I had seen in an earlier vision, approached me, flying in like a bird about the time of evening worship.

"He stood before me and said, 'Daniel, I have come to make things plain to you. You had no sooner started your prayer when the answer was given. And now I'm here to deliver the answer to you. You are much loved! So listen carefully to the answer, the plain meaning of what is revealed:

"'Seventy sevens are set for your people and for your holy city to throttle rebellion, stop sin, wipe out crime, set things right forever, confirm what the prophet saw, and anoint The Holy of Holies.

"'Here is what you must understand: From the time the word goes out to rebuild Jerusalem until the coming of the Anointed Leader, there will be seven sevens. The rebuilding will take sixty-two sevens, including building streets and digging a moat. Those will be rough times. After the sixty-two sevens, the Anointed Leader will be killed—the end of him. The city and Sanctuary will be laid in ruins by the army of the newly arriving leader. The end will come in a rush, like a flood. War will rage right up to the end, desolation the order of the day.

"'Then for one seven, he will forge many and strong alliances, but halfway through the seven he will banish worship and prayers. At the place of worship, a desecrating obscenity will be set up and remain until finally the desecrator himself is decisively destroyed.'"

10

A VISION OF A BIG WAR

In the third year of the reign of King Cyrus of Persia, a message was made plain to Daniel, whose Babylonian name was Belteshazzar. The message was true. It dealt with a big war. He understood the message, the understanding coming by revelation:

"During those days, I, Daniel, went into mourning over Jerusalem for three weeks. I ate only plain and simple food, no seasoning or meat or wine. I neither bathed nor shaved until the three weeks were up.

"On the twenty-fourth day of the first month I was standing on the bank of the great river, the Tigris. I looked up and to my surprise saw a man dressed in linen with a belt of pure gold around his waist. His body was hard and glistening, as if sculpted from a precious stone, his face radiant, his eyes bright and penetrating like torches, his arms and feet glistening like polished bronze, and his voice, deep and resonant, sounded like a huge choir of voices.

"I, Daniel, was the only one to see this. The men who were with me, although they didn't see it, were overcome with fear and ran off and hid, fearing the worst. Left alone after the appearance, abandoned by my friends, I went weak in the knees, the blood drained from my face.

"I heard his voice. At the sound of it I fainted, fell flat on the ground, face in the dirt. A hand touched me and pulled me to my hands and knees.

"'Daniel,' he said, 'man of quality, listen carefully to my message. And get up on your feet. Stand at attention. I've been sent to bring you news.'

"When he had said this, I stood up, but I was still shaking.

"'Relax, Daniel,' he continued, 'don't be afraid. From the moment you decided to humble yourself to receive understanding, your prayer was heard, and I set out to come to you. But I was waylaid by the angel-prince of the kingdom of Persia and was delayed for a good three weeks. But then Michael, one of the chief angel-princes, intervened to help me. I left him there with the prince of the kingdom of Persia. And now I'm here to help you understand what will eventually happen to your people. The vision has to do with what's ahead.'

"While he was saying all this, I looked at the ground and said nothing. Then I was surprised by something like a human hand that touched my lips. I opened my mouth and started talking to the messenger: 'When I saw you, master, I was terror-stricken. My knees turned to water. I couldn't move. How can I, a lowly servant, speak to you, my master? I'm paralyzed. I can hardly breathe!'

"Then this humanlike figure touched me again and gave me strength. He said, 'Don't be afraid, friend. Peace. Everything is going to be all right. Take courage. Be strong.'

"Even as he spoke, courage surged up within me. I said, 'Go ahead, let my master speak. You've given me courage.'

"He said, 'Do you know why I've come here to you? I now have to go back to fight against the angel-prince of Persia, and when I get him out of the way, the angel-prince of Greece will arrive. But first let me tell you what's written in The True Book. No one helps me in my fight against these beings except Michael, your angel-prince.

☩

11

"'And I, in my turn, have been helping him out as best I can ever since the first year in the reign of Darius the Mede.'

The Kings of the South and the North

"'But now let me tell you the truth of how things stand: Three more kings of Persia will show up, and then a fourth will become richer than all of them. When he senses that he is powerful enough as a result of his wealth, he will go to war against the entire kingdom of Greece.

"'Then a powerful king will show up and take over a huge territory and run things just as he pleases. But at the height of his power, with everything seemingly under control, his kingdom will split into four parts, like the four points of the compass. But his heirs won't get in on it. There will be no continuity with his kingship. Others will tear it to pieces and grab whatever they can get for themselves.

"'Next the king of the south will grow strong, but one of his princes will grow stronger than he and rule an even larger territory. After a few years, the two of them will make a pact, and the daughter of the king of the south will marry the king of the north to cement the peace agreement. But her influence will weaken and her child will not survive. She and her servants, her child, and her husband will be betrayed.

"'Sometime later a member of the royal family will show up and take over. He will take command of his army and invade the defenses of the king of the north and win a resounding victory. He will load up their tin gods and all the gold and silver trinkets that go with them and cart them off to Egypt. Eventually, the king of the north will recover and invade the country of the king of the south, but unsuccessfully. He will have to retreat.

"'But then his sons will raise a huge army and rush down like a flood, a torrential attack, on the defenses of the south.

"'Furious, the king of the south will come out and engage the king of the north and his huge army in battle and rout them. As the corpses are cleared from the field, the king, inflamed with bloodlust, will go on a bloodletting rampage, massacring tens of thousands. But his victory won't last long, for the king of the north will put together another army bigger than the last one, and after a few years he'll come back to do battle again with his immense army and endless supplies.

"'In those times, many others will get into the act and go off to fight against the king of the south. Hotheads from your own people, drunk on dreams, will join them. But they'll sputter out.

"'When the king of the north arrives, he'll build siege works and capture the outpost fortress city. The armies of the south will fall to pieces before him. Not even their famous commando shock troops will slow down the attacker. He'll march in big as you please, as if he owned the place. He'll take over that beautiful country, Palestine, and make himself at home in it. Then he'll proceed to get everything, lock, stock, and barrel, in his control. He'll cook up a peace treaty and even give his daughter in marriage to the king of the south in a plot to destroy him totally. But the plot will fizzle. It won't succeed.

"'Later, he'll turn his attention to the coastal regions and capture a bunch of prisoners, but a general will step in and put a stop to his bullying ways. The bully will be bullied! He'll go back home and tend to his own military affairs. But by then he'll be washed up and soon will be heard of no more.

"He will be replaced shortly by a real loser, his rule, reputation, and authority already in shreds. And he won't last long. He'll slip out of history quietly, without even a fight.

"'His place will be taken by a reject, a man spurned and passed over for advancement. He'll surprise everyone, seemingly coming out of nowhere, and will seize the kingdom. He'll come in like a steamroller, flattening the opposition. Even the Prince of the Covenant will be crushed. After negotiating a cease-fire, he'll betray its terms. With a few henchmen, he'll take total control. Arbitrarily and impulsively, he'll invade the richest provinces. He'll surpass all his ancestors, near and distant, in his rape of the country, grabbing and looting, living with his cronies in corrupt and lavish luxury.

"'He will make plans against the fortress cities, but they'll turn out to be shortsighted. He'll get a great army together, all charged up to fight the king of the south. The king of the south in response will get his army—an even greater army—in place, ready to fight. But he won't be able to sustain that intensity for long because of the treacherous intrigue in his own ranks, his court having been honeycombed with vicious plots. His army will be smashed, the battlefield filled with corpses.

"'The two kings, each with evil designs on the other, will sit at the conference table and trade lies. Nothing will come of the treaty, which is nothing but a tissue of lies anyway. But that's not the end of it. There's more to this story.

"'The king of the north will go home loaded down with plunder, but his mind will be set on destroying the holy covenant as he passes through the country on his way home.

"'One year later he will mount a fresh invasion of the south. But the second invasion won't compare to the first. When the Roman ships arrive, he will turn tail and go back home. But as he passes through the country, he will be filled with anger at the holy covenant. He will take up with all those who betray the holy covenant, favoring them. The bodyguards surrounding him will march in and desecrate the Sanctuary and citadel. They'll throw out the daily worship and set up in its place the obscene sacrilege. The king of the north will play up to those who betray the holy covenant, corrupting them even further with his seductive talk, but those who stay courageously loyal to their God will take a strong stand.

"'Those who keep their heads on straight will teach the crowds right from wrong by their example. They'll be put to severe testing for a season: some killed, some burned, some exiled, some robbed. When the testing is intense, they'll get some help, but not much. Many of the helpers will be halfhearted at best. The testing will refine, cleanse, and purify those who keep their heads on straight and stay true, for there is still more to come.

"'Meanwhile, the king of the north will do whatever he pleases. He'll puff himself up and posture himself as greater than any god. He will even dare to brag and boast in defiance of the God of gods. And he'll get by with it for a while—until this time of wrathful judgment is completed, for what is decreed must be done. He will have no respect for the gods of his ancestors, not even that popular favorite among women, Adonis. Contemptuous of every god and goddess, the king of the north will puff himself up greater than all of them. He'll even stoop to despising the God of the holy ones, and in the place where God is worshiped he will put on exhibit, with a lavish show of silver and gold and jewels, a new god that no one has ever heard of. Marching under the banner of a strange god, he will attack the key fortresses. He will promote everyone who falls into line behind this god, putting them in positions of power and paying them off with grants of land.

"'In the final wrap-up of this story, the king of the south will confront him. But the king of the north will come at him like a tornado. Unleashing chariots and horses and an armada of ships, he'll blow away anything in his path. As he enters the beautiful land, people will fall before him like dominoes. Only Edom, Moab, and a few Ammonites will escape. As he reaches out, grabbing country after country, not even Egypt will be exempt. He will confiscate the treasuries of Egyptian gold and silver and other valuables. The Libyans and Ethiopians will fall in with him. Then disturbing reports will come in from the north and east that will throw him into a panic. Towering in rage, he'll rush to stamp out the threat. But he'll no sooner have pitched camp between the Mediterranean Sea and the Holy Mountain—all those royal tents!—than he'll meet his end. And not a soul around who can help!

12

THE WORST TROUBLE THE WORLD HAS EVER SEEN

"'That's when Michael, the great angel-prince, champion of your people, will step in. It will be a time of trouble, the worst trouble the world has ever seen. But your people will be saved from the trouble, every last one found written in the Book. Many who have been long dead and buried will wake up, some to eternal life, others to eternal shame.

"'Men and women who have lived wisely and well will shine brilliantly, like the cloudless, star-strewn night skies. And those who put others on the right path to life will glow like stars forever.

"'This is a confidential report, Daniel, for your eyes and ears only. Keep it secret. Put the book under lock and key until the end. In the interim there is going to be a lot of frantic running around, trying to figure out what's going on.'

✝

"As I, Daniel, took all this in, two figures appeared, one standing on this bank of the river and one on the other bank. One of them asked a third man who was dressed in linen and who straddled the river, 'How long is this astonishing story to go on?'

"The man dressed in linen, who straddled the river, raised both hands to the skies. I heard him solemnly swear by the Eternal One that it would be a time, two times, and half a time, that when the oppressor of the holy people was brought down the story would be complete.

"I heard all this plainly enough, but I didn't understand it. So I asked, 'Master, can you explain this to me?'

"'Go on about your business, Daniel,' he said. 'The message is confidential and under lock and key until the end, until things are about to be wrapped up. The populace will be washed clean and made like new. But the wicked will just keep on being wicked, without a clue about what is happening. Those who live wisely and well will understand what's going on.'

✝

"From the time that the daily worship is banished from the Temple and the obscene desecration is set up in its place, there will be 1,290 days.

"Blessed are those who patiently make it through the 1,335 days.

"And you? Go about your business without fretting or worrying. Relax. When it's all over, you will be on your feet to receive your reward."

HOSEA

W e live in a world awash in love stories. Most of them are lies. They are not love stories at all—they are lust stories, sex-fantasy stories, domination stories. From the cradle we are fed on lies about love.

This would be bad enough if it only messed up human relationships—man and woman, parent and child, friend and friend—but it also messes up God-relationships. The huge, mountainous reality of all existence is that God is love, that God loves the world. Each single detail of the real world that we face and deal with day after day is permeated by this love.

But when our minds and imaginations are crippled with lies about love, we have a hard time understanding this fundamental ingredient of daily living, "love," either as a noun or as a verb. And if the basic orienting phrase "God is love" is plastered over with cultural graffiti that obscure and deface the truth of the way the world is, we are not going to get very far in living well. We require true stories of love if we are to live truly.

Hosea is the prophet of love, but not love as we imagine or fantasize it. He was a parable of God's love for his people lived out as God revealed and enacted it—a lived parable. It is an astonishing story: a prophet commanded to marry a common whore and have children with her. It is an even more astonishing message: God loves us in just this way—goes after us at our worst, keeps after us until he gets us, and makes lovers of men and women who know nothing of real love. Once we absorb this story and the words that flow from it, we will know God far more accurately. And we will be well on our way to being cured of all the sentimentalized and neurotic distortions of love that incapacitate us from dealing with the God who loves us and loving the neighbors who don't love us.

HOSEA

1

This is GOD's Message to Hosea son of Beeri. It came to him during the royal reigns of Judah's kings Uzziah, Jotham, Ahaz, and Hezekiah. This was also the time that Jeroboam son of Joash was king over Israel.

THIS WHOLE COUNTRY HAS BECOME A WHOREHOUSE

The first time GOD spoke to Hosea he said:

"Find a whore and marry her.
    Make this whore the mother of your children.
And here's why: This whole country
    has become a whorehouse, unfaithful to me, GOD."

Hosea did it. He picked Gomer daughter of Diblaim. She got pregnant and gave him a son.
    Then GOD told him:

"Name him Jezreel. It won't be long now before
    I'll make the people of Israel pay for the massacre at Jezreel.
    I'm calling it quits on the kingdom of Israel.
Payday is coming! I'm going to chop Israel's bows and arrows
    into kindling in the valley of Jezreel."

✠

Gomer got pregnant again. This time she had a daughter. GOD told Hosea:

"Name this one No-Mercy. I'm fed up with Israel.
    I've run out of mercy. There's no more forgiveness.
Judah's another story. I'll continue having mercy on them.
    I'll save them. It will be their GOD who saves them,
Not their armaments and armies,
    not their horsepower and manpower."

✠

After Gomer had weaned No-Mercy, she got pregnant yet again and had a son. GOD said:

"Name him Nobody. You've become nobodies to me,
    and I, God, am a nobody to you.

"But down the road the population of Israel is going to explode past
counting, like sand on the ocean beaches. In the very place where they were
once named Nobody, they will be named God's Somebody. Everybody in
Judah and everybody in Israel will be assembled as one people. They'll
choose a single leader. There'll be no stopping them—a great day in Jezreel!

⫟

2

"Rename your brothers 'God's Somebody.'
    Rename your sisters 'All Mercy.'

WILD WEEKENDS AND UNHOLY HOLIDAYS

"Haul your mother into court. Accuse her!
    She's no longer my wife.
    I'm no longer her husband.
Tell her to quit dressing like a whore,
    displaying her breasts for sale.
If she refuses, I'll rip off her clothes
    and expose her, naked as a newborn.
I'll turn her skin into dried-out leather,
    her body into a badlands landscape,
    a rack of bones in the desert.
I'll have nothing to do with her children,
    born one and all in a whorehouse.
Face it: Your mother's been a whore,
    bringing bastard children into the world.
She said, 'I'm off to see my lovers!
    They'll wine and dine me,
Dress and caress me,
    perfume and adorn me!'
But I'll fix her: I'll dump her in a field of thistles,
    then lose her in a dead-end alley.
She'll go on the hunt for her lovers
    but not bring down a single one.
She'll look high and low

but won't find a one. Then she'll say,
'I'm going back to my husband, the one I started out with.
    That was a better life by far than this one.'
She didn't know that it was I all along
    who wined and dined and adorned her,
That I was the one who dressed her up
    in the big-city fashions and jewelry
    that she wasted on wild Baal-orgies.
I'm about to bring her up short: No more wining and dining!
    Silk lingerie and gowns are a thing of the past.
I'll expose her genitals to the public.
    All her fly-by-night lovers will be helpless to help her.
Party time is over. I'm calling a halt to the whole business,
    her wild weekends and unholy holidays.
I'll wreck her sumptuous gardens and ornamental fountains,
    of which she bragged, 'Whoring paid for all this!'
They will soon be dumping grounds for garbage,
    feeding grounds for stray dogs and cats.
I'll make her pay for her indulgence in promiscuous religion—
    all that sensuous Baal worship
And all the promiscuous sex that went with it,
    stalking her lovers, dressed to kill,
And not a thought for me."
    GOD's Message!

TO START ALL OVER AGAIN

"And now, here's what I'm going to do:
    I'm going to start all over again.
I'm taking her back out into the wilderness
    where we had our first date, and I'll court her.
I'll give her bouquets of roses.
    I'll turn Heartbreak Valley into Acres of Hope.
She'll respond like she did as a young girl,
    those days when she was fresh out of Egypt.

☩

"At that time"—this is GOD's Message still—
    "you'll address me, 'Dear husband!'

439

Never again will you address me,
    'My slave-master!'
I'll wash your mouth out with soap,
    get rid of all the dirty false-god names,
    not so much as a whisper of those names again.
At the same time I'll make a peace treaty between you
    and wild animals and birds and reptiles,
And get rid of all weapons of war.
    Think of it! Safe from beasts and bullies!
And then I'll marry you for good—forever!
    I'll marry you true and proper, in love and tenderness.
Yes, I'll marry you and neither leave you nor let you go.
    You'll know me, GOD, for who I really am.

✠

"On the very same day, I'll answer"—this is GOD's Message—
    "I'll answer the sky, sky will answer earth,
Earth will answer grain and wine and olive oil,
    and they'll all answer Jezreel.
I'll plant her in the good earth.
    I'll have mercy on No-Mercy.
I'll say to Nobody, 'You're my dear Somebody,'
    and he'll say 'You're my God!'"

3

IN TIME THEY'LL COME BACK

Then GOD ordered me, "Start all over: Love your wife again,
    your wife who's in bed with her latest boyfriend, your
        cheating wife.
Love her the way I, GOD, love the Israelite people,
    even as they flirt and party with every god that takes their fancy."

I did it. I paid good money to get her back.
    It cost me the price of a slave.
Then I told her, "From now on you're living with me.
    No more whoring, no more sleeping around.
    You're living with me and I'm living with you."

✠

The people of Israel are going to live a long time
    stripped of security and protection,
without religion and comfort,
    godless and prayerless.
But in time they'll come back, these Israelites,
    come back looking for their GOD and their David-King.
They'll come back chastened to reverence
        before GOD and his good gifts, ready for the End of the story of
            his love.

4

NO ONE IS FAITHFUL

Attention all Israelites! GOD's Message!
    GOD indicts the whole population:
"No one is faithful. No one loves.
    No one knows the first thing about God.
All this cussing and lying and killing, theft and loose sex,
    sheer anarchy, one murder after another!
And because of all this, the very land itself weeps
    and everything in it is grief-stricken—
animals in the fields and birds on the wing,
    even the fish in the sea are listless, lifeless.

✠

"But don't look for someone to blame.
    No finger pointing!
You, priest, are the one in the dock.
    You stumble around in broad daylight,
And then the prophets take over and stumble all night.
    Your mother is as bad as you.
My people are ruined
    because they don't know what's right or true.
Because you've turned your back on knowledge,
    I've turned my back on you priests.
Because you refuse to recognize the revelation of God,

I'm no longer recognizing your children.
The more priests, the more sin.
    They traded in their glory for shame.
They pig out on my people's sins.
    They can't wait for the latest in evil.
The result: You can't tell the people from the priests,
    the priests from the people.
I'm on my way to make them both pay
    and take the consequences of the bad lives they've lived.
They'll eat and be as hungry as ever,
    have sex and get no satisfaction.
They walked out on me, their GOD,
    for a life of rutting with whores.

THEY MAKE A PICNIC OUT OF RELIGION

"Wine and whiskey
    leave my people in a stupor.
They ask questions of a dead tree,
    expect answers from a sturdy walking stick.
Drunk on sex, they can't find their way home.
    They've replaced their God with their genitals.
They worship on the tops of mountains,
    make a picnic out of religion.
Under the oaks and elms on the hills
    they stretch out and take it easy.
Before you know it, your daughters are whores
    and the wives of your sons are sleeping around.
But I'm not going after your whoring daughters
    or the adulterous wives of your sons.
It's the men who pick up the whores that I'm after,
    the men who worship at the holy whorehouses—
    a stupid people, ruined by whores!

✠

"You've ruined your own life, Israel—
    but don't drag Judah down with you!
Don't go to the sex shrine at Gilgal,
    don't go to that sin city Bethel,

442

Don't go around saying 'GOD bless you' and not mean it,
    taking God's name in vain.
Israel is stubborn as a mule.
    How can GOD lead him like a lamb to open pasture?
Ephraim is addicted to idols.
    Let him go.
When the beer runs out,
    it's sex, sex, and more sex.
Bold and sordid debauchery—
    how they love it!
The whirlwind has them in its clutches.
    Their sex-worship leaves them finally impotent.

5

THEY WOULDN'T RECOGNIZE GOD IF THEY SAW HIM

"Listen to this, priests!
    Attention, people of Israel!
Royal family—all ears!
    You're in charge of justice around here.
But what have you done? Exploited people at Mizpah,
    ripped them off on Tabor,
Victimized them at Shittim.
    I'm going to punish the lot of you.

"I know you, Ephraim, inside and out.
    Yes, Israel, I see right through you!
Ephraim, you've played your sex-and-religion games long enough.
    All Israel is thoroughly polluted.
They couldn't turn to God if they wanted to.
    Their evil life is a bad habit.
Every breath they take is a whore's breath.
    They wouldn't recognize GOD if they saw me.

"Bloated by arrogance, big as a house,
    they're a public disgrace,
The lot of them—Israel, Ephraim, Judah—
    lurching and weaving down their guilty streets.
When they decide to get their lives together

443

and go off looking for GOD once again,
They'll find it's too late.
    I, GOD, will be long gone.
They've played fast and loose with me for too long,
    filling the country with their bastard offspring.
A plague of locusts will
    devastate their violated land.

"Blow the ram's-horn shofar in Gibeah,
    the bugle in Ramah!
Signal the invasion of Sin City!
    Scare the daylights out of Benjamin!
Ephraim will be left wasted,
    a lifeless moonscape.
I'm telling it straight, the unvarnished truth,
    to the tribes of Israel.

"Israel's rulers are crooks and thieves,
    cheating the people of their land,
And I'm angry, good and angry.
    Every inch of their bodies is going to feel my anger.

"Brutal Ephraim is himself brutalized—
    a taste of his own medicine!
He was so determined
    to do it his own worthless way.
Therefore I'm pus to Ephraim,
    dry rot in the house of Judah.

"When Ephraim saw he was sick
    and Judah saw his pus-filled sores,
Ephraim went running to Assyria,
    went for help to the big king.
But he can't heal you.
    He can't cure your oozing sores.

"I'm a grizzly charging Ephraim,
    a grizzly with cubs charging Judah.
I'll rip them to pieces—yes, I will!
    No one can stop me now.

I'll drag them off.
No one can help them.
Then I'll go back to where I came from
until they come to their senses.
When they finally hit rock bottom,
maybe they'll come looking for me."

6

GANGS OF PRIESTS ASSAULTING WORSHIPERS

"Come on, let's go back to GOD.
He hurt us, but he'll heal us.
He hit us hard,
but he'll put us right again.
In a couple of days we'll feel better.
By the third day he'll have made us brand-new,
Alive and on our feet,
fit to face him.
We're ready to study GOD,
eager for God-knowledge.
As sure as dawn breaks,
so sure is his daily arrival.
He comes as rain comes,
as spring rain refreshing the ground."

✛

"What am I to do with you, Ephraim?
What do I make of you, Judah?
Your declarations of love last no longer
than morning mist and predawn dew.
That's why I use prophets to shake you to attention,
why my words cut you to the quick:
To wake you up to my judgment
blazing like light.
I'm after love that lasts, not more religion.
I want you to know GOD, not go to more prayer meetings.
You broke the covenant—just like Adam!
You broke faith with me—ungrateful wretches!

445

"Gilead has become Crime City—
      blood on the sidewalks, blood on the streets.
It used to be robbers who mugged pedestrians.
      Now it's gangs of priests
Assaulting worshipers on their way to Shechem.
      Nothing is sacred to them.

"I saw a shocking thing in the country of Israel:
      Ephraim worshiping in a religious whorehouse,
      and Israel in the mud right there with him.

"You're as bad as the worst of them, Judah.
      You've been sowing wild oats. Now it's harvest time.

7

DESPITE ALL THE SIGNS, ISRAEL IGNORES GOD

"Every time I gave Israel a fresh start,
      wiped the slate clean and got them going again,
Ephraim soon filled the slate with new sins,
      the treachery of Samaria written out in bold print.
Two-faced and double-tongued,
      they steal you blind, pick you clean.
It never crosses their mind
      that I keep account of their every crime.
They're mud-spattered head to toe with the residue of sin.
      I see who they are and what they've done.

"They entertain the king with their evil circus,
      delight the princes with their acrobatic lies.
They're a bunch of overheated adulterers,
      like an oven that holds its heat
From the kneading of the dough
      to the rising of the bread.
On the royal holiday the princes get drunk
      on wine and the frenzy of the mocking mob.
They're like wood stoves,
      red-hot with lust.
Through the night their passion is banked;
      in the morning it blazes up, flames hungrily licking.

446

Murderous and volcanic,
    they incinerate their rulers.
Their kings fall one by one,
    and no one pays any attention to me.

"Ephraim mingles with the pagans, dissipating himself.
    Ephraim is half-baked.
Strangers suck him dry
    but he doesn't even notice.
His hair has turned gray—
    he doesn't notice.
Bloated by arrogance, big as a house,
    Israel's a public disgrace.
Israel lumbers along oblivious to GOD,
    despite all the signs, ignoring GOD.

"Ephraim is bird-brained,
    mindless, clueless,
First chirping after Egypt,
    then fluttering after Assyria.
I'll throw my net over them. I'll clip their wings.
    I'll teach them to mind me!
Doom! They've run away from home.
    Now they're *really* in trouble! They've *defied* me.
And I'm supposed to help them
    while they feed me a line of lies?
Instead of crying out to me in heartfelt prayer,
    they whoop it up in bed with their whores,
Gash themselves bloody in their sex-and-religion orgies,
    but turn their backs on me.
I'm the one who gave them good minds and healthy bodies,
    and how am I repaid? With evil scheming!
They turn, but not to me—
    turn here, then there, like a weather vane.
Their rulers will be cut down, murdered—
    just deserts for their mocking blasphemies.
And the final sentence?
    Ridicule in the court of world opinion.

8

ALTARS FOR SINNING

"Blow the trumpet! Sound the alarm!
    Vultures are circling over God's people,
Who have broken my covenant
    and defied my revelation.
Predictably, Israel cries out, 'My God! We know you!'
    But they don't act like it.
Israel will have nothing to do with what's good,
    and now the enemy is after them.

"They crown kings, but without asking me.
    They set up princes but don't let me in on it.
Instead, they make idols, using silver and gold,
    idols that will be their ruin.
Throw that gold calf-god on the trash heap, Samaria!
    I'm seething with anger against that rubbish!
How long before they shape up?
    And they're Israelites!
A sculptor made that thing—
    it's not God.
That Samaritan calf
    will be broken to bits.
Look at them! Planting wind-seeds,
    they'll harvest tornadoes.
Wheat with no head
    produces no flour.
And even if it did,
    strangers would gulp it down.
Israel is swallowed up and spit out.
    Among the pagans they're a piece of junk.
They trotted off to Assyria:
    Why, even wild donkeys stick to their own kind,
    but donkey-Ephraim goes out and *pays* to get lovers.
Now, because of their whoring life among the pagans,
    I'm going to gather them together and confront them.
They're going to reap the consequences soon,
    feel what it's like to be oppressed by the big king.

"Ephraim has built a lot of altars,
    and then uses them for sinning.
        Can you believe it? Altars for sinning!
I write out my revelation for them in detail
    and they pretend they can't read it.
They offer sacrifices to me
    and then they feast on the meat.
        GOD is not pleased!
I'm fed up—I'll keep remembering their guilt.
    I'll punish their sins
    and send them back to Egypt.
Israel has forgotten his Maker
    and gotten busy making palaces.
        Judah has gone in for a lot of fortress cities.
I'm sending fire on their cities
    to burn down their fortifications."

9

STARVED FOR GOD

Don't waste your life in wild orgies, Israel.
    Don't party away your life with the heathen.
You walk away from your God at the drop of a hat
    and like a whore sell yourself promiscuously
    at every sex-and-religion party on the street.
All that party food won't fill you up.
    You'll end up hungrier than ever.
At this rate you'll not last long in GOD's land:
    Some of you are going to end up bankrupt in Egypt.
    Some of you will be disillusioned in Assyria.
As refugees in Egypt and Assyria,
    you won't have much chance to worship GOD—
Sentenced to rations of bread and water,
    and your souls polluted by the spirit-dirty air.
You'll be starved for GOD,
    exiled from GOD's own country.
Will you be homesick for the old Holy Days?
    Will you miss festival worship of GOD?
Be warned! When you escape from the frying pan of disaster,

you'll fall into the fire of Egypt.
 Egypt will give you a fine funeral!
What use will all your god-inspired silver be then
 as you eke out a living in a field of weeds?

✠

Time's up. Doom's at the doorstep.
 It's payday!
Did Israel bluster, "The prophet is crazy!
 The 'man of the Spirit' is nuts!"?
Think again. Because of your great guilt,
 you're in big trouble.
The prophet is looking out for Ephraim,
 working under God's orders.
But everyone is trying to trip him up.
 He's hated right in God's house, of all places.
The people are going from bad to worse,
 rivaling that ancient and unspeakable crime at Gibeah.
God's keeping track of their guilt.
 He'll make them pay for their sins.

THEY TOOK TO SIN LIKE A PIG TO FILTH

"Long ago when I came upon Israel,
 it was like finding grapes out in the desert.
When I found your ancestors, it was like finding
 a fig tree bearing fruit for the first time.
But when they arrived at Baal-peor, that pagan shrine,
 they took to sin like a pig to filth,
  wallowing in the mud with their newfound friends.
Ephraim is fickle and scattered, like a flock of blackbirds,
 their beauty dissipated in confusion and clamor,
Frenetic and noisy, frigid and barren,
 and nothing to show for it—neither conception nor childbirth.
Even if they did give birth, I'd declare them
 unfit parents and take away their children!
Yes indeed—a black day for them
 when I turn my back and walk off!

I see Ephraim letting his children run wild.
  He might just as well take them and kill them outright!"

Give it to them, GOD! But what?
  Give them a dried-up womb and shriveled breasts.

"All their evil came out into the open
  at the pagan shrine at Gilgal. Oh, how I hated them there!
Because of their evil practices,
  I'll kick them off my land.
I'm wasting no more love on them.
  Their leaders are a bunch of rebellious adolescents.
Ephraim is hit hard—
  roots withered, no more fruit.
Even if by some miracle they had children,
  the dear babies wouldn't live—I'd make sure of that!"

My God has washed his hands of them.
  They wouldn't listen.
They're doomed to be wanderers,
  vagabonds among the godless nations.

10

YOU THOUGHT YOU COULD DO IT ALL ON YOUR OWN

Israel was once a lush vine,
  bountiful in grapes.
The more lavish the harvest,
  the more promiscuous the worship.
The more money they got,
  the more they squandered on gods-in-their-own-image.
Their sweet smiles are sheer lies.
  They're guilty as sin.
God will smash their worship shrines,
  pulverize their god-images.

They go around saying,
  "Who needs a king?
We couldn't care less about GOD,
  so why bother with a king!

What difference would he make?"
They talk big,
>lie through their teeth,
>make deals.
But their high-sounding words
>turn out to be empty words, litter in the gutters.

The people of Samaria travel over to Crime City
>to worship the golden calf-god.
They go all out, prancing and hollering,
>taken in by their showmen priests.
They act so important around the calf-god,
>but are oblivious to the sham, the shame.
They have plans to take it to Assyria,
>present it as a gift to the great king.
And so Ephraim makes a fool of himself,
>disgraces Israel with his stupid idols.

Samaria is history. Its king
>is a dead branch floating down the river.
Israel's favorite sin centers
>will all be torn down.
Thistles and crabgrass
>will decorate their ruined altars.
Then they'll say to the mountains, "Bury us!"
>and to the hills, "Fall on us!"

You got your start in sin at Gibeah—
>that ancient, unspeakable, shocking sin—
And you've been at it ever since.
>And Gibeah will mark the end of it
>in a war to end all the sinning.
I'll come to teach them a lesson.
>Nations will gang up on them,
Making them learn the hard way
>the sum of Gibeah plus Gibeah.

Ephraim was a trained heifer
>that loved to thresh.
Passing by and seeing her strong, sleek neck,

I wanted to harness Ephraim
And put him to work in the fields—
    Judah plowing, Jacob harrowing:
Sow righteousness,
    reap love.
It's time to till the ready earth,
    it's time to dig in with GOD,
Until he arrives
    with righteousness ripe for harvest.
But instead you plowed wicked ways,
    reaped a crop of evil and ate a salad of lies.
You thought you could do it all on your own,
    flush with weapons and manpower.
But the volcano of war will erupt among your people.
    All your defense posts will be leveled
As viciously as king Shalman
    leveled the town of Beth-arba,
When mothers and their babies
    were smashed on the rocks.
That's what's ahead for you, you so-called people of God,
    because of your off-the-charts evil.
Some morning you're going to wake up
    and find Israel, king and kingdom, a blank—nothing.

11

ISRAEL PLAYED AT RELIGION WITH TOY GODS

"When Israel was only a child, I loved him.
    I called out, 'My son!'—called him out of Egypt.
But when others called him,
    he ran off and left me.
He worshiped the popular sex gods,
    he played at religion with toy gods.
Still, I stuck with him. I led Ephraim.
    I rescued him from human bondage,
But he never acknowledged my help,
    never admitted that I was the one pulling his wagon,
That I lifted him, like a baby, to my cheek,
    that I bent down to feed him.

Now he wants to go *back* to Egypt or go over to Assyria—
    anything but return to me!
That's why his cities are unsafe—the murder rate skyrockets
    and every plan to improve things falls to pieces.
My people are hell-bent on leaving me.
    They pray to god Baal for help.
    He doesn't lift a finger to help them.
But how can I give up on you, Ephraim?
    How can I turn you loose, Israel?
How can I leave you to be ruined like Admah,
    devastated like luckless Zeboim?
I can't bear to even think such thoughts.
    My insides churn in protest.
And so I'm not going to act on my anger.
    I'm not going to destroy Ephraim.
And why? Because I am God and not a human.
    I'm The Holy One and I'm here—in your very midst.

"The people will end up following GOD.
    I will roar like a lion—
Oh, how I'll roar!
    My frightened children will come running from the west.
Like frightened birds they'll come from Egypt,
    from Assyria like scared doves.
I'll move them back into their homes."
    GOD's Word!

SOUL-DESTROYING LIES

Ephraim tells lies right and left.
    Not a word of Israel can be trusted.
Judah, meanwhile, is no better,
    addicted to cheap gods.

✛

12

Ephraim, obsessed with god-fantasies,
    chases ghosts and phantoms.
He tells lies nonstop,
    soul-destroying lies.

Both Ephraim and Judah made deals with Assyria
    and tried to get an inside track with Egypt.
GOD is bringing charges against Israel.
    Jacob's children are hauled into court to be punished.
In the womb, that heel, Jacob, got the best of his brother.
    When he grew up, he tried to get the best of GOD.
But GOD would not be bested.
    GOD bested him.
Brought to his knees,
    Jacob wept and prayed.
GOD found him at Bethel.
    That's where he spoke with him.
GOD is God-of-the-Angel-Armies,
    GOD-Revealed, GOD-Known.

☩

What are you waiting for? Return to your God!
    Commit yourself in love, in justice!
Wait for your God,
    and don't give up on him—ever!

The businessmen engage in wholesale fraud.
    They love to rip people off!
Ephraim boasted, "Look, I'm rich!
    I've made it big!
And look how well I've covered my tracks:
    not a hint of fraud, not a sign of sin!"

"But not so fast! I'm GOD, *your* God!
    Your God from the days in Egypt!
I'm going to put you back to living in tents,
    as in the old days when your worshiped in the wilderness.
I speak through the prophets
    to give clear pictures of the way things are.
    Using prophets, I tell revealing stories.
I show Gilead rampant with religious scandal
    and Gilgal teeming with empty-headed religion.
I expose their worship centers as
    stinking piles of garbage in their gardens."

Are you going to repeat the life of your ancestor Jacob?
  He ran off guilty to Aram,
Then sold his soul to get ahead,
  and made it big through treachery and deceit.
Your real identity is formed through God-sent prophets,
  who led you out of Egypt and served as faithful pastors.
As it is, Ephraim has continually
  and inexcusably insulted God.
Now he has to pay for his life-destroying ways.
  His Master will do to him what *he* has done.

13

RELIGION CUSTOMIZED TO TASTE

God once let loose against Ephraim
  a terrifying sentence against Israel:
Caught and convicted
  in the lewd sex-worship of Baal—they died!
And now they're back in the sin business again,
  manufacturing god-images they can use,
Religion customized to taste. Professionals see to it:
  Anything you want in a god you can get.
Can you believe it? They sacrifice live babies to these dead gods—
  kill living babies and kiss golden calves!
And now there's nothing left to these people:
  hollow men, desiccated women,
Like scraps of paper blown down the street,
  like smoke in a gusty wind.

"I'm still your GOD,
  the God who saved you out of Egypt.
I'm the only real God you've ever known.
  I'm the one and only God who delivers.
I took care of you during the wilderness hard times,
  those years when you had nothing.
I took care of you, took care of all your needs,
  gave you everything you needed.
You were spoiled. You thought you didn't need me.
  You forgot me.

"I'll charge them like a lion,
    like a leopard stalking in the brush.
I'll jump them like a sow grizzly robbed of her cubs.
    I'll rip out their guts.
Coyotes will make a meal of them.
    Crows will clean their bones.
I'm going to destroy you, Israel.
    Who is going to stop me?
Where is your trusty king you thought would save you?
    Where are all the local leaders you wanted so badly?
All these rulers you insisted on having,
    demanding, 'Give me a king! Give me leaders!'?
Well, long ago I gave you a king, but I wasn't happy about it.
    Now, fed up, I've gotten rid of him.
I have a detailed record of your infidelities—
    Ephraim's sin documented and stored in a safe-deposit box.

"When birth pangs signaled it was time to be born,
    Ephraim was too stupid to come out of the womb.
When the passage into life opened up,
    he didn't show.
Shall I intervene and pull them into life?
    Shall I snatch them from a certain death?
Who is afraid of you, Death?
    Who cares about your threats, Tomb?
In the end I'm abolishing regret,
    banishing sorrow,
Even though Ephraim ran wild,
    the black sheep of the family.

"God's tornado is on its way,
    roaring out of the desert.
It will devastate the country,
    leaving a trail of ruin and wreckage.
The cities will be gutted,
    dear possessions gone for good.
Now Samaria has to face the charges
    because she has rebelled against her God:
Her people will be killed, babies smashed on the rocks,
    pregnant women ripped open."

14

COME BACK! RETURN TO YOUR GOD!

Oh Israel, come back! Return to your GOD!
   You're down but you're not out.
Prepare your confession
   and come back to GOD.
Pray to him, "Take away our sin,
   accept our confession.
Receive as restitution
   our repentant prayers.
Assyria won't save us;
   horses won't get us where we want to go.
We'll never again say 'our god'
   to something we've made or made up.
You're our last hope. Is it not true
   that in you the orphan finds mercy?"

✠

"I will heal their waywardness.
   I will love them lavishly. My anger is played out.
I will make a fresh start with Israel.
   He'll burst into bloom like a crocus in the spring.
He'll put down deep oak tree roots,
   he'll become a forest of oaks!
He'll become splendid—like a giant sequoia,
   his fragrance like a grove of cedars!
Those who live near him will be blessed by him,
   be blessed and prosper like golden grain.
Everyone will be talking about them,
   spreading their fame as the vintage children of God.
Ephraim is finished with gods that are no-gods.
   From now on I'm the one who answers and satisfies him.
I am like a luxuriant fruit tree.
   Everything you need is to be found in me."

✠

If you want to live well,
    make sure you understand all of this.
If you know what's good for you,
    you'll learn this inside and out.
GOD's paths get you where you want to go.
    Right-living people walk them easily;
      wrong-living people are always tripping and stumbling.

JOEL

W hen disaster strikes, understanding of God is at risk. Unexpected illness or death, national catastrophe, social disruption, personal loss, plague or epidemic, devastation by flood or drought, turn men and women who haven't given God a thought in years into instant theologians. Rumors fly: "God is absent" . . . "God is angry" . . . "God is playing favorites, and I'm not the favorite" . . . "God is ineffectual" . . . "God is holding a grudge from a long time ago, and now we're paying for it" . . .

It is the task of the prophet to stand up at such moments of catastrophe and clarify who God is and how he acts. If the prophet is good—that is, accurate and true—the disaster becomes a lever for prying people's lives loose from their sins and setting them free for God. Joel is one of the good ones: He used a current event in Israel as a text to call his people to an immediate awareness that there wasn't a day that went by that they weren't dealing with God. We are always dealing with God.

The event that Joel used as his text was a terrible locust plague that was devastating the crops of Israel, creating an agricultural disaster of major proportions. He compared it to a massive military invasion. But any catastrophe would have served him as well. He projected it onto a big screen and used it to focus the reality of God in the lives of his people. Then he expanded the focus to include everything and everyone *everywhere*—the whole world crowded into Decision Valley for God's verdict. This powerful picture has kept God's people alert to the eternal consequences of their decisions for many centuries.

There is a sense in which catastrophe doesn't introduce anything new into our lives. It simply exposes the moral or spiritual reality that already exists but was hidden beneath an overlay of routine, self-preoccupation, and business as usual. Then suddenly, there it is before us: a moral universe in which our accumulated decisions—on what we say and do, on how we treat others, on whether or not we will obey God's commands—are set in the stark light of God's judgment.

In our everyday experience, right and wrong and the decisions we make about them seldom come to us neatly packaged and precisely defined. Joel's prophetic words continue to reverberate down through the generations, making the ultimate connection between anything, small or large, that disrupts our daily routine, and God, giving us fresh opportunity to reorient our lives in faithful obedience. Joel gives us opportunity for "deathbed repentance" before we die, while there is still time and space for a lot of good living to the glory of God.

JOEL

1

GET IN TOUCH WITH REALITY—AND WEEP!
GOD's Message to Joel son of Pethuel:

Attention, elder statesmen! Listen closely,
    everyone, whoever and wherever you are!
Have you ever heard of anything like this?
    Has anything like this ever happened before—ever?
Make sure you tell your children,
    and your children tell their children,
And their children *their* children.
    Don't let this message die out.

What the chewing locust left,
    the gobbling locust ate;
What the gobbling locust left,
    the munching locust ate;
What the munching locust left,
    the chomping locust ate.

Sober up, you drunks!
    Get in touch with reality—and weep!
Your supply of booze is cut off.
    You're on the wagon, like it or not.
My country's being invaded
    by an army invincible, past numbering,
Teeth like those of a lion,
    fangs like those of a tiger.
It has ruined my vineyards,
    stripped my orchards,
And clear-cut the country.
    The landscape's a moonscape.

Weep like a young virgin dressed in black,
    mourning the loss of her fiancé.
Without grain and grapes,

worship has been brought to a standstill
    in the Sanctuary of GOD.
The priests are at a loss.
    GOD's ministers don't know what to do.
The fields are sterile.
    The very ground grieves.
The wheat fields are lifeless,
    vineyards dried up, olive oil gone.

Dirt farmers, despair!
    Grape growers, wring your hands!
Lament the loss of wheat and barley.
    All crops have failed.
Vineyards dried up,
    fig trees withered,
Pomegranates, date palms, and apple trees—
    deadwood everywhere!
And joy is dried up and withered
    in the hearts of the people.

NOTHING'S GOING ON IN THE PLACE OF WORSHIP

And also you priests,
    put on your robes and join the outcry.
You who lead people in worship,
    lead them in lament.
Spend the night dressed in gunnysacks,
    you servants of my God.
Nothing's going on in the place of worship,
    no offerings, no prayers—nothing.
Declare a holy fast, call a special meeting,
    get the leaders together,
Round up everyone in the country.
    Get them into GOD's Sanctuary for serious prayer to GOD.

What a day! Doomsday!
    GOD's Judgment Day has come.
The Strong God has arrived.
    This is serious business!
Food is just a memory at our tables,

as are joy and singing from God's Sanctuary.
The seeds in the field are dead,
    barns deserted,
Grain silos abandoned.
        Who needs them? The crops have failed!
The farm animals groan — oh, how they groan!
        The cattle mill around.
There's nothing for them to eat.
        Not even the sheep find anything.

GOD! I pray, I cry out to you!
        The fields are burning up,
The country is a dust bowl,
        forest and prairie fires rage unchecked.
Wild animals, dying of thirst,
        look to you for a drink.
Springs and streams are dried up.
        The whole country is burning up.

2

THE LOCUST ARMY

Blow the ram's-horn trumpet in Zion!
        Trumpet the alarm on my holy mountain!
Shake the country up!
        GOD's Judgment's on its way — the Day's almost here!
A black day! A Doomsday!
        Clouds with no silver lining!
Like dawn light moving over the mountains,
        a huge army is coming.
There's never been anything like it
        and never will be again.
Wildfire burns everything before this army
        and fire licks up everything in its wake.
Before it arrives, the country is like the Garden of Eden.
        When it leaves, it is Death Valley.
        Nothing escapes unscathed.

The locust army seems all horses—
  galloping horses, an army of horses.
It sounds like thunder
  leaping on mountain ridges,
Or like the roar of wildfire
  through grass and brush,
Or like an invincible army shouting for blood,
  ready to fight, straining at the bit.
At the sight of this army,
  the people panic, faces white with terror.

The invaders charge.
  They climb barricades. Nothing stops them.
Each soldier does what he's told,
  so disciplined, so determined.
They don't get in each other's way.
  Each one knows his job and does it.
Undaunted and fearless,
  unswerving, unstoppable.
They storm the city,
  swarm its defenses,
Loot the houses,
  breaking down doors, smashing windows.
They arrive like an earthquake,
  sweep through like a tornado.
Sun and moon turn out their lights,
  stars black out.
GOD himself bellows in thunder
  as he commands his forces.
Look at the size of that army!
  And the strength of those who obey him!
GOD's Judgment Day—great and terrible.
  Who can possibly survive this?

CHANGE YOUR LIFE

But there's also this, it's not too late—
  GOD's personal Message!—
"Come back to me and really mean it!
  Come fasting and weeping, sorry for your sins!"

Change your life, not just your clothes.
    Come back to GOD, *your* God.
And here's why: God is kind and merciful.
    He takes a deep breath, puts up with a lot,
This most patient God, extravagant in love,
    always ready to cancel catastrophe.
Who knows? Maybe he'll do it now,
    maybe he'll turn around and show pity.
Maybe, when all's said and done,
    there'll be blessings full and robust for your GOD!

☩

Blow the ram's-horn trumpet in Zion!
    Declare a day of repentance, a holy fast day.
Call a public meeting.
    Get everyone there. Consecrate the congregation.
Make sure the elders come,
    but bring in the children, too, even the nursing babies,
Even men and women on their honeymoon—
    interrupt them and get them there.
Between Sanctuary entrance and altar,
    let the priests, GOD's servants, weep tears of repentance.
Let them intercede: "Have mercy, GOD, on your people!
    Don't abandon your heritage to contempt.
Don't let the pagans take over and rule them
    and sneer, 'And so where is this God of theirs?'"

☩

At that, GOD went into action to get his land back.
    He took pity on his people.
GOD answered and spoke to his people,
    "Look, listen—I'm sending a gift:
Grain and wine and olive oil.
    The fast is over—eat your fill!
I won't expose you any longer
    to contempt among the pagans.
I'll head off the final enemy coming out of the north
    and dump them in a wasteland.

Half of them will end up in the Dead Sea,
    the other half in the Mediterranean.
There they'll rot, a stench to high heaven.
    The bigger the enemy, the stronger the stench!"

THE TREES ARE BEARING FRUIT AGAIN

Fear not, earth! Be glad and celebrate!
    GOD has done great things.
Fear not, wild animals!
    The fields and meadows are greening up.
The trees are bearing fruit again:
    a bumper crop of fig trees and vines!
Children of Zion, celebrate!
    Be glad in your GOD.
He's giving you a teacher
    to train you how to live right—
Teaching, like rain out of heaven, showers of words
    to refresh and nourish your soul, just as he used to do.
And plenty of food for your body—silos full of grain,
    casks of wine and barrels of olive oil.

✠

"I'll make up for the years of the locust,
    the great locust devastation—
Locusts savage, locusts deadly,
    fierce locusts, locusts of doom,
That great locust invasion
    I sent your way.
You'll eat your fill of good food.
    You'll be full of praises to your GOD,
The God who has set you back on your heels in wonder.
    Never again will my people be despised.
You'll know without question
    that I'm in the thick of life with Israel,
That I'm your GOD, yes, *your* GOD,
    the one and only real God.
Never again will my people be despised.

469

THE SUN TURNING BLACK AND THE MOON BLOOD-RED

"And that's just the beginning: After that—

"I will pour out my Spirit
    on every kind of people:
Your sons will prophesy,
    also your daughters.
Your old men will dream,
    your young men will see visions.
I'll even pour out my Spirit on the servants,
    men and women both.
I'll set wonders in the sky above
    and signs on the earth below:
Blood and fire and billowing smoke,
    the sun turning black and the moon blood-red,
Before the Judgment Day of GOD,
    the Day tremendous and awesome.
Whoever calls, 'Help, GOD!'
    gets help.
On Mount Zion and in Jerusalem
    there will be a great rescue—just as GOD said.
Included in the survivors
    are those that GOD calls.

3

GOD IS A SAFE HIDING PLACE

"In those days, yes, at that very time
    when I put life back together again for Judah and Jerusalem,
I'll assemble all the godless nations.
    I'll lead them down into Judgment Valley
And put them all on trial, and judge them one and all
    because of their treatment of my own people Israel.
They scattered my people all over the pagan world
    and grabbed my land for themselves.
They threw dice for my people
    and used them for barter.
They would trade a boy for a whore,
    sell a girl for a bottle of wine when they wanted a drink.

✛

"As for you, Tyre and Sidon and Philistia,
    why should I bother with you?
Are you trying to get back at me
    for something I did to you?
If you are, forget it.
    I'll see to it that it boomerangs on you.
You robbed me, cleaned me out of silver and gold,
    carted off everything valuable to furnish your own temples.
You sold the people of Judah and Jerusalem
    into slavery to the Greeks in faraway places.
But I'm going to reverse your crime.
    I'm going to free those slaves.
I'll have done to you what you did to them:
    I'll sell your children as slaves to your neighbors,
And they'll sell them to the far-off Sabeans."
    GOD's Verdict.

✛

Announce this to the godless nations:
    Prepare for battle!
Soldiers at attention!
    Present arms! Advance!
Turn your shovels into swords,
    turn your hoes into spears.
Let the weak one throw out his chest
    and say, "I'm tough, I'm a fighter."
Hurry up, pagans! Wherever you are, get a move on!
    Get your act together.
Prepare to be
    shattered by GOD!

Let the pagan nations set out
    for Judgment Valley.
There I'll take my place at the bench
    and judge all the surrounding nations.

"Swing the sickle—
    the harvest is ready.
Stomp on the grapes—
    the winepress is full.
The wine vats are full,
    overflowing with vintage evil.

"Mass confusion, mob uproar—
    in Decision Valley!
GOD's Judgment Day has arrived
    in Decision Valley.

"The sky turns black,
    sun and moon go dark, stars burn out.
GOD roars from Zion, shouts from Jerusalem.
    Earth and sky quake in terror.
But GOD is a safe hiding place,
    a granite safe house for the children of Israel.
Then you'll know for sure
    that I'm *your* GOD,
Living in Zion,
    my sacred mountain.
Jerusalem will be a sacred city,
    posted: 'NO TRESPASSING.'

MILK RIVERING OUT OF THE HILLS

"What a day!
    Wine streaming off the mountains,
Milk rivering out of the hills,
    water flowing everywhere in Judah,
A fountain pouring out of GOD's Sanctuary,
    watering all the parks and gardens!
But Egypt will be reduced to weeds in a vacant lot,
    Edom turned into barren badlands,
All because of brutalities to the Judean people,
    the atrocities and murders of helpless innocents.
Meanwhile, Judah will be filled with people,
    Jerusalem inhabited forever.
The sins I haven't already forgiven, I'll forgive."
    GOD has moved into Zion for good.

#

More people are exploited and abused in the cause of religion than in any other way. Sex, money, and power all take a back seat to religion as a source of evil. Religion is the most dangerous energy source known to humankind. The moment a person (or government or religion or organization) is convinced that God is either ordering or sanctioning a cause or project, anything goes. The history, worldwide, of religion-fueled hate, killing, and oppression is staggering. The biblical prophets are in the front line of those doing something about it.

The biblical prophets continue to be the most powerful and effective voices ever heard on this earth for keeping religion honest, humble, and compassionate. Prophets sniff out injustice, especially injustice that is dressed up in religious garb. They sniff it out a mile away. Prophets see through hypocrisy, especially hypocrisy that assumes a religious pose. Prophets are not impressed by position or power or authority. They aren't taken in by numbers, size, or appearances of success.

They pay little attention to what men and women say about God or do for God. They listen to God and rigorously test all human language and action against what they hear. Among these prophets, Amos towers as defender of the down-trodden poor and accuser of the powerful rich who use God's name to legitimize their sin.

None of us can be trusted in this business. If we pray and worship God and associate with others who likewise pray and worship God, we absolutely must keep company with these biblical prophets. We are required to submit all our words and acts to their passionate scrutiny to prevent the perversion of our religion into something self-serving. A spiritual life that doesn't give a large place to the prophet-articulated justice will end up making us worse instead of better, separating us from God's ways instead of drawing us into them.

AMOS

1

The Message of Amos, one of the shepherds of Tekoa, that he received on behalf of Israel. It came to him in visions during the time that Uzziah was king of Judah and Jeroboam II son of Joash was king of Israel, two years before the big earthquake.

SWALLOWING THE SAME OLD LIES

The Message:

GOD roars from Zion,
 shouts from Jerusalem!
The thunderclap voice withers the pastures tended by shepherds,
 shrivels Mount Carmel's proud peak.

 GOD's Message:

"Because of the three great sins of Damascus
 —make that four—I'm not putting up with her any longer.
She pounded Gilead to a pulp, pounded her senseless
 with iron hammers and mauls.
For that, I'm setting the palace of Hazael on fire.
 I'm torching Ben-hadad's forts.
I'm going to smash the Damascus gates
 and banish the crime king who lives in Sin Valley,
 the vice boss who gives orders from Paradise Palace.
The people of the land will be sent back
 to where they came from—to Kir."
 GOD's Decree.

 GOD's Message:

"Because of the three great sins of Gaza
 —make that four—I'm not putting up with her any longer.
She deported whole towns
 and then sold the people to Edom.
For that, I'm burning down the walls of Gaza,
 burning up all her forts.

I'll banish the crime king from Ashdod,
    the vice boss from Ashkelon.
I'll raise my fist against Ekron,
        and what's left of the Philistines will die."
            GOD's Decree.

    GOD's Message:

"Because of the three great sins of Tyre
        —make that four—I'm not putting up with her any longer.
She deported whole towns to Edom,
    breaking the treaty she had with her kin.
For that, I'm burning down the walls of Tyre,
    burning up all her forts."

    GOD's Message:

"Because of the three great sins of Edom
        —make that four—I'm not putting up with her any longer.
She hunts down her brother to murder him.
    She has no pity, she has no heart.
Her anger rampages day and night.
    Her meanness never takes a timeout.
For that, I'm burning down her capital, Teman,
    burning up the forts of Bozrah."

    GOD's Message:

"Because of the three great sins of Ammon
        —make that four—I'm not putting up with her any longer.
She ripped open pregnant women in Gilead
    to get more land for herself.
For that, I'm burning down the walls of her capital, Rabbah,
    burning up her forts.
Battle shouts! war whoops!
    with a tornado to finish things off!
The king has been carted off to exile,
        the king and his princes with him."
            GOD's Decree.

✠

2

GOD's Message:

"Because of the three great sins of Moab
    —make that four—I'm not putting up with her any longer.
She violated the corpse of Edom's king,
    burning it to cinders.
For that, I'm burning down Moab,
    burning down the forts of Kerioth.
Moab will die in the shouting,
    go out in the blare of war trumpets.
I'll remove the king from the center
    and kill all his princes with him."
            GOD's Decree.

GOD's Message:

"Because of the three great sins of Judah
    —make that four—I'm not putting up with them any longer.
They rejected GOD's revelation,
    refused to keep my commands.
But they swallowed the same old lies
    that got their ancestors onto dead-end roads.
For that, I'm burning down Judah,
    burning down all the forts of Jerusalem."

DESTROYED FROM THE ROOTS UP

GOD's Message:

"Because of the three great sins of Israel
    —make that four—I'm not putting up with them any longer.
They buy and sell upstanding people.
    People for them are only *things*—ways of making money.
They'd sell a poor man for a pair of shoes.
    They'd sell their own grandmother!
They grind the penniless into the dirt,
    shove the luckless into the ditch.
Everyone and his brother sleeps with the 'sacred whore'—

a sacrilege against my Holy Name.
Stuff they've extorted from the poor
    is piled up at the shrine of their god,
While they sit around drinking wine
    they've conned from their victims.

"In contrast, I was always on your side.
    I destroyed the Amorites who confronted you,
Amorites with the stature of great cedars,
    tough as thick oaks.
I destroyed them from the top branches down.
    I destroyed them from the roots up.
And yes, I'm the One who delivered you from Egypt,
    led you safely through the wilderness for forty years
And then handed you the country of the Amorites
    like a piece of cake on a platter.
I raised up some of your young men to be prophets,
    set aside your best youth for training in holiness.
Isn't this so, Israel?"
    GOD's Decree.

"But you made the youth-in-training break training,
    and you told the young prophets, 'Don't prophesy!'
You're too much for me.
    I'm hard-pressed—to the breaking point.
I'm like a wagon piled high and overloaded,
    creaking and groaning.

"When I go into action, what will you do?
    There's no place to run no matter how fast you run.
The strength of the strong won't count.
    Fighters won't make it.
Skilled archers won't make it.
    Fast runners won't make it.
Chariot drivers won't make it.
    Even the bravest of all your warriors
Won't make it.
    He'll run off for dear life, stripped naked."
      GOD's Decree.

3

THE LION HAS ROARED

Listen to this, Israel. GOD is calling you to account—and I mean *all* of you, everyone connected with the family that he delivered out of Egypt. Listen!

"Out of all the families on earth,
     I picked *you*.
Therefore, because of your special calling,
     I'm holding you responsible for all your sins."

Do two people walk hand in hand
     if they aren't going to the same place?
Does a lion roar in the forest
     if there's no carcass to devour?
Does a young lion growl with pleasure
     if he hasn't caught his supper?
Does a bird fall to the ground
     if it hasn't been hit with a stone?
Does a trap spring shut
     if nothing trips it?
When the alarm goes off in the city,
     aren't people alarmed?
And when disaster strikes the city,
     doesn't GOD stand behind it?
The fact is, GOD, the Master, does nothing
     without first telling his prophets the whole story.

The lion has roared—
     who isn't frightened?
GOD has spoken—
     what prophet can keep quiet?

✛

Announce to the forts of Assyria,
     announce to the forts of Egypt—
Tell them, "Gather on the Samaritan mountains, take a good,
          hard look:

what a snake pit of brutality and terror!
They can't—or won't—do one thing right." GOD said so.
    "They stockpile violence and blight.
Therefore"—this is GOD's Word—"an enemy will surround
       the country.
    He'll strip you of your power and plunder your forts."

    GOD's Message:

"In the same way that a shepherd
    trying to save a lamb from a lion
Manages to recover
    just a pair of legs or the scrap of an ear,
So will little be saved of the Israelites
    who live in Samaria—
A couple of old chairs at most,
    the broken leg of a table.

"Listen and bring witness against Jacob's family"—
    this is God's Word, GOD-of-the-Angel-Armies!
"Note well! The day I make Israel pay for its sins,
    pay for the sin-altars of worship at Bethel,
The horned altars will all be dehorned
    and scattered around.
I'll tear down the winter palace,
    smash the summer palace—all your fancy buildings.
The luxury homes will be demolished,
    all those pretentious houses."
       GOD's Decree.

4

YOU NEVER GOT HUNGRY FOR GOD

"Listen to this, you cows of Bashan
    grazing on the slopes of Samaria.
You women! Mean to the poor,
    cruel to the down-and-out!
Indolent and pampered, you demand of your husbands,
    'Bring us a tall, cool drink!'

"This is serious—I, GOD, have sworn by my holiness!
    Be well warned: Judgment Day is coming!
They're going to rope you up and haul you off,
    keep the stragglers in line with cattle prods.
They'll drag you through the ruined city walls,
    forcing you out single file,
And kick you to kingdom come."
    GOD's Decree.

"Come along to Bethel and sin!
    And then to Gilgal and sin some more!
Bring your sacrifices for morning worship.
    Every third day bring your tithe.
Burn pure sacrifices—thank offerings.
    Speak up—announce freewill offerings!
That's the sort of religious show
    you Israelites just love."
    GOD's Decree.

"You know, don't you, that I'm the One
    who emptied your pantries and cleaned out your cupboards,
Who left you hungry and standing in bread lines?
    But you never got hungry for me. You continued to ignore me."
    GOD's Decree.

"Yes, and I'm the One who stopped the rains
    three months short of harvest.
I'd make it rain on one village
    but not on another.
I'd make it rain on one field
    but not on another—and that one would dry up.
People would stagger from village to village
    crazed for water and never quenching their thirst.
But you never got thirsty for me.
    You ignored me."
    GOD's Decree.

"I hit your crops with disease
    and withered your orchards and gardens.
Locusts devoured your olive and fig trees,

but you continued to ignore me."
    God's Decree.

"I revisited you with the old Egyptian plagues,
    killed your choice young men and prize horses.
The stink of rot in your camps was so strong
    that you held your noses—
But you didn't notice me.
    You continued to ignore me."
      God's Decree.

"I hit you with earthquake and fire,
    left you devastated like Sodom and Gomorrah.
You were like a burning stick
    snatched from the flames.
But you never looked my way.
    You continued to ignore me."
      God's Decree.

"All this I have done to you, Israel,
    and this is why I have done it.
Time's up, oh Israel!
    Prepare to meet your God!"

Look who's here: Mountain-Shaper! Wind-Maker!
    He laid out the whole plot before Adam.
He brings everything out of nothing,
    like dawn out of darkness.
He strides across the alpine ridges.
    His name is God, God-of-the-Angel-Armies.

5

ALL SHOW, NO SUBSTANCE

Listen to this, family of Israel,
    this Message I'm sending in bold print, this tragic warning:

"Virgin Israel has fallen flat on her face.
    She'll never stand up again.

She's been left where she's fallen.
No one offers to help her up."

This is the Message, GOD's Word:

"The city that marches out with a thousand
will end up with a hundred.
The city that marches out with a hundred
will end up with ten. Oh, family of Israel!"

GOD's Message to the family of Israel:

"Seek me and live.
Don't fool around at those shrines of Bethel,
Don't waste time taking trips to Gilgal,
and don't bother going down to Beer-sheba.
Gilgal is here today and gone tomorrow
and Bethel is all show, no substance."

So seek GOD and live! You don't want to end up
with nothing to show for your life
But a pile of ashes, a house burned to the ground.
For God will send just such a fire,
and the firefighters will show up too late.

RAW TRUTH IS NEVER POPULAR

Woe to you who turn justice to vinegar
and stomp righteousness into the mud.
Do you realize where you are? You're in a cosmos
star-flung with constellations by God,
A world God wakes up each morning
and puts to bed each night.
God dips water from the ocean
and gives the land a drink.
GOD, God-revealed, does all this.
And he can destroy it as easily as make it.
He can turn this vast wonder into total waste.

People hate this kind of talk.
Raw truth is never popular.
But here it is, bluntly spoken:

Because you run roughshod over the poor
 and take the bread right out of their mouths,
You're never going to move into
 the luxury homes you have built.
You're never going to drink wine
 from the expensive vineyards you've planted.
I know precisely the extent of your violations,
 the enormity of your sins. Appalling!
You bully right-living people,
 taking bribes right and left and kicking the poor when they're
  down.

Justice is a lost cause. Evil is epidemic.
 Decent people throw up their hands.
Protest and rebuke are useless,
 a waste of breath.

Seek good and not evil—
 and live!
You talk about GOD, the God-of-the-Angel-Armies,
 being your best friend.
Well, *live* like it,
 and maybe it will happen.

Hate evil and love good,
 then work it out in the public square.
Maybe GOD, the God-of-the-Angel-Armies,
 will notice your remnant and be gracious.

Now again, my Master's Message, GOD, God-of-the-Angel-Armies:

"Go out into the streets and lament loudly!
 Fill the malls and shops with cries of doom!
Weep loudly, 'Not me! Not us, Not now!'
 Empty offices, stores, factories, workplaces.
Enlist everyone in the general lament.
 I want to hear it loud and clear when I make my visit."
  GOD's Decree.

TIME TO FACE HARD REALITY, NOT FANTASY

Woe to all of you who want GOD's Judgment Day!
  Why would you want to see GOD, want him to come?
When GOD comes, it will be bad news before it's good news,
  the worst of times, not the best of times.
Here's what it's like: A man runs from a lion
  right into the jaws of a bear.
A woman goes home after a hard day's work
  and is raped by a neighbor.
At GOD's coming we face hard reality, not fantasy—
  a black cloud with no silver lining.

"I can't stand your religious meetings.
  I'm fed up with your conferences and conventions.
I want nothing to do with your religion projects,
  your pretentious slogans and goals.
I'm sick of your fund-raising schemes,
  your public relations and image making.
I've had all I can take of your noisy ego-music.
  When was the last time you sang to *me*!
Do you know what I want?
  I want justice—oceans of it.
I want fairness—rivers of it.
  That's what I want. That's *all* I want.

"Didn't you, dear family of Israel, worship me faithfully for forty years in the wilderness, bringing the sacrifices and offerings I commanded? How is it you've stooped to dragging gimcrack statues of your so-called rulers around, hauling the cheap images of all your star-gods here and there? Since you like them so much, you can take them with you when I drive you into exile beyond Damascus." GOD's Message, God-of-the-Angel-Armies.

6

THOSE WHO LIVE ONLY FOR TODAY

Woe to you who think you live on easy street in Zion,
  who think Mount Samaria is the good life.

You assume you're at the top of the heap,
     voted the number-one best place to live.
Well, wake up and look around. Get off your pedestal.
     Take a look at Calneh.
Go and visit Great Hamath.
     Look in on Gath of the Philistines.
Doesn't that take you off your high horse?
     Compared to them, you're not much, are you?

Woe to you who are rushing headlong to disaster!
     Catastrophe is just around the corner!
Woe to those who live in luxury
     and expect everyone else to serve them!
Woe to those who live only for today,
     indifferent to the fate of others!
Woe to the playboys, the playgirls,
     who think life is a party held just for them!
Woe to those addicted to feeling good—life without pain!
     those obsessed with looking good—life without wrinkles!
They could not care less
     about their country going to ruin.

But here's what's *really* coming:
     a forced march into exile.
They'll leave the country whining,
     a rag-tag bunch of good-for-nothings.

You've Made a Shambles of Justice

God, the Master, has sworn, and solemnly stands by his Word.
     The God-of-the-Angel-Armies speaks:

"I hate the arrogance of Jacob.
     I have nothing but contempt for his forts.
I'm about to hand over the city
     and everyone in it."

Ten men are in a house, all dead. A relative comes and gets the bodies to prepare them for a decent burial. He discovers a survivor huddled in a closet and asks, "Are there any more?" The answer: "Not a soul. But hush! God must not be mentioned in this desecrated place."

Note well: GOD issues the orders.
>He'll knock large houses to smithereens.
>He'll smash little houses to bits.

Do you hold a horse race in a field of rocks?
>Do you plow the sea with oxen?
You'd cripple the horses
>and drown the oxen.
And yet you've made a shambles of justice,
>a bloated corpse of righteousness,
Bragging of your trivial pursuits,
>beating up on the weak and crowing, "Look what I've done!"

"Enjoy it while you can, you Israelites.
>I've got a pagan army on the move against you"
>—this is your GOD speaking, God-of-the-Angel-Armies—
"And they'll make hash of you,
>from one end of the country to the other."

7

TO DIE HOMELESS AND FRIENDLESS

GOD, my Master, showed me this vision: He was preparing a locust swarm. The first cutting, which went to the king, was complete, and the second crop was just sprouting. The locusts ate everything green. Not even a blade of grass was left.

I called out, "GOD, my Master! Excuse me, but what's going to come of Jacob? He's so small."

GOD gave in.

"It won't happen," he said.

✠

GOD showed me this vision: Oh! GOD, my Master GOD was calling up a firestorm. It burned up the ocean. Then it burned up the Promised Land.

I said, "GOD, my Master! Hold it—please! What's going to come of Jacob? He's so small."

GOD gave in.

"All right, this won't happen either," GOD, my Master, said.

☩

GOD showed me this vision: My Master was standing beside a wall. In his hand he held a plumb line.

GOD said to me, "What do you see, Amos?"

I said, "A plumb line."

Then my Master said, "Look what I've done. I've hung a plumb line in the midst of my people Israel. I've spared them for the last time. This is it!

"Isaac's sex-and-religion shrines will be smashed,
Israel's unholy shrines will be knocked to pieces.
I'm raising my sword against the royal family of Jeroboam."

Amaziah, priest at the shrine at Bethel, sent a message to Jeroboam, king of Israel:

"Amos is plotting to get rid of you; and he's doing it as an insider, working from within Israel. His talk will destroy the country. He's got to be silenced. Do you know what Amos is saying?

"'Jeroboam will be killed.
Israel is headed for exile.'"

Then Amaziah confronted Amos: "Seer, be on your way! Get out of here and go back to Judah where you came from! Hang out there. Do your preaching there. But no more preaching at Bethel! Don't show your face here again. This is the king's chapel. This is a royal shrine."

But Amos stood up to Amaziah: "I never set up to be a preacher, never had plans to be a preacher. I raised cattle and I pruned trees. Then GOD took me off the farm and said, 'Go preach to my people Israel.'

"So listen to GOD's Word. You tell me, 'Don't preach to Israel. Don't say anything against the family of Isaac.' But here's what GOD is telling you:

"'Your wife will become a whore in town.
Your children will get killed.
Your land will be auctioned off.
You will die homeless and friendless.
And Israel will be hauled off to exile, far from *home*.'"

8

You Who Give Little and Take Much

My Master God showed me this vision: A bowl of fresh fruit.
>He said, "What do you see, Amos?"
>I said, "A bowl of fresh, ripe fruit."
>God said, "Right. So, I'm calling it quits with my people Israel. I'm
no longer acting as if everything is just fine."

"The royal singers will wail when it happens."
>My Master God said so.
"Corpses will be strewn here, there, and everywhere.
>Hush!"

Listen to this, you who walk all over the weak,
>you who treat poor people as less than nothing,
Who say, "When's my next paycheck coming
>so I can go out and live it up?
How long till the weekend
>when I can go out and have a good time?"
Who give little and take much,
>and never do an honest day's work.
You exploit the poor, using them—
>and then, when they're used up, you discard them.

God swears against the arrogance of Jacob:
>"I'm keeping track of their every last sin."
God's oath will shake earth's foundations,
>dissolve the whole world into tears.
God's oath will sweep in like a river that rises,
>flooding houses and lands,
And then recedes,
>leaving behind a sea of mud.

"On Judgment Day, watch out!"
>These are the words of God, my Master.
"I'll turn off the sun at noon.
>In the middle of the day the earth will go black.

I'll turn your parties into funerals
 and make every song you sing a dirge.
Everyone will walk around in rags,
 with sunken eyes and bald heads.
Think of the worst that could happen
 —your only son, say, murdered.
That's a hint of Judgment Day
 —that and much more.

"Oh yes, Judgment Day is coming!"
 These are the words of my Master GOD.
"I'll send a famine through the whole country.
 It won't be food or water that's lacking, but my Word.
People will drift from one end of the country to the other,
 roam to the north, wander to the east.
They'll go anywhere, listen to anyone,
 hoping to hear GOD's Word—but they won't hear it.

"On Judgment Day,
 lovely young girls will faint of Word-thirst,
 robust young men will faint of God-thirst,
Along with those who take oaths at the Samaria Sin-and-Sex Center,
 saying, 'As the lord god of Dan is my witness!'
 and 'The lady goddess of Beer-sheba bless you!'
Their lives will fall to pieces.
 They'll never put it together again."

9

ISRAEL THROWN INTO A SIEVE

I saw my Master standing beside the altar at the shrine. He said:

"Hit the tops of the shrine's pillars,
 make the floor shake.
The roof's about to fall on the heads of the people,
 and whoever's still alive, I'll kill.
No one will get away,
 no runaways will make it.
If they dig their way down into the underworld,
 I'll find them and bring them up.

If they climb to the stars,
    I'll find them and bring them down.
If they hide out at the top of Mount Carmel,
    I'll find them and bring them back.
If they dive to the bottom of the ocean,
    I'll send Dragon to swallow them up.
If they're captured alive by their enemies,
    I'll send Sword to kill them.
I've made up my mind
    to hurt them, not help them."

My Master, GOD-of-the-Angel-Armies,
    touches the earth, a mere touch, and it trembles.
    The whole world goes into mourning.
Earth swells like the Nile at flood stage;
    then the water subsides, like the great Nile of Egypt.
God builds his palace—towers soaring high in the skies,
    foundations set on the rock-firm earth.
He calls ocean waters and they come,
    then he ladles them out on the earth.
      GOD, your God, does all this.

✠

"Do you Israelites think you're any better than the faroff Cushites?"
GOD's Decree.

"Am I not involved with all nations? Didn't I bring Israel up from Egypt, the Philistines from Caphtor, the Arameans from Qir? But you can be sure that I, GOD, the Master, have my eye on the Kingdom of Sin. I'm going to wipe it off the face of the earth. Still, I won't totally destroy the family of Jacob." GOD's Decree.

"I'm still giving the orders around here. I'm throwing Israel into a sieve among all the nations and shaking them good, shaking out all the sin, all the sinners. No real grain will be lost, but all the sinners will be sifted out and thrown away, the people who say, 'Nothing bad will ever happen in our lifetime. It won't even come close.'

BLESSINGS LIKE WINE POURING OFF THE MOUNTAINS

"But also on that Judgment Day I will restore David's house that has fallen to pieces. I'll repair the holes in the roof, replace the broken windows, fix it up like new. David's people will be strong again and seize what's left of enemy Edom, plus everyone else under my sovereign judgment." GOD's Decree. He will do this.

"Yes indeed, it won't be long now." GOD's Decree.

"Things are going to happen so fast your head will swim, one thing fast on the heels of the other. You won't be able to keep up. Everything will be happening at once—and everywhere you look, blessings! Blessings like wine pouring off the mountains and hills. I'll make everything right again for my people Israel:

"They'll rebuild their ruined cities.
They'll plant vineyards and drink good wine.
They'll work their gardens and eat fresh vegetables.
And I'll plant *them*, plant them on their own land.
They'll never again be uprooted from the land I've given them."

GOD, your God, says so.

OBADIAH

It takes the entire Bible to read any part of the Bible. Even the
brief walk-on appearance of Obadiah has its place. No one,
whether in or out of the Bible, is without significance. It was
Obadiah's assignment to give voice to God's word of judgment
against Edom.

Back in the early stages of the biblical narrative, we are told
the story of the twins Jacob and Esau (Genesis 25–36). They
came out of the womb fighting. Jacob was ancestor to the people
of Israel, Esau ancestor to the people of Edom. The two neighbor-
ing peoples, Israel mostly to the west of the Jordan River and
Dead Sea and Edom to the southeast, never did get along. They
had a long history of war and rivalry. When Israel was taken into
exile—first the northern kingdom by the Assyrians in 721 B.C.
and later the southern kingdom by the Babylonians in 586 B.C.—
Edom stood across the fence and watched, glad to see her old
relative get beat up.

At first reading, this brief but intense prophecy of Obadiah,
targeted at Edom, is a broadside indictment of Edom's cruel
injustice to God's chosen people. Edom is the villain and God's
covenant people the victim.

But the last line of the prophecy takes a giant step out of
the centuries of hate and rivalry and invective. Israel, so often
a victim of Edomite aggression through the centuries, is suddenly revealed to be saved from the injustices of the past and
taking up a position of rule over their ancient enemies the
Edomites. But instead of doing to others what had been done
to them and continuing the cycle of violence that they had
been caught in, they are presented as taking over the reins of
government and administering God's justice justly. They find
themselves in a new context—God's kingdom—and realize
that they have a new vocation—to represent God's rule. It is
not much (one verse out of twenty-one!), but it is a glimmer
(it *is* the final verse!).

On the Day of Judgment, dark retaliation and invective do
not get the last word. Only the first rays of the light of justice
appear here. But these rays will eventually add up to a kingdom
of light, in which all nations will be judged justly from the eternal throne in heaven.

OBADIAH

YOUR WORLD WILL COLLAPSE

Obadiah's Message to Edom
    from GOD, the Master.
We got the news straight from GOD
    by a special messenger sent out to the godless nations:

"On your feet, prepare for battle;
    get ready to make war on Edom!

☩

"Listen to this, Edom:
    I'm turning you to a no-account,
    the runt of the godless nations, despised.
You thought you were so great,
    perched high among the rocks, king of the mountain,
Thinking to yourself,
    'Nobody can get to me! Nobody can touch me!'
Think again. Even if, like an eagle,
    you hang out on a high cliff-face,
Even if you build your nest in the stars,
    I'll bring you down to earth."
        GOD's sure Word.

"If thieves crept up on you,
    they'd rob you blind—isn't that so?
If they mugged you on the streets at night,
    they'd pick you clean—isn't that so?
Oh, they'll take Esau apart, piece by piece,
    empty his purse and pockets.
All your old partners will drive you to the edge.
    Your old friends will lie to your face.
Your old drinking buddies will stab you in the back.
    Your world will collapse. You won't know what hit you.
So don't be surprised"—it's GOD's sure Word!—
    "when I wipe out all sages from Edom
    and rid the Esau mountains of its famous wise men.

Your great heroes will desert you, Teman.
    There'll be nobody left in Esau's mountains.
Because of the murderous history compiled
    against your brother Jacob,
You will be looked down on by everyone.
    You'll lose your place in history.
On that day you stood there and didn't do anything.
    Strangers took your brother's army into exile.
Godless foreigners invaded and pillaged Jerusalem.
    You stood there and watched.
    You were as bad as they were.
You shouldn't have gloated over your brother
    when he was down-and-out.
You shouldn't have laughed and joked at Judah's sons
    when they were face down in the mud.
You shouldn't have talked so big
    when everything was so bad.
You shouldn't have taken advantage of my people
    when their lives had fallen apart.
You of all people should not have been amused
    by their troubles, their wrecked nation.
You shouldn't have taken the shirt off their back
    when they were knocked flat, defenseless.
And you shouldn't have stood waiting at the outskirts
    and cut off refugees,
And traitorously turned in helpless survivors
    who had lost everything.

☩

"GOD's Judgment Day is near
    for all the godless nations.
As you have done, it will be done to you.
    What you did will boomerang back
    and hit your own head.
Just as you partied on my holy mountain,
    all the godless nations will drink God's wrath.
They'll drink and drink and drink—
    they'll drink themselves to death.
But not so on Mount Zion—there's respite there!

a safe and holy place!
The family of Jacob will take back their possessions
    from those who took them from them.
That's when the family of Jacob will catch fire,
    the family of Joseph become fierce flame,
    while the family of Esau will be straw.
Esau will go up in flames,
    nothing left of Esau but a pile of ashes."
        GOD said it, and it is so.

☩

People from the south will take over the Esau mountains;
    people from the foothills will overrun the Philistines.
They'll take the farms of Ephraim and Samaria,
    and Benjamin will take Gilead.
Earlier, Israelite exiles will come back
    and take Canaanite land to the north at Zarephath.
Jerusalem exiles from the far northwest in Sepharad
    will come back and take the cities in the south.
The remnant of the saved in Mount Zion
    will go into the mountains of Esau
And rule justly and fairly,
    a rule that honors GOD's kingdom.

JONAH

Everybody knows about Jonah. People who have never read the Bible know enough about Jonah to laugh at a joke about him and the "whale." Jonah has entered our folklore. There is a playful aspect to his story, a kind of slapstick clumsiness about Jonah as he bumbles his way along, trying, but always unsuccessfully, to avoid God.

But the playfulness is not frivolous. This is deadly serious. While we are smiling or laughing at Jonah, we drop the guard with which we are trying to keep God at a comfortable distance, and suddenly we find ourselves caught in the purposes and commands of God. All of us. No exceptions.

Stories are the most prominent biblical way of helping us see ourselves in "the God story," which always gets around to the story of God making and saving us. Stories, in contrast to abstract statements of truth, tease us into becoming participants in what is being said. We find ourselves involved in the action. We may start out as spectators or critics, but if the story is good (and the biblical stories are very good!), we find ourselves no longer just listening to but inhabiting the story.

One reason that the Jonah story is so enduringly important for nurturing the life of faith in us is that Jonah is not a hero too high and mighty for us to identify with—he doesn't do anything great. Instead of being held up as an ideal to admire, we find Jonah as a companion in our ineptness. Here is someone on our level. Even when Jonah does it right (like preaching, finally, in Nineveh) he does it wrong (by getting angry at God). But the whole time, God is working within and around Jonah's very ineptness and accomplishing his purposes in him. Most of us need a biblical friend or two like Jonah.

JONAH

1

RUNNING AWAY FROM GOD

One day long ago, GOD's Word came to Jonah, Amittai's son: "Up on your feet and on your way to the big city of Nineveh! Preach to them. They're in a bad way and I can't ignore it any longer."

But Jonah got up and went the other direction to Tarshish, running away from GOD. He went down to the port of Joppa and found a ship headed for Tarshish. He paid the fare and went on board, joining those going to Tarshish—as far away from GOD as he could get.

But GOD sent a huge storm at sea, the waves towering.

The ship was about to break into pieces. The sailors were terrified. They called out in desperation to their gods. They threw everything they were carrying overboard to lighten the ship. Meanwhile, Jonah had gone down into the hold of the ship to take a nap. He was sound asleep. The captain came to him and said, "What's this? Sleeping! Get up! Pray to your god! Maybe your god will see we're in trouble and rescue us."

Then the sailors said to one another, "Let's get to the bottom of this. Let's draw straws to identify the culprit on this ship who's responsible for this disaster."

So they drew straws. Jonah got the short straw.

Then they grilled him: "Confess. Why this disaster? What is your work? Where do you come from? What country? What family?"

He told them, "I'm a Hebrew. I worship GOD, the God of heaven who made sea and land."

At that, the men were frightened, really frightened, and said, "What on earth have you done!" As Jonah talked, the sailors realized that he was running away from GOD.

They said to him, "What are we going to do with you—to get rid of this storm?" By this time the sea was wild, totally out of control.

Jonah said, "Throw me overboard, into the sea. Then the storm will stop. It's all my fault. I'm the cause of the storm. Get rid of me and you'll get rid of the storm."

But no. The men tried rowing back to shore. They made no headway. The storm only got worse and worse, wild and raging.

Then they prayed to GOD, "Oh GOD! Don't let us drown because of this man's life, and don't blame us for his death. You are GOD. Do what you think is best."

They took Jonah and threw him overboard. Immediately the sea was quieted down.

The sailors were impressed, no longer terrified by the sea, but in awe of GOD. They worshiped GOD, offered a sacrifice, and made vows.

2

AT THE BOTTOM OF THE SEA

Then GOD assigned a huge fish to swallow Jonah. Jonah was in the fish's belly three days and nights. Then Jonah prayed to his God from the belly of the fish. He prayed:

"In trouble, deep trouble, I prayed to GOD.
> He answered me.
From the belly of the grave I cried, 'Help!'
> You heard my cry.
You threw me into ocean's depths,
> into a watery grave,
With ocean waves, ocean breakers
> crashing over me.
I said, 'I've been thrown away,
> thrown out, out of your sight.
I'll never again lay eyes
> on your Holy Temple.'
Ocean gripped me by the throat.
> The ancient Abyss grabbed me and held tight.
My head was all tangled in seaweed
> at the bottom of the sea where the mountains take root.
I was as far down as a body can go,
> and the gates were slamming shut behind me forever—
Yet you pulled me up from that grave alive,
> oh GOD, my God!
When my life was slipping away,
> I remembered GOD,
And my prayer got through to you,
> made it all the way to your Holy Temple.
Those who worship hollow gods, god-frauds,
> walk away from their only true love.

But I'm worshiping you, GOD,
    calling out in thanksgiving!
And I'll do what I promised I'd do!
    Salvation belongs to GOD!"

Then GOD spoke to the fish, and it vomited up Jonah on the seashore.

3

MAYBE GOD WILL CHANGE HIS MIND

Next, GOD spoke to Jonah a second time: "Up on your feet and on your way to the big city of Nineveh! Preach to them. They're in a bad way and I can't ignore it any longer."

This time Jonah started off straight for Nineveh, obeying GOD's orders to the letter.

Nineveh was a big city, very big—it took three days to walk across it.

Jonah entered the city, went one day's walk and preached, "In forty days Nineveh will be smashed."

The people of Nineveh listened, and trusted God. They proclaimed a city-wide fast and dressed in burlap to show their repentance. Everyone did it—rich and poor, famous and obscure, leaders and followers.

When the message reached the king of Nineveh, he got up off his throne, threw down his royal robes, dressed in burlap, and sat down in the dirt. Then he issued a public proclamation throughout Nineveh, authorized by him and his leaders: "Not one drop of water, not one bite of food for man, woman, or animal, including your herds and flocks! Dress them all, both people and animals, in burlap, and send up a cry for help to God. Everyone must turn around, turn back from an evil life and the violent ways that stain their hands. Who knows? Maybe God will turn around and change his mind about us, quit being angry with us and let us live!"

God saw what they had done, that they had turned away from their evil lives. He *did* change his mind about them. What he said he would do to them he didn't do.

4

"I KNEW THIS WAS GOING TO HAPPEN!"

Jonah was furious. He lost his temper. He yelled at GOD, "GOD! I knew it—when I was back home, I knew this was going to happen! That's why I ran off to Tarshish! I knew you were sheer grace and mercy, not easily angered, rich in love, and ready at the drop of a hat to turn your plans of punishment into a program of forgiveness!

"So, GOD, if you won't kill them, kill *me*! I'm better off dead!"

GOD said, "What do you have to be angry about?"

But Jonah just left. He went out of the city to the east and sat down in a sulk. He put together a makeshift shelter of leafy branches and sat there in the shade to see what would happen to the city.

GOD arranged for a broad-leafed tree to spring up. It grew over Jonah to cool him off and get him out of his angry sulk. Jonah was pleased and enjoyed the shade. Life was looking up.

But then God sent a worm. By dawn of the next day, the worm had bored into the shade tree and it withered away. The sun came up and God sent a hot, blistering wind from the east. The sun beat down on Jonah's head and he started to faint. He prayed to die: "I'm better off dead!"

Then God said to Jonah, "What right do you have to get angry about this shade tree?"

Jonah said, "Plenty of right. It's made me angry enough to die!"

GOD said, "What's this? How is it that you can change your feelings from pleasure to anger overnight about a mere shade tree that you did nothing to get? You neither planted nor watered it. It grew up one night and died the next night. So, why can't I likewise change what I feel about Nineveh from anger to pleasure, this big city of more than a hundred and twenty thousand childlike people who don't yet know right from wrong, to say nothing of all the innocent animals?"

MICAH

Prophets use words to remake the world. The world—
heaven and earth, men and women, animals and
birds—was made in the first place by God's Word.
Prophets, arriving on the scene and finding that world in ruins,
finding a world of moral rubble and spiritual disorder, take up
the work of words again to rebuild what human disobedience
and mistrust demolished. These prophets learn their speech
from God. Their words are God-grounded, God-energized,
God-passionate. As their words enter the language of our communities, men and women find themselves in the presence of
God, who enters the mess of human sin to rebuke and renew.

Left to ourselves we turn God into an object, something
we can deal with, some *thing* we can use to our benefit,
whether that thing is a feeling or an idea or an image.
Prophets scorn all such stuff. They train us to respond to
God's presence and voice.

Micah, the final member of that powerful quartet of writing prophets who burst on the world scene in the eighth
century B.C. (Isaiah, Hosea, and Amos were the others), like
virtually all his fellow prophets—those charged with keeping
people alive to God and alert to listening to the voice of God—
was a master of metaphor. This means that he used words not
simply to define or identify what can be seen, touched, smelled,
heard, or tasted, but to plunge us into a world of *presence*. To
experience presence is to enter that far larger world of reality
that our sensory experiences point to but cannot describe—the
realities of love and compassion, justice and faithfulness, sin
and evil . . . and God. Mostly God. The realities that are Word-
evoked are where most of the world's action takes place. There
are no "mere words."

MICAH

1

GOD's Message as it came to Micah of Moresheth. It came during the
reigns of Jotham, Ahaz, and Hezekiah, kings of Judah. It had to do with
what was going on in Samaria and Jerusalem.

GOD TAKES THE WITNESS STAND

Listen, people—all of you.
   Listen, earth, and everyone in it:
The Master, GOD, takes the witness stand against you,
   the Master from his Holy Temple.

✝

Look, here he comes! GOD, from his place!
   He comes down and strides across mountains and hills.
Mountains sink under his feet,
   valleys split apart;
The rock mountains crumble into gravel,
   the river valleys leak like sieves.
All this because of Jacob's sin,
   because Israel's family did wrong.
You ask, "So what is Jacob's sin?"
   Just look at Samaria—isn't it obvious?
And all the sex-and-religion shrines in Judah—
   isn't Jerusalem responsible?

✝

"I'm turning Samaria into a heap of rubble,
   a vacant lot littered with garbage.
I'll dump the stones from her buildings in the valley
   and leave her abandoned foundations exposed.
All her carved and cast gods and goddesses
   will be sold for stove wood and scrap metal,
All her sacred fertility groves
   burned to the ground,

507

All the sticks and stones she worshiped as gods,
> destroyed.
These were her earnings from her life as a whore.
> This is what happens to the fees of a whore."

⳾

This is why I lament and mourn.
> This is why I go around in rags and barefoot.
This is why I howl like a pack of coyotes,
> and moan like a mournful owl in the night.
GOD has inflicted punishing wounds;
> Judah has been wounded with no healing in sight.
Judgment has marched through the city gates.
> Jerusalem must face the charges.

⳾

Don't gossip about this in Telltown.
> Don't waste your tears.
In Dustville,
> roll in the dust.
In Alarmtown,
> the alarm is sounded.
The citizens of Exitburgh
> will never get out alive.
Lament, Last-Stand City:
> There's nothing in you left standing.
The villagers of Bittertown
> wait in vain for sweet peace.
Harsh judgment has come from GOD
> and entered Peace City.
All you who live in Chariotville,
> get in your chariots for flight.
You led the daughter of Zion
> into trusting not God but chariots.
Similar sins in Israel
> also got their start in you.
Go ahead and give your goodbye gifts
> to Goodbyeville.

Miragetown beckoned
    but disappointed Israel's kings.
Inheritance City
    has lost its inheritance.
Glorytown
    has seen its last of glory.
Shave your heads in mourning
    over the loss of your precious towns.
Go bald as a goose egg—they've gone
    into exile and aren't coming back.

2

GOD HAS HAD ENOUGH

Doom to those who plot evil,
    who go to bed dreaming up crimes!
As soon at it's morning,
    they're off, full of energy, doing what they've planned.
They covet fields and grab them,
    find homes and take them.
They bully the neighbor and his family,
    see people only for what they can get out of them.
GOD has had enough. He says,
    "I have some plans of my own:
Disaster because of this interbreeding evil!
    Your necks are on the line.
You're not walking away from this.
    It's doomsday for you.
Mocking ballads will be sung of you,
    and you yourselves will sing the blues:
'Our lives are ruined,
    our homes and lands auctioned off.
They take everything, leave us nothing!
    All is sold to the highest bidder.'"
And there'll be no one to stand up for you,
    no one to speak for you before GOD and his jury.

✠

"Don't preach," say the preachers.
 "Don't preach such stuff.
Nothing bad will happen to us.
 Talk like *this* to the family of Jacob?
Does GOD lose his temper?
 Is this the way he acts?
Isn't he on the side of good people?
 Doesn't he help those who help themselves?"

    ✠

"What do you mean, 'good people'!
 You're the enemy of my people!
You rob unsuspecting people
 out for an evening stroll.
You take their coats off their backs
 like soldiers who plunder the defenseless.
You drive the women of my people
 out of their ample homes.
You make victims of the children
 and leave them vulnerable to violence and vice.
Get out of here, the lot of you.
 You can't take it easy here!
You've polluted this place,
 and now *you're* polluted—ruined!
If someone showed up with a good smile and glib tongue
 and told lies from morning to night—
'I'll preach sermons that will tell you
 how you can get anything you want from God:
More money, the best wines . . . you name it'—
 you'd hire him on the spot as your preacher!

    ✠

"I'm calling a meeting, Jacob.
 I want everyone back—all the survivors of Israel.
I'll get them together in one place—
 like sheep in a fold, like cattle in a corral—
 a milling throng of homebound people!
Then I, GOD, will burst all confinements

and lead them out into the open.
They'll follow their King.
    I will be out in front leading them."

3

HATERS OF GOOD, LOVERS OF EVIL

Then I said:

"Listen, leaders of Jacob, leaders of Israel:
    Don't you know anything of justice?
Haters of good, lovers of evil:
    Isn't justice in your job description?
But you skin my people alive.
    You rip the meat off their bones.
You break up the bones, chop the meat,
    and throw it in a pot for cannibal stew."

The time's coming, though, when these same leaders
    will cry out for help to GOD, but he won't listen.
He'll turn his face the other way
    because of their history of evil.

✝

Here is GOD's Message to the prophets,
    the preachers who lie to my people:
"For as long as they're well paid and well fed,
    the prophets preach, 'Isn't life wonderful! Peace to all!'
But if you don't pay up and jump on their bandwagon,
    their 'God bless you' turns into 'God damn you.'
Therefore, you're going blind. You'll see nothing.
    You'll live in deep shadows and know nothing.
The sun has set on the prophets.
    They've had their day; from now on it's night.
Visionaries will be confused,
    experts will be all mixed up.
They'll hide behind their reputations and make lame excuses
    to cover up their God-ignorance."

✠

But me—I'm filled with GOD's power,
    filled with GOD's Spirit of justice and strength,
Ready to confront Jacob's crime
    and Israel's sin.

The leaders of Jacob and
    the leaders of Israel are
Leaders contemptuous of justice,
    who twist and distort right living,
Leaders who build Zion by killing people,
    who expand Jerusalem by committing crimes.
Judges sell verdicts to the highest bidder,
    priests mass-market their teaching,
    prophets preach for high fees,
All the while posturing and pretending
    dependence on GOD:
"We've got GOD on our side.
    He'll protect us from disaster."
Because of people like you,
    Zion will be turned back into farmland,
Jerusalem end up as a pile of rubble,
    and instead of the Temple on the mountain,
    a few scraggly scrub pines.

4

THE MAKING OF GOD'S PEOPLE

But when all is said and done,
    GOD's Temple on the mountain,
Firmly fixed, will dominate all mountains,
    towering above surrounding hills.
People will stream to it
    and many nations set out for it,
Saying, "Come, let's climb GOD's mountain.
    Let's go to the Temple of Jacob's God.
He will teach us how to live.
    We'll know how to live God's way."

True teaching will issue from Zion,
   GOD's revelation from Jerusalem.
He'll establish justice in the rabble of nations
   and settle disputes in faraway places.
They'll trade in their swords for shovels,
   their spears for rakes and hoes.
Nations will quit fighting each other,
   quit learning how to kill one another.
Each man will sit under his own shade tree,
   each woman in safety will tend her own garden.
GOD-of-the-Angel-Armies says so,
   and he means what he says.

Meanwhile, all the other people live however they wish,
   picking and choosing their gods.
But we live honoring GOD,
   and we're loyal to our God for ever and ever.

"On that great day," GOD says,
   "I will round up all the hurt and homeless,
   everyone I have bruised or banished.
I will transform the battered into a company of the elite.
   I will make a strong nation out of the long lost,
A showcase exhibit of GOD's rule in action,
   as I rule from Mount Zion, from here to eternity.

"And you stragglers around Jerusalem,
   eking out a living in shantytowns:
The glory that once was will be again.
   Jerusalem's daughter will be the kingdom center."

✠

So why the doomsday hysterics?
   You still have a king, don't you?
But maybe he's not doing his job
   and you're panicked like a woman in labor.
Well, go ahead—twist and scream, Daughter Jerusalem.
   You *are* like a woman in childbirth.
You'll soon be out of the city, on your way

and camping in the open country.
And then you'll arrive in Babylon.
   What you lost in Jerusalem will be found in Babylon.
GOD will give you new life again.
   He'll redeem you from your enemies.

But for right now, they're ganged up against you,
   many godless peoples, saying,
"Kick her when she's down! Violate her!
   We want to see Zion grovel in the dirt."
These blasphemers have no idea
   what GOD is thinking and doing in this.
They don't know that this is the making of GOD's people,
   that they are wheat being threshed, gold being refined.

On your feet, Daughter of Zion! Be threshed of chaff,
   be refined of dross.
I'm remaking you into a people invincible,
   into God's juggernaut to crush the godless peoples.
You'll bring their plunder as holy offerings to GOD,
   their wealth to the Master of the earth.

5

THE LEADER WHO WILL SHEPHERD-RULE ISRAEL

But for now, prepare for the worst, victim daughter!
   The siege is set against us.
They humiliate Israel's king,
   slapping him around like a rag doll.

But you, Bethlehem, David's country,
   the runt of the litter—
From you will come the leader
   who will shepherd-rule Israel.
He'll be no upstart, no pretender.
   His family tree is ancient and distinguished.
Meanwhile, Israel will be in foster homes
   until the birth pangs are over and the child is born,
And the scattered brothers come back

514

home to the family of Israel.
He will stand tall in his shepherd-rule by GOD's strength,
　　centered in the majesty of GOD-Revealed.
And the people will have a good and safe home,
　　for the whole world will hold him in respect—
Peacemaker of the world!

And if some bullying Assyrian shows up,
　　invades and violates our land, don't worry.
We'll put him in his place, send him packing,
　　and watch his every move.
Shepherd-rule will extend as far as needed,
　　to Assyria and all other Nimrod-bullies.
Our shepherd-ruler will save us from old or new enemies,
　　from anyone who invades or violates our land.

The purged and select company of Jacob will be
　　like an island in the sea of peoples.
They'll be like dew from GOD,
　　like summer showers
Not mentioned in the weather forecast,
　　not subject to calculation or control.

Yes, the purged and select company of Jacob will be
　　like an island in the sea of peoples,
Like the king of beasts among wild beasts,
　　like a young lion loose in a flock of sheep,
Killing and devouring the lambs
　　and no one able to stop him.
With your arms raised in triumph over your foes,
　　your enemies will be no more!

✠

"The day is coming"
　　—GOD's Decree—
"When there will be no more war. None.
　　I'll slaughter your war horses and demolish your chariots.
I'll dismantle military posts
　　and level your fortifications.

I'll abolish your religious black markets,
    your underworld traffic in black magic.
I will smash your carved and cast gods
    and chop down your phallic posts.
No more taking control of the world,
    worshiping what you do or make.
I'll root out your sacred sex-and-power centers
    and destroy the God-defiant.
In raging anger, I'll make a clean sweep
    of godless nations who haven't listened."

6

WHAT GOD IS LOOKING FOR

Listen now, listen to GOD:

"Take your stand in court.
    If you have a complaint, tell the mountains;
    make your case to the hills.
And now, Mountains, hear GOD's case;
    listen, Jury Earth—
For I am bringing charges against my people.
    I am building a case against Israel.

"Dear people, how have I done you wrong?
    Have I burdened you, worn you out? Answer!
I delivered you from a bad life in Egypt;
    I paid a good price to get you out of slavery.
I sent Moses to lead you—
    and Aaron and Miriam to boot!
Remember what Balak king of Moab tried to pull,
    and how Balaam son of Beor turned the tables on him.
Remember all those stories about Shittim and Gilgal.
    Keep all GOD's salvation stories fresh and present."

How can I stand up before GOD
    and show proper respect to the high God?
Should I bring an armload of offerings
    topped off with yearling calves?

Would GOD be impressed with thousands of rams,
    with buckets and barrels of olive oil?
Would he be moved if I sacrificed my first-born child,
    my precious baby, to cancel my sin?

✢

But he's already made it plain how to live, what to do,
    what GOD is looking for in men and women.
It's quite simple: Do what is fair and just to your neighbor,
    be compassionate and loyal in your love,
And don't take yourself too seriously—
    take God seriously.

Attention! GOD calls out to the city!
    If you know what's good for you, you'll listen.
So listen, all of you!
    This is serious business.

✢

"Do you expect me to overlook obscene wealth
    you've piled up by cheating and fraud?
Do you think I'll tolerate shady deals
    and shifty scheming?
I'm tired of the violent rich
    bullying their way with bluffs and lies.
I'm fed up. Beginning now, you're finished.
    You'll pay for your sins down to your last cent.
No matter how much you get, it will never be enough—
    hollow stomachs, empty hearts.
No matter how hard you work, you'll have nothing to show for it—
    bankrupt lives, wasted souls.
You'll plant grass
    but never get a lawn.
You'll make jelly
    but never spread it on your bread.
You'll press apples
    but never drink the cider.
You have lived by the standards of your king, Omri,

517

the decadent lifestyle of the family of Ahab.
Because you've slavishly followed their fashions,
    I'm forcing you into bankruptcy.
Your way of life will be laughed at, a tasteless joke.
    Your lives will be derided as futile and fake."

7

Stick Around to See What God Will Do

I'm overwhelmed with sorrow!
    sunk in a swamp of despair!
I'm like someone who goes to the garden
    to pick cabbages and carrots and corn
And returns empty-handed,
    finds nothing for soup or sandwich or salad.
There's not a decent person in sight.
    Right-living humans are extinct.
They're all out for one another's blood,
    animals preying on each other.
They've all become experts in evil.
    Corrupt leaders demand bribes.
The powerful rich
    make sure they get what they want.
The best and brightest are thistles.
    The top of the line is crabgrass.
But no longer: It's exam time.
    Look at them slinking away in disgrace!
Don't trust your neighbor,
    don't confide in your friend.
Watch your words,
    even with your spouse.
Neighborhoods and families are falling to pieces.
    The closer they are—sons, daughters, in-laws—
The worse they can be.
    Your own family is the enemy.

✚

But me, I'm not giving up.
    I'm sticking around to see what God will do.

I'm waiting for God to make things right.
I'm counting on God to listen to me.

SPREADING YOUR WINGS

Don't, enemy, crow over me.
I'm down, but I'm not out.
I'm sitting in the dark right now,
but GOD is my light.
I can take GOD's punishing rage.
I deserve it—I sinned.
But it's not forever. He's on my side
and is going to get me out of this.
He'll turn on the lights and show me his ways.
I'll see the whole picture and how right he is.
And my enemy will see it, too,
and be discredited—yes, disgraced!
This enemy who kept taunting,
"So where is this GOD of yours?"
I'm going to see it with these, my own eyes—
my enemy disgraced, trash in the gutter.

✛

Oh, that will be a day! A day for rebuilding your city,
a day for stretching your arms, spreading your wings!
All your dispersed and scattered people will come back,
old friends and family from faraway places,
From Assyria in the east to Egypt in the west,
from across the seas and out of the mountains.
But there'll be a reversal for everyone else—massive depopulation—
because of the way they lived, the things they did.

Shepherd, oh GOD, your people with your staff,
your dear and precious flock.
Uniquely yours in a grove of trees,
centered in lotus land.
Let them graze in lush Bashan
as in the old days in green Gilead.
Reproduce the miracle-wonders

of our exodus from Egypt.
And the godless nations: Put them in their place—
    humiliated in their arrogance, speechless and clueless.
Make them slink like snakes, crawl like cockroaches,
    come out of their holes from under their rocks
And face our GOD.
    Fill them with holy fear and trembling.

✛

Where is the god who can compare with you—
    wiping the slate clean of guilt,
Turning a blind eye, a deaf ear,
    to the past sins of your purged and precious people?
You don't nurse your anger and don't stay angry long,
    for mercy is your specialty. That's what you love most.
And compassion is on its way to us.
    You'll stamp out our wrongdoing.
You'll sink our sins
    to the bottom of the ocean.
You'll stay true to your word to Father Jacob
    and continue the compassion you showed
        Grandfather Abraham—
Everything you promised our ancestors
    from a long time ago.

NAHUM

The stage of history is large. Larger-than-life figures appear on this stage from time to time, swaggering about, brandishing weapons and money, terrorizing and bullying. These figures are not, as they suppose themselves to be, at the center of the stage—not, in fact, anywhere near the center. But they make a lot of noise and are able to call attention to themselves. They often manage to get a significant number of people watching and even admiring: big nations, huge armies, important people. At any given moment a few superpower nations and their rulers dominate the daily news. Every century a few of these names are left carved on its park benches, marking rather futile, and in retrospect pitiable, attempts at immortality.

The danger is that the noise of these pretenders to power will distract us from what is going on quietly at the center of the stage in the person and action of God. God's characteristic way of working is in quietness and through prayer. "I speak," says poet George Meredith, "of the unremarked forces that split the heart and make the pavement toss—forces concealed in quiet people and plants." If we are conditioned to respond to noise and size, we will miss God's word and action.

From time to time, God assigns someone to pay attention to one or other of these persons or nations or movements just long enough to get the rest of us to *quit* paying so much attention to them and get back to the main action: *God*! Nahum drew that assignment in the seventh century B.C. Assyria had the whole world terrorized. At the time that Nahum delivered his prophecy, Assyria (and its capital, Nineveh) appeared invincible. A world free of Assyrian domination was unimaginable. Nahum's task was to make it imaginable—to free God's people from Assyrian paralysis, free them to believe in and pray to a sovereign God. Nahum's preaching, his Spirit-born metaphors, his God-shaped syntax, knocked Assyria off her high horse and cleared the field of Nineveh-distraction so that Israel could see that despite her world reputation, Assyria didn't amount to much. Israel could now attend to what was *really* going on.

Because Nahum has a single message—doom to Nineveh/Assyria—it is easy to misunderstand the prophet as simply a Nineveh hater. But Nahum writes and preaches out of the large context in which Israel's sins are denounced as vigorously as those of any of her enemies. The effect of Nahum is not to foment religious hate against the enemy but to say, "Don't admire or be intimidated by this enemy. They are going to be judged by the very same standards applied to us."

NAHUM

1

GOD IS SERIOUS BUSINESS

A report on the problem of Nineveh, the way God gave Nahum of Elkosh to see it:

GOD is serious business.
    He won't be trifled with.
He avenges his foes.
    He stands up against his enemies, fierce and raging.
But GOD doesn't lose his temper.
    He's powerful, but it's a patient power.
Still, no one gets by with anything.
    Sooner or later, everyone pays.
Tornadoes and hurricanes
    are the wake of his passage,
Storm clouds are the dust
    he shakes off his feet.
He yells at the sea: It dries up.
    All the rivers run dry.
The Bashan and Carmel mountains shrivel,
    the Lebanon orchards shrivel.
Mountains quake in their roots,
    hills dissolve into mud flats.
Earth shakes in fear of GOD.
    The whole world's in a panic.
Who can face such towering anger?
    Who can stand up to this fierce rage?
His anger spills out like a river of lava,
    his fury shatters boulders.

GOD is good,
    a hiding place in tough times.
He recognizes and welcomes
    anyone looking for help,
No matter how desperate the trouble.
    But cozy islands of escape

He wipes right off the map.
  No one gets away from God.
Why waste time conniving against GOD?
  He's putting an end to all such scheming.
For troublemakers, no second chances.
  Like a pile of dry brush,
Soaked in oil,
  they'll go up in flames.

A THINK TANK FOR LIES

Nineveh's an anthill
  of evil plots against GOD,
A think tank for lies
  that seduce and betray.

And GOD has something to say about all this:
  "Even though you're on top of the world,
With all the applause and all the votes,
  you'll be mowed down flat.

"I've afflicted you, Judah, true,
  but I won't afflict you again.
From now on I'm taking the yoke from your neck
  and splitting it up for kindling.
I'm cutting you free
  from the ropes of your bondage."

✠

GOD's orders on Nineveh:

"You're the end of the line.
  It's all over with Nineveh.
I'm gutting your temple.
  Your gods and goddesses go in the trash.
I'm digging your grave. It's an unmarked grave.
  You're nothing—no, you're *less* than nothing!"

Look! Striding across the mountains—
  a messenger bringing the latest good news: peace!

525

A holiday, Judah! Celebrate!
Worship and recommit to God!
No more worries about *this* enemy.
This one is history. Close the books.

2

ISRAEL'S BEEN TO HELL AND BACK

The juggernaut's coming!
Post guards, lay in supplies.
Get yourselves together,
get ready for the big battle.

☦

GOD has restored the Pride of Jacob,
the Pride of Israel.
Israel's lived through hard times.
He's been to hell and back.

Weapons flash in the sun,
the soldiers splendid in battle dress,
Chariots burnished and glistening,
ready to charge,
A spiked forest of brandished spears,
lethal on the horizon.
The chariots pour into the streets.
They fill the public squares,
Flaming like torches in the sun,
like lightning darting and flashing.
The Assyrian king rallies his men,
but they stagger and stumble.
They run to the ramparts
to stem the tide, but it's too late.
Soldiers pour through the gates.
The palace is demolished.
Soon it's all over:
Nineveh stripped, Nineveh doomed,
Maids and slaves moaning like doves,

beating their breasts.
Nineveh is a tub
from which they've pulled the plug.
Cries go up, "Do something! Do something!"
    but it's too late. Nineveh's soon empty—nothing.
Other cries come: "Plunder the silver!
    Plunder the gold!
A bonanza of plunder!
    Take everything you want!"
Doom! Damnation! Desolation!
    Hearts sink,
    knees fold,
    stomachs retch,
    faces blanch.
So, what happened to the famous
    and fierce Assyrian lion
And all those cute Assyrian cubs?
    To the lion and lioness
Cozy with their cubs,
    fierce and fearless?
To the lion who always returned from the hunt
    with fresh kills for lioness and cubs,
The lion lair heaped with bloody meat,
    blood and bones for the royal lion feast?

⊹

"Assyria, I'm your enemy,"
    says GOD-of-the-Angel-Armies.
"I'll torch your chariots. They'll go up in smoke.
    'Lion Country' will be strewn with carcasses.
The war business is over—you're out of work:
    You'll have no more wars to report,
No more victories to announce.
    You're out of war work forever."

3

LET THE NATIONS GET THEIR FILL OF THE UGLY TRUTH

Doom to Murder City—
     full of lies, bursting with loot, addicted to violence!
Horns blaring, wheels clattering,
     horses rearing, chariots lurching,
Horsemen galloping,
     brandishing swords and spears,
Dead bodies rotting in the street,
     corpses stacked like cordwood,
Bodies in every gutter and alley,
     clogging every intersection!
And whores! Whores without end!
     Whore City,
Fatally seductive, you're the Witch of Seduction,
     luring nations to their ruin with your evil spells.

✠

"I'm your enemy, Whore Nineveh—
     I, GOD-of-the-Angel-Armies!
I'll strip you of your seductive silk robes
     and expose you on the world stage.
I'll let the nations get their fill of the ugly truth
     of who you really are and have been all along.
I'll pelt you with dog dung
     and place you on a pedestal: 'Slut on Exhibit.'
Everyone who sees you will gag and say,
     'Nineveh's a pigsty:
What on earth did we ever see in her?
     Who would give her a second look? Ugh!'"

PAST THE POINT OF NO RETURN

Do you think you're superior to Egyptian Thebes,
     proudly invincible on the River Nile,
Protected by the great River,
     walled in by the River, secure?
Ethiopia stood guard to the south,

Egypt to the north.
Put and Libya, strong friends,
    were ready to step in and help.
But you know what happened to her:
    The whole city was marched off to a refugee camp,
Her babies smashed to death
    in public view on the streets,
Her prize leaders auctioned off,
    her celebrities put in chain gangs.
Expect the same treatment, Nineveh.
    You'll soon be staggering like a bunch of drunks,
Wondering what hit you,
    looking for a place to sleep it off.
All your forts are like peach trees,
    the lush peaches ripe, ready for the picking.
One shake of the tree and they fall
    straight into hungry mouths.
Face it: Your warriors are wimps.
    You're sitting ducks.
Your borders are gaping doors, inviting
    your enemies in. And who's to stop them?

✛

Store up water for the siege.
    Shore up your defenses.
Get down to basics: Work the clay
    and make bricks.
Sorry. Too late.
    Enemy fire will burn you up.
Swords will cut you to pieces.
    You'll be chewed up as if by locusts.

✛

Yes, as if by locusts—a fitting fate,
    for you yourselves are a locust plague.
You've multiplied shops and shopkeepers—
    more buyers and sellers than stars in the sky!
A plague of locusts, cleaning out the neighborhood
    and then flying off.

Your bureaucrats are locusts,
    your brokers and bankers are locusts.
Early on, they're all at your service,
    full of smiles and promises,
But later when you return with questions or complaints,
    you'll find they've flown off and are nowhere to be found.

King of Assyria! Your shepherd-leaders,
    in charge of caring for your people,
Are busy doing everything else but.
    They're not doing their job,
And your people are scattered and lost.
    There's no one to look after them.
You're past the point of no return.
    Your wound is fatal.
When the story of your fate gets out,
    the whole world will applaud and cry "Encore!"
Your cruel evil has seeped
    into every nook and cranny of the world.
    Everyone has felt it and suffered.

HABAKKUK

L iving by faith is a bewildering venture. We rarely know what's coming next, and not many things turn out the way we anticipate. It is natural to assume that since I am God's chosen and beloved, I will get favorable treatment from the God who favors me so extravagantly. It is not unreasonable to expect that from the time that I become his follower, I will be exempt from dead ends, muddy detours, and cruel treatment from the travelers I meet daily who are walking the other direction. That God-followers don't get preferential treatment in life always comes as a surprise. But it's also a surprise to find that there are a few men and women *within* the Bible who show up alongside us at such moments.

The prophet Habakkuk is one of them, and a most welcome companion he is. Most prophets, most of the time, speak God's Word *to us*. They are preachers calling us to listen to God's words of judgment and salvation, confrontation and comfort. They face us with God as he is, not as we imagine him to be. Most prophets are in-your-face assertive, not given to tact, not diplomatic, as they insist that we pay attention to God. But Habakkuk speaks our word *to God*. He gives voice to our bewilderment, articulates our puzzled attempts to make sense of things, faces God with our disappointment with God. He insists that God pay attention to us, and he insists with a prophet's characteristic no-nonsense bluntness.

The circumstance that aroused Habakkuk took place in the seventh century B.C. The prophet realized that God was going to use the godless military machine of Babylon to bring God's judgment on God's own people—using a godless nation to punish a godly nation! It didn't make sense, and Habakkuk was quick and bold to say so. He dared to voice his feelings that God didn't know his own God business. Not a day has passed since then that one of us hasn't picked up and repeated Habakkuk's bafflement: "God, you don't seem to make sense!"

But this prophet companion who stands at our side does something even more important: He waits and he listens. It is in his waiting and listening—which then turns into his praying—that he found himself inhabiting the large world of God's sovereignty. Only there did he eventually realize that the believing-in-God life, the steady trusting-in-God life, is the full life, the only real life. Habakkuk started out exactly where we start out with our puzzled complaints and God-accusations, but he didn't stay there. He ended up in a world, along with us, where every detail in our lives of love for God is worked into something good.

HABAKKUK

1

JUSTICE IS A JOKE

The problem as God gave Habakkuk to see it:

GOD, how long do I have to cry out for help
    before you listen?
How many times do I have to yell, "Help! Murder! Police!"
    before you come to the rescue?
Why do you force me to look at evil,
    stare trouble in the face day after day?
Anarchy and violence break out,
    quarrels and fights all over the place.
Law and order fall to pieces.
    Justice is a joke.
The wicked have the righteous hamstrung
    and stand justice on its head.

GOD SAYS, "LOOK!"

"Look around at the godless nations.
    Look long and hard. Brace yourself for a shock.
Something's about to take place
    and you're going to find it hard to believe.
I'm about to raise up Babylonians to punish you,
    Babylonians, fierce and ferocious—
World-conquering Babylon,
    grabbing up nations right and left,
A dreadful and terrible people,
    making up its own rules as it goes.
Their horses run like the wind,
    attack like bloodthirsty wolves.
A stampede of galloping horses
    thunders out of nowhere.
They descend like vultures
    circling in on carrion.
They're out to kill. Death is on their minds.
    They collect victims like squirrels gathering nuts.

They mock kings,
    poke fun at generals,
Spit on forts,
    and leave them in the dust.
They'll all be blown away by the wind.
    Brazen in sin, they call strength their god."

WHY IS GOD SILENT NOW?

GOD, you're from eternity, aren't you?
    Holy God, we aren't going to die, are we?
GOD, you chose *Babylonians* for your judgment work?
    Rock-Solid God, you gave *them* the job of discipline?
But you can't be serious!
    You can't condone evil!
So why don't you do something about this?
    Why are you silent *now*?
This outrage! Evil men swallow up the righteous
    and you stand around and *watch*!

✠

You're treating men and women
    as so many fish in the ocean,
Swimming without direction,
    swimming but not getting anywhere.
Then this evil Babylonian arrives and goes fishing.
    He pulls in a good catch.
He catches his limit and fills his creel—
    a good day of fishing! He's happy!
He praises his rod and reel,
    piles his fishing gear on an altar and worships it!
It's made his day,
    and he's going to eat well tonight!

✠

Are you going to let this go on and on?
    Will you let this Babylonian fisherman
Fish like a weekend angler,
    killing people as if they're nothing but fish?

✠

2

What's God going to say to my questions? I'm braced for the worst.
   I'll climb to the lookout tower and scan the horizon.
I'll wait to see what God says,
   how he'll answer my complaint.

FULL OF SELF, BUT SOUL-EMPTY

And then GOD answered: "Write this.
   Write what you see.
Write it out in big block letters
   so that it can be read on the run.
This vision-message is a witness
   pointing to what's coming.
It aches for the coming—it can hardly wait!
   And it doesn't lie.
If it seems slow in coming, wait.
   It's on its way. It will come right on time.

✛

"Look at that man, bloated by self-importance—
   full of himself but soul-empty.
But the person in right standing before God
   through loyal and steady believing
   is fully alive, *really* alive.

"Note well: Money deceives.
   The arrogant rich don't last.
They are more hungry for wealth
   than the grave is for cadavers.
Like death, they always want more,
   but the 'more' they get is dead bodies.
They are cemeteries filled with dead nations,
   graveyards filled with corpses.
Don't give people like this a second thought.
   Soon the whole world will be taunting them:

"'Who do you think you are—
   getting rich by stealing and extortion?

How long do you think
 you can get away with this?'
Indeed, how long before your victims wake up,
 stand up and make *you* the victim?
You've plundered nation after nation.
 Now you'll get a taste of your own medicine.
All the survivors are out to plunder you,
 a payback for all your murders and massacres.

"Who do you think you are—
 recklessly grabbing and looting,
Living it up, acting like king of the mountain,
 acting above it all, above trials and troubles?
You've engineered the ruin of your own house.
 In ruining others you've ruined yourself.
You've undermined your foundations,
 rotted out your own soul.
The bricks of your house will speak up and accuse you.
 The woodwork will step forward with evidence.

"Who do you think you are—
 building a town by murder, a city with crime?
Don't you know that GOD-of-the-Angel-Armies
 makes sure nothing comes of that but ashes,
Makes sure the harder you work
 at that kind of thing, the less you are?
Meanwhile the earth fills up
 with awareness of GOD's glory
 as the waters cover the sea.

"Who do you think you are—
 inviting your neighbors to your drunken parties,
Giving them too much to drink,
 roping them into your sexual orgies?
You thought you were having the time of your life.
 Wrong! It's a time of disgrace.
All the time you were drinking,
 you were drinking from the cup of God's wrath.
You'll wake up holding your throbbing head, hung over—
 hung over from Lebanon violence,

Hung over from animal massacres,
    hung over from murder and mayhem,
From multiple violations
    of place and people.

"What's the use of a carved god
    so skillfully carved by its sculptor?
What good is a fancy cast god
    when all it tells is lies?
What sense does it make to be a pious god-maker
    who makes gods that can't even talk?
Who do you think you are—
    saying to a stick of wood, 'Wake up,'
Or to a dumb stone, 'Get up'?
    Can they teach you anything about anything?
There's nothing to them but surface.
    There's nothing on the inside.

"But oh! GOD is in his holy Temple!
    Quiet everyone—a holy silence. Listen!"

3

GOD RACING ON THE CREST OF THE WAVES

A prayer of the prophet Habakkuk, with orchestra:

GOD, I've heard what our ancestors say about you,
    and I'm stopped in my tracks, down on my knees.
Do among us what you did among them.
    Work among us as you worked among them.
And as you bring judgment, as you surely must,
    remember mercy.

✠

God's on his way again,
    retracing the old salvation route,
Coming up from the south through Teman,
    the Holy One from Mount Paran.

Skies are blazing with his splendor,
    his praises sounding through the earth,
His cloud-brightness like dawn, exploding, spreading,
    forked-lightning shooting from his hand—
    what power hidden in that fist!
Plague marches before him,
    pestilence at his heels!
He stops. He shakes Earth.
    He looks around. Nations tremble.
The age-old mountains fall to pieces;
    ancient hills collapse like a spent balloon.
The paths God takes are older
    than the oldest mountains and hills.
I saw everyone worried, in a panic:
    Old wilderness adversaries,
Cushan and Midian, were terrified,
    hoping he wouldn't notice them.

☩

GOD, is it River you're mad at?
    Angry at old River?
Were you raging at Sea when you rode
    horse and chariot through to salvation?
You unfurled your bow
    and let loose a volley of arrows.
    You split Earth with rivers.
Mountains saw what was coming.
    They twisted in pain.
Flood Waters poured in.
    Ocean roared and reared huge waves.
Sun and Moon stopped in their tracks.
    Your flashing arrows stopped them,
    your lightning-strike spears impaled them.
Angry, you stomped through Earth.
    Furious, you crushed the godless nations.
You were out to save your people,
    to save your specially chosen people.
You beat the stuffing
    out of King Wicked,

Stripped him naked
    from head to toe,
Set his severed head on his own spear
    and blew away his army.
Scattered they were to the four winds—
    and ended up food for the sharks!
You galloped through the Sea on your horses,
    racing on the crest of the waves.
When I heard it, my stomach did flips.
    I stammered and stuttered.
My bones turned to water.
    I staggered and stumbled.
I sit back and wait for Doomsday
    to descend on our attackers.

✠

Though the cherry trees don't blossom
    and the strawberries don't ripen,
Though the apples are worm-eaten
    and the wheat fields stunted,
Though the sheep pens are sheepless
    and the cattle barns empty,
I'm singing joyful praise to GOD.
    I'm turning cartwheels of joy to my Savior God.
Counting on GOD's Rule to prevail,
    I take heart and gain strength.
I run like a deer.
    I feel like I'm king of the mountain!

(For congregational use, with a full orchestra.)

ZEPHANIAH

ZEPHANIAH

W e humans keep looking for a religion that will give us
access to God without having to bother with people.
We want to go to God for comfort and inspiration
when we're fed up with the men and women and children
around us. We want God to give us an edge in the dog-eat-dog
competition of daily life.

This determination to get ourselves a religion that gives us
an inside track with God but leaves us free to deal with people
however we like is age-old. It is the sort of religion that has
been promoted and marketed with both zeal and skill throughout human history. Business is always booming.

It is also the sort of religion that the biblical prophets are
determined to root out. They are dead set against it.

Because the root of the solid spiritual life is embedded in a
relationship between people and God, it is easy to develop the
misunderstanding that my spiritual life is something personal
between God and me—a private thing to be nurtured by
prayers and singing, spiritual readings that comfort and inspire,
and worship with like-minded friends. If we think this way for
very long, we will assume that the way we treat the people we
don't like or who don't like us has nothing to do with God.

That's when the prophets step in and interrupt us, insisting,
"Everything you do or think or feel has to do with God. Every
person you meet has to do with God." We live in a vast world of
interconnectedness, and the connections have consequences,
either in things or in people—and all the consequences come
together in God. The biblical phrase for the coming together of
the consequences is Judgment Day.

We can't be reminded too often or too forcefully of this
reckoning. Zephaniah's voice in the choir of prophets sustains
the intensity, the urgency.

ZEPHANIAH

1

No Longer Giving God a Thought or a Prayer

God's Message to Zephaniah son of Cushi, son of Gedaliah, son of Amariah, son of Hezekiah. It came during the reign of Josiah son of Amon, who was king of Judah:

"I'm going to make a clean sweep of the earth,
    a thorough housecleaning." God's Decree.

"Men and women and animals,
    including birds and fish—
Anything and everything that causes sin—will go,
    but especially people.

✝

"I'll start with Judah
    and everybody who lives in Jerusalem.
I'll sweep the place clean of every trace
    of the sex-and-religion Baal shrines and their priests.
I'll get rid of the people who sneak up to their rooftops at night
    to worship the star gods and goddesses;
Also those who continue to worship God
    but cover their bases by worshiping other king-gods as well;
Not to mention those who've dumped God altogether,
    no longer giving him a thought or offering a prayer.

✝

"Quiet now!
    Reverent silence before me, God, the Master!
Time's up. My Judgment Day is near:
    The Holy Day is all set, the invited guests made holy.
On the Holy Day, God's Judgment Day,
    I will punish the leaders and the royal sons;
I will punish those who dress up like foreign priests and priestesses,

543

Who introduce pagan prayers and practices;
And I'll punish all who import pagan superstitions
   that turn holy places into hellholes.
Judgment Day!" GOD's Decree!
   "Cries of panic from the city's Fish Gate,
Cries of terror from the city's Second Quarter,
   sounds of great crashing from the hills!
Wail, you shopkeepers on Market Street!
   Moneymaking has had its day. The god Money is dead.
On Judgment Day,
   I'll search through every closet and alley in Jerusalem.
I'll find and punish those who are sitting it out, fat and lazy,
   amusing themselves and taking it easy,
Who think, 'GOD doesn't do anything, good or bad.
   He isn't involved, so neither are we.'
But just wait. They'll lose everything they have,
   money and house and land.
They'll build a house and never move in.
   They'll plant vineyards and never taste the wine.

A DAY OF DARKNESS AT NOON

"The Great Judgment Day of GOD is almost here.
   It's countdown time: . . . seven, six, five, four . . .
Bitter and noisy cries on my Judgment Day,
   even strong men screaming for help.
Judgment Day is payday—my anger paid out:
   a day of distress and anguish,
   a day of catastrophic doom,
   a day of darkness at noon,
   a day of black storm clouds,
   a day of bloodcurdling war cries,
   as forts are assaulted,
   as defenses are smashed.
I'll make things so bad they won't know what hit them.
   They'll walk around groping like the blind.
   They've sinned against GOD!
Their blood will be poured out like old dishwater,
   their guts shoveled into slop buckets.
Don't plan on buying your way out.

Your money is worthless for this.
This is the Day of GOD's Judgment—my *wrath*!
    I *care* about sin with fiery passion—
A fire to burn up the corrupted world,
    a wildfire finish to the corrupting people."

2

SEEK GOD

So get yourselves together. Shape up!
    You're a nation without a clue about what it wants.
Do it before you're blown away
    like leaves in a windstorm,
Before GOD's Judgment-anger
    sweeps down on you,
Before GOD's Judgment Day wrath
    descends with full force.

✠

Seek GOD, all you quietly disciplined people
    who live by GOD's justice.
Seek GOD's right ways. Seek a quiet and disciplined life.
    Perhaps you'll be hidden on the Day of GOD's anger.

ALL EARTH-MADE GODS WILL BLOW AWAY

Gaza is scheduled for demolition,
    Ashdod will be cleaned out by high noon,
    Ekron pulled out by the roots.
Doom to the seaside people,
    the seafaring people from Crete!
The Word of GOD is bad news for you
    who settled Canaan, the Philistine country:
"You're slated for destruction—
    no survivors!"

✠

The lands of the seafarers
    will become pastureland,

A country for shepherds and sheep.
    What's left of the family of Judah will get it.
Day after day they'll pasture by the sea,
    and go home in the evening to Ashkelon to sleep.
Their very own GOD will look out for them.
    He'll make things as good as before.

✠

"I've heard the crude taunts of Moab,
    the mockeries flung by Ammon,
The cruel talk they've used to put down my people,
    their self-important strutting along Israel's borders.
Therefore, as sure as I am the living God," says
        GOD-of-the-Angel-Armies,
    Israel's personal God,
"Moab will become a ruin like Sodom,
    Ammon a ghost town like Gomorrah,
One a field of rocks, the other a sterile salt flat,
    a moonscape forever.
What's left of my people will finish them off,
    will pick them clean and take over.
This is what they get for their bloated pride,
    their taunts and mockeries of the people
    of GOD-of-the-Angel-Armies.
GOD will be seen as truly terrible—a Holy Terror.
    All earth-made gods will shrivel up and blow away;
And everyone, wherever they are, far or near,
    will fall to the ground and worship him.
Also you Ethiopians,
    you too will die—I'll see to it."

✠

Then GOD will reach into the north
    and destroy Assyria.
He will waste Nineveh,
    leave her dry and treeless as a desert.
The ghost town of a city,
    the haunt of wild animals,

Nineveh will be home to raccoons and coyotes—
    they'll bed down in its ruins.
Owls will hoot in the windows, ravens will croak in the doorways—
    all that fancy woodwork now a perch for birds.
Can this be the famous Fun City
    that had it made,
That boasted, "I'm the Number-One City!
    I'm King of the Mountain!"
So why is the place deserted,
    a lair for wild animals?
Passersby hardly give it a look;
    they dismiss it with a gesture.

3

SEWER CITY

Doom to the rebellious city,
    the home of oppressors—Sewer City!
The city that wouldn't take advice,
    wouldn't accept correction,
Wouldn't trust GOD,
    wouldn't even get close to her own god!
Her very own leaders
    are rapacious lions,
Her judges are rapacious timber wolves
    out every morning prowling for a fresh kill.
Her prophets are out for what they can get.
    They're opportunists—you can't trust them.
Her priests desecrate the Sanctuary.
    They use God's law as a weapon to maim and kill souls.
Yet GOD remains righteous in her midst,
    untouched by the evil.
He stays at it, day after day, meting out justice.
    At evening he's still at it, strong as ever.
But evil men and women, without conscience
    and without shame, persist in evil.

✝

"So I cut off the godless nations.
     I knocked down their defense posts,
Filled her roads with rubble
     so no one could get through.
Her cities were bombed-out ruins,
     unlivable and unlived in.

"I thought, 'Surely she'll honor me now,
     accept my discipline and correction,
Find a way of escape from the trouble she's in,
     find relief from the punishment I'm bringing.'
But it didn't faze her. Bright and early
     she was up at it again, doing the same old things.

"Well, if that's what you want, stick around."
     GOD's Decree.
"Your day in court is coming,
     but remember I'll be there to bring evidence.
I'll bring all the nations to the courtroom,
     round up all the kingdoms,
And let them feel the brunt of my anger,
     my raging wrath.
My zeal is a fire
     that will purge and purify the earth.

GOD IS IN CHARGE AT THE CENTER

"In the end I will turn things around for the people.
     I'll give them a language undistorted, unpolluted,
Words to address GOD in worship
     and, united, to serve me with their shoulders to the wheel.
They'll come from beyond the Ethiopian rivers,
     they'll come praying—
All my scattered, exiled people
     will come home with offerings for worship.
You'll no longer have to be ashamed
     of all those acts of rebellion.
I'll have gotten rid of your arrogant leaders.
     No more pious strutting on my holy hill!
I'll leave a core of people among you

who are poor in spirit—
What's left of Israel that's really Israel.
They'll make their home in GOD.
This core holy people
    will not do wrong.
They won't lie,
    won't use words to flatter or seduce.
Content with who they are and where they are,
    unanxious, they'll live at peace."

✠

So sing, Daughter Zion!
    Raise the rafters, Israel!
Daughter Jerusalem,
    be happy! celebrate!
GOD has reversed his judgments against you
    and sent your enemies off chasing their tails.
From now on, GOD is Israel's king,
    in charge at the center.
There's nothing to fear from evil
    ever again!

GOD IS PRESENT AMONG YOU

Jerusalem will be told:
    "Don't be afraid.
Dear Zion,
    don't despair.
Your GOD is present among you,
    a strong Warrior there to save you.
Happy to have you back, he'll calm you with his love
    and delight you with his songs."

✠

"The accumulated sorrows of your exile
    will dissipate.
I, your God, will get rid of them for you.
    You've carried those burdens long enough.

At the same time, I'll get rid of all those
    who've made your life miserable.
I'll heal the maimed;
    I'll bring home the homeless.
In the very countries where they were hated
    they will be venerated.
On Judgment Day
    I'll bring you back home—a great family gathering!
You'll be famous and honored
    all over the world.
You'll see it with your own eyes—
    all those painful partings turned into reunions!"
        GOD's Promise.

HAGGAI

P laces of worship are a problem. And the problem does not seem to be architectural. Grand Gothic cathedrals that dominate a city don't ensure that the worship of God dominates that city. Unpainted, ramshackle, clapboard sheds perched precariously on the edge of a prairie don't guarantee a congregation of humble saints in denim. As we look over the centuries of the many and various building projects in God's name—wilderness tabernacle, revival tent, Gothic cathedral, wayside chapel, synagogue, temple, meeting house, storefront mission, the catacombs—there doesn't seem to be any connection between the buildings themselves and the belief and behavior of the people who assemble in them.

In noticing this, it is not uncommon for us to be dismissive of the buildings themselves by saying, "A place of worship is not a building; it's people," or, "I prefer worshiping God in the great cathedral of the outdoors." These pronouncements are often tagged with the scriptural punch line, "The God who made the universe doesn't live in custom-made shrines," which is supposed to end the discussion. God doesn't live in build-ings—period. That's what we often say.

But then there is Haggai to account for. Haggai was digni-fied with the title "prophet" (therefore we must take him seriously). His single task, carried out in a three-and-a-half-month mission, was to get God's people to work at rebuilding God's Temple (the same Temple that had been destroyed by God's decree only seventy or so years earlier).

Compared with the great prophets who preached repen-tance and salvation, Haggai's message doesn't sound very "spiritual." But in God's economy it is perhaps unwise to rank our assigned work as either more or less spiritual. We are not angels; we inhabit space. Material—bricks and mortar, boards and nails—keeps us grounded and connected with the ordinary world in which we necessarily live out our extraordinary beliefs. Haggai keeps us in touch with those times in our lives when repairing the building where we worship is an act of obedience every bit as important as praying in that place of worship.

HAGGAI

1

CAUGHT UP WITH TAKING CARE OF YOUR OWN HOUSES

On the first day of the sixth month of the second year in the reign of King Darius of Persia, GOD's Message was delivered by the prophet Haggai to the governor of Judah, Zerubbabel son of Shealtiel, and to the high priest, Joshua son of Jehozadak:

A Message from GOD-of-the-Angel-Armies: "The people procrastinate. They say this isn't the right time to rebuild my Temple, the Temple of GOD."

Shortly after that, GOD said more and Haggai spoke it: "How is it that it's the 'right time' for you to live in your fine new homes while the Home, GOD's Temple, is in ruins?"

And then a little later, GOD-of-the-Angel-Armies spoke out again:

"Take a good, hard look at your life.
    Think it over.
You have spent a lot of money,
    but you haven't much to show for it.
You keep filling your plates,
    but you never get filled up.
You keep drinking and drinking and drinking,
    but you're always thirsty.
You put on layer after layer of clothes,
    but you can't get warm.
And the people who work for you,
    what are they getting out of it?
Not much—
    a leaky, rusted-out bucket, that's what.

That's why GOD-of-the-Angel-Armies said:

"Take a good, hard look at your life.
    Think it over."

✠

553

Then GOD said:

"Here's what I want you to do:
  Climb into the hills and cut some timber.
Bring it down and rebuild the Temple.
  Do it just for me. Honor me.
You've had great ambitions for yourselves,
  but nothing has come of it.
The little you have brought to my Temple
  I've blown away—there was nothing to it.

"And why?" (This is a Message from GOD-of-the-Angel-Armies, remember.) "Because while you've run around, caught up with taking care of your own houses, my Home is in ruins. That's why. Because of your stinginess. And so I've given you a dry summer and a skimpy crop. I've matched your tight-fisted stinginess by decreeing a season of drought, drying up fields and hills, withering gardens and orchards, stunting vegetables and fruit. Nothing—not man or woman, not animal or crop—is going to thrive."

✝

Then the governor, Zerubbabel son of Shealtiel, and the high priest, Joshua son of Jehozadak, and all the people with them listened, really listened, to the voice of their GOD. When GOD sent the prophet Haggai to them, they paid attention to him. In listening to Haggai, they honored GOD.

Then Haggai, GOD's messenger, preached GOD's Message to the people: "I am with you!" GOD's Word.

This is how GOD got Zerubbabel, Joshua, and all the people moving—got them working on the Temple of GOD-of-the-Angel-Armies. This happened on the twenty-fourth day of the sixth month in the second year of King Darius.

2

THIS TEMPLE WILL END UP BETTER THAN IT STARTED OUT

On the twenty-first day of the seventh month, the Word of GOD came through the prophet Haggai: "Tell Governor Zerubbabel son of Shealtiel and High Priest Joshua son of Jehozadak and all the people: 'Is there anyone here who saw the Temple the way it used to be, all glorious? And what do you see now? Not much, right?

"'So get to work, Zerubbabel!'—GOD is speaking.

"'Get to work, Joshua son of Jehozadak—high priest!'

"'Get to work, all you people!'—GOD is speaking.

"'Yes, get to work! For I am with you.' The GOD-of-the-Angel-Armies is speaking! 'Put into action the word I covenanted with you when you left Egypt. I'm living and breathing among you right now. Don't be timid. Don't hold back.'

"This is what GOD-of-the-Angel-Armies said: 'Before you know it, I will shake up sky and earth, ocean and fields. And I'll shake down all the godless nations. They'll bring bushels of wealth and I will fill this Temple with splendor.' GOD-of-the-Angel-Armies says so.

"'This Temple is going to end up far better than it started out, a glorious beginning but an even more glorious finish: a place in which I will hand out wholeness and holiness.' Decree of GOD-of-the-Angel-Armies."

✠

On the twenty-fourth day of the ninth month (again, this was in the second year of Darius), GOD's Message came to Haggai: "GOD-of-the-Angel-Armies speaks: Consult the priests for a ruling. If someone carries a piece of sacred meat in his pocket, meat that is set apart for sacrifice on the altar, and the pocket touches a loaf of bread, a dish of stew, a bottle of wine or oil, or any other food, will these foods be made holy by such contact?"

The priests said, "No."

Then Haggai said, "How about someone who is contaminated by touching a corpse—if that person touches one of these foods, will it be contaminated?"

The priests said, "Yes, it will be contaminated."

Then Haggai said, "'So, this people is contaminated. Their nation is contaminated. Everything they do is contaminated. Whatever they do for me is contaminated.' GOD says so.

"'Think back. Before you set out to lay the first foundation stones for the rebuilding of my Temple, how did it go with you? Isn't it true that your foot-dragging, halfhearted efforts at rebuilding the Temple of GOD were reflected in a sluggish, halfway return on your crops—half the grain you were used to getting, half the wine? I hit you with drought and blight and hail. Everything you were doing got hit. But it didn't seem to faze you. You continued to ignore me.' GOD's Decree.

"'Now think ahead from this same date—this twenty-fourth day of the ninth month. Think ahead from when the Temple rebuilding was launched. Has anything in your fields—vine, fig tree, pomegranate, olive tree—failed to flourish? From now on you can count on a blessing.'"

✝

GOD's Message came a second time to Haggai on that most memorable day, the twenty-fourth day of the ninth month: "Speak to Zerubbabel, the governor of Judah:

"'I am about to shake up everything, to turn everything upside down and start over from top to bottom—overthrow governments, destroy foreign powers, dismantle the world of weapons and armaments, throw armies into confusion, so that they end up killing one another. And on that day'"—this is GOD's Message—"'I will take you, oh Zerubbabel son of Shealtiel, as my personal servant and I will set you as a signet ring, the sign of my sovereign presence and authority. I've looked over the field and chosen you for this work.'" The Message of GOD-of-the-Angel-Armies.

ZECHARIAH

Zechariah shared with his contemporary Haggai the prophetic task of getting the people of Judah to rebuild their ruined Temple. Their preaching pulled the people out of self-preoccupation and got them working together as a people of God. There was a job to do, and the two prophets teamed up to make sure it got done.

But Zechariah did more than that. For the people were faced with more than a ruined Temple and city. Their self-identity as the people of God was in ruins. For a century they had been knocked around by the world powers, kicked and mocked, used and abused. This once-proud people, their glorious sacred history starred with the names of Abraham, Moses, Samuel, David, and Isaiah, had been treated with contempt for so long that they were in danger of losing all connection with that past, losing their magnificent identity as God's people.

Zechariah was a major factor in recovering the magnificence from the ruins of a degrading exile. Zechariah reinvigorated their imaginations with his visions and messages. The visions provided images of a sovereign God that worked their way into the lives of the people, countering the long ordeal of debasement and ridicule. The messages forged a fresh vocabulary that gave energy and credibility to the long-term purposes of God being worked out in their lives.

But that isn't the end of it. Zechariah's enigmatic visions, working at multiple levels, and his poetically charged messages are at work still, like time capsules in the lives of God's people, continuing to release insight and hope and clarity for the people whom God is using to work out his purposes in a world that has no language for God and the purposes of God.

ZECHARIAH

1

In the eighth month of the second year in the reign of Darius, GOD's Message came to the prophet Zechariah son of Berechiah, son of Iddo: "GOD was very angry with your ancestors. So give to the people this Message from GOD-of-the-Angel-Armies: 'Come back to me and I'll come back to you. Don't be like your parents. The old-time prophets called out to them, "A Message from GOD-of-the-Angel-Armies: Leave your evil life. Quit your evil practices." But they ignored everything I said to them, stubbornly refused to listen.'

"And where are your ancestors now? Dead and buried. And the prophets who preached to them? Also dead and buried. But the Message that my servants the prophets spoke, that isn't dead and buried. That Message did its work on your ancestors, did it not? It woke them up and they came back, saying, 'He did what he said he would do, sure enough. We didn't get by with a thing.'"

FIRST VISION: FOUR RIDERS

On the twenty-fourth day of the eleventh month in the second year of the reign of Darius, the Message of GOD was given to the prophet Zechariah son of Berechiah, son of Iddo:

One night I looked out and saw a man astride a red horse. He was in the shadows in a grove of birches. Behind him were more horses—a red, a chestnut, and a white.

I said, "Sir, what are these horses doing here? What's the meaning of this?"

The Angel-Messenger said, "Let me show you."

Then the rider in the birch grove spoke up, "These are the riders that GOD sent to check things out on earth."

They reported their findings to the Angel of GOD in the birch grove: "We have looked over the whole earth and all is well. Everything's under control."

The Angel of GOD reported back, "Oh GOD-of-the-Angel-Armies, how long are you going to stay angry with Jerusalem and the cities of Judah? When are you going to let up? Isn't seventy years long enough?"

GOD reassured the Angel-Messenger—good words, comforting words—who then addressed me: "Tell them this. Tell them that GOD-of-the-Angel-Armies has spoken. This is GOD's Message: 'I care deeply for Jerusalem and Zion. I feel very possessive of them. But I'm thoroughly angry with the godless nations that act as if they own the whole world. I was only moderately angry earlier, but now they've gone too far. I'm going into action.

"'I've come back to Jerusalem, but with compassion this time.'
    This is GOD speaking.
'I'll see to it that my Temple is rebuilt.'
    A Decree of GOD-of-the-Angel-Armies!
'The rebuilding operation is already staked out.'
    Say it again—a Decree of GOD-of-the-Angel-Armies:
'My cities will prosper again,
    GOD will comfort Zion again,
    Jerusalem will be back in my favor again.'"

SECOND VISION: FOUR HORNS AND FOUR BLACKSMITHS

I looked up, and was surprised by another vision: four horns!
    I asked the Messenger-Angel, "And what's the meaning of this?"
    He said, "These are the powers that have scattered Judah, Israel, and Jerusalem abroad."
    Then GOD expanded the vision to include four blacksmiths.
    I asked, "And what are these all about?"
    He said, "Since the 'horns' scattered Judah so badly that no one had any hope left, these blacksmiths have arrived to combat the horns. They'll dehorn the godless nations who used their horns to scatter Judah to the four winds."

2

THIRD VISION: THE MAN WITH THE TAPE MEASURE

I looked up and was surprised to see
    a man holding a tape measure in his hand.
I said, "What are you up to?"
    "I'm on my way," he said, "to survey Jerusalem,
    to measure its width and length."
Just then the Messenger-Angel on his way out
    met another angel coming in and said,
"Run! Tell the Surveyor, 'Jerusalem will burst its walls—

bursting with people, bursting with animals.
And I'll be right there with her'—GOD's Decree—'a wall of fire
around unwalled Jerusalem and a radiant presence within.'"

✠

"Up on your feet! Get out of there—and now!" GOD says so.
"Return from your far exile.
I scattered you to the four winds." GOD's Decree.
"Escape from Babylon, Zion, and come home—now!"

✠

GOD-of-the-Angel-Armies, the One of Glory who sent me on my mission, commenting on the godless nations who stripped you and left you homeless, said, "Anyone who hits you, hits me—bloodies my nose, blackens my eye. Yes, and at the right time I'll give the signal and they'll be stripped and thrown out by their own servants." Then you'll know for sure that GOD-of-the-Angel-Armies sent me on this mission.

✠

"Shout and celebrate, Daughter of Zion!
I'm on my way. I'm moving into your neighborhood!"
GOD's Decree.

✠

Many godless nations will be linked up with GOD at that time. ("They will become my family! I'll live in their homes!") And then you'll know for sure that GOD-of-the-Angel-Armies sent me on this mission. GOD will reclaim his Judah inheritance in the Holy Land. He'll again make clear that Jerusalem is his choice.

✠

Quiet, everyone! Shh! Silence before GOD. Something's afoot in his holy house. He's on the move!

3

FOURTH VISION: JOSHUA'S NEW CLOTHES

Next the Messenger-Angel showed me the high priest Joshua. He was standing before GOD's Angel where the Accuser showed up to accuse him. Then GOD said to the Accuser, "I, GOD, rebuke you, Accuser! I rebuke you and choose Jerusalem. Surprise! Everything is going up in flames, but I reach in and pull out Jerusalem!"

Joshua, standing before the angel, was dressed in dirty clothes. The angel spoke to his attendants, "Get him out of those filthy clothes," and then said to Joshua, "Look, I've stripped you of your sin and dressed you up in clean clothes."

I spoke up and said, "How about a clean new turban for his head also?" And they did it—put a clean new turban on his head. Then they finished dressing him, with GOD's Angel looking on.

GOD's Angel then charged Joshua, "Orders from GOD-of-the-Angel-Armies: 'If you live the way I tell you and remain obedient in my service, then you'll make the decisions around here and oversee my affairs. And all my attendants standing here will be at your service.

"'Careful, High Priest Joshua—both you and your friends sitting here with you, for your friends are in on this, too! Here's what I'm doing next: I'm introducing my servant Branch. And note this: This stone that I'm placing before Joshua, a single stone with seven eyes'—Decree of GOD-of-the-Angel-Armies—'I'll engrave with these words: "I'll strip this land of its filthy sin, all at once, in a single day."

"'At that time, everyone will get along with one another, with friendly visits across the fence, friendly visits on one another's porches.'"

4

FIFTH VISION: A LAMPSTAND AND TWO OLIVE TREES

The Messenger-Angel again called me to attention. It was like being wakened out of deep sleep.

He said, "What do you see?"

I answered, "I see a lampstand of solid gold with a bowl on top. Seven lamps, each with seven spouts, are set on the bowl. And there are two olive trees, one on either side of the bowl."

Then I asked the Messenger-Angel, "What does this mean, sir?"

The Messenger-Angel said, "Can't you tell?"

"No, sir," I said.

Then he said, "This is GOD'S Message to Zerubbabel: 'You can't force these things. They only come about through my Spirit,' says GOD-of-the-Angel-Armies. 'So, big mountain, who do you think you are? Next to Zerubbabel you're nothing but a molehill. He'll proceed to set the Cornerstone in place, accompanied by cheers: "Yes! Yes! Do it!"'"

After that, the Word of GOD came to me: "Zerubbabel started rebuilding this Temple and he will complete it. That will be your confirmation that GOD-of-the-Angel-Armies sent me to you. Does anyone dare despise this day of small beginnings? They'll change their tune when they see Zerubbabel setting the last stone in place!"

Going back to the vision, the Messenger-Angel said, "The seven lamps are the eyes of GOD probing the dark corners of the world like searchlights."

"And the two olive trees on either side of the lampstand?" I asked. "What's the meaning of them? And while you're at it, the two branches of the olive trees that feed oil to the lamps—what do they mean?"

He said, "You haven't figured that out?"

I said, "No, sir."

He said, "These are the two who stand beside the Master of the whole earth and supply golden lamp oil worldwide."

5

SIXTH VISION: THE FLYING BOOK

I looked up again and saw—surprise!—a book on the wing! A book flying!

The Messenger-Angel said to me, "What do you see now?"

I said, "I see a book flying, a huge book—thirty feet long and fifteen wide!"

He told me, "This book is the verdict going out worldwide against thieves and liars. The first half of the book disposes of everyone who steals; the second half takes care of everyone who lies. I launched it"—Decree of GOD-of-the-Angel-Armies—"and so it will fly into the house of every thief and every liar. It will land in each house and tear it down, timbers and stones."

SEVENTH VISION: A WOMAN IN A BASKET

The Messenger-Angel appeared and said, "Look up. Tell me what you see."

I said, "What in the world is that?"

He said, "This is a bushel basket on a journey. It holds the sin of everyone, everywhere."

Then the lid made of lead was removed from the basket—and there was a woman sitting in it!

He said, "This is Miss Wicked." He pushed her back down into the basket and clamped the lead lid over her.

Then I looked up and to my surprise saw two women flying. On outstretched wings they airlifted the bushel basket into the sky.

I said to the Messenger-Angel, "Where are they taking the bushel basket?"

He said, "East to the land of Shinar. They will build a garage to house it. When it's finished, the basket will be stored there."

6

EIGHTH VISION: FOUR CHARIOTS

Once again I looked up—another strange sight! Four chariots charging out from between two mountains. The mountains were bronze.

The first chariot was drawn by red horses, the second chariot by black horses, the third chariot by white horses, and the fourth chariot by dappled horses. All the horses were powerful.

I asked the Messenger-Angel, "Sir, what's the meaning here?"

The angel answered, "These are the four winds of heaven, which originate with the Master of the whole earth. The black horses are headed north with the white ones right after them. The dappled horses are headed south." The powerful horses galloped out, bursting with energy, eager to patrol through the earth. The Messenger-Angel commanded: "On your way! Survey the earth!" and they were off in every direction.

Then he called to me and said, "Look at them go! The ones going north are conveying a sense of my Spirit, serene and secure. No more trouble from that direction."

A MAN NAMED BRANCH

Then this Message from GOD came to me: "Take up a collection from the exiles. Target Heldai, Tobiah, and Jedaiah. They've just arrived from Babylon. You'll find them at the home of Josiah son of Zephaniah. Collect silver and gold from them and fashion crowns. Place one on the head of Joshua son of Jehozadak, the high priest, and give him this message:

"'A Message from GOD-of-the-Angel-Armies. Be alert. We have a man here whose name is Branch. He will branch out from where he is and build the Temple of GOD. Yes, he's the one. He'll build the Temple of GOD. Then he'll assume the role of royalty, take his place on the throne and rule—a priest sitting on the throne!—showing that king and priest can coexist in harmony.'

"The other crown will be in the Temple of GOD as a symbol of royalty, under the custodial care of Helem, Tobiah, Jedaiah, and Hen son of Zephaniah.

"People will come from faraway places to pitch in and rebuild the Temple of GOD. This will confirm that GOD-of-the-Angel-Armies did, in fact, send me to you. All this follows as you put your minds to a life of responsive obedience to the voice of your GOD."

7

"YOU'RE INTERESTED IN RELIGION, I'M INTERESTED IN PEOPLE"

On the fourth day of the ninth month, in the fourth year of the reign of King Darius, GOD's Message again came to Zechariah.

The town of Bethel had sent a delegation headed by Sarezer and Regem-Melech to pray for GOD's blessing and to confer with the priests of the Temple of GOD-of-the-Angel-Armies, and also with the prophets. They posed this question: "Should we plan for a day of mourning and abstinence next August, the seventieth anniversary of Jerusalem's fall, as we have been doing all these years?"

GOD-of-the-Angel-Armies gave me this Message for them, for all the people and for the priests: "When you held days of fasting every fifth and seventh month all these seventy years, were you doing it for me? And when you held feasts, was that for me? Hardly. You're interested in religion, I'm interested in people.

"There's nothing new to say on the subject. Don't you still have the message of the earlier prophets from the time when Jerusalem was still a thriving, bustling city and the outlying countryside, the Negev and Shephelah, was populated? [This is the message that GOD gave Zechariah.] Well, the message hasn't changed. GOD-of-the-Angel-Armies said then and says now:

"'Treat one another justly.
Love your neighbors.

Be compassionate with each other.
Don't take advantage of widows, orphans, visitors, and the poor.
Don't plot and scheme against one another—that's evil.'

"But did your ancestors listen? No, they set their jaws in defiance. They shut their ears. They steeled themselves against GOD's revelation and the Spirit-filled sermons preached by the earlier prophets by order of GOD-of-the-Angel-Armies. And GOD became angry, really angry, because he told them everything plainly and they wouldn't listen to a word he said.

"So [this is what GOD-of-the-Angel-Armies said] if they won't listen to me, I won't listen to them. I scattered them to the four winds. They ended up strangers wherever they were. Their 'promised land' became a vacant lot—weeds and tin cans and thistles. Not a sign of life. They turned a dreamland into a wasteland."

8

REBUILDING THE TEMPLE

And then these Messages from GOD-of-the-Angel-Armies:

A Message from GOD-of-the-Angel-Armies:

"I am zealous for Zion—I *care*!
    I'm angry about Zion—I'm *involved*!"

⊹

GOD's Message:

"I've come back to Zion,
    I've moved back to Jerusalem.
Jerusalem's new names will be Truth City,
    and Mountain of GOD-of-the-Angel-Armies,
    and Mount Holiness."

⊹

A Message from GOD-of-the-Angel-Armies:
    "Old men and old women will come back to Jerusalem, sit on benches on the streets and spin tales, move around safely with their canes—a good city to grow old in. And boys and girls will fill the public parks, laughing and playing—a good city to grow up in."

✠

A Message from GOD-of-the-Angel-Armies:

"Do the problems of returning and rebuilding by just a few survivors seem too much? But is anything too much for me? Not if I have
my say."

✠

A Message from GOD-of-the-Angel-Armies:

"I'll collect my people from countries to the east and countries to the
west. I'll bring them back and move them into Jerusalem. They'll be my
people and I'll be their God. I'll stick with them and do right by them."

✠

A Message from GOD-of-the-Angel-Armies:

"Get a grip on things. Hold tight, you who are listening to what I
say through the preaching of the prophets. The Temple of GOD-of-the-
Angel-Armies has been reestablished. The Temple is being rebuilt.
We've come through a hard time: You worked for a pittance and were
lucky to get that; the streets were dangerous; you could never let down
your guard; I had turned the world into an armed camp.

"But things have changed. I'm taking the side of my core of surviving people":

"Sowing and harvesting will resume,
Vines will grow grapes,
Gardens will flourish,
Dew and rain will make everything green.

"My core survivors will get everything they need—and more. You've
gotten a reputation as a bad-news people, you people of Judah and Israel,
but I'm coming to save you. From now on, you're the good-news people.
Don't be afraid. Keep a firm grip on what I'm doing."

KEEP YOUR LIVES SIMPLE AND HONEST

A Message from GOD-of-the-Angel-Armies:

"In the same way that I decided to punish you when your ancestors made me angry, and didn't pull my punches, at this time I've

decided to bless Jerusalem and the country of Judah. Don't be afraid. And now here's what I want you to do: Tell the truth, the whole truth, when you speak. Do the right thing by one another, both personally and in your courts. Don't cook up plans to take unfair advantage of others. Don't do or say what isn't so. I hate all that stuff. Keep your lives simple and honest." Decree of GOD.

⁜

Again I received a Message from GOD-of-the-Angel-Armies:
    "The days of mourning set for the fourth, fifth, seventh, and tenth months will be turned into days of feasting for Judah—celebration and holiday. Embrace truth! Love peace!"

⁜

A Message from GOD-of-the-Angel-Armies:
    "People and their leaders will come from all over to see what's going on. The leaders will confer with one another: 'Shouldn't we try to get in on this? Get in on GOD's blessings? Pray to GOD-of-the-Angel-Armies? What's keeping us? Let's go!'
    "Lots of people, powerful nations—they'll come to Jerusalem looking for what they can get from GOD-of-the-Angel-Armies, looking to get a blessing from GOD."

⁜

A Message from GOD-of-the-Angel-Armies:
    "At that time, ten men speaking a variety of languages will grab the sleeve of one Jew, hold tight, and say, 'Let us go with you. We've heard that God is with you.'"

9

THE WHOLE WORLD HAS ITS EYES ON GOD
War Bulletin:

GOD's Message challenges the country of Hadrach.
    It will settle on Damascus.

The whole world has its eyes on GOD.
    Israel isn't the only one.
That includes Hamath at the border,
    and Tyre and Sidon, clever as they think they are.
Tyre has put together quite a kingdom for herself;
    she has stacked up silver like cordwood,
    piled gold high as haystacks.
But God will certainly bankrupt her;
    he will dump all that wealth into the ocean
    and burn up what's left in a big fire.
Ashkelon will see it and panic,
    Gaza will wring its hands,
    Ekron will face a dead end.
Gaza's king will die.
    Ashkelon will be emptied out,
    And a villain will take over in Ashdod.

"I'll take proud Philistia down a peg:
    I'll make him spit out his bloody booty
    and abandon his vile ways."
What's left will be all God's—a core of survivors,
    a family brought together in Judah—
But enemies like Ekron will go the way of the Jebusites,
    into the dustbin of history.
"I will set up camp in my home country
    and defend it against invaders.
Nobody is going to hurt my people ever again.
    I'm keeping my eye on them.

A HUMBLE KING RIDING A DONKEY

"Shout and cheer, Daughter Zion!
    Raise the roof, Daughter Jerusalem!
Your king is coming!
    a good king who makes all things right,
    a humble king riding a donkey,
    a mere colt of a donkey.
I've had it with war—no more chariots in Ephraim,
    no more war horses in Jerusalem,
    no more swords and spears, bows and arrows.

He will offer peace to the nations,
    a peaceful rule worldwide,
    from the four winds to the seven seas.

"And you, because of my blood covenant with you,
    I'll release your prisoners from their hopeless cells.
Come home, hope-filled prisoners!
    This very day I'm declaring a double bonus—
    everything you lost returned twice-over!
Judah is now my weapon, the bow I'll pull,
    setting Ephraim as an arrow to the string.
I'll wake up your sons, oh Zion,
    to counter your sons, oh Greece.
From now on
    people are my swords."

Then GOD will come into view,
    his arrows flashing like lightning!
Master GOD will blast his trumpet
    and set out in a whirlwind.
GOD-of-the-Angel-Armies will protect them—
    all-out war,
The war to end all wars,
    no holds barred.
Their GOD will save the day. He'll rescue them.
    They'll become like sheep, gentle and soft,
Or like gemstones in a crown,
    catching all the colors of the sun.
Then how they'll shine! shimmer! glow!
    the young men robust, the young women lovely!

10

GOD'S WORK OF REBUILDING

Pray to GOD for rain—it's time for the spring rain—
    to GOD, the rainmaker,
Spring thunderstorm maker,
    maker of grain and barley.

"Store-bought gods babble gibberish.
    Religious experts spout rubbish.

They pontificate hot air.
 Their prescriptions are nothing but smoke.
And so the people wander like lost sheep,
 poor lost sheep without a shepherd.
I'm furious with the so-called shepherds.
 They're worse than billy goats, and I'll treat them like goats."

✠

GOD-of-the-Angel-Armies will step in
 and take care of his flock, the people of Judah.
He'll revive their spirits,
 make them proud to be on God's side.
God will use them in his work of rebuilding,
 use them as foundations and pillars,
Use them as tools and instruments,
 use them to oversee his work.
They'll be a work force to be proud of, working as one,
 their heads held high, striding through swamps and mud,
Courageous and vigorous because GOD is with them,
 undeterred by the world's thugs.

✠

"I'll put muscle in the people of Judah;
 I'll save the people of Joseph.
I know their pain and will make them good as new.
 They'll get a fresh start, as if nothing had ever happened.
And why? Because I am their very own GOD,
 I'll do what needs to be done for them.
The people of Ephraim will be famous,
 their lives brimming with joy.
Their children will get in on it, too—
 oh, let them feel blessed by GOD!
I'll whistle and they'll all come running.
 I've set them free—oh, how they'll flourish!
Even though I scattered them to the far corners of earth,
 they'll remember me in the faraway places.
They'll keep the story alive in their children,
 and they will come back.

I'll bring them back from the Egyptian west
    and round them up from the Assyrian east.
I'll bring them back to sweet Gilead,
    back to leafy Lebanon.
Every square foot of land
    will be marked by homecoming.
They'll sail through troubled seas, brush aside brash ocean waves.
    Roaring rivers will turn to a trickle.
Gaudy Assyria will be stripped bare,
    bully Egypt exposed as a fraud.
But my people—oh, I'll make them strong, GOD-strong!
    and they'll live my way." GOD says so!

✝

11

Open your borders to the immigrants, proud Lebanon!
    Your sentinel trees will burn.
Weep, great pine trees! Mourn, you sister cedars!
    Your towering trees are cordwood.
Weep Bashan oak trees!
    Your thick forest is now a field of stumps.
Do you hear the wailing of shepherds?
    They've lost everything they once owned.
Do you hear the outrage of the lions?
    The mighty jungle of the Jordan is wasted.
Make room for the returning exiles!

BREAKING THE BEAUTIFUL COVENANT

GOD commanded me, "Shepherd the sheep that are soon to be slaughtered. The people who buy them will butcher them for quick and easy money. What's worse, they'll get away with it. The people who sell them will say, 'Lucky me! God's on my side; I've got it made!' They have shepherds who couldn't care less about them."

GOD's Decree: "I'm washing my hands of the people of this land. From now on they're all on their own. It's dog-eat-dog, survival of the fittest, and the devil take the hindmost. Don't look for help from me."

So I took over from the crass, money-grubbing owners, and shepherded the sheep marked for slaughter. I got myself two shepherd staffs. I named one Lovely and the other Harmony. Then I went to work shepherding the sheep. Within a month I got rid of the corrupt shepherds. I got tired of putting up with them—and they couldn't stand me.

And then I got tired of the sheep and said, "I've had it with you—no more shepherding from me. If you die, you die; if you're attacked, you're attacked. Whoever survives can eat what's left."

Then I took the staff named Lovely and broke it across my knee, breaking the beautiful covenant I had made with all the peoples. In one stroke, both staff and covenant were broken. The money-hungry owners saw me do it and knew GOD was behind it.

Then I addressed them: "Pay me what you think I'm worth." They paid me an insulting sum, counting out thirty silver coins.

GOD told me, "Throw it in the poor box." This stingy wage was all they thought of me and my work! So I took the thirty silver coins and threw them into the poor box in GOD's Temple.

Then I broke the other staff, Harmony, across my knee, breaking the concord between Judah and Israel.

GOD then said, "Dress up like a stupid shepherd. I'm going to install just such a shepherd in this land—a shepherd indifferent to victims, who ignores the lost, abandons the injured, and disdains decent citizens. He'll only be in it for what he can get out of it, using and abusing any and all.

"Doom to you, useless shepherd,
    walking off and leaving the sheep!
A curse on your arm!
    A curse on your right eye!
Your arm will hang limp and useless.
    Your right eye will go stone blind."

12

HOME AGAIN IN JERUSALEM

War Bulletin:

GOD's Message concerning Israel, GOD's Decree—the very GOD who threw the skies into space, set earth on a firm foundation, and breathed his own life into men and women: "Watch for this: I'm about to turn

Jerusalem into a cup of strong drink that will have the people who have set siege to Judah and Jerusalem staggering in a drunken stupor.

"On the Big Day, I'll turn Jerusalem into a huge stone blocking the way for everyone. All who try to lift it will rupture themselves. All the pagan nations will come together and try to get rid of it.

"On the Big Day"—this is GOD speaking—"I'll throw all the war horses into a crazed panic, and their riders along with them. But I'll keep my eye on Judah, watching out for her at the same time that I make the enemy horses go blind. The families of Judah will then realize, 'Why, our leaders are strong and able through GOD-of-the-Angel-Armies, their personal God.'

"On the Big Day, I'll turn the families of Judah into something like a burning match in a tinder-dry forest, like a fiercely flaming torch in a barn full of hay. They'll burn up everything and everyone in sight—people to the right, people to the left—while Jerusalem fills up with people moving in and making themselves at home—home again in Jerusalem.

"I, GOD, will begin by restoring the common households of Judah so that the glory of David's family and the leaders in Jerusalem won't overshadow the ordinary people in Judah. On the Big Day, I'll look after everyone who lives in Jerusalem so that the lowliest, weakest person will be as glorious as David and the family of David itself will be godlike, like the Angel of GOD leading the people.

"On the Big Day, I'll make a clean sweep of all the godless nations that fought against Jerusalem.

"Next I'll deal with the family of David and those who live in Jerusalem. I'll pour a spirit of grace and prayer over them. They'll then be able to recognize me as the One they so grievously wounded—that piercing spear-thrust! And they'll weep—oh, how they'll weep! Deep mourning as of a parent grieving the loss of the firstborn child. The lamentation in Jerusalem that day will be massive, as famous as the lamentation over Hadad-Rimmon on the fields of Megiddo:

"Everyone will weep and grieve,
    the land and everyone in it:
The family of David off by itself
    and their women off by themselves;
The family of Nathan off by itself
    and their women off by themselves;
The family of Levi off by itself
    and their women off by themselves;

The family of Shimei off by itself
    and their women off by themselves;
And all the rest of the families off by themselves
    and their women off by themselves.

13

WASHING AWAY SINS

"On the Big Day, a fountain will be opened for the family of David and all the leaders of Jerusalem for washing away their sins, for scrubbing their stained and soiled lives clean.

"On the Big Day"—this is GOD-of-the-Angel-Armies speaking— "I will wipe out the store-bought gods, erase their names from memory. People will forget they ever heard of them. And I'll get rid of the prophets who polluted the air with their diseased words. If anyone dares persist in spreading diseased, polluting words, his very own parents will step in and say, 'That's it! You're finished! Your lies about GOD put everyone in danger,' and then they'll stab him to death in the very act of prophesying lies about GOD—his own parents, mind you!

"On the Big Day, the lying prophets will be publicly exposed and humiliated. Then they'll wish they'd never swindled people with their 'visions.' No more masquerading in prophet clothes. But they'll deny they've even heard of such things: 'Me, a prophet? Not me. I'm a farmer— grew up on the farm.' And if someone says, 'And so where did you get that black eye?' they'll say, 'I ran into a door at a friend's house.'

✢

"Sword, get moving against my shepherd,
    against my close associate!"
        Decree of GOD-of-the-Angel-Armies.
"Kill the shepherd! Scatter the sheep!
    The back of my hand against even the lambs!
All across the country"—GOD's Decree—
    "two-thirds will be devastated
    and one-third survive.
I'll deliver the surviving third to the refinery fires.
    I'll refine them as silver is refined,
    test them for purity as gold is tested.

Then they'll pray to me by name
    and I'll answer them personally.
I'll say, 'That's my people.'
    They'll say, 'GOD—my God!'"

14

THE DAY IS COMING

Note well: GOD's Judgment Day is on the way:
    "Plunder will be piled high and handed out.
I'm bringing all the godless nations
    to war against Jerusalem—
Houses plundered,
    women raped,
Half the city taken into exile,
    the other half left behind."

But then GOD will march out against the godless nations and fight—
a great war! That's the Day he'll take his stand on the Mount of Olives,
facing Jerusalem from the east. The Mount of Olives will be split right
down the middle, from east to west, leaving a wide valley. Half the mountain will shift north, the other half south. Then you will run for your lives
down the valley, your escape route that will take you all the way to Azal.
You'll run for your lives, just as you ran on the day of the great earthquake
in the days of Uzziah, king of Judah. Then my GOD will arrive and all
the holy angels with him.

What a Day that will be! No more cold nights—in fact, no more
nights! The Day is coming—the timing is GOD's—when it will be continuous day. Every evening will be a fresh morning.

What a Day that will be! Fresh flowing rivers out of Jerusalem, half
to the eastern sea, half to the western sea, flowing year-round, summer
and winter!

GOD will be king over all the earth, one GOD and only one. What
a Day that will be!

✝

The land will stretch out spaciously around Jerusalem—to Geba in the
north and Rimmon in the south, with Jerusalem towering at the center, and the commanding city gates—Gate of Benjamin to First Gate

to Corner Gate to Hananel Tower to the Royal Winery—ringing the city full of people. Never again will Jerusalem be totally destroyed. From now on it will be a safe city.

But this is what will happen to all who fought against Jerusalem: GOD will visit them with a terrible plague. People's flesh will rot off their bones while they are walking around; their eyes will rot in their sockets and their tongues in their mouths; people will be dying on their feet! Mass hysteria when that happens—total panic! Fellow soldiers fighting and killing each other—holy terror! And then Judah will jump into the fray!

Treasures from all the nations will be piled high—gold, silver, the latest fashions. The plague will also hit the animals—horses, mules, camels, donkeys. Everything alive in the military camps will be hit by the plague.

✝

All the survivors from the godless nations that fought against Jerusalem will travel to Jerusalem every year to worship the King, GOD-of-the-Angel-Armies, and celebrate the Feast of Booths. If any of these survivors fail to make the annual pilgrimage to Jerusalem to worship the King, GOD-of-the-Angel-Armies, there will be no rain. If the Egyptians don't make the pilgrimage and worship, there will be no rain for them. Every nation that does not go up to celebrate the Feast of Booths will be hit with the plague. Egypt and any other nation that does not make pilgrimage to celebrate the Feast of Booths gets punished.

On that Day, the Big Day, all the horses' harness bells will be inscribed "Holy to GOD." The cooking pots in the Temple of GOD will be as sacred as chalices and plates on the altar. In fact, all the pots and pans in all the kitchens of Jerusalem and Judah will be holy to GOD-of-the-Angel-Armies. People who come to worship, preparing meals and sacrifices, will use them. On that Big Day there will be no buying or selling in the Temple of GOD-of-the-Angel-Armies.

MALACHI

Most of life is not lived in crisis—which is a good thing. Not many of us would be able to sustain a life of perpetual pain or loss or ecstasy or challenge. But crisis has this to say for it: In time of crisis everything, absolutely everything, is important and significant. Life itself is on the line. No word is casual, no action marginal. And almost always, God and our relation with God is on the front page.

But during the humdrum times, when things are, as we tend to say, "normal," our interest in God is crowded to the margins of our lives and we become preoccupied with ourselves. "Religion" during such times is trivialized into asking "God-questions"—calling God into question or complaining about him, treating the worship of God as a mere hobby or diversion, managing our personal affairs (such as marriage) for our own convenience and disregarding what God has to say about them, going about our usual activities as if God were not involved in such dailiness.

The prophecy of Malachi is made to order for just such conditions. Malachi creates a crisis at a time when we are unaware of crisis. He wakes us up to the crisis of God during the times when the only thing we are concerned with is us. He keeps us on our toes, listening for God, waiting in anticipation for God, ready to respond to God, who is always coming to us.

Malachi gets in the last word of Holy Scripture in the Old Testament. The final sentences in his message to us evoke the gigantic figures of Moses and Elijah—Moses to keep us rooted in what God has done and said in the past, Elijah to keep us alert to what God will do in the days ahead. By leaving us in the company of mighty Moses and fiery Elijah, Malachi considerably reduces the danger of our trivializing matters of God and the soul.

MALACHI

1

No More of This So-Called Worship!

A Message. God's Word to Israel through Malachi:

God said, "I love you."

You replied, "Really? How have you loved us?"

"Look at history" (this is God's answer). "Look at how differently I've treated you, Jacob, from Esau: I loved Jacob and hated Esau. I reduced pretentious Esau to a molehill, turned his whole country into a ghost town."

When Edom (Esau) said, "We've been knocked down, but we'll get up and start over, good as new," God-of-the-Angel-Armies said, "Just try it and see how far you get. When I knock you down, you stay down. People will take one look at you and say, 'Land of Evil!' and 'the God-cursed tribe!'

"Yes, take a good look. Then you'll see how faithfully I've loved you and you'll want even more, saying, 'May God be even greater, beyond the borders of Israel!'

✝

"Isn't it true that a son honors his father and a worker his master? So if I'm your Father, where's the honor? If I'm your Master, where's the respect?" God-of-the-Angel-Armies is calling you on the carpet: "You priests despise me!

"You say, 'Not so! How do we despise you?'

"By your shoddy, sloppy, defiling worship.

"You ask, 'What do you mean, "defiling"? What's defiling about it?'

"When you say, 'The altar of God is not important anymore; worship of God is no longer a priority,' that's defiling. And when you offer worthless animals for sacrifices in worship, animals that you're trying to get rid of—blind and sick and crippled animals—isn't that defiling? Try a trick like that with your banker or your senator—how far do you think it will get you?" God-of-the-Angel-Armies asks you.

"Get on your knees and pray that I will be gracious to you. You priests have gotten everyone in trouble. With this kind of conduct, do you think I'll pay attention to you?" God-of-the-Angel-Armies asks you.

"Why doesn't one of you just shut the Temple doors and lock them? Then none of you can get in and play at religion with this silly, empty-headed worship. I am not pleased. The GOD-of-the-Angel-Armies is not pleased. And I don't want any more of this so-called worship!

OFFERING GOD SOMETHING HAND-ME-DOWN, BROKEN, OR USELESS

"I am honored all over the world. And there are people who know how to worship me all over the world, who honor me by bringing their best to me. They're saying it everywhere: 'God is greater, this GOD-of-the-Angel-Armies.'

"All except you. Instead of honoring me, you profane me. You profane me when you say, 'Worship is not important, and what we bring to worship is of no account,' and when you say, 'I'm bored—this doesn't do anything for me.' You act so superior, sticking your noses in the air—act superior to *me*, GOD-of-the-Angel-Armies! And when you do offer something to me, it's a hand-me-down, or broken, or useless. Do you think I'm going to accept it? This is GOD speaking to you!

"A curse on the person who makes a big show of doing something great for me—an expensive sacrifice, say—and then at the last minute brings in something puny and worthless! I'm a great king, GOD-of-the-Angel-Armies, honored far and wide, and I'll not put up with it!

2

DESECRATING THE HOLINESS OF GOD

"And now this indictment, you priests! If you refuse to obediently listen, and if you refuse to honor me, GOD-of-the-Angel-Armies, in worship, then I'll put you under a curse. I'll exchange all your blessings for curses. In fact, the curses are already at work because you're not serious about honoring me. Yes, and the curse will extend to you children. I'm going to plaster your faces with rotting garbage, garbage thrown out from your feasts. That's what you have to look forward to!

"Maybe that will wake you up. Maybe then you'll realize that I'm indicting you in order to put new life into my covenant with the priests of Levi, the covenant of GOD-of-the-Angel-Armies. My covenant with Levi was to give life and peace. I kept my covenant with him, and he honored me. He stood in reverent awe before me. He taught the truth and did not lie. He walked with me in peace and uprightness. He kept many out of the ditch, kept them on the road.

"It's the job of priests to teach the truth. People are supposed to look to them for guidance. The priest is the messenger of GOD-of-the-Angel-Armies. But you priests have abandoned the way of priests. Your teaching has messed up many lives. You have corrupted the covenant of priest Levi. GOD-of-the-Angel-Armies says so. And so I am showing you up for who you are. Everyone will be disgusted with you and avoid you because you don't live the way I told you to live, and you don't teach my revelation truly and impartially."

Don't we all come from one Father? Aren't we all created by the same God? So why can't we get along? Why do we desecrate the covenant of our ancestors that binds us together?

Judah has cheated on GOD—a sickening violation of trust in Israel and Jerusalem: Judah has desecrated the holiness of GOD by falling in love and running off with foreign women, women who worship alien gods. GOD's curse on those who do this! Drive them out of house and home! They're no longer fit to be part of the community no matter how many offerings they bring to GOD-of-the-Angel-Armies.

And here's a second offense: You fill the place of worship with your whining and sniveling because you don't get what you want from GOD. Do you know why? Simple. Because GOD was there as a witness when you spoke your marriage vows to your young bride, and now you've broken those vows, broken the faith-bond with your vowed companion, your covenant wife. GOD, not you, made marriage. His Spirit inhabits even the smallest details of marriage. And what does he want from marriage? Children of God, that's what. So guard the spirit of marriage within you. Don't cheat on your spouse.

"I hate divorce," says the GOD of Israel. GOD-of-the-Angel-Armies says, "I hate the violent dismembering of the 'one flesh' of marriage." So watch yourselves. Don't let your guard down. Don't cheat.

You make GOD tired with all your talk.

"How do we tire him out?" you ask.

By saying, "GOD loves sinners and sin alike. GOD loves all." And also by saying, "Judgment? GOD's too nice to judge."

3

THE MASTER YOU'VE BEEN LOOKING FOR

"Look! I'm sending my messenger on ahead to clear the way for me. Suddenly, out of the blue, the Leader you've been looking for will enter his Temple—yes, the Messenger of the Covenant, the one you've been waiting for. Look! He's on his way!" A Message from the mouth of GOD-of-the-Angel-Armies.

But who will be able to stand up to that coming? Who can survive his appearance?

He'll be like white-hot fire from the smelter's furnace. He'll be like the strongest lye soap at the laundry. He'll take his place as a refiner of silver, as a cleanser of dirty clothes. He'll scrub the Levite priests clean, refine them like gold and silver, until they're fit for GOD, fit to present offerings of righteousness. Then, and only then, will Judah and Jerusalem be fit and pleasing to GOD, as they used to be in the years long ago.

⊹

"Yes, I'm on my way to visit you with Judgment. I'll present compelling evidence against sorcerers, adulterers, liars, those who exploit workers, those who take advantage of widows and orphans, those who are inhospitable to the homeless—anyone and everyone who doesn't honor me." A Message from GOD-of-the-Angel-Armies.

⊹

"I am GOD—yes, I AM. I haven't changed. And because I haven't changed, you, the descendants of Jacob, haven't been destroyed. You have a long history of ignoring my commands. You haven't done a thing I've told you. Return to me so I can return to you," says GOD-of-the-Angel-Armies.

"You ask, 'But how do we return?'

"Begin by being honest. Do honest people rob God? But you rob me day after day.

"You ask, 'How have we robbed you?'

"The tithe and the offering—that's how! And now you're under a curse—the whole lot of you—because you're robbing me. Bring your full tithe to the Temple treasury so there will be ample provisions in my Temple. Test me in this and see if I don't open up heaven itself to you and pour out blessings beyond your wildest dreams. For my part, I will defend you against marauders, protect your wheat fields and vegetable gardens against plunderers." The Message of GOD-of-the-Angel-Armies.

"You'll be voted 'Happiest Nation.' You'll experience what it's like to be a country of grace." GOD-of-the-Angel-Armies says so.

The Difference Between Serving God and Not Serving Him

God says, "You have spoken hard, rude words to me.

"You ask, 'When did we ever do that?'

"When you said, 'It doesn't pay to serve God. What do we ever get out of it? When we did what he said and went around with long faces, serious about God-of-the-Angel-Armies, what difference did it make? Those who take life into their own hands are the lucky ones. They break all the rules and get ahead anyway. They push God to the limit and get by with it.'"

Then those whose lives honored God got together and talked it over. God saw what they were doing and listened in. A book was opened in God's presence and minutes were taken of the meeting, with the names of the God-fearers written down, all the names of those who honored God's name.

God-of-the-Angel-Armies said, "They're mine, all mine. They'll get special treatment when I go into action. I treat them with the same consideration and kindness that parents give the child who honors them. Once more you'll see the difference it makes between being a person who does the right thing and one who doesn't, between serving God and not serving him.

4

The Sun of Righteousness Will Dawn

"Count on it: The day is coming, raging like a forest fire. All the arrogant people who do evil things will be burned up like stove wood, burned to a crisp, nothing left but scorched earth and ash—a black day. But for you, sunrise! The sun of righteousness will dawn on those who honor my name, healing radiating from its wings. You will be bursting with energy, like colts frisky and frolicking. And you'll tromp on the wicked. They'll be nothing but ashes under your feet on that Day." God-of-the-Angel-Armies says so.

"Remember and keep the revelation I gave through my servant Moses, the revelation I commanded at Horeb for all Israel, all the rules and procedures for right living.

"But also look ahead: I'm sending Elijah the prophet to clear the way for the Big Day of God—the decisive Judgment Day! He will convince parents to look after their children and children to look up to their parents. If they refuse, I'll come and put the land under a curse."